# Christianity Comes to the ✝ Americas

## 1492–1776

# Christianity Comes to the ✝ Americas

## 1492–1776

CHARLES H. LIPPY

ROBERT CHOQUETTE

STAFFORD POOLE

A GINIGER BOOK

*Published in association with Paragon House*

First paperback edition, 1992
Published in the United States by

Paragon House
90 Fifth Avenue
New York, N.Y. 10011

Copyright © 1992 by Paragon House

Figures from *Historical Atlas of Religion in America* by Edwin S. Gaustad. Copyright © 1962,
1976 by Edwin S. Gaustad. Reprinted by permission of HarperCollins Publishers.

Expansion of Colonial Settlements, 1492-1800. From *A History of Latin America* by Hubert
Herring. Copyright © 1968 by Helen Baldwin Herring, executrix of the estate of Hubert Herring.
Copyright © 1955, 1961 by Hubert Herring. Reprinted by permission of Alfred A.
Knopf, Inc.

Fragment of Cantino Sailing Chart, 1502, accurately read from the color reproduction in the
"Historia da Colonizacao" and copied by Enrique Uribe-White, Bogota, 1942. Reprinted by
permission of The Map Division, The New York Library, Astor, Lenox, and Tilden Foundations.

Mendicant Establishments, Mexico, 1570. From *The Spiritual Conquest of Mexico, An Essay on the
Apostolate and the Evangelizing Methods of the Mendicant Orders in New Spain, 1523-1572.*
Copyright © 1966, University of California Press, Berkeley, California. Used by permission of
University of California Press.

Colonial Brazil. From *Colonial Roots of Modern Brazil* by Dauril Alden. Copyright ©
University of California Press, 1973. Used by permission of University of California Press.

America Sive Novi Orbis No Va Descripto, 1584. From Abraham Ortelius, *Theatrvm orbis
terrarvm, Antverpiae*...Christophorum Plantinum. Reprinted by permission of the Map
Division, The New York Public Library, Astor, Lenox, and Tilden Foundations.

Excerpt from Cortez letter from *Hernan Cortez: Letters from Mexico*, translated by Anthony
Pagden. Copyright © 1986 Yale University Press. Used by permission of Yale University Press.

Library of Congress Cataloging-in-Publication Data

Lippy, Charles H.
   Christianity comes to the Americas, 1492-1776 / Charles H. Lippy, Robert Choquette,
Stafford Poole.1st ed.
      p.    cm.
   "A Giniger book."
   Includes bibliographical references and index.
   ISBN 1-55778-501-5
   1. North America—Church history. 2. South America—Church
history. 3. Church history—Modern period, 1500–    I. Choquette,
Robert. II. Poole, Stafford. III. Title.
   BR500.L54   1992
277—dc20                                                                    91-15675
                                                                              CIP


Manufactured in the United States of America
10  9  8  7  6  5  4  3  2  1

# CONTENTS

# LIST OF MAPS AND CHARTS

## PART I

Figure 1: Expansion of Colonial Settlements, 1492–1800
Figure 2: Fragment of Cantino Sailing Chart, 1502
Figure 3: Mendicant Establishments in Mexico, 1570
Figure 4: Colonial Brazil
Figure 5: Americae Sive Novi Orbis No Va Descriptio, 1570

## PART II

Figure 6: Leading Explorers of New France
Figure 7: Missions in Acadia, 1604–1776
Figure 8: Missions in Canada I, 1615–1776, The Eastern Provinces
Figure 9: Missions in Canada II, 1615–1776, Lakes Ontario and Erie
Figure 10: Missions on the Great Lakes, 1640–1776, Lakes Huron, Michigan, and Superior
Figure 11: Missions in the Mississippi Valley, 1673–1776

## PART III

Figure 12: Churches in America, 1650
Figure 13: Number of Churches, 1660
Figure 14: Number of Churches, 1700
Figure 15: Number of Churches, 1740
Figure 16: Number of Churches, 1780
Figure 17: Anglican Churches, 1750
Figure 18: Baptist Churches, 1750
Figure 19: Congregational Churches, 1750
Figure 20: Lutheran Churches, 1750
Figure 21: Presbyterian Churches, 1750
Figure 22: Reformed Churches, 1750
Figure 23: Roman Catholic Churches, 1750

# INTRODUCTION

"Gold, Glory, and the Gospel." This alliterative phrase was memorized by generations of school children in the United States as a concise summary of the motives that spurred Europeans to invade, conquer, and colonize in the New World following Christopher Columbus's voyage to the West in 1492. While the phrase is catchy, it greatly oversimplifies the complex reasons behind the European conquest and settlement of South and North America. But it does highlight one vital component in the story: that of the coming of Christianity— "the Gospel"—to the Americas. The many dimensions of that part of colonial history form the focus of this book.

The book, written by three specialists, details the story of Christianity for each of the areas that became identified with the three European nations that emerged triumphant in the craze for conquest and colonization in the Americas—Spain, France, and Britain. While other nations such as Portugal and the Netherlands carved territories for themselves in the New World, these three dominated. All three were lands where Christianity, with its compulsion to proclaim the Gospel, enjoyed a favored position. But the style of Christianity varied. After the Protestant Reformation started remaking the religious map of Europe, France and Spain remained generally within the Roman Catholic fold, while a tangled mix of politics and piety drew Britain into the Protestant ranks. Yet even within Spain and France, the nuances of Catholic practice took a different form that was linked with both the drama of the emergence of the modern nation-state and the complexity of relations between royal prerogative and religious influence, political power and papal power. Such intrigue provides part of the backdrop for the story that unfolds here.

All three sections begin with the quest for empire that cascaded across the emerging nation-states of Europe following Columbus's 1492 voyage. The Spanish and the Portuguese were the first to carve for themselves an enduring presence in the New World. The French and the English followed soon after with major exploration, though their first permanent settlements in North America did not materialize until the seventeenth century. This book takes the story of Christianity's coming to the Americas through 1776, when much of British America declared its independence from its European mother country and became the United States. The Age of Revolutions that ensued would see the severance of ties with European powers in much of the Americas, though even in the twentieth century there remain some areas with more than nominal links to European nations. But the declaration of American independence is a convenient point to end this story, for it marked the beginning of another story, the development of Christianity in the New World as an entity in its own right.

In the colonial era, because the religious situations in Spain, France, and Britain differed, the ways in which conquerors and colonists brought Christianity to the New World also differed. Yet there are some common strands. In all parts of the Americas, Europeans had to confront a radically different environment in which to cultivate Christianity. The two major factors were the land itself and the peoples inhabiting it. The vast expanse of the New World that the Puritans who came to British North America were fond of calling a "wilderness" contained no network of towns and roads connecting places together as they did in Europe; here, vast amounts of terrain were unoccupied by humans. The signs that Europeans had come to identify with civilization— from the architecture of towns and cities to established structures of government—were by and large missing.

Thus in every area of the New World it proved impossible merely to transplant European Christian institutions, Catholic or Protestant, in the Americas. Rather, one had to start afresh in a strange atmosphere that had no heritage of Christianity stretching back some fifteen centuries. One had to construct Christianity in a cultural setting that offered few, if any, buttresses for its being. The collision of European Christianity, regardless of its form, with the environment of the New World is part of the story whether one examines Ibero-America, French America, or British America. Adaptation, modification, and the construction of new ways of operating or indeed of implanting Christianity became the unstated norm in the New World. Of course, precisely how those processes occurred varied, as the analysis that follows makes plain.

Christianity's coming to the Americas was also always related to the political intrigues in Europe that involved those nations seeking to establish colonial empires in the New World. Among the earliest was the rivalry between the Spanish and Portuguese for the presumed right to conquer and colonize in South America that was resolved only in part (and not really to the satisfaction of any) by papal intervention. In time, all too frequently the contest for empire erupted into military conflict, especially when there were questions of royal succession in Europe. Antagonism between the Spanish and the British was only partially contained by the British defeat of the Spanish Armada in 1588. Until the eighteenth century, the bulk of hostilities was carried out in Europe, with only relatively minor consequences for colonial life. But in what Europeans called the Seven Years' War, known in British North America as the French and Indian War (1756–1763), parts of the New World saw considerable military action. The net result of that confrontation was the extension of British control over most of French America and the whittling away of some of Spanish America.

When Protestant Britain took over Catholic Canada, many felt that the future of Catholic Christianity there was endangered. The reason is simple. Not only did nationalism breed suspicion of other countries, religious differences between Catholics and Protestants fostered distrust. Many of the Protestants who came to British America were staunchly anti-Catholic, and hostile attitudes toward the French and the Spanish were nurtured by misunderstanding and distrust of Catholicism. Hence the British conquest of Canada also brought concern in Britain's North American colonies about the future of Protestant Christianity, which ultimately fed into the move for independence that gave birth to the United States.

The story of Christianity's coming to the Americas is indeed a dramatic one. At times a tale of heroes and heroines who sacrificed the relative comforts of European life and often their lives to bring the gospel to the New World, it is also frequently an account of conquest and destruction of native American societies and their religious life. Caught in struggles for influence, if not control, as colonial empires expanded, Christian leaders were drawn into political involvement as they sought to build a missionary church. For Catholics in Ibero-America and French America, such political intrigue occasionally included jockeying with ecclesiastical authorities in Europe as well as with secular powers in both the colonies and the mother country.

In British America, religious differences between colonists, especially those of a Puritan stripe, and the Church of England brought a different sort of relationship to both local and royal authorities, one that also meant political affairs were a lively concern of religious leaders. Throughout the Americas Christians were confronted with constructing their religious life in an alien context, what appeared an uncivilized wilderness fraught with both danger and possibility. Everywhere European models and sometimes accepted European Christian practices faced modification in the light of local circumstances. As well, political and military struggles among the colonial powers themselves often had significant impact on the fortunes of Christianity in the New World. But by 1776, the year of the founding of the San Francisco mission and the independence of the United States, Christianity throughout the Americas was no longer primarily a missionary enterprise, though it still was technically regarded as such in many circles, but a flourishing, organized religion. Christians had persevered, and Christianity had both endured in the Americas and in a variety of forms had become the dominant religious style. Such it remains.

CHARLES H. LIPPY

# ✝ Part I

## Iberian Catholicism Comes to the Americas

BY STAFFORD POOLE

# 1

# THE IBERIAN BACKGROUND

When Christopher Columbus set foot on the island he called San Salvador on 12 October 1492, he unalterably changed the course of history for two hemispheres. The mutual impact—ecological, human, religious, economic, and even nutritional—continues to this day. It is undeniable that the religious factor has been influential, even dominant, in the subsequent history of Ibero-America. Conquest, settlement, and missionary endeavors not only advanced together but at times were inseparable, for the missions were a vanguard of empire. Any understanding of Christianity in Ibero-America, therefore, presupposes a knowledge of the nations from which that Christianity came. The mentality, organization, and religion of the two exploring and colonizing Iberian states—Spain and Portugal—sheds light on the great enterprise of the Indies, the impact of which still affects millions of people.

## CASTILE

Spain was the European country most deeply involved in this encounter between two hitherto separate worlds. Since 1492 uncounted numbers of people have used its language, worshiped according to its religion, and lived by its institutions. An understanding of Spanish history and outlook is essential to understanding not only the evangelization of Spanish America but also its contemporary people, society, and institutions.

The determinative factor in the history of mainland Spain, comparable to the frontier in British America, was the *reconquista* (reconquest) of the peninsula from the long Moorish domination. The Moors, recent and fervent converts to Islam, entered the Visigothic kingdom of Spain in 711 and within seven years almost entirely subjugated it. The reconquista was a centuries-long crusade by the Christians (in this context they did not call themselves Spaniards or Portuguese) to drive out the Moors. By the thirteenth century most of

3

the Iberian peninsula had been reclaimed, with the exception of the kingdom of Granada in the southeast. This struggle helped to define Spanish character and mentality, both in myth and in reality. Militant religiosity, individualism, courage, fatalism, stoicism, arrogance, ethnocentric nationalism, a strong sense of personal honor (*pundonor*), and the use of force for religious ends were the heritage of the last great European crusade.

Yet Spain, as it is known today, did not exist. Throughout most of the fifteenth century the peninsula was divided into a number of small states: Navarre, Castile-León, Aragon, Portugal, and the Moorish kingdom of Granada. Castile was an unstable kingdom, plagued by dynastic wars and fractious nobles. In 1469 the marriage of Ferdinand, heir to the throne of Aragon, and Isabella, heir to the throne of Castile, set in motion a train of events that would lead to the formation of an identifiable Spain as the first modern nation-state. Isabella's accession to the throne of Castile was the occasion of one final dynastic war in that kingdom (in which her enemies were supported by the king of Portugal), which ended with her triumph at the battle of Toro (1476).

The marriage of Ferdinand and Isabella, the Catholic Monarchs (*los reyes católicos*), united the sovereigns, not the realms. Even in the sixteenth century it was still common to speak of "the Spains." Castile and Aragon remained separate, and each monarch had clearly defined limits in the territory of the other. Ferdinand and Isabella complemented each other to an extraordinary degree, with the strengths of one compensating for the weaknesses of the other. Historians today dispute whether they were the last medieval monarchs or the first modern ones. There is no denying, however, that they were a formative force in the development of the Spanish empire. The rebellious nobility was pacified or bought off. An efficient and talented bureaucracy, eventually to be one of the best in Europe, began to emerge as a potent force in Castilian society. The church came more and more under royal control. The reconquista was renewed with a war against Granada and carried through to victory. On 2 January 1492 the last Moorish ruler on the peninsula surrendered the keys of the Alhambra ("I give you the keys to paradise"), and the Catholic Monarchs enjoyed unparalleled prestige throughout Europe. With the triumph of the reconquista the power of the monarchs was dramatically increased. One of the witnesses to the surrender was a Genoese sailor and mapmaker whose Spanish name was Cristóbal Colón, known in the English-speaking world as Christopher Columbus.

The death of Isabella in 1504 and then of Ferdinand twelve years later led to a renewal of dynastic instability. Their son-in-law, Philip I, died prematurely and his wife, their daughter Juana, suffered a mental breakdown that incapacitated her for rule. The heir to both kingdoms was the young grandson of Ferdinand and Isabella, Charles of Burgundy (1500–1558). In Castile, under the regencies of Cardinal Francisco Jiménez de Cisneros and then of Ferdinand and finally a second regency of Cisneros, the cities grew restive. When the young king, Charles I (later Charles V of the Holy Roman Empire), showed little understanding of the needs of his Castilian subjects, a revolt broke out (1520–1521). Called the *comunero* revolt because it was led by the cities or communes, it was the last major challenge to royal authority in that century. After it had been suppressed, Charles wisely followed a policy of accommodation. He himself became more Spanish in his temperament, language, and outlook and saw to it that his son, the future Philip II, was raised as a thoroughgoing Spaniard.

Both as king of Spain and as Holy Roman Emperor Charles I ruled the largest European kingdom since that of Charlemagne in the early Middle Ages. His Spanish inheritance embraced Flanders and Burgundy (modern-day Netherlands and Belgium), Castile, Aragon, Navarre, the former Moorish kingdom of Granada, Naples, Sicily, Sardinia, and the Duchy of Milan, together with hereditary rights over Hungary and Bohemia. After his election as emperor, he also ruled what is modern Germany. His reign, however, was troubled by incessant religious, diplomatic, and military problems. In Germany, shortly before Charles's election Martin Luther launched his religious revolution, one of the first challenges the young emperor faced. Eventually it led to civil war within the empire and the permanent religious division of Europe. His reign saw a continuous state of hostility with Francis I of France in the Habsburg–Valois wars. In the east the Turks occupied most of the Balkans and posed a threat to the ancestral Habsburg lands in Austria. At the same time *conquistadores* were adding to his realms in the New World—and also adding to his administrative and governmental responsibilities. In April 1521, while Luther faced Charles at the Diet of Worms, Fernando Cortés was preparing to lay siege to the Aztec capital of Tenochtitlán. It is small wonder that Charles, in his farewell speech to his nobles at the end of his reign, reflected that his life had been one long journey.

In the sixteenth century, even as the various Iberian kingdoms under Habsburg control were being melded into the one nation of Spain, many attitudes remained medieval. Even at the height of sixteenth-century absolutism, the king's role was still defined in medieval terms. He was not just a supreme legislator or executive; his primary function was to dispense justice to his subjects. All else flowed from that. Subjects with grievances could freely petition the monarch, and they showed an amazing willingness to do so. As a result Spanish society tended toward corporatism, a congeries of special-interest or pressure groups, each of which received a hearing from the crown for its petitions. There was no representative body as such. The Castilian *cortes* represented a select number of cities and was called primarily for financial reasons; that is, when the crown needed more money from the cities. Royal policy was for the most part tactically flexible, though the principle of protecting and enhancing the crown's power remained fixed. A decree issued in one year in response to agitation by religious orders in the New World might be repealed or modified a few years later in response to complaints by bishops in the same area. Government thus reflected the medieval social contract: loyalty and service in return for justice and leadership. When the contract was violated, Spaniards did not hesitate to revolt. Despite the move toward unification, localism remained strong. Since Castile was the kingdom that held the monopoly on New World discovery, conquests, and government, its impact was the greatest. Political loyalties tended to be strongly local in Castile. Those of an individual were to his lord, his city, or his province, often called his "little fatherland" (*patria chica*).

## THE CHURCH IN CASTILE

Catholicism in Castile had many features unique to that kingdom. It was never to be directly affected by the Reformation or other major European religious movements, except in an oblique way. It developed in ways that were distinct, enhanced by a self-imposed isolation. In the early part of the sixteenth century it did nevertheless feel the impact of current European thought; many churchmen were influenced by the thought of Erasmus of Rotterdam, the preeminent humanist of the day. This thought emphasized the ethical aspects of religion, downplayed the institutional and liturgical, and was strongly opposed to the extremes of popular piety, especially in such areas as pilgrimages and devotion to the saints. In general, it favored simplicity in religion. (A strong reaction against Erasmianism in midcentury, especially on the part of the Inquisition, doomed it to extinction.)

Castilian religion was local in nature and of a folk or superstitious variety. A wide number of local shrines and chapels, each with its own special devotion and history of apparitions, dotted the countryside. The average person, particularly in the rural areas, was poorly instructed in religion. Sunday sermons were rare or unknown, and their legislation by the Council of Trent (1545–1563) was regarded as a major innovation. There was no organized form of catechizing young people. Life centered around the local church, its festivals, celebrations, and pilgrimages. Religious observance was often externalized, yet it was also deeply mystical and in the sixteenth century produced some of the greatest religious literature of modern times. Sexual morality was frequently divorced from formal religious precepts. Castilian Catholicism was as paradoxical and contradictory as the Castilians themselves: formalized and external, personal and mystical, compassionate and brutal.

In the cities, however, the church in Castile was strongly hierarchical and clerical. Some dioceses were wealthy and powerful. In the sixteenth century Toledo, the richest see in the kingdom, had a private army of some two thousand soldiers. The structure of bishops and cathedral and collegiate chapters was well defined, and the clergy constituted a clear and prestigious state in a stratified society. The growth of the universities (twenty-one were founded in Spain in the sixteenth century alone) produced a highly educated clergy, at least for the urban areas. The universities, especially Salamanca, brought about a renaissance of scholastic theology that was to be very influential in

Spanish attitudes in the New World. The famous university of Alcalá de Henares, founded by Cardinal Cisneros in the early sixteenth century, was an attempt to prepare both an educated and a spiritual clergy for Castile. The university graduates, whose degrees were often in canon or civil law, were to be found in the cities (rural clergy were often poorly educated) and frequently functioned as government bureaucrats. The proportion of clergy to the general population was quite high, although it is impossible today to arrive at an absolutely accurate number.

*The religious orders.* In addition to the diocesan clergy there were the religious orders. (The term *religious* refers both to the orders and their members.) The original form of the religious life had been the monastery, a freestanding, autonomous house whose members were called monks. The various monasteries were united only in observing a common rule. Monastic orders, of which the Benedictines are the best known, were not primarily clerical; that is, the majority of their membership were not necessarily priests or clerics. The monks' primary function was prayer and contemplation, leavened by physical labor, and ordinarily they did not have a specific ministry outside the monastery. In Spanish America the term *monastery* came to indicate any house of any religious order, just as *convent* meant religious houses of both men and women.

In the Middle Ages new forms of the religious life appeared. One was the clerks regular, communities of priests established for a specific ministry and living under a rule. The foremost example of clerks regular in the sixteenth century were the Jesuits. Another innovation was that of the friars, who were not attached to autonomous houses but to larger, transnational communities divided into provinces of which the houses were constituent parts. In general they were not considered clerical communities, even though they often had a majority of priest members. Although they had active ministries, especially preaching and teaching, their primary emphasis was on communitarian prayer. Because they theoretically lived by begging, they were called mendicants. Their organization was more flexible than that of the monastic orders. The supreme authority was held by a superior general or minister general. Thus the mendicants were more international in scope than the older monastic orders or orders of clerks regular. This gave them more independence and, in the case of Castile, put them somewhat outside royal control.

The principal mendicant groups were the Franciscans, the Dominicans, and the Augustinians. The Franciscans (Order of Friars Minor) had been founded in the early thirteenth century by Francis of Assisi, with a special orientation toward poverty and preaching. The Dominicans (Order of Preachers) had been founded at about the same time by the Castilian Domingo de Guzmán for the purpose of preaching and converting heretics. The Augustinians had a more complex history, which involved the union of several groups that followed the rule of Saint Augustine. Though not originally mendicants, they were so classed by the sixteenth century.

The primary function of the mendicants was preaching and teaching. This, together with their flexibility, mobility, superior education, and intense zeal made them ideal for the work of the missions. The mendicants, and in a special way the Franciscans, were vitally important to the evangelization of the New World; all three played major roles in the evangelization of Spanish America. Two other orders, which were not properly mendicants and which played lesser roles, were the Hieronymites (Order of Saint Jerome or Jerónimos) and the Mercedarians.

The Society of Jesus (Jesuits) originated after the conquest of the New World was all but complete. Founded by Saint Ignatius of Loyola in 1534 and approved by the papacy six years later, at the very beginning of the Catholic Reformation, they were neither monks nor friars. Ignatius introduced an even greater element of flexibility and mobility into the religious life. The Jesuits made education and missions their primary responsibilities, while their rapid expansion enabled them to extend their work throughout the world in an amazingly short time. Arriving in Peru in 1568 and New Spain in 1572, they were soon conducting an extensive system of preparatory schools and expanding into new mission territories. Along with the Franciscans, the Jesuits were the most important missionary force in Spanish-America.

*The Patronato Real.* Catholicism in Castile was very much a state church. From the time of Ferdinand and Isabella, the crown came to exercise more and more control over the church, a control known globally as the *patronato real*, or right of royal patronage. It was not a single, well-defined entity but an uneven evolutionary development, a system rather than a law, the result of tradition, growth, papal concessions, and extortion. Nor was it unique to Castile. Throughout Europe the monarchs and the emerging nation-states were increasing their control over the Church and its functions. Although at times the papacy had successfully resisted this tendency, as in the famous investiture controversy of the twelfth century, the Church was inevitably becoming more closely linked to the state in most of Europe. The key element in all these systems was the right to nominate bishops. By the time of the French Revolution the Church had become a department of the state in most European monarchies.

The patronato had medieval antecedents and was based on the concept that churches were supported more by endowments than by alms from the faithful. Patronage consisted of endowing a place of worship in return for certain rights for the patron, usually that of nominating the pastor or chaplain. By the sixteenth century it had become common in Spain for heads of families to endow churches or chaplaincies so that family members could hold the positions of pastor or chaplain. Under Ferdinand and Isabella this individual patronage began to develop into a national system. To a certain extent this was the result of events to which the monarchs reacted. It was, however, also part of an overall policy of control, an attempt to bring peninsular institutions under the governance of the crown. This process was particularly marked in Castile, though it was not unique to that kingdom.

The groundwork for the extended patronato was laid in 1482 when Pope Sixtus IV attempted to appoint a worldly nephew, an Italian, as bishop of Cuenca in Spain. The Catholic monarchs resisted so strongly that the pope was forced to give them the right to nominate candidates for vacant dioceses. This was not a formal presentation but a petition (supplication), with the pope granting the spiritual and ecclesiastical jurisdiction. A major advance came four years later when Pope Innocent VIII attempted a similar appointment. Again the monarchs resisted. Since the war against Granada was in progress, they succeeded in wresting from the pope the right of patronage over churches, dioceses, and benefices that would result from the conquest of Granada. Because of the cost of the war, they were also given the right to one third of the tithes collected from Christians in order to defray the expenses of the war. The funds were also to be used to endow churches. Alexander VI's bull *Inter Caetera* of 1493 (discussed below) carried the system a step further by imposing a religious vicariate and laying the basis for a closer union of throne and altar.

Because of the financial outlay involved in missionary work in the New World, Alexander VI, in the bull *Eximiae Devotionis* (1501) allowed the monarchs to collect all tithes in the New World. In 1512 a complex schedule whereby these were redonated to the church was devised. The most sweeping grant of powers came from Pope Julius II. In 1504 he attempted to bypass the crown by appointing bishops to the New World without consultation. Ferdinand resisted this and after the death of Isabella in that year refused to allow any papally appointed bishops to take their sees. In order to have bishops for the Spanish dependencies, the pope had to yield. In the bull *Universalis Ecclesiae* (1508) he gave the crown the right of formal presentation of candidates for all ecclesiastical offices in the Indies: archbishops, bishops, abbots, canons. In 1543 the crown received the right to draw the boundary lines of dioceses, a move necessitated by Rome's ignorance of New World geography. Like many Castilian institutions imported to the New World, the patronato was stronger in the colonies than in the mother country.

Under Philip II (1556–1598) governmental control of the church reached such a level that Spanish Catholicism was almost a national church. The crown approved the decrees of all provincial councils, financed the church, was responsible for the construction and maintenance of ecclesiastical buildings, and mediated disputes among churchmen. No papal letters could enter Spanish dominions without royal approval (*pase regio*). These were personal rights of the ruler of Castile, but they were often exercised through governmental agencies such as the Council of the Indies. With the establishment of the viceregal system, beginning in New Spain in 1535, the viceroys in their capacities as "vice-kings," claimed comparable rights. Thus, if the king had the right to draw the boundaries of dioceses, the viceroys argued that they had the same right with regard to parishes.

The only serious attack on the patronato in the sixteenth century came in 1568 when Pope Saint Pius V moved to put missionary activity under papal control. The papacy wanted to send nuncios to the Spanish possessions in the New World, whereas the crown wanted to create the position of Patriarch of the Indies as a means of limiting papal intervention. Philip II managed to frustrate the papal initiatives and the patronato system remained intact down to and even after the independence period. Though the title of patriarch was bestowed in some cases, it remained essentially honorary. In 1573 the rights of the patronato were codified in a document called the *Cédula general del patronazgo real*, which was primarily the work of Philip II's influential adviser Juan de Ovando. Among other things it attempted to make the religious orders subservient to the bishops and viceroys and allowed the latter to intrude themselves into all types of ecclesiastical affairs. In 1622, with the foundation of the Congregation for the Propagation of the Faith, the papacy attempted to regain control of Catholic missions throughout the world. In the New World this had some success in Brazil but none whatever in Spanish America.

There was little resistance to the patronato on the part of bishops, the notable exception being Domingo de Salazar, the first bishop of the Philippines (1579–1594). Almost all others accepted it as the normal order of things. There was, however, disagreement among churchmen and jurists as to the nature of the royal rights. One school, the regalists, believed that the patronato was inherent in the concept of sovereignty and not the result of concessions by the papacy. For them it was laic in origin, and hence the powers of the patronato could be delegated. The papalists, on the other hand, believed that the rights were papal in origin and could not be delegated. The question was not merely academic. When the nations of Spanish America became independent in the nineteenth century, many of them maintained the regalist stance that the patronato derived from sovereignty and that as a result the rights had passed from the crown of Castile to the newly independent states.

*The Spanish Inquisition.* The most famous, and probably the most effective, instrument of royal control in Spain was the Inquisition. It has become famous, or infamous, through literature, history, and popular lore, and at one time there was scarcely another word that could raise such dread in an Anglo-Saxon heart. The legends and shadows linger, as in the lamentably nonhistorical and misleading twentieth-century musical *Man of La Mancha*. The Spanish Inquisition is one of the most difficult topics in history to treat with any degree of objectivity.

In the history of the Church there have been three kinds of Inquisition. The first, called the episcopal, belonged to bishops by right of their office. The second, called the Roman, was established by the papacy in the Middle Ages to deal with the rise of heresy. It was governed by the papacy and was usually administered by Dominicans. The medieval or Roman Inquisition had never existed in Castile and was generally ineffective in Aragon. The Spanish Inquisition, founded in 1480 by the papacy at the request of Ferdinand and Isabella, was a distinct institution that was unique to their kingdoms. It was the only institution outside the monarchy itself that reached into every part of Spain, and it superseded the episcopal Inquisition.

The original purpose of the Spanish Inquisition was not so much to ferret out unorthodox teaching as to deal with "New Christians," converts to Catholicism whose sincerity was suspect and who were viewed as a threat to both church and state. These included *conversos*, Jewish converts, and *moriscos*, Moslem converts. Because of a wave of violent anti-Semitism that swept over Castile and Aragon from 1391 on, large numbers of Jews sought refuge in conversion. The same thing happened again in 1492, when the crown offered all non-Christian Jews the choice between conversion and expulsion. Together with those who converted out of conviction, they constituted a large minority in the church. Many conversos found their way into the religious orders and high positions in the church; the famous Pablo de Santa María (d. 1435), grand rabbi of Burgos, converted to Catholicism, became a priest and then bishop of the city. His son, Alfonso (1384–1456), succeeded him as bishop. The moriscos were proportionately fewer but stood out because of their retention of Arabic language, dress, and customs.

Popular hostility and a suspicion that the conversos represented a danger to orthodoxy were primary motives for the foundation of the Spanish Inquisition. Still, the new tribunal met opposition throughout the two kingdoms. The Aragonese viewed it as a foreign importation from Castile and were hostile to it. Many Spaniards regarded it as a violation of traditional Spanish liberties, especially in its secret procedures, the inability to confront accusers, and inheritance of penalties (such as infamy) from parents to children. Though this hostility reached even the point of riots, the Holy Office eventually became fixed on all the kingdoms of Spain, the only institution under the monarchy with such power. It was not introduced into the New World, however, until much later: 1568 in Peru, 1570 in New Spain. It effectively restrained the spread of unorthodox thought but at the cost of limiting Spanish intellectual and spiritual development.

The Inquisition maintained strict censorship over books of a devotional or theological nature but not, paradoxically, over scientific works. The Galileo case would not have occurred in Spain, where the Copernican theory was freely taught in the universities. The Inquisition also avoided prosecutions for witchcraft, a subject on which it had generally enlightened views. In 1526 the authorities of the Inquisition called a general meeting to discuss what should be done about the supposed prevalence of witches in the area near the French border. The majority opinion was that witchcraft existed only in the imaginations of the accused. The renewal of interest in witchcraft that swept Europe in the midsixteenth century was greeted with skepticism by the Inquisition. This moderate policy seems to have undergone some change in the seventeenth century. In 1610 some witches were burned in Logroño, the first known instance of such a punishment by the Inquisition. In general, however, it was regarded as either a mental aberration or a manifestation of popular superstition.

One of the Inquisition's most powerful weapons was secrecy. Arrests were generally made at night by its officers (*alguaciles* or *familiares*). The accused was allowed to write a list of enemies who may have denounced him but was never permitted to face his accusers. Theoretically, torture was employed only once, but by a legalism the one time could be indefinitely prolonged. Sentences were given at a public ceremony called an *auto-de-fé* (act of faith) and usually consisted of public penance, pilgrimages, floggings, the galleys, or imprisonment in a religious house. Those to be punished came to the auto clothed in a chasublelike garment called the *sambenito* and wearing a miterlike cap, often decorated with flames. The death penalty could be inflicted only on those who refused to recant heresy or who relapsed—that is, fell back into heresy after being reconciled. Since the Church by its own law could not inflict capital punishment, the condemned was handed over to the "secular arm" for the final penalty. This was almost always burning at the stake, although as an act of mercy the condemned were often strangled first. The sambenitos of those reconciled or punished were displayed in the local church, so that subsequent generations would know who belonged to tainted or suspect lineage.

Out of the general cultural and religious hostility to the conversos and moriscos grew the concept of purity of blood (*limpieza de sangre*). This meant that one's immediate ancestry was not contaminated by any mixture of Jewish or Moorish blood or by descent from someone condemned by the Inquisition; in the New World this also came to include Indian and black ancestry. Those who did not meet the proper criteria were systematically excluded from higher ecclesiastical positions (except, paradoxically, that of bishop) and from the prestigious fraternities (*colegios*) at the major universities. Orthodoxy became a matter of lineage as well as belief. Although this discrimination extended to all the suspect minorities, it was strongest against the Jews. In both Spain and Spanish America in the sixteenth century there was a crypto-Jewish subculture that led a precarious and perilous existence.

## CASTILE UNDER PHILIP II

In 1556, weary and prematurely aged by his manifold responsibilities, Charles I abdicated and retired to the monastery of Yuste. The Caroline empire was divided between his son Philip II and Charles's brother Ferdinand. In addition to Spain, Philip received the Italian possessions, the New World, and, in an unwise move, the Low Countries. In 1580 he occupied the vacant throne of Portugal, and for the first time since the Roman Empire the entire Iberian peninsula was under one rule. It was once more the *Hispania* of ancient times, and only after 1580 did Philip II begin to call himself king of Spain.

The reign of Philip II (1556–1598) saw both the apogee and the decline of Spanish power. Within the kingdoms of Spain power was centered more and more in the king, and this in turn meant Castile. In Aragon the monarch's power was more limited because of the traditional rights and privileges (*fueros*) enjoyed by that kingdom. A major innovation was the establishment of the first royal capital at Madrid, which was chosen primarily because of its centralized geographic location. Prior to the 1560s, Spanish monarchs had been peripatetic, traveling from one part of the kingdom to another, knowing their subjects and being known by them. Under Philip II the court became static. Philip built an extensive palace-cum-monastery north of Madrid, San Lorenzo de El Escorial, where he made his fixed residence. Like Versailles in seventeenth-century France, it became not only the center of administration and bureaucracy but also the focus of political life in Spain.

Under Philip the *letrados*, royal civil servants trained in law at the great universities, came to dominate the governmental bureaucracy. Dependent totally on the king for their positions, they challenged the old nobility for power in a struggle of talent against lineage. They brought an increased efficiency and rationality to chaotic and haphazard governmental administration. They also formed an old-boy network from their university years onward and advanced one another's careers. They also came to prominence in the Church and some of the most important and effective bishops in Spanish America came from the ranks of the letrados.

The search for uniformity and control gave added prestige and power to the Inquisition, an institution that Philip both favored and controlled. Fearful of heresy and the intrusion of any heterodox ideas, he even recalled Spanish students from foreign universities. Statutes of limpieza de sangre became more numerous and more exacting, and suspicion of conversos grew. Again the paradox: Whereas conversos were excluded from most cathedral chapters and higher university and governmental positions, they could become bishops. Appointments to the latter offices still had to go through Rome. Stranger still, some of Philip II's closest and most influential advisers, such as Antonio Pérez and Mateo Vázquez de Leca, were of suspect lineage.

Philip II's reign was racked by disasters, especially in foreign policy. His almost total lack of understanding of the Low Countries led to a revolt that for the better part of forty years exhausted Spanish financial and human resources. His attempt to dethrone Elizabeth I of England led to the catastrophe of the Armada in 1588. Within Spain his repressive policies led to a revolt by the Moriscos of the Alpujarras region. His meddling in the religious conflicts in France was equally fruitless. Accompanying all this was a continuous series of financial crises. Three times during his reign—1557, 1575, and 1596—the crown had to suspend interest payments on its debts, the equivalent of bankruptcy. Neither Philip nor his advisers were ever able to find a way out of the quagmire of debt into which the crown continued to sink.

Yet at the same time this was a glorious period in Spanish history, the *siglo de oro*. From the religious point of view it was the age of the great saints and mystics: Ignatius of Loyola, Teresa of Avila, John of the Cross, Luis de León,

Luis de Granada, and Juan de Avila. They not only produced a great body of religious work, they were outstanding writers and poets as well. During the sixteenth and early seventeenth centuries Spain experienced a theological renaissance, much of it centered in the university of Salamanca. Francisco de Vitoria, Domingo de Soto, Melchor Cano, Domingo Bañez, Juan de Mariana, and Francisco Suárez were among the great creative theologians of that period. They were especially effective in advancing thought on political power, human rights, and international law. Cervantes began his writings during this reign, El Greco painted for the churches and chapels of Toledo, and Lope de Vega produced a great body of drama. It is not surprising that the reign of Philip II was regarded by many Spaniards as one of the great periods in their history.

## PORTUGAL

The neighboring kingdom of Portugal had a similar historical background, but one which took a course distinct from that of its Castilian neighbor. Portugal from the Minho to the Tagus had been freed from Moorish domination by the Castilian kings Ferdinand I (1055–1064) and Alfonso VI (1093). Alfonso awarded the territory to his son-in-law, but after the latter's death there was a period of civil war. Aspirations for independence from Castile were born in the early twelfth century. In 1139 Afonso Enrique defeated five Moorish kings at the battle of Ourique, and by 1142 Portugal had constituted itself a kingdom. In 1143 Afonso accepted vassalage to the pope, thus securing papal recognition for his claim. Four years later he wrested Lisbon from the Moors and made it his capital.

### SUBSEQUENT RULERS

The kings of Portugal continued their southward expansion at the expense of the Moors. The fact that this paralleled a similar expansion in Castile brought the two kingdoms into conflict. The rulers of Castile never gave up the dream of annexing Portugal, and it remained one of their chief aims throughout the fourteenth and fifteenth centuries. With the establishment of a new dynasty, the Aviz, in 1385, Portuguese independence was assured.

In the fifteenth century, while Castile was being rent by dynastic and feudalistic wars, Portugal was enjoying relative peace and prosperity. Although the Portuguese had visited the Canary Islands as early as 1341, these eventually became a Castilian possession. From 1415 on, however, Portugal became a notable exploring and colonizing power. In this it preceded Castile, at least chronologically. Also in 1415, as part of a campaign to carry the crusade against the Moslems into their home territory, the Portuguese captured Ceuta, in modern Spanish Morocco. The outstanding figure of that period was Prince Henry the Navigator (1394–1460), a patron of explorers and seafarers. He founded a naval school at Sagres, to which he invited experts from all over Europe. He also sponsored expeditions of exploration down the African coast, gradually extending them farther and adding to geographical knowledge. The ships often contained Franciscan and Augustinian missionaries. The Madeiras were annexed in 1418 and the Azores in 1431. In 1441 Antônio Gonsalves brought back the first Africans and gave Portugal the dubious distinction of introducing black slavery into Europe. Such names as Gold Coast, Ivory Coast, and Sierra Leone were holdovers from that period. In 1487 Bartolomeu Dias rounded the Cape of Good Hope, an achievement that distracted the Portuguese king from the westward project then being presented to him by Christopher Columbus. In 1497–1498 Vasco da Gama reached India and opened a whole new chapter in Portuguese exploration and trade. Merchants and missionaries went to the Far East, and for a few decades of the sixteenth century Lisbon became one of the richest trading centers in Europe. However, the period from the death of King Manoel I (1521) until that of King Enrique II (1580) was one of general political decline.

A key element in Portuguese expansion was the attempted conquest of Morocco. King Sebastião (1557–1578), Philip II's nephew, was the last to make a major effort. An ill-conceived and poorly planned expedition ended at the battle of Alcázarquivir in 1578. The king disappeared and though he was presumed to be dead, tales of reappearance continued to be told. Since he was childless, he was succeeded by his great uncle Enrique II (1578–1580). The new king was sixty-six years old and a cardinal vowed to celibacy, so he also died without a direct heir. After his death Philip II, who had a strong claim to the throne through his mother, annexed Portugal. Although Castilian rule was relatively benign and accepted by a portion of the population, it was still foreign. In 1640 João IV overthrew Spanish domination and established the reign of the house of Bragança.

The church in Portugal supported the campaign for independence from Castile in the twelfth century. Despite this and despite the flourishing of religious life in the thirteenth century, there were conflicts between church and state over the former's property holdings. As in other parts of Europe, there was also antagonism toward the church's system of independent lawcourts. The mendicant orders, after their introduction into Portugal, were favored by the crown and became very influential. A religious decline seems to have set in during the fourteenth century, with a revival toward the end of that century. As in Castile, the church gradually became subordinated to the state through the growth of a native patronato called the *padroado*. The Portuguese right of patronage had an earlier history than that of Spain, assuming a clear shape as early as 1418. Missionary interest was never so strong in Portugal as in Castile, and it declined notably during the sixteenth century. It was most successful in Brazil. In 1496 all non-Christian Jews and Moors were expelled from Portugal and in 1536 the Inquisition introduced. It was never, however, introduced into the Portuguese New World.

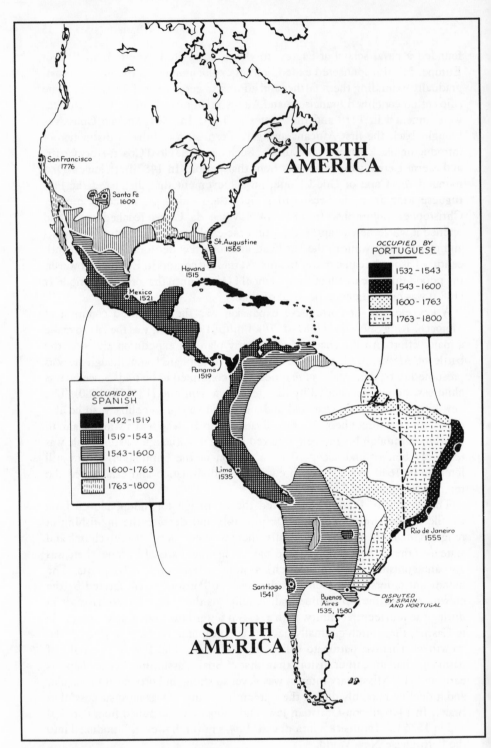

Expansion of Colonial Settlements, 1492–1800

# EXPANSION AND
# EVANGELIZATION:
# CENTRAL AND NORTH AMERICA,
# 1492–1600

## CASTILE IN AMERICA

It was not Spain that undertook the discovery and conquest of the New World but the kingdom of Castile. When Columbus signed a contract with the monarchs in April 1492, it was to Castile that the government and ultimate control of the discoveries and conquests were given. Legally Aragonese were regarded as foreigners in the Indies. As a result Castilian institutions and attitudes came to dominate the Spanish New World.

This New World was a widely divergent and disparate one, geographically, climatically, ethnically. The misnamed "Indians" were not one consistent group. They included the Inuits of the far north, the plains Indians of the present-day United States, the Caribs and Arawaks first encountered by the Spaniards in the Caribbean, the Mexica (Aztecs), Tarascans, and Mayas of Mexico, the varied Inca groups of Peru, the jungle Indians of the Amazon, the Guaranís of Paraguay, and the Araucanians of Chile. These groups were diverse in almost every way. They constructed magnificent civilizations, like the Mayas, Aztecs, and Incas, and they were warlike cannibals, like the Guaraní. Their languages were vastly different, often differing from village to village. Their religious beliefs were just as varied. There was simple animism among less advanced groups and sophisticated theological teachings, with accompanying cosmogonies, among others. This dizzying diversity presented one of the greatest challenges to the Castilian missionaries.

Even before Columbus returned to Spain, word of his achievement had reached Ferdinand and Isabella. They immediately sent communications to Rome, seeking papal approval for their discoveries. This led to two papal bulls, both called *Inter Caetera*, issued by the Spanish Pope Alexander VI. The first was drawn up toward the end of April 1493, dated 3 May, and was in the hands of the monarchs by 28 May. It granted the requested confirmation. The second was issued on 28 June but backdated to 4 May and was apparently in response to Portuguese protests that the first bull impinged on that kingdom's prerogatives. The second *Inter Caetera* added to the first the famous Line of Demarcation, drawn vertically down the Atlantic Ocean, which delineated the boundary line between Spanish and Portuguese discoveries.

*Inter Caetera* has been the object of intense historical scrutiny. The question arises as to why the Catholic Monarchs, who were usually so eager to restrict papal authority in their kingdoms, should have sought the pope's approval for their discoveries. One explanation was that they wanted to forestall any action by the Portuguese, who had traditionally sought papal approval of their conquests and whose king, João II, claimed that Columbus's discoveries lay within areas that belonged to Portugal by the treaty of Alcoçovas (1479). According to this theory the pope was giving a canonical confirmation to a political reality. Some claim that it was a recognition of the pope's right to depose non-Christian rulers. Still others assert that it was based on a medieval concept of the pope as having dominion over islands but not kingdoms, and that what Columbus had discovered was a mass of islands near the Asiatic mainland.[1] Another theory holds that it "was not, then, an assertion of long-dead papal claims to world domination but rather a carefully worded statement which balanced the rights of the infidels, the papal responsibility for preaching the Gospel, and the political realities of aggressive expansionism."[2]

Whatever the explanation, one thing is clear: the bull imposed on Castile a religious and missionary vicariate. The monarchs were charged with the christianization of the peoples of these newly discovered lands. This in turn gave rise to the contention of many jurists and humanitarians that evangelization was the only justification for the Spanish presence in the Indies. Despite lapses in practice, the Spanish crown in the sixteenth century took this obligation seriously. (See Chapter 5.)

Interestingly enough, the papal donation was not accepted by the other Catholic powers of Europe. In October 1493 Alexander VI, in the bull *Dudum Siquidem*, attempted to disavow all Portuguese claims. This led to negotiations between the Spanish and Portuguese crowns, culminating in the Treaty of Tordesillas (1494). A purely secular, diplomatic affair, this agreement moved the line of demarcation three hundred leagues westward (thus giving Portugal a claim to part of Brazil) and excluded the pope from any role in the interpretation of the treaty.

The first priest to set foot in the New World was Bernal Buyl, or Boyl (1445–?), a Benedictine who had become a Minim friar and who accompanied Columbus on his second voyage with the title of vicar apostolic (1493). An intelligent and pious man, Buyl soon ran afoul of the autocratic and vain Columbus, especially over the latter's treatment of the Indians and the colonists. Buyl eventually returned to Spain and resigned his position.

## THE CARIBBEAN, 1493–1521

The first area of Spanish domination was the Caribbean: Española (modern Haiti and Dominican Republic, often called Hispaniola in English), Cuba, Puerto Rico, and the coasts of Venezuela and Panama. In the early period of this domination, approximately 1493 to 1518, the results were dreadful for the natives. European diseases, culture shock, exploitation, and enslavement resulted in the almost total extermination of the Indian races. As a result the opportunity for evangelization was restricted. There was intense missionary activity in the beginning, but as the objects of this activity—the Indians— died off, so too did the missionary incentive.

### ESPAÑOLA

The restoration of peace and order on Española following the turbulent years of Columbus's rule and increased royal control that began with the appointment of governor Nicolás de Ovando in 1501 permitted a more orderly evangelization. A royal instruction of 20 and 29 May 1503 laid down some of the basic guidelines for evangelization, some of which would remain in force throughout the entire period of Spanish rule. One of these was the policy later called *congregación*, the gathering of scattered or seminomadic peoples into villages and towns, each of which would have a church and resident priest to take care of the natives' religious instruction. There were also to be schools for the literary and religious instruction of children. The Indians were to be kept as much as possible from the vices and low morals of Europeans. Hospitals for poor Indians and Spaniards were also to be built. (See page 39 for a more complete discussion of congregación and reduction.)

At first the church in the Caribbean was under the ecclesiastical rule of the archdiocese of Seville. In 1504 Pope Julius II erected an archdiocese, that of Yaguata near the port of Santo Domingo, on Española, together with two dependent (or suffragan) dioceses. As matters turned out, only one of the bishops was actually appointed. An archdiocese with suffragans was too ambitious for a colony with a small European population. The full ecclesiastical organization would have to wait until 1511, when the diocese of Santo Domingo was established. The first bishop of Santo Domingo was Fray Diego de Padilla, who died before being consecrated. The first resident bishop on Española was an Italian, Alessandro Geraldini. He was appointed in 1516 but did not arrive until some years later. His administration was not a successful one, for he seems to have been poorly qualified for his task. Not until 1545 did

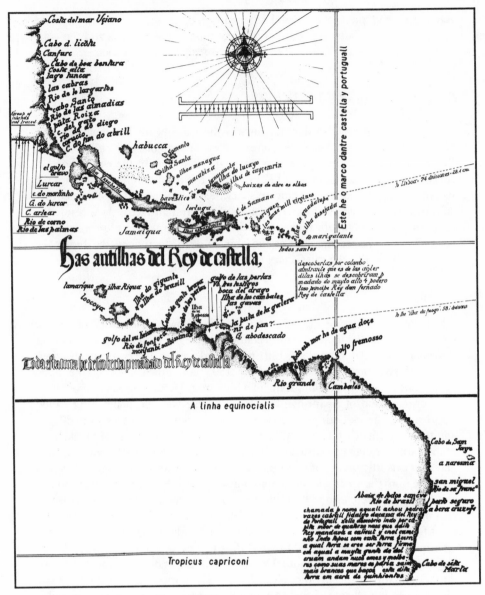

Fragment of Cantino Sailing Chart, 1502

Santo Domingo become an archdiocese, with modern Cuba, Puerto Rico, Colombia, Venezuela, and Honduras as suffragans.

The real missionary work on Española was done by mendicants. This, too, was to be characteristic of Spanish evangelization throughout the New World, for the friars were the essential element in the missionary enterprise. The

Franciscans were the first to come (1500) and by 1505 they were well enough established for their mission to become a province. In 1510 the first Dominicans, including the soon-to-be-famous Antonio de Montesinos, departed for the new field and soon proved themselves active missionaries. The mendicants, in contrast with the diocesan clergy, did not depend on a fixed living, or benefice. They enjoyed a greater mobility and in general had the reputation of being holier, better educated, and more zealous than their diocesan counterparts. The Dominicans on Española also proved themselves the enemies of Spanish exploitation of the Indians, a subject dealt with in Chapter 5.

Until Charles I forbade foreign priests to work in the Indies in 1530 (an order that was never seriously enforced), different nationalities, such as Flemings and Germans, were represented in the mission field. In 1514 an Irish diocesan priest, Achilles Holden, was teaching grammar in the cathedral school on Española.

## PUERTO RICO

San Juan in Puerto Rico was the third diocese to be established in the Caribbean. The island had been occupied by the Spaniards in 1509–1510 under the leadership of Juan Ponce de León. The first bishop of San Juan, and the first one to set foot in the New World, was Alonso Manso. Unfortunately, very little is known about him or his apostolic activity. His previous career as canon preacher of the archdiocese of Salamanca does not seem to have prepared him for the rigors of missionary life on a tropical island. His task was not made easier by the fact that in 1513 there were only two other priests on the island. He did, however, succeed in establishing a school for clerics and laity. He died in 1534 and a new bishop was not named until 1542.

## CUBA

In 1508 the Spaniards finally verified the fact that Cuba was an island, not part of the mainland. Three years later an expedition under the command of Diego de Velázquez and including what would become some of the most famous names in the New World—Fernando Cortés, Pedro de Alvarado, Bernal Díaz del Castillo, and their chaplain, Bartolomé de las Casas—set out to conquer the island. As elsewhere the conquest was accompanied by atrocities, later described in blazing, indignant detail by Las Casas. In ecclesiastical matters Cuba was at first subject to Española. From 1508 until 1514 Las Casas settled down to the comfortable life of a gentleman-cleric-farmer, while most of the apostolic activity seems to have been carried on by the mendicants.

In 1517 a diocese was erected, situated first at Baracoa and then at Santiago. The first bishop, Juan de Ubite (1517–1525), never came to the island. The first resident bishop was Miguel Ramírez, a Dominican, who arrived in 1528. He soon achieved a bad reputation for greed and mismanagement and was recalled to Spain in 1532. His successor, Diego Sarmiento, a Carthusian, was able to accomplish a great deal more in the short period before his death in 1537. By that time the Church in Cuba was predominantly a Spanish one and missionary activity became distinctly secondary. By midcentury there were no more than five thousand Indians left, and these soon became part of the growing mestizo (mixed white–Indian) class.

## THE SPANISH MAIN

### THE ISTHMUS

The first settlement of Spaniards on the mainland was along the coast of modern Panama. In 1508 the crown granted two independent contracts to Diego de Nicuesa and Alonso de Ojeda to conquer and colonize the lands of the isthmus region. Ojeda's attempts to settle the mainland near Cartagena met bitter defeat at the hands of the natives, as did a later attempt at Urabá that cost him his life. In 1510 an expedition led by Nicuesa arrived at Nombre de Dios and established a settlement. In that same year an expedition under Martín de Enciso left Española, with Vasco Núñez de Balboa as a stowaway (he was fleeing creditors), and established a fort at Santa María la Antigua at Darién on the Gulf of Urabá. The settlers soon elected Balboa their governor. When Nicuesa came to demand the removal of the colony from an area that techni-cally belonged to him, he and his men were put to sea in untrustworthy vessels and were never heard from again. In 1513, lured south by reports of a fabu-lously rich kingdom called Peru, Balboa discovered the Pacific Ocean—which, because of the twisted geography of the peninsula, he called the South Sea. The Spaniards had been given their first clear clue that the lands they had discovered were not the outlying areas of Asia but an entirely new continent. This would be confirmed by the [Ferdinand] Magellan expedition of 1519–1522. Balboa, unjustly blamed for the deaths of Nicuesa and his men, was executed by the new governor, his father-in-law Pedro Arias de Avila, more commonly known as Pedrarias Dávila, one of the most loathsome of the Span-iards in the Indies.

Some Franciscans accompanied Ojeda on his voyage to the isthmus. There is evidence that about the year 1511 they founded a house in Darién, their first on the mainland. In 1514 six members of the order accompanied Pedrarias Dávila to Tierra Firme, of which he had been appointed governor. One of their number was Juan de Quevedo, who in the previous year had been named bishop of the newly founded diocese of Santa María la Antigua at Darién, but he did not arrive until 1514. They were soon joined by others from Española and set up what may have been the first permanent Franciscan residence on the mainland. When, in 1519, Dávila moved his capital to the newly founded city of Panamá, the missionaries had to follow him. In 1522 the Mercedarians founded a house in Panama City, as did the Dominicans a few years later. Their work was hindered by the freebooting and slave-catching expeditions of the

Spaniards. In Quevedo's words, the Indians were like the Moors of Granada, "who because of the bad treatment they have received, wherever they see Christians off their guard, they killed them, something that before they would not dare think of."[3] The Franciscans eventually abandoned the mission and returned to Española.

## FLORIDA

The other part of the mainland that the Spaniards attempted to colonize at this time was in the present-day United States. In 1513 an expedition of conquerors and colonists led by Juan Ponce de León left Puerto Rico for the north, without any priests in their company. Having arrived in the Easter season (*pascua florida*) and because of the abundant vegetation, he named the country Florida. The three major Indian tribes of the region were primitive and warlike. (The more advanced Seminoles, who today are so closely associated with Florida, had not yet arrived.) The hostility of the natives proved too much and the expedition had to return to Puerto Rico. Not until 1521 did Ponce de León attempt a return. With two hundred men, including some friars and secular (diocesan) priests, he almost immediately encountered hostile natives and received the wounds from which he later died. An expedition in 1526 led by Juan Vázquez de Ayllón, which included two Dominican priests and a brother, also failed.

In 1528 an expedition of some six hundred colonists led by Pánfilo de Narváez, who some years earlier had lost an eye in a skirmish with Cortés's troops, landed at Tampa Bay. With him were a number of priests, including five Franciscans. One of the Franciscans bore the title of bishop-elect of Florida, though he never had the opportunity to exercise it. Some of the men, drawn inland by the reports of gold, lost contact with their ships, which returned to Cuba without them. Thus began one of the most incredible odysseys of the Spanish conquest. The abandoned Spaniards made boats out of horsehide and set sail along the Gulf coast toward Pánuco on the Mexican coast, which they believed to be nearby. Eventually some eighty survivors were cast up on the Texas coast, where their numbers dwindled to four, including the famous Alvar Núñez Cabeza de Vaca and a black slave, Esteban. They began an epic wandering, sometimes as slaves of the Indians, sometimes posing as medicine men and traders, until they arrived in Mexico City eight years after landing in Florida.

In May 1539 another expedition of six hundred colonists led by Hernando de Soto landed near Tampa. This expedition included twelve priests, eight of them secular and four religious. Four of the secular priests died within the first year. Led on by reports from the Indians, who found that the easiest way to get rid of the Spaniards was by telling them of great wealth to be found farther on, part of the expedition went through Georgia as far as South Carolina. Disappointed in their search for wealth, they returned to the Gulf near present-day

Mobile. In 1541 they resumed their march, discovered the Mississippi (which they named Río Espíritu Santo, or River of the Holy Spirit), and crossed into Arkansas. It was all in vain. De Soto died in 1542 and was buried in the river. Only five of the twelve priests made it back to New Spain, and very little missionary work had been accomplished.

In 1549 the Dominican Luis Cáncer de Barbastro and several companions undertook a mission attempt in Florida based on the idea of peaceful evangelization without military help. Cáncer had been strongly influenced by Bartolomé de las Casas and had participated with the latter in a similar experiment in New Spain. Cáncer was almost immediately killed by Calusa Indians. Ten years later Tristán de Luna led an armada of thirteen ships, five hundred soldiers, a thousand colonists, and five Dominican priests and one brother from Veracruz to found settlements in Alabama and the Carolinas. Shortly after landing at Pensacola, the expedition was all but destroyed by a hurricane. An attempt by part of the company to establish a colony on the Carolina coast met the same fate. Not surprisingly, there were few opportunities for missionary work. Two of the Dominicans on this expedition survived to later become bishops, Pedro de Feria in Chiapas, Mexico, and Domingo de Salazar in Manila.

What finally brought about permanent Spanish settlement, as so often happened in the New World, was the threat of intrusion by another power. In the 1560s French Huguenots (Calvinists) under Jean Ribault began settling in what is modern South Carolina. The French Huguenot leader, Admiral Gaspar de Coligny, was searching for a place of refuge for his co-religionists and a way of blocking Spanish Catholic expansion. In the face of this threat the crown ordered the capable but ruthless sea captain Pedro Menéndez de Avilés to suppress piratical activity and stop the French. His expedition was better planned than those of his predecessors and included four diocesan priests. In 1563 he established an outpost in Florida, where the first mass in the continental United States was celebrated on 25 August, the feast of Saint Augustine of Hippo. The presidio was thus named San Agustín. (Today called St. Augustine, it is the oldest continuously inhabited city in the United States.) Menéndez de Avilés took care of the French threat in another way, by attacking and massacring them. What he did was cruel, although unfortunately not unusual for the age. He then set up fortifications around the peninsula and brought in colonists and missionaries. Two Dominicans came in 1566 and were sent north to Chesapeake Bay, but a storm prevented their landing. By 1565 Florida was safely in Spanish hands for the next two centuries.

In that same year Menéndez de Avilés asked the Jesuits to send additional missionaries and three of them arrived in the following year. Up to that time the missionary work had been carried on by diocesan priests, an unusual situation in the Spanish empire. After the Jesuits' leader, Father Pedro Martínez, was killed by hostile Indians, the others returned to Havana. Early in 1567 two Jesuit priests and two brothers arrived, to be joined the following year by an even larger band. They then extended their work as far as South Carolina and even Virginia, but the martyrdom of six of their number was a fatal blow. In addition, their missionary work proved difficult because of the nomadic habits of the Indians. In 1572 the remainder were sent to New Spain to help inaugurate the Jesuit apostolate there. The only priests left in Florida were a small number of diocesans.

In 1573 the Franciscans came to Florida to replace the Jesuits. They were few in number and the mission did not begin to show real progress until 1587 when thirteen Franciscans, led by Fray Alonso Reinoso, arrived at St. Augustine. Even then the mission led a precarious existence until 1595, when a new group arrived under the leadership of Fray Francisco Marrón. The missions now took on a stable character. The mission centers with resident friars were called *doctrinas*; outlying chapels were called *visitas*. The Franciscan missionary activity was imperiled again in 1597 when the Guale Indians, in what is present-day Georgia, rebelled against their missionaries and killed some of them. The Indians had been outraged over the friars' attempts to enforce monogamy. The revolt was soon put down.

In 1598, a priest named Ricardo Artur (Richard Arthur) became pastor of the church in St. Augustine, the first known Irish priest to work in what is now the United States. In that same year a hospital was built, the first one within the present boundaries of this country. (The subsequent history of the Florida missions is given in Chapter 6.)

## GEORGIA AND SOUTH CAROLINA

The modern state of Georgia was part of the Spanish colony of Florida. Jesuits and Franciscans founded missions along the Atlantic coast and worked there throughout the sixteenth and seventeenth centuries. In what is now South Carolina, Lucas Vázquez de Ayllón in 1526 established a short-lived colony of five hundred men, women, and children near Winyah Bay. He was accompanied by two Dominicans, Antonio Cervantes and Antonio de Montesinos. The latter has achieved lasting fame as the man who inaugurated the campaign in favor of the Indians against Spanish exploitation. Vázquez de Ayllón died and the bickering colonists returned to Española. Until 1586, however, the Spaniards maintained a colony at Santa Elena (Parris Island) and near there Juan Rogel, a Jesuit, conducted a mission among the Indians. The Jesuits were succeeded by the Franciscans in 1578 and kept up their contacts with the Indians until 1675, when the English presence came to dominate the area.

## VENEZUELA AND COLOMBIA

These areas were first evangelized by Franciscans from Peru. Although individual friars had visited Colombia in 1534 and 1540, the order was not fully established there until 1550. The first two bishops of Bogotá were Franciscans,

Juan de los Barrios and Luis Zapata. From there the friars began the evangelization of the outer areas, including Santa Marta, the Chocó region, and Los Llanos. In 1565 the independent Franciscan province of Santa Fe de Bogotá was created. In Venezuela the Franciscans carried out a successful mission at Cumaná, on the coast, between 1514 and 1522 but did not begin the full penetration of the area until 1575. The missions of Píritu, named for the small city where they were centered, became major missionary activities in the seventeenth century.

## MEXICO

In 1516 the Spanish began to explore the eastern coast of modern Mexico and in the process opened up the next great period in their conquest of the New World. The first, unsuccessful probes whetted their appetites for further exploration and booty. They also brought the Spaniards their first contacts with an advanced native civilization and religion. Their first impression of the latter was negative for the sight of temples splattered with the blood of human sacrifice came as a shock. (This process would be repeated, although with differences, in South America.) The conquest of Mexico also marked a great step forward in the missionary enterprise, for it was the field in which would be developed a process of evangelization that, with modifications, would be used throughout Spanish America in the colonial period.

### ANCESTRAL CIVILIZATIONS

Civilization in what is now Mexico began on the Gulf coast near La Venta with a people called the Olmecs ("dwellers in the land of rubber"), much of whose history and culture is now shrouded in mystery. Many characteristics of later civilizations—the ceremonial ballgame, cities as ceremonial centers, the calendar, and a bar-dot system of computation—probably originated with this people. When Olmec civilization declined, perhaps in a revolt against a dominant military-priestly caste, it passed to a number of other centers: Monte Albán in the Zapotec country, Teotihuacán north of Mexico City, the Huastec area to the northeast of Mexico City, and the highland Mayan concentrations in Guatemala. Like all the cultures in Central and North America, these relied on maize, first hybridized about 2000 B.C.E., as the staple that made settled life possible. All went through a cyclical process of preclassic, classic, and postclassic periods of rise and decline.

Of these successor states the most important from viewpoint of subsequent history was Teotihuacán ("the place where the gods meet"). There is not much agreement among historians about the chronology of the teotihuacano civilization, which probably lasted from 200 B.C.E. until about the eighth or ninth century of the common era. The chief deity was Tlaloc, the rain god. The language was probably an early form of Nahuatl, ancestral to that spoken later by the Aztecs. Religion was characterized by a certain amount of human sacrifice. The teotihuacanos developed the construction of pyramids.

Like many of the civilizations of the central plateau, that of Teotihuacán was overthrown by less civilized, barbarian tribes from the north, globally called Chichimecas ("people of dog lineage," perhaps a reference to a totem). In a pattern that was to be repeated, the conquerors settled around the lakes of the Valley of Mexico (Anáhuac, "the place next to the waters"), absorbed the language and culture of the conquered, and eventually fused with them to create a new civilization. In the ninth century the foremost of these invaders were the Toltecs, who founded the city of Tollan—probably modern Tula in the state of Hidalgo. There is little certainty about the nature of Toltec rule of civilization because both became heavily overlaid with legend. Probably a warlike people with a military/theocratic government, they extended their rule over a large part of the central plateau.

In a real sense the Toltecs were more important for what they represented than for what they were. The city of Tollan, which reached its zenith around 1000 to 1100, passed into legend and came to embrace a concept (like Jerusalem, Rome, or Hollywood) rather than a geographic location. It symbolized greatness in the arts and technology. Similarly, the term *Toltec* came to represent an idealized master race of builders, artists, and technicians. Later peoples mythologized the Toltecs as the inventors of all technological advances, hence to have or to claim descent from the Toltecs meant legitimacy and prestige. The Toltecs were legendary by the time the Aztecs arrived in the plateau, and the name came to mean artisan or mechanic. They were seen through a mist of legend and idealization as *the* great people of the plateau.

The chief Toltec deity was Quetzalcóatl ("plumed serpent"), originally identified with both the wind and the planet Venus. The stories and legends that grew up around him are of incredible complexity, in part because Toltec kings tended to take the name of the god. As a result there is confusion over the individuals named and whether the narration refers to historic events, religious myths, or a combination of both. Quetzalcóatl was a benevolent, peaceful deity whose sacrifices consisted of butterflies and feathers. Opposed to him was the grim Tezcatlipoca ("smoking mirror"), warlike and demanding human sacrifice. A myth, which may reflect a historic religious struggle, relates that Tezcatlipoca maneuvered the downfall of Quetzalcóatl, who left Tollan for the east. There he departed over the waters. The story that he was a white person with a beard who promised to return to regain his kingdom was probably a postconquest development.

As Toltec power declined, it was not able to withstand the incursions of new Chichimecas. After a period of confusion and war, a number of new city-states arose in the area immediately surrounding the lakes of Anáhuac. Chief among these were Culhuacán, whose people, the Culhuas, claimed descent from the Toltecs and so had an aura of legitimacy; Azcatpotzalco, peopled by the

Tepanecs; Xochimilco, Cholula, and Texcoco. These states engaged in wars and alliances and had most of the cultural characteristics that had begun with the Olmecs and been transmitted through successor states. In the thirteenth and fourteenth centuries these states would face a new and far more ominous invasion.

### THE MEXICA

Aztlán, a semilegendary homeland to the northwest of Mexico City, gave rise to the people who called themselves Mexica. Aztecs was their original name but it died out and was replaced by *Mexica* (approximately pronounced Meh-SHEE-ca), which may be derived from an eponymous tribal leader named Mictli. In the seventeenth century the Jesuit historian Francisco Clavigero revived the term *Aztec*. The precise origins of some of these names is not clear. Sometime in the thirteenth century these people left their homeland and began a long series of wanderings, led by their chief deity Huitzilopochtli. Associated with rain, human sacrifice, and the Lord of the Daylight Sky, he was a militant deity who guided the people through oracles delivered by the priests. They entered the Valley of Mexico sometime toward the end of the thirteenth or beginning of the fourteenth century and became vassals of Azcatpotzalco. Regarded by the other peoples as rude, uncouth, and uncivilized—in part because of their great emphasis on human sacrifice—they were often driven from one spot to another.

The Mexica were a strong, resourceful, militant, brutal, and aggressive people with a messianic sense of their own destiny. When the Culhuas of Azcatpotzalco forced them to settle in a miserable, marshy area of the lakes, they flourished. They joined their patrons in a war against Xochimilco in the early fourteenth century and proved their worth by displaying the ears of the enemies they had killed. Fearful of their growing strength, the Culhuas forced the Mexica to migrate. Some time around 1322 the Mexica went on another exodus until they found the place promised them by Huitzilopochtli: the place where they saw an eagle on a prickly pear cactus devouring a serpent. (The serpent is not mentioned in some versions of the story. The cactus [*nopalli*] represented the earth, sun and sky, that is, Huitzilopochtli; the serpent, earth and moisture; the prickly pear fruit [*tuna*], human hearts. This was to become the national symbol of Mexico.)

The place the god had given them was an island, where they founded the city of Tenochtitlán. It was a good strategic location and became the center from which Mexica rule extended throughout central Mexico. Intensive agriculture, and hence a large population, was made possible by reed and mud rafts called *chinantli*, hispanized to *chinampas*. Trade was developed with the mainland. About the year 1372 the simple tribal government was replaced by a monarchy, although it continued to be elective throughout the rest of their history. The Mexica began as vassals of the local states, then became allies and finally masters.

The Mexica empire took its clear shape toward the end of the fifteenth century. It was not an empire in the modern sense but rather a confederation of three city-states: Tenochtitlán, Texcoco, and Tlacopan. The Mexica, of course, were dominant. Territories conquered by the Mexica were not usually incorporated into Tenochtitlán. More commonly they were tributary states, one of the tributes being human sacrifices. Trade extended to the Gulf coast, with the merchants often acting as the advance guard of military conquest. Mexica society became more and more stratified, with the emperor growing remote and locked in elaborate ceremonial. All of this had been achieved within the space of a hundred or a hundred fifty years.

Tenochtitlán grew into a magnificent city connected to the mainland by causeways and an aqueduct. Dominating its center was the temple of Huitzilopochtli, perched atop an awesome pyramid. At its dedication in 1487 from eight thousand to twenty thousand victims were sacrificed. The city was clean, far more so than any contemporary European city, but was subject to flooding from the lakes. In 1519, when Fernando Cortés made his appearance at Veracruz, the emperor was Moctezoma II Xocoyotzin ("the younger")—ruthless, devious, superstitious, and ultimately tragic.

The religion of the Mexica was a complex polytheism. This complexity arose in part from their custom of adopting divinities of conquered tribes; they later experienced difficulty in grasping the exclusive claims of Christianity. Their lives were ceremonial, often bloody. Their ancestral god, Huitzilopochtli, had to be nourished by human hearts procured by human sacrifice. Though ritual cannibalism was practiced, its magnitude has often been exaggerated. Priests constituted a special stratum in society and were celibate. The Aztecs believed in the afterlife but its form depended on the manner of death, not on behavior during life. Death by drowning, for example, meant that one was dear to the water god. The Mexica believed that the world had been created, destroyed, and recreated over the course of time. Hence they viewed the world as an unsettled, threatened place with only a precarious existence, with a resulting fatalism of outlook.

Some elements in Mexica religion seemed to correspond with Catholicism. The cross, symbolic of the four points of the compass, was one. There was also a form of baptism. It was customary to make a form of confession, usually late in life, to the goddess Tlazoteotl ("beloved goddess"), who was also known as the "eater of filth" (that is, sins). Early missionaries were struck by these similarities and often exaggerated them. These later provided the basis for the claim that the native religion was a decadent form of Christianity that had first been preached to them in apostolic times, particularly by the Apostle Thomas, whom Mexican patriots tried to identify with Quetzalcóatl. More important for subsequent missionary work, however, were the differences in the two religious systems. The Mexica believed in a dialectical process that took place between order and chaos. The world, they believed, had been successively destroyed and recreated. Hence their ritual did not involve sin or redemption but was an attempt to stave off destruction and disorder. The Mexica and Christian concepts of sin were very dissimilar, and the natives had no real idea of redemption or the afterlife as understood by Christians.

## THE SPANISH INVASION

After the initial explorations of the mainland coast, Diego Velázquez, the governor of Cuba, decided to launch a major expedition to Mexico. As leader he chose the aggressive and talented young mayor of Santiago, Fernando Cortés. A native of Extremadura, Cortés had briefly studied law and then come to the New World as a young man. As a reward for his role in the conquest of Cuba, he became a moderately wealthy landowner. Resourceful and intensely ambitious, he quickly began to worry Velázquez, who finally determined to replace him. Fearing that his great opportunity for wealth and glory was about to be taken from him, Cortés surreptitiously led the expedition out of Cuba and took it to eastern Mexico. Realizing his perilous legal position, for he was technically an outlaw, he founded the city of Veracruz on Good Friday 1519 and had himself elected mayor, thereby putting a gloss of legality on his audacity.

With slightly more than four hundred men, he pushed inland. Moctezoma II played a devious diplomatic game to persuade the Spaniards to leave, but ultimately he was no match for the wily Spanish captain. Within a short while Cortés had made the emperor his prisoner and through him was ruling a restive and hostile population. The catalyst for disaster was the arrival at Veracruz of a contingent of soldiers sent by Governor Velázquez of Cuba to arrest the insubordinate Cortés. The latter rushed off to the coast, leaving the impulsive Pedro de Alvarado in charge of Tenochtitlán. In a dangerous night battle Cortés overcame the Velázquez forces and won most of them to his side. On his return to Tenochtitlán, he discovered that Alvarado and his men had instigated a massacre that caused a revolt among the Aztecs. The Spaniards were besieged in the imperial palace, where the Aztecs allowed Cortés and his men to join them before again closing the ring. During the course of the siege Moctezoma received wounds from which he never recovered. As the situation became desperate, Cortés decided to attempt a nighttime breakout. The stratagem almost succeeded but, warned by an elderly woman who had gone out to draw water, the Aztecs fell on the Spaniards with full fury in what became known as the sad night (*la noche triste*). Very few made their escape. The Aztecs, however, failed to follow up their victory, partly out of a conviction that they had an ultimate triumph, partly because of the ravages of smallpox that had arrived with the Spaniards.

Even so, Cortés and his companions would never have survived the defeat if their allies, the Indians of Tlaxcala, sworn enemies of the Aztecs, had not remained loyal. Cortés now resolved to renew the siege, but this time by controlling the lake that surrounded Tenochtitlán. In an incredible achievement he brought supplies to the shore of the lake and there built an entire fleet of brigantines. With these he was eventually able to isolate the city and cut off its water supply. Even then the conquest necessitated the block-by-block destruction of the once-beautiful capital. Finally, on 13 August 1521, the feast of Saint Hippolytus (later the patron of Mexico City), Tenochtitlán fell and the young emperor Cuauhtémoc was captured.

Except for the Yucatán, the rest of what is modern Mexico was conquered in a surprisingly short time. The collapse of the Aztec empire brought with it the immediate control of much of central Mexico without the need for conquest. Tlaxcala was already allied with the Spaniards—an alliance based on submission, not equality. In 1521 Gonzalo de Sandoval conquered Coatzacoalcos. In that same year Luis Martín, after an unsuccessful attempt to conquer the Zapotecs of Oaxaca, had better success against the Mayas of Chiapas. Cristóbal de Olid subdued the Tarascans of Michoacán (who had successfully resisted Aztec domination) and explored the Pacific coast as far as Colima. In 1529 the despicable Nuño de Guzmán, in order to regain credit with the crown, carried on a bloody campaign through Jalisco and Sonora.

## THE EVANGELIZATION OF NEW SPAIN

Farsighted and statesmanlike, Cortés envisioned the establishment of a new empire consisting of Spaniards and Indians living and working together. It was a vision that unfortunately was never realized. He also saw it as a Christian empire, where the work of evangelization would be carried on by friars. Like many Spaniards of his age, he did not trust the bishops and diocesan clergy. On 15 October 1524 he wrote to Charles I:

> If we have bishops and other dignities, they will only follow the customs which, for our sins, they pursue these days, of squandering the goods of the Church on pomp and ceremony, and other vices, and leaving entailed estates to their sons or kinsmen. And the evil here would be still greater, for the natives of these parts had in their time religious persons administering their rites and ceremonies who were so severe in the observance of both chastity and honesty that if any one of them was held by anyone to have transgressed he was put to death. If these people were now to see the affairs of the Church and the service of God in the hands of canons or other dignitaries, and saw them indulge in the vices and profanities now common in Spain, knowing that such men were the ministers of God, it would bring our Faith into much contempt, and they would hold it a mockery; this would cause such harm that I believe any further preaching would be of no avail.[4]

In 1523 three Flemish Franciscans arrived in New Spain. One of these, the lay brother Pedro de Gante (Peter of Ghent), became one of the most notable figures in the history of the colony because of his educational efforts among the Indians. In 1524 twelve Franciscans arrived in Veracruz and walked the entire distance to Mexico City. As they traveled in their tattered habits, one of them, Fray Toribio de Benavente, heard the Indians repeating the word *motolinia*. Learning that the word meant "poor," he assumed it as his surname and is still known by it today. The number, of course, was quite significant and they became known as "The Twelve" or "The Twelve Apostles." When they arrived in Mexico City, the Indians were astounded to see Cortés and other conquistadores kneel to kiss their hands and the hems of their robes. What Robert Ricard called "the Spiritual Conquest of Mexico" had begun.[5]

It was in New Spain, as the colony was called, that the missionary methods of the Spanish church and state were perfected. With variations these methods would be used throughout the Spanish dominions until the nineteenth century, in places and forms as varied as the Jesuit reductions in Paraguay and the Franciscan missions in California.

The field of the apostolate in New Spain was varied and difficult. In the south it began with the highlands of Chiapas and Guatemala, difficult of access and with a cold, damp climate. The Gulf coast was low, tropical, and humid, an unhealthy area with many endemic diseases. The central highlands, including Mexico City, had a temperate climate and fertile lands. To the north lay a vast desert populated by the wild, nomadic Indians collectively called Chichimecas. The population was just as varied: in the south, the Mayas, heirs to a wonderful culture that had decayed, a people stubbornly resistant to outside influence; in the southwest and west, the Zapotecs and Tarascans; in the central valley the Nahuas and Otomis. All of these peoples had to be approached in their own languages. It was a daunting missionary challenge.

The first Dominicans, also twelve in number, arrived in New Spain in 1526. The Augustinians, the third major group of friars, came in 1533. The mendicants played the major role in the evangelization of the newly conquered land. As Ricard has said, the Church in New Spain was a "Church of friars."[6] Because the friars carried the burden of the missionary enterprise, the Holy See granted them many privileges, sometimes of an extraordinary nature. The most important of these were given in a bull of Adrian VI called *Exponi nobis nuper* (10 May 1522) but more popularly known as the *Omnímoda*. It granted mendicants who were more than two days' journey from a bishop "all of our authority in both fora," which was the equivalent of the authority of a bishop with the exception of ordination to major orders (there is some disagreement about confirmation). It was, in Robert Padden's trenchant phrase, "a very piece of the rock of Peter."[7] Obviously, when the diocesan structure, with its bishops, chapters, and parish priests, began to overlap with that of the mendicants, controversy would ensue. The disputes between the bishops and the regulars was a constant and disruptive element in the history of Mexican Catholicism.

The need to prepare missionaries to work among the natives led to a wide variety of studies. This was the principal motivation for the many linguistic and ethnic works, such as Molina's *Vocabulario* and Sahagún's *General History of the Things of New Spain*. Molina's dictionary of Spanish and Nahuatl is one of the best available and is still used in Nahuatl-language courses. Sahagún's history, which has been described as a dictionary in action, was an exhaustive and pioneering work in ethnology and Sahagún is considered the founder of that science in Mexico. Without the *General History* our knowledge of prehispanic Mexico would be badly hampered.

In general the linguistic preparation of the mendicants was quite extensive. Each order rather naturally concentrated on the languages spoken in its district. Nahuatl, the Aztec language, was the closest thing to a lingua franca of the missions. Many missionaries saw it, not Spanish, as the most appropriate language of evangelization. Not until the eighteenth century, as part of the enlightenment reforms of Charles III, was an ultimately unsuccessful attempt made to impose Spanish on the natives.

The preparation of the missionaries demanded close contact with the natives and an understanding of both pre- and postconquest culture. The Franciscans in a special way worked very closely with the natives, with the result that the evangelization of New Spain was not just a one-directional matter. The friars absorbed as well as instructed. The result was a phenomenon in the sixteenth century that has only been recognized and accepted in the twentieth: the missionary who is missionized. Christianization was a matter not just of imposition but also one of fusion. Louise Burkhart has described it well as "the friar whose sympathies come to lie with the Indians against the colonists and the ecclesiastical hierarchy, against an Old World perceived as corrupt, and who adopts Indian ways in order to fulfill his mission."[8] In varying degrees this process occurred throughout Ibero-America.

The Franciscans branched out from Mexico City very early after the conquest and soon evangelized large areas in the central plateau. The Dominican presence was less extensive and was centered in two areas: the Valley of Mexico, including Puebla and Morelos, and the Zapotec and Mixtec lands with the city of Oaxaca as center. The Augustinians, who arrived later, worked in the same areas but had to content themselves with those localities that the other two orders had not yet occupied, with foci in the west and near north. The Augustinians earned a rather negative reputation because of their grandiose and costly monasteries.

The structure of dioceses and diocesan bishops lagged behind that of the religious. The first bishopric in New Spain was erected in Tlaxcala in 1526, among the Indians whose support made the Spanish conquest possible. Julián Garcés, a Dominican, was named the first bishop. The real religious center, of

Topia(F)

●DURANGO(F)               Peñol Blanco(F)

●Nombre de Dios(F)

●Sombrerete (F)

●ZACATECAS(F)

M      E      X      I

●Sentispac (F)

●Juchipila (F)

●Jalisco(F)

Ahuacatlán (F)●

●Etzatlán(F)                    San Miguel el Grande(F)●

GUADALAJARA(F)●
                        ●Tonalá(F)                              Querétaro(F)●
Tlajomulco(F)●
Cocula(F)●          ●Poncitlán(F)                              Apaseo(F)●
          Chapala(F)●          Ocotlán(F)
          Axixic(F)●
Zacoalco(F)●                                          Yuriria(A)●
Amacueca(F)●                                          Cuitzeo(A)●          Acámbaro(F)●
                    ●Atoyac (F)          Huango(A)●          ●Ucareo(A)
Autlán(F)●                    Jacona(A)●                    Zinapécuaro(F)●          Jerécuaro(F
          ●Zapotlán(F)          Zacapú(F)●          Cucupao(F)●●Charo(A)
Zapotitlán (F)●          Tarécuato(F)●          Santa Fe(F)●          Tajimaroa(F)●
                              Erongañcuaro(F)●          VALLADOLID(F,A)
                    ●Tuxpan (F)          Pátzcuaro(F)●          ●Tiripitío(A)
                                          Uruapan(F)●          Tzintzuntzan (F)
          ●Colima(F)

                                          ●Tacámbaro(A)

                                          Cupándaro(A)●

(A).  Augustinian
(F)  Franciscan
(D)  Dominican

C     O

TAMPICO(F)

Xilitla(A)

Tantoyuca(A)

Chapulhuacán(A)
Huejutla(A)
Pahuatlán(A)

Culhuacán(A)

Molango(A)

Metztitlán(A)

Chapantongo(A)

Ixmiquilpan(A)

Tututepec(A)

Actopan(A)

Atotonilco(A)

Huauchinango(A)

Acatlán(A)

Tula(F)

Tulancingo(F)

Jilotepec(F)

Tezontepec(A)

Epazoyuca(F)
Zempoala(F)

Otumba(F)

Tepeapulco(F)

Acolman(A)

Apan(F)

Cuautitlán(F)

Teotihuacán(A)

Ecatepec(D)

Tepetlaoztoc(D)

Atzcapotzalco(D)

Tetzcoco(F)

Huexotla(F)

oyoacán(D)

MEXICO

Chalco(D)

Chimalhuacán(D)

TLAXCALA(F)

oluca(F)

Coatepec Chalco(D)

Xochimilco(F)

Huejotzingo(F)

Ocuila(A)

Mexquic(A)

Tlalmanalco(F)

Tenango(D)

Amecameca(F,D)

Malinalco(A)

Totolapan(A)

Cholula(F)

PUEBLA(F,D)

Quecholac(F)

Tepoztlán(D)

Tetela(D)

Atlixco(F)

Acatzingo(F)

Cuernavaca(F)

Cuautinchan(F)

Tepeaca(F)

Tlayacapan(A)

Hueyapan(D)

Tecamachalco(F)

Yautepec(D)

Tecali(F)

Yecapixtla(A)

Jantetelco(A)

Atlatlahuca(F)

Ocuituco(A)

Oaxtepec(D)

Izúcar(Iztucan)(D)

Tehuacán(F)

Zacualpan(A)

Chietla(A)

Tepeji(D)

Chiautla(A)

Zapotitlán(F)

Teutila(D)

Tonalá(D)

Coixtlahuaca(D)

Tlapa(A)

Tamazulapan(D)

Tanetze(D)

Teposcocula(D)

Yanhuitlán(D)

Villa Alta(D)

Tecomaxtlahuaca(D)

Achlutla(D)

Ixtepexi(D)

Totontepec(D)

Tlaxiaco(D)

Etla(D)

OAXACA(D)

Cuilapan(D)

Ocotlán(D)

Nejapa(D)

Jalapa(D)

Coatlán(D)

Tehuantepec(D)

Huaxolotitlán

Huamelula(D)

course, was to be Mexico City. On 12 December 1527 Juan de Zumárraga was named bishop of Mexico and protector of the Indians. A Basque, he was born in Durango around the year 1468. Nothing is known of his early life. He entered the Franciscan order, probably in the province of Concepción, at a young age. From 1520 to 1523 he was the provincial minister of his province, and in 1527 he was guardian (superior) of the convent of Abrojo. In that year, almost accidentally, he came to the attention of Charles I, who was attending a cortes (Castilian assembly) at Valladolid. Impressed by the Franciscan's qualities, the king appointed him *ad hoc* inquisitor to investigate cases of suspected witchcraft. The results of the investigation are not known. On 12 December 1527, the king nominated him to be bishop of the newly created diocese of Mexico, with the additional title of protector of the Indians. At the king's direction, without waiting to be consecrated bishop, he left Spain and arrived in New Spain on 6 December 1528.

The bishop-elect found a colony that was in the process of being destroyed by corrupt and tyrannical government, known to history as the first audiencia. In Spain an *audiencia* had been an appellate court, but in the New World it united this function to that of a legislative council and later an advisory board for the viceroy. Throughout the colonial period it was an extremely powerful body; the boundaries of modern Latin American countries tend to follow the jurisdictional limits of the colonial audiencia districts.

Zumárraga immediately became involved in a stormy dispute with the judges of the first audiencia. He finally succeeded in smuggling a letter, carried by a Basque sailor, to Spain. The result was the deposition of the first audiencia in favor of the second audiencia, one of whose members was Vasco de Quiroga, a layman who later became bishop of Michoacán. In 1535 the governmental system was regularized still more by the creation of the post of viceroy. Viceregal organization would last until independence.

Zumárraga returned to Spain in 1532, was consecrated bishop at Valladolid the following year, and returned to the colony in 1534. He became justly famous for his solicitude for the Indians—but it was a solicitude like that of many Spanish churchmen then and later, paternalistic and sometimes authoritarian. In his capacity as inquisitor ordinary he was responsible for the execution in 1539 of Don Carlos of Texcoco, an Indian leader, on the charge of heresy. He also believed in some sort of compulsory labor for the Indians, specifically the encomienda that was so vigorously denounced by the pro-Indian faction.

In 1547 the diocese of Mexico was raised to the status of an archdiocese, or metropolitan see. This meant that it was now independent of the archdiocese of Seville and that it had dependent dioceses of its own, called suffragans. The diocesan structure began to spread throughout New Spain and with it came more cohesion in the missionary enterprise, illustrated by the increasing number of meetings and councils.

Zumárraga's successor was Alonso de Montúfar, a Dominican, who was appointed in 1551 but did not take possession of his see until three years later. Montúfar was born at Loja, Spain, in 1489. At fifteen he entered the Dominican order and was professed in 1514. In 1524 he began his theological studies at the Dominican convent of Santa Cruz in Granada, the same one in which he had entered the order. He later became a theological consultant to the Inquisition and was sixty-one when he was nominated to the see of Mexico. He entered Mexico City on 23 June 1554, in the company of his friend and fellow Dominican Bartolomé de Ledesma, who became the vicar general of the archdiocese and administered it during Montúfar's prolonged illness. (Ledesma later became bishop of Oaxaca.) Montúfar died on 7 March 1572. The archbishop experienced a great deal of difficulty with the religious. He was responsible for the convocation of the first Mexican Provincial Council of 1555, which attempted to bring order and discipline to the nascent church, and the second council of 1565, an indifferent affair that did little more than accept the decrees of the Council of Trent.

The real organizer of the Mexican church was its third archbishop, Pedro Moya de Contreras (?–1591?). A student of law at the university of Salamanca and the first inquisitor of Mexico, he was the consummate letrado administrator. He convoked the third Mexican Provincial Council (1585), whose decrees formed a code of canon law for the Mexican church. They were later extended to Central America and the Philippines and in some areas remained in effect until the nineteenth century. A prelate very much in the spirit of Trent, he sought the good of the Indians (albeit in a paternalistic way), promoted discipline and education among the clergy, and made pastoral visitations of his archdiocese, some parts of which had not seen a bishop in decades. Unfortunately, after his departure for Spain in 1586, the archdiocese did not receive another resident bishop for almost twenty years.

## MISSIONARY METHODS

The original form of missionary activity, inherited from the Caribbean, was the encomienda-doctrina system. The *encomienda* was a grant of Indians to a Spaniard in return for his services to the crown. The grant brought with it two rights, tribute and free labor, and two obligations, military service in times of emergency (there was no standing army until 1762) and support of a church and priest for the instruction of the Indians. Whatever it may have been in theory, in practice it was subject to the most appalling abuses. The pro-Indian campaigners such as Las Casas saw it as the source of all abuses against the Indians. The crown also disliked it because, even though it was not feudal in the strict sense of the term (it did not, for example, grant rights to rule or administer justice), it was close enough to cause concern. After 1542 the labor component was removed. Devastating epidemics, especially in 1544 and 1576, drastically lessened the native population and even depopulated whole villages. Tribute fell off, and the encomienda had to compete with an emerging economy for native labor, which became scarcer. This, together with the agitation of the humanitarians and the suspicions of the crown, brought the encomienda to heel. Although some encomiendas remained after the sixteenth century, they were no longer important.

After 1573 the focus of missionary work became the presidio/mission system which proved itself on the northern frontier of New Spain and became the basis for all future evangelization. It emerged out of Spanish contact with the fierce and nomadic Chichimeca Indians to the north of Mexico City. With the discovery of silver in the Zacatecas region around 1545, Spanish settlement began to move northward. The Chichimecas proved a formidable obstacle, and the colonists raised demand for a total war of extermination and enslavement (*guerra a fuego y a sangre*, war by fire and blood). The crown did not yield to these demands, contenting itself with limited and ineffectual military expeditions. The third Mexican Provincial Council of 1585 roundly denounced war against the Chichimecas and called for a peaceful program of conversion and assimilation.

The presidio/mission system that was eventually adopted consisted of a fort with enough soldiers to protect the missionaries. Christian Indians, especially the Tlaxcalans, were brought in as settlers to act as liaison with the hostiles. Great emphasis was laid on the disinterestedness of the missionaries, and for that reason the system relied heavily on mendicants and Jesuits. The Indians were brought together in involuntary isolation from Spaniards and taught not only religion but also crafts and a European life-style. The aim of the mission was not just conversion but also to incorporate the native into Spanish life. The financial support of the missions came primarily from the crown. The system proved successful in the Chichimeca territories and was refined in subsequent undertakings. It was the model of future mission enterprises, from the Jesuit reductions of Paraguay to the Franciscan missions of California. While the presence of soldiers helped protect the missionaries and the Christian natives, it also proved an obstacle to evangelization. Officers often engaged in acrimonious disputes with the friars or priests over respective areas of authority, and the soldiers were only too ready to pacify supposedly rebellious Indians when it involved the accumulation of booty or slaves.

In general the Nahuas (the global name for the Indians of the central plateau, who shared a common language and culture) did not actively resist christianization. Their past history had accustomed them to accepting alien gods into their pantheon, though they had difficulty understanding the exclusive claims of the Christian deity. Their reaction was more of an accommodation, an acceptance of Christianity but mingling it with elements of their native religion and culture. In general, from the end of the sixteenth century on, the clergy tended to accept the status quo rather than attempt to alter it radically. Other peoples, such as the Mayas of Chiapas and Yucatán, were traditionally more conservative and tenacious of their old ways. Their Christianity was more heavily mixed with pagan and preconquest elements than was that of the central area and has remained so.

## A HOUSE DIVIDED

The religious presented a solid front in their disputes with the bishops, but their solidarity collapsed when they began to fight with each other. There was an intense rivalry among the mendicant orders that subsided only when they faced a common enemy. The religious found themselves in a position of power that they had nowhere else in the world. Their enemies called this a form of religious imperialism, the carving out of domains and fiefs in the new land. Although the crown tried to restrain their power, especially by means of the Ordenanza General del Patronazgo Real of 1573, they were never entirely successful. The religious were essential to the missionary enterprise, which the crown took seriously if only because it was the major basis for Spanish rule. When the religious threatened to leave the mission fields rather than give up their privileges, the crown had to take their threat seriously. The imperialism of the mendicants reached its peak in 1556 when they divided New Spain among them, with each order having exclusive control of designated areas. This caused intense disgust to their enemies, especially since the individual orders were not always fully able to serve the lands assigned them.

A major difficulty faced in evangelization, and another source of controversy, was the fact that the Indians were often seminomadic or lived in small, scattered villages. The solution to this was a policy called *congregación*, or resettlement, whereby the nomads were brought together in villages and the smaller villages were combined. In general the bishops and diocesan clergy favored this policy because it was favorable to the development of diocesan parishes. The religious, often supported by the viceroys, opposed it for the same reason: Diocesan parishes interfered with the religious' control. Europeans of that century, in their belief that their way of life was the only civilized one, were oblivious to the culture shock that such abrupt uprooting from traditional patterns of living caused.

A special point of contention between the bishops and the religious was the status of *doctrinas*. These were churches in Indian villages where all or most of the natives had embraced Christianity, perhaps for a generation or more, and so had passed beyond the purely missionary stage. In reality they had become Indian parishes, though according to the letter of canon law they were still missions. In the sixteenth century parish work was considered incompatible with the religious life. The bishops believed that the mendicants should move out of the doctrinas and on to new missionary areas. The doctrinas would be yielded to the bishops and the diocesan clergy and would become parishes in the strict, canonical sense of the term. The truth was that the bishops could not live with a situation in which so many de facto parishes were outside their control. The religious resisted, claiming that they alone had the good interests of the natives at heart and they alone had sufficient knowledge of the native languages. The struggle continued throughout the sixteenth century without any clearly definable outcome. The shift in favor of the bishops began with the *Cédula general* but complete domination of the religious by the crown was not achieved until the eighteenth century.

Bishops and religious also differed over other questions, such as jurisdiction over marriage cases, congregación, and tithes. The bishops were chagrined that the religious would settle disputes over the validity of marriages (a function ordinarily reserved to bishops) and accused them of marrying and unmarrying the Indians too easily. The religious would respond with the privileges of the Omnímoda. The bishops favored the policy of congregación and the payment of tithes by the Indians because this brought the Indians more directly under their control and provided financial support for the diocesan structure. For exactly the same reason the religious opposed them.

There were also major differences in the approach to missionary tactics. The Franciscans, strongly influenced by millenarian and apocalyptic ideas, saw the New World, with its innocent and receptive natives, as the site of an ideal Christian commonwealth free of the taint and corruption of the Old World. And because many of them believed that this would also be a sign of the end of the world and viewed baptism as essential for salvation, they emphasized mass baptism without the need for an extensive preliminary instruction. The Dominicans and Augustinians, on the other hand, believed in delaying baptism until the neophytes had been thoroughly instructed. Even granted that the number of baptisms reported by the Franciscans was highly exaggerated, they seem to have baptized in very large numbers with little or no preparation.

One of the reasons for the lack of a catechumenate or proper prebaptismal instruction was that such a thing was not known in sixteenth-century missions. After a rudimentary instruction, baptism was administered, to be followed by a lengthier and fuller catechesis. This catechesis was often restricted to rote memorization of the Our Father, Hail Mary, Creed, the Ten Commandments, and vivid depictions of hell. The Augustinians demanded a better preparation and so in the beginning baptized fewer Indians.

In the early days not all sacraments were administered to the Indians. Confirmation and the Anointing of the Sick (Extreme Unction) were not regularly administered both because of a lack of holy oils and because of doubts about the Indians' capacity to receive them. (The special case of ordination to the priesthood will be considered later.) A special problem in the earlier days was that of polygamy among the natives and the validity of their marriages. Polygamy did not really die out until some ten to twenty years after the conquest. In general the religious favored the validity of native marriages, the diocesans did not.

Another source of disagreement among the missionaries concerned their attitude toward the native cultures. The two extremes were represented by those who believed that the native cultures and beliefs were diabolically inspired and hence should be uprooted—the "root and branch" approach—and those who took a more gradual approach. Inevitably this brings up the question: To what extent were the missionaries guilty of destroying prehispanic writings and art? Quite clearly many did so, although the famous legend that Zumárraga burned the great library of Texcoco is just that, a legend.[9] Undoubtedly much prehispanic learning and history was lost both to the excessive zeal of missionaries and to the vagaries of conquest. On the other hand, mendicants such as Sahagún, Motolinía, and Las Casas were responsible for preserving much of this material. They believed that only by knowing the religious and historical background of the natives could they effectively evangelize them. Without them the history of Mexico before Cortés could hardly be written. It should also be noted that the Aztecs themselves were guilty of that sort of destruction. "Once secure, the Aztecs destroyed all the records and reconstructed their history with accounts favorable to themselves."[10]

## THE CRIOLLOS

A source of tension among the mendicants came with the changing composition of their membership. As the sixteenth century advanced there emerged a new class in society, the *criollos*, full-blooded Europeans born in the New World. Technically the only difference between them and native-born Spaniards (called *peninsulares*) was the place of birth. Yet in practice there were many differences. Because of their birth outside the Iberian peninsula, criollos were held to be in some way inferior, a situation sometimes blamed on geography (they were born too close to the sun) or climate (which made them lazy). Hence a sense of inferiority, not always subtle, was part of the criollo inheritance. Thus, for example, all higher offices in New Spain were monopolized by peninsulares. Of the 171 bishops and archbishops in New Spain in the colonial period, only a handful were criollos. A similar situation prevailed in civil government. The criollos' resentment of their second-class status was a major factor in the wars for independence.

The mendicants, especially the Franciscans, were the first to feel the antagonism between the peninsulares and criollos. In addition, some of the peninsulares after years of working in the New World came to identify with the criollos. When large numbers of the latter began entering the orders, the former feared that the religious life was going to be swamped and diluted by members who did not have the true spirit of religion. Their presence was considered destructive of the spirit and rule of the orders. Among the Franciscans the antagonism reached such a pitch that each side attempted to swamp the other by recruiting members from its group. Finally, a compromise was reached, called the *alternativa*, whereby the office of provincial alternated between peninsulares and criollos.

EDUCATION

This was a major priority for the early churchmen in New Spain. The Franciscans, with great optimism and zeal, established a college of Santa Cruz for Indian boys at Tlaltelolco, north of Mexico City. Its purpose was to give them the equivalent of a European classical education, with the ultimate purpose of forming a native clergy. In this it succeeded and some of its graduates, such as Antonio Valeriano, were famous as Latinists and scholars. The project ultimately failed, in part because of opposition by the Spanish colonists, who quickly realized that an educated Indian class was incompatible with exploitation. In addition, the decision by the bishops of New Spain in 1585 not to ordain Indians to the priesthood made a classical education unnecessary. On a more practical level the famous Franciscan lay brother, Pedro de Gante, inaugurated a system of craft education that gained him everlasting fame in Mexican history. The educational endeavors of the other mendicant orders, such as the Augustinian college of San Pablo, were devoted almost entirely to the education of their own members. Paradoxically, the Dominicans, heirs to a great intellectual tradition, did not found a single secondary school in their missions and were opposed to the idea of teaching the natives Latin.

One of Zumárraga's major ambitions was the creation of a university in Mexico City. The exuberant growth of Spanish universities of this time and the pride taken by their graduates, especially those of Salamanca, gave rise to a mentality that wanted to create the same situation in the New World. At the same time a university would be a source of vocations to the priesthood, since in the Spanish system it was preeminently a place of clerical formation. Difficulties prevented the foundation of the university during Zumárraga's lifetime and not until 1551 was a royal order issued for its establishment. It formally opened two years later. In 1596 Pope Clement VII extended to it all the privileges and rights enjoyed by the university of Salamanca, to which Philip II later added those enjoyed by San Marcos in Lima, and so it was known as The Royal and Pontifical University of Mexico. In structure and curriculum it was modeled on the university of Salamanca, not surprising in view of the fact that the majority of ecclesiastical and civil officials in New Spain were alumni of that preeminent Castilian institution.

Probably the greatest single educational force in the colonial New World was the Society of Jesus. Arriving in Peru in 1568 and New Spain in 1572, the Jesuits soon inaugurated a number of outstanding schools for the colonials. In Mexico City the colegio de San Pedro y San Pablo, later known as San Ildefonso, became the center for criollo education. It was eventually matched in fame by the Jesuit college in Valladolid, modern Michoacán. Other colleges were founded throughout New Spain. The Jesuit program laid heavy emphasis on classical humanism. Despite some efforts to get the Jesuits involved in the university, this ultimately failed and the Jesuit colleges remained essentially preparatory schools. During the colonial period the Jesuits founded twenty-five colleges, eleven seminaries, and six houses for priests. The Jesuits also engaged in extensive mission activity, primarily to the north of Mexico City. (This will be dealt with in Chapter 4 as part of the northward expansion of New Spain.)

## HOSPITALS

A major charitable work in New Spain was the establishment of hospitals. The term included not only the care of the sick but also, in the original significance of hospice, the care of travelers. In his last will Cortés founded the Hospital de Jesús in Mexico City, whose chapel today holds his tomb. In 1541 Zumárraga founded the Hospital del Amor de Dios, which was also known as the Hospital de las Bubas, because it cared for the poor afflicted with venereal diseases. There was a hospital for Indians, called the royal hospital, with the king as its chief patron. The first Mexican Provincial Council of 1555 decreed the establishment of hospitals in all towns and villages to receive the poor and the sick. There is evidence that by 1583 every principal town in the archdiocese of Mexico had a hospital.

Especially notable were the hospital-pueblos founded at Santa Fe by Vasco de Quiroga while he was still a layman. They were not only hospitals in the modern sense of the term but also cooperatives, modeled on Thomas More's *Utopia* and Plato's *Republic*. Quiroga, like Zumárraga, was strongly influenced by the ideas of the great Renaissance humanist Erasmus of Rotterdam. In 1532 he moved to Michoacán, where he established similar institutions among the Tarascan Indians, and in 1539 was named bishop. Each village or commune was self-governing and specialized in a particular craft. In addition to provisions for sick care, they included schools, workshops, and dwellings for the Indians. The natives were also taught Christianity and fundamental European methods of farming. They shared equally in the profits from their enterprises, and their lives also centered around communal religious devotions. Quiroga's experiment was the prototype of later Spanish mission methods, including the missions of Alta California and the reductions of Paraguay. Quiroga died in 1565, leaving behind him a glowing reputation as a humanitarian and churchman. The Tarascan Indians of Michoacán still remember him as Tata Vasco—"Daddy Vasco"—and many villages still pursue the crafts he taught them.

## THE INQUISITION IN NEW SPAIN

In the aftermath of the Council of Trent and the worldwide Catholic Reformation, the Church in New Spain grew more structured, bureaucratic, and more under royal control. It is significant that in the period between 1570 and 1585 the Jesuits arrived in New Spain, the Inquisition was established, the patronato was codified, the first diocesan priest was named archbishop of Mexico, and the third Provincial Council drew up a law code for the Church. In part this was because the reform program of the Church coincided with the policies of the Spanish crown, for example, the subordination of the religious to the bishops, greater control of popular devotion, reform and rational administration, and a greater emphasis on law in the life of both Church and state.

A major instrument of governmental and ecclesiastical control was clearly the Inquisition. It was established in 1571, half a century after the conquest, with Pedro Moya de Contreras as the first inquisitor. Up to that time inquisitorial functions had belonged to the individual bishops. The Inquisition at first concerned itself with Protestant corsairs, some of whom had been stranded in New Spain and lived there in relative freedom. These were rounded up and given various sentences. The Inquisition was also concerned about books and iconography. Later it began to ferret out crypto-Jews or persons of Jewish sympathy, the most famous being some members of the Carvajal family. At a later period also it began to deal with moral offenses such as bigamy, blasphemy, and moral lapses among the clergy. Though the Inquisition was never as active in New Spain as in the old country, it constantly sought to extend its power.

As powerful as the Inquisition was in theory, its importance should not be exaggerated. The tribunal was not particularly welcomed in the colony, particularly by the viceroy Martín Enríquez de Almansa, because its intrusion upset a delicate balance of power within colonial society. Enríquez tried to restrict the influence of the Inquisition to such an extent that Moya de Contreras accused him of treating it with contempt. The audiencia, which functioned both as a law court and advisory council to the viceroy, found itself in competition with the Inquisition over jurisdiction in criminal cases. Bishops looked askance at an institution that intruded on their own power. The Indians were exempt from the authority of the Spanish Inquisition, though they remained subject to the inquisitorial powers of the bishops.

Like many other colonial institutions, the Inquisition tended to decline in later ages, especially in the seventeenth and eighteenth centuries. In part this was because it was afflicted with a great deal of corruption, a problem that plagued the tribunal in all the Spanish dominions. There is a historical debate as to the precise strength of the Inquisition in later times. Some have seen it as a continued check on independent thought and creativity. Others regard it as having become ineffective, plagued by corruption, subject to economic pressure from merchants, and declining into formalism. The widespread circulation of Enlightenment thought in the eighteenth century, especially among clergy, indicates that it was unsuccessful in keeping out subversive doctrines.

## OUR LADY OF GUADALUPE

It is impossible to write about religion in Mexico without referring to the premier religious factor in its history: devotion to Our Lady of Guadalupe. In

December 1531, according to the traditional account, the Virgin Mary appeared to an Indian peasant, Juan Diego, at a place called Tepeyac, while he was going to Tlaltelolco to hear mass and religious instruction. The Virgin directed him to go to the bishop-elect of Mexico, Juan de Zumárraga, and tell him to have a chapel built on that spot. Meeting initial skepticism from the bishop-elect, Juan Diego returned home. In a subsequent apparition the Virgin told him that his uncle Juan Bernardino, who was mortally ill, would recover and that in response to the bishop-elect's request she would provide a sign. Juan Diego was instructed to gather roses from the top of a promontory where flowers did not grow and take them in his mantle to Zumárraga. When he opened the mantle (*tilmatl* in Nahuatl) before Zumárraga, the picture of the Virgin was imprinted on it. The bishop-elect immediately put it in his private oratory and before the end of the year had built the first chapel at Tepeyac (later called Guadalupe), to which the entire city of Mexico made pilgrimage.

The account follows closely the pattern to be found in hundreds of apparition stories in Spain and the New World at that time. The Virgin is a compassionate and loving mother, in contrast to her angry and judging son. She comes to the aid of the oppressed and marginalized of society. Her message meets with initial disbelief but after a miraculous sign it is accepted by Church authorities. The account explains the origin of a shrine or a devotion.

The traditional account is not without difficulties. The assertion that Juan Diego went from his native village of Cuauhtitlán to the Franciscan house at Tlaltelolco does not accord with present-day research, which locates the Franciscans at Cuauhtitlán and not at Tlaltelolco in 1531. Similarly, the use of a Spanish name, Guadalupe, associated with a major devotion in Extremadura, presents problems. The claim that Zumárraga heard a Nahuatl word he interpreted as "Guadalupe" cannot be taken seriously. All accounts, even those in Nahuatl, use the Spanish term. The conclusion is inescapable that the shrine antedated the formulation of the account.

A still more formidable problem is the total lack of any reliable, datable record of the apparitions prior to 1648. The lack of any mention of them in Zumárraga's letters may be attributable to the fact that not all his correspondence has survived, but his failure to refer to Guadalupe in his will is more significant. In that century any Spaniard who founded a chapel or had a special devotion would have left money either for masses or a chaplaincy. This silence concerning the apparitions is maintained by all major religious figures and writers of the sixteenth century. When reference is made to the shrine or to the devotion of Our Lady of Guadalupe, no mention is made of the apparition account or Juan Diego.

In 1556 the Franciscan provincial Francisco de Bustamante delivered a scathing condemnation of the devotion, stating that it was pagan in origin, that it was "new," and that the image had been painted by an Indian. Neither in his sermon, however, nor in the investigation later made of it did anyone mention the apparition account. In 1571 the English corsair Miles Philips left a description of the shrine but without mentioning the apparitions. When the viceroy of New Spain, Martín Enríquez de Almansa, was asked in 1575 to give an account of the shrine to the Council of the Indies, he made no reference to the apparitions. Instead, he stated that the chapel had been built about 1555 and that the devotion had become popular after a herdsman claimed to have been cured there.

In general the devotion was condemned by the friars and supported by the bishops and diocesan clergy, but without reference to any apparitions. Bernardino de Sahagún called it "suspect" and decried the fact that the Indians equated it with the worship of Tonantzin, the mother goddess of the Mexica, whose shrine had been on the hill of Tepeyac. In the sixteenth century there was a vague tradition of an apparition around the years 1555–1556, but they were not associated with the bestowal of an image. In fact, it seems that at the time the devotion at Guadalupe was twofold. For the Spaniards it was devotion to the Virgin of Extremadura, the land from which the majority of conquistadores and settlers came. For the Indians it was a devotion to the successor of Tonantzin.

In 1648 a priest named Miguel Sánchez published the story of the apparitions for the first time. There is abundant evidence that prior to that time the account was unknown in New Spain. The following year another priest, Luis Lasso de la Vega, published a Nahuatl version of the story. Known as the *Nican Mopohua* from its opening words, it—rather than Sánchez's account—has become the standard version. However, attempts to show that it was contemporary with Juan Diego have been unsuccessful. In the years that followed, the devotion spread very rapidly, particularly among the criollos. In the eighteenth century there was a conscious effort to spread it among the Indians. The claim that mass conversions of Indians followed on the apparitions in 1531 is without foundation. Eventually, of course, it became popular outside Mexico, and in 1945 Pope Pius XII proclaimed Our Lady of Guadalupe patroness of the Americas.

As touching and poignant as the story is, it remains, from the historical point of view, just a story. In all probability it was a legend that grew up among the Indians in the late sixteenth or more probably early seventeenth century to explain the origin of the shrine and to bring comfort to an oppressed people.

## THE WOMEN OF NEW SPAIN

For most of the sixteenth century men outnumbered women in New Spain. Spanish women, especially those of a higher social stratum, were reluctant to migrate. Spanish men, whether they had left wives and children behind or not, turned to the available Indian women, less frequently to black women, usually in casual or unblessed unions. This begot a new class of mixed white/Indian, called *mestizo*, almost invariably the offspring of a Spanish father and an Indian mother, and the offspring of black and white, called *mulatto*. Though the terms were primarily racial, throughout the century they were synonymous with illegitimate. When marriage did take place in New Spain, it was sometimes bigamous, with the Spanish men conveniently ignoring the existence of spouse and family in the home peninsula.

In Castilian society of the sixteenth century the role of a woman was defined by convention, law, religion, and prejudice. It was sharply circumscribed. Spanish women basically had two alternatives in life, marriage or the convent. A Latin aphorism of the times was *aut maritus, aut murus* (a husband or the cloister). Both required dowries, and the question of providing adequate dowries was an important one. A major social problem in the later sixteenth century was that of upper-class women whose straitened circumstances deprived them of dowries, thus removing from them both alternatives. To remedy this Archbishop Moya de Contreras founded the convent of Jesús María just for young ladies in that situation. He and the viceroy Martín Enríquez de Almansa also used some of the surplus funds from the chapel at Guadalupe to supply dowries for needy girls.

Marriages were usually arranged by families on the basis of social and financial advantage. Romantic love was not ordinarily an important factor. It is somewhat surprising, therefore, to find that in the sixteenth century the Church strongly supported freedom of marital choice. In cases where young couples wanted to marry against the wishes of parents, ecclesiastics often gave shelter and performed their marriages. Ecclesiastical courts pronounced in favor of freedom of choice and would invoke the aid of civil law to enforce their decisions. This situation began to change in the seventeenth century, when civil authorities grew reluctant to enforce ecclesiastical verdicts and the weight of convention began to favor parental authority.

In spite of the restrictions set by convention and society, many women did manage to make their mark and to exercise influence. The life of Sor Juana Inés de la Cruz (detailed later), was an example, albeit unique, of this. A certain level of financial independence came to women from their dowries, which protected them from their husbands' debts and which reverted to them after the husband's death. Women, especially widows, were sometimes able to use their dowry funds to enhance family fortunes by investment in real estate and by providing funds for entrepreneurs. The encomienda, acquired through widowhood or inheritance, was sometimes a source of financial independence for widows, who often administered them personally. Widows who inherited them were theoretically required to remarry within a year or so, but this was not enforced.

Also helpful to women was the custom of *compadrazgo* or ritual sponsorship. Originally it applied to the spiritual relationship with sponsors in baptism, confirmation, and marriage (at that time it was customary, but not required, to have sponsors for married couples). In Spanish America this was expanded into a network of complex social relationships that included mutual obligations of help, financial aid, security, and support in times of need and danger. For women it provided masculine help and protection without at the same time depriving the women of their independence.

Education for women was primarily aimed at training them for roles in the home. Lower-class women could find work in various trades or businesses, some of them regarded as unsavory. Ironically, the best educational opportunities for women were to be found in convents.

It is difficult to establish with total certitude the attitudes and behavior of that time in regard to sexuality. In theory the Church's sexual teaching was clear and rigid, especially in the aftermath of the Council of Trent. Virginity was considered superior to marriage. Any sexual activity outside marriage, solitary or with another (fornication), was sinful. So also was adultery, sexual intercourse in which one of the partners was married. Homosexuality and bestiality were regarded as contrary to nature and eventually came under the jurisdiction of the Inquisition. Incest was also condemned, but the word was often used very loosely to indicate sexual relations between even distant relatives. Deviations from these norms, however, are to be found in documentary evidence. Inquisition records show rather frequent instances of priests' preaching that simple fornication was not a sin, an idea that seems to have been commonplace among many laity. Solicitation to sexual sins by priests in the confessional was not confined to isolated cases. The frequent references by church authorities to men who kidnapped girls from their parents' homes would seem to reflect a genuine social problem, except that at times the kidnapping was fictitious. Concubinage, whether (in Spanish America) with native women or with a mistress, was common.

## CONVENTS

The convent was a very important social institution throughout the Spanish empire. A convent was considered a sign of distinction for cities and hence had a civic importance. Popularly regarded as centers of moral and religious uplift, they were dedicated to prayer and contemplation, not to ministries such as teaching or hospitals. The outlook throughout the Catholic world at that time was that nunneries were cloistered. It was not until the next century in France that sisters (not nuns in the strict sense of the term) began to exercise specific ministries.

Convents were also urban, in contrast to many of the mendicants' monasteries, which were often founded in rural districts in order to be near the Indians. The convents were supported by individual patrons, endowments, and the dowries of the nuns. Some convents became wealthy and were extensive property owners by reason of bequests from the laity. As their funds increased, they moved into the purchase of urban real estate. In the absence of banks as they are known today, convents and other ecclesiastical institutions functioned as moneylenders and as such had a significant economic impact.

The way in which women were recruited, or placed, in convents in the sixteenth century can arouse both surprise and repugnance in a modern reader. However, stories of upper-class families using convents as dumping grounds for surplus daughters are exaggerated, if only because of the expense of dowries and subsequent support of the nun, all of which fell to the family. It should also be kept in mind that the concept of a vocation as a freely chosen response to a divine call was not well developed at the time. Men entered the Church as part of a career choice, and women could go into convents with little or no aptitude for the life. The results were often negative for both the convent and the woman. Upper-class nuns would sometimes live comfortably, accompanied by servants or slaves, and subject to minimal supervision, though most convents in New Spain seem to have been stricter. The rigors of convent life were often alleviated by the fact that so many of the nuns were related to each other. Nuns were also able to have personal funds, called *reservas*, which were sometimes invested through legal representatives. Theatrical and musical productions provided recreation, and the convent often provided the only accessible means of achieving an education. Many women found convent life less oppressive than married life.

The first convent in New Spain was Nuestra Señora de la Concepción, founded between 1540 and 1550. They were soon to be found throughout New Spain and wherever Spanish rule went. Outside Mexico City the founders were often wealthy criollos, especially owners of ranches (*haciendas*) and mines. By the eighteenth century monasteries and nunneries had come to dominate the real estate market in Mexico City itself and were a powerful economic factor throughout the land.

## COFRADÍAS

Another important institution was the *cofradía*, the brotherhood or confraternity. These were organizations of men with certain things in common (the same trade or craft or even race) who came together for a religious purpose. Originally they had arisen from the *gremios* (trade guilds) of the Spanish Middle Ages. Gradually they became distinct, though there was always a certain degree of overlapping. Each cofradía had a charter granted by ecclesiastical or civil authority that specified its purpose, nature, functions, and officers. Among the functions were supplying burials for poor members and giving financial aid to their widows. Others included financing the maintenance of churches, chapels, and hospitals; organization of festivals, especially for their patronal feasts; and works of charity. In return for the fraternal aspects of the cofradía members also enjoyed certain privileges, such as indulgences or special burial places. The institution of the cofradía, which came to be found throughout Latin America, has not been given the study it deserves, but it also played an important social and economic role. Cofradías for Indians and blacks, for example, provided social identity and economic support. Others, particularly in the cities, were sometimes quite wealthy and in the absence of a banking system provided loans, especially to their members, after the manner of a modern credit union.

The Spanish missionary endeavor in the New World got off to a faltering start in the Caribbean and went through its formative stage in New Spain. The frightful devastation of the native races in Española, Cuba, and the other areas of the Caribbean left the missionaries without a people to evangelize. The Church in those areas became primarily a Spanish one, with some work being done among the black slaves who were imported to replace the Indians and among the remnants of the natives themselves.

The situation was quite different in New Spain, where the basic format of the missions was established. By the end of the sixteenth century it had not only been clarified, but it had passed through its greatest period and begun to lose some of its fervor. The patterns formulated in New Spain, however, were those that were to be followed, with adaptations and growth, throughout the rest of Spanish America. These included the use of the native languages, the presidio/mission system, the doctrinas, educational institutions for both Spaniards and natives, the dominance of the religious, the financial support of the missions, and the policy of regrouping or congregación. Some of the less desirable aspects of the system, such as the venomous antagonism between bishops and religious and increasing royal control, were also exported to the rest of Spanish America.

# 3

# EXPANSION
# AND EVANGELIZATION:
# SOUTH AMERICA, 1492–1600

## PERU

To the south the Spaniards encountered a civilization as brilliant as that of the
Aztecs, though less sanguinary. Though the Spaniards already had considerable experience both in colonizing and in evangelization, their domination and
christianization of Peru got off to a much shakier start than that of New Spain.
Both civil government and missionary methods drew on the experience of New
Spain, so there was less need of devising new ones. In general it can also be said
that the missionary endeavor in Peru and in the rest of South America has not
been studied as intensely as that of New Spain. This is especially true of
English-language studies.

### THE INCAS

The history of pre-Inca Andean cultures is obscure. The ancestral cultures
probably originated around Lake Titicaca in the Bolivian altiplano, but most of
them seem to have been extinct by the time of the Incas. The flow of
civilization was from the highlands to the coastal areas. Inca history began with
a semilegendary chieftain called Manco Capac who led his tribe into the valley
of Cuzco in the mid-thirteenth century. He soon formed alliances with three
other tribes. The four groups came to constitute the Inca empire but retained
their distinct identities down to the Spanish conquest. *Inca*, a term of unknown
origin originally applied to the ruler of the confederation (*Sapa Inca*), eventually came to be applied to all the peoples of the empire. In point of fact, the
empire was made of numerous linguistic and ethnic groups, of which the

original four were the most important. The polity now known as the Inca empire called itself *Tahuantinsuyo*—"four quarters."

The expansion of the empire outside the area of Cuzco began in the reign of a remarkable ruler named Viracocha Inca. He not only raided outside his area, as did other chieftains, but he also assumed administrative control of the peoples he defeated. In 1438 his son, Inca Yupanqui, known as Pachacuti, defeated an invading army of Chancas and then forced his father to give him the royal title.

Pachacuti was a military genius who in a series of campaigns extended the empire to the borders of Ecuador in the north and to Lake Titicaca in the south. He also instituted important changes in Inca society, changes that paralleled those taking place at the same time in among the Aztecs. He established Inca colonies in conquered regions to dilute rebelliousness, and efforts were made to weaken local religions by centering everything in Cuzco. Those who willingly accepted Inca rule were made Incas by adoption (called *orejones*, "big ears," by the Spaniards because of their large earplugs). Pachacuti locked the office of emperor in rigid protocol. In a process similar to that among the Mexica, the emperor became more and more remote. Even dead emperors retained their status; their mummies had their own households (*panaca*), with living attendants. Pachacuti also introduced and embellished the ceremonial of everyday life. Inca society had a rigid, stratified caste system that centered about the *ayllus* (clans). Cuzco was rebuilt into a magnificent imperial capital.

The greatest weakness of the empire was the lack of a clear process for succession. Originally the office of chieftain (*sinchi*) had been elective, as it had been among the Aztecs. Although the emperors came to dominate the process of election more and more, some sort of tribal consent was still necessary. Succession did not necessarily or even commonly descend from father to son. Legitimacy was secured by a system of brother-sister marriages, though most emperors also had concubines and numerous illegitimate children. Additional problems arose from the discontent of conquered peoples and palace intrigues.

Despite its weaknesses, the Inca empire was a remarkable achievement. Technically all property belonged to the state. There were great accomplishments in art, architecture, and engineering. The use of terraced fields for Andean agriculture, suspension bridges, construction without mortar, fine pottery, and goldsmithing all testify to the level of Inca achievements. In addition there was an elaborate network of roads and a system of runners who acted as couriers. Though the Incas had no written language, they devised a system of knotted cords that made the sending of messages practical. The economy was planned and regulated. There was total absorption of the individual into the state, with little or no room left for individual initiative on the local level. One result was a great deal of security and very little crime.

The ancestral god of the Incas was the sun (*Inti*), from whom the emperor claimed descent. Pachacuti sought to diminish this cult, even though it established the legitimacy of his rule, in favor of the monotheistic Viracocha, the creator-god. In part this was the result of his desire to impose uniformity on the empire, but it had only modest success. The priesthood was never so strong in Peru as it was in Mexico.

In 1493 a young boy, Huayna Capac, succeeded to the imperial rule. At that time the empire extended from present-day Quito in the north to Chile in the south and Lake Titicaca in the southeast. Huayna Capac spent sixteen years in campaigns and in quelling revolts. It was during his reign that the first news of Spaniards reached Peru. Something else came from the Spaniards: an epidemic. Precisely what the disease was is not clear but, entering Peru from the Spanish possessions to the north, it devastated the immunologically unprotected natives and decimated the nobility and the army.

Before his death in 1527 Huayna Capac made a disastrous change in the order of succession. This had already been settled on his oldest legitimate son, Huascar, but at the last minute the emperor changed it in favor of another son, Ninan Cuyochi, who died of the epidemic shortly after his father's death. Huascar, in violation of Inca tradition, proclaimed himself emperor in Cuzco. This seizure of power was soon contested by his half-brother Atahuallpa, the imperial viceroy in Quito. A bitter and destructive civil war broke out in 1530, ending with Huascar's defeat two years later. By that time the Spaniards had been in Peru for a year. Thus, at the very time that the empire needed all its resources to meet a foreign invasion, it was devastated by an epidemic and internal conflict.

## THE CONQUEST OF PERU

After his discovery of the South Sea Vasco Núñez de Balboa planned an expedition to Peru but his death in 1519 prevented it. In 1522 there were some tentative and ultimately unsuccessful Spanish explorations of the north coast of Peru. After that the governor of Darién, Pedrarias Dávila, father-in-law and executioner of Balboa, gave a contract of exploration and conquest to a newly formed partnership of three men. The most famous of these was Francisco Pizarro, an illiterate, illegitimate, and uncouth swineherd from Extremadura. Already middle-aged, he had had vast experience in the New World. The second was Diego de Almagro, who matched Pizarro in almost every way except that he was a Castilian. Both men were brave, ruthless, and over fifty years of age. The third partner was Hernando de Luque, a well-to-do priest, who was the principal financial backer of the expedition and who, together with other financial rewards, was promised a bishopric. Together with Pedrarias, they were probably as unsavory a group as ever infested the New World.

Their first expedition in 1524 was unsuccessful, though it did produce enough gold to justify a second one. The second expedition, in 1526, was somewhat more successful. At one point Pizarro and his men were stranded on the island of Gallo off the coast of Ecuador. When Almagro returned to Panama for supplies and reinforcements, he found that Pedrarias had been replaced by a new governor, Pedro de los Ríos, who was antagonistic to Pizarro. Ríos detained Almagro and sent ships to bring Pizarro back. It was at that point that Pizarro made his famous stand, drawing a line in the sand with his sword and challenging his men to join him. Thirteen did so. Ríos was initially angry with this act of defiance, but Almagro and Luque calmed him to the extent that he sent a ship to help Pizarro. With that Pizarro went south, captured Túmbez, and returned to Panama with the conviction that Peru should be his. In 1528 he returned to Spain and received royal approval for the conquest. Two years later he returned to Panama, accompanied by two brothers, one half-brother, and several cousins. In 1529 Luque received his reward when he was appointed bishop of the newly created see of Túmbez and was named, apparently without intentional irony, protector of the Indians. (He did not enjoy his rewards for long; he died in 1532.)

The third expedition finally sailed in 1531. In late 1532 it reached Cajamarca, where Pizarro met Atahuallpa. He treacherously attacked the natives and imprisoned the emperor. As a ransom Atahuallpa offered a roomful of gold and silver. It was delivered, but it was not enough to save the emperor's life, for in an act of blatant treachery Pizarro had him executed in August 1533. In Cuzco Pizarro set up Manco Capac as puppet Inca and gave most of the municipal positions to his relatives. In 1535 he founded Lima (officially, the City of the Kings) as his capital. In the meantime the Spaniards continued to extend their conquest. In 1540 Pedro de Valdivia went to the southern reach of the Inca empire, in what is now Chile, where in the following year he founded the city of Santiago. The southern part of the region, however, lay outside Spanish domination because of the fierce resistance of the Araucanian Indians.

CIVIL WAR

Pizarro had none of the diplomatic skill or vision of Cortés. Given the centralized nature of the Inca government and the docility of its people, it would have been an easy thing for him to control the empire. Coarse, uncouth, and treacherous, he was interested primarily in immediate ends and gratification. In addition he had to deal with a formidable adversary in the person of Almagro, with whom he soon fell out. Almagro disliked the entire Pizarro clan and felt that he had been cheated out of his rightful rewards. In 1536 a native revolt broke out and the Indians laid siege to Cuzco for a year. Almagro, who had just explored Chile in an expedition that set new standards for hardship and suffering, returned in time to raise the siege. He then claimed the city for himself.

The result was civil war. In 1538 Almagro was defeated and executed and the two factions were irreparably divided. The almagristas rallied around Diego's son, Almagro el Mozo. The war continued in a desultory fashion until 1541, when the almagristas succeeded in assassinating Pizarro. The leadership of the

Pizarro faction fell to his brother, Gonzalo. In 1542 the almagristas were defeated by the Spanish governor, Vaca de Castro, who was allied with the pizarristas.

From civil war the colonists moved to insurrection. The catalyst was the New Laws, a set of ordinances enacted by the crown in 1542 that attempted to reconcile humanitarian concern for the Indians with the need to assert firmer royal control over the dependencies. The colonials quite correctly saw the laws as a direct threat to their hard-won riches and security. To enforce them, the Spanish crown appointed a viceroy, Blasco Núñez Vela, and an audiencia for Peru. Unfortunately, all of them were incompetent. In reaction to the New Laws the colonists rose in revolt in 1544, with the idea of making Gonzalo king of Peru. In a confused series of actions, Gonzalo defeated the royal forces and Vela was killed (1546). The colonists were treated to the spectacle of a conquistador carrying the late viceroy's head through the streets of Quito. Gonzalo set himself up in Lima and began to live in semiregal style. The crown, in the meantime, appointed a governor who proved more than a match for the pizarristas, a priest named Pedro de la Gasca who also doubled as soldier and administrator. He arrived in 1547 with the title of president of the audiencia and the authority to govern and set about reestablishing royal authority. The result was renewed civil war, in which the colonists were defeated and Gonzalo executed (1548). With the situation under control, Gasca returned to Spain in 1550 and the crown appointed a second viceroy. This was Antonio de Mendoza, who had just filled the same office in New Spain but who died in the following year.

Mendoza's two successors as viceroy proved just as capable and firmly established Spanish rule in Peru. Andrés Hurtado de Mendoza, the marqués de Cañete (1556–1560), and Francisco de Toledo (1567–1581) perfected the colonial administration. Toledo was brusque, authoritarian, and determined to impose order on what had been a turbulent colony. He suppressed the revolt of the Inca Túpac Amaru, a lineal descendant of Huayna Capac, and the last of the royal descendants was executed. Although active Indian resistance was ended, at least temporarily, the majority of the natives retreated into the Andes to be far from their tormentors. The viceroy attempted a total break with the Indian past by commissioning historical studies that demonstrated the illegitimacy of Inca rule. He made an extensive tour of his viceroyalty (in fact, he spent most of his term outside Lima) and came to know most of it firsthand. On the basis of this personal knowledge he was able to organize colonial administration to a high peak of efficiency.

## MISSIONS IN PERU

As is clear, the conquest of Peru went in a vastly different direction, and with far greater turbulence, than that of New Spain. For a period of almost sixteen years the country was racked by conquest, civil war, and rebellion. The establishment of a stable civil administration took longer than in New Spain. Peru, moreover, continued to be plagued by Indian revolts into the eighteenth century.

Such a situation would hardly seem propitious for consolidation or advance of any sort, yet surprisingly such did take place, even during the time of the civil wars. Settlers arrived and began the process of building a society that would come to fruition only after a number of years. The discovery of silver at Potosí in 1545 and of mercury at Huancavelica laid the basis for a booming economy. Francisco Pizarro had brought with him specific royal instructions about the extirpation of idolatry and the conversion of the Indians. Like Cortés, he sometimes showed an immoderate zeal in the destruction of idols. The treacherous and ruthless Pizarro also built churches and attempted to educate the sons of Indian nobles in Christianity. The process of destroying the pagan temples and idols was accelerated by the fact that they were often the repositories of treasure.

The missionary task was to be far more difficult than in New Spain. Geography alone presented a formidable obstacle. Many of the natives lived in remote mountainous regions that were almost inaccessible. The language problem was more acute than in Mexico because, despite the prevalence of Quechua and Aymará, there was nothing comparable to Nahuatl as a lingua franca. Some dialects were spoken only in individual villages. The Indians themselves proved resistant to conversion and were stubbornly conservative. Even when Christianity was accepted, it was often little more than a veneer over a basic paganism. Spanish exploitation, especially the establishment of the encomienda, which was introduced by Pizarro, and later a system of conscript labor called the *mita*, also intensified native resistance. As in New Spain, the bishops had conflicts with both the mendicants and the civil authorities.

The first missionaries in Peru were Dominicans, some of whom had accompanied the armies of Francisco Pizarro. Although the Dominicans played a major role in the evangelization of Peru, their work has not been given the study it deserves. The Franciscans came later, but for them the Peruvian mission was secondary to that of New Spain, which held priority in both time and interest. It is difficult to date the arrival of the Franciscans, but it seems to have been no later than 1532 when, accompanied by Dominicans, they came to inaugurate the mission. The Franciscans made Quito their earliest headquarters (1537–1545). Despite the disturbances of the civil war, more Franciscans came to Peru and in 1545 they established themselves in the city of Lima.

The first Franciscans were itinerant missionaries who went from village to village instructing the Indians in Christianity. At midcentury the friars began to build their residences among the Indians and concentrated their efforts on the local native population. As in New Spain, the missions soon became doctrinas, a midway station between missions and parishes in the technical sense. Again, as in New Spain, this situation caused a great deal of tension, not only with bishops and diocesan clergy but also among the Franciscans themselves, many of whom were ill-prepared for such work.

The missionary effort was hampered not only by a lack of priests but by the poor quality of those who came. As a result the friars turned to Indian cate-chists, called *alguaciles* or *fiscales de doctrina*, who gave elementary instruction and brought the Indians together for religious services. The conversion rate did eventually rise, so that by the 1570s there were doctrinas in many areas. In general, however, the missionary effort in Peru in the sixteenth century had more difficult beginnings than that in New Spain. Among the reasons for this were the difficulties caused by geography, including high mountains and impassable streams, and the presence of Spanish marauders, whose raids and exploitation turned the natives against all intruders.

The missionary methods used by the Franciscans in Peru were based on those that had been devised for New Spain. These included compulsory attendance at religious instructions, with a system of monitoring attendance or lack of it. (In New Spain well into the seventeenth century, Indians who were late for instruction or mass were customarily given five or six blows with a stick.) This was later enacted into law by the first Provincial Council of Lima in 1551. Instruction was often given through interpreters, at least until the friars had learned the native languages, and relied strongly on gestures, signs, and pictures. Liturgy was designed to impress the natives with its beauty and splendor, often with lavish processions and candlelight ceremonies. Songs and hymns were also used to communicate Christian doctrine. As in New Spain, the basic catechesis was very simple, emphasizing repetition of the Lord's Prayer, the Hail Mary, the Salve Regina, the Creed, the Ten Commandments, and the seven capital sins. As in New Spain, there were superficial resem-blances between Andean native religious practices and Catholicism, including such elements as fasting, confession of sins, atonement, and restitution. Mis-sionaries often tended to see these as evidence of a previous evangelization in apostolic times (in New Spain this was credited to the apostle Thomas) and of native religions as a corrupted form of Christianity. There is no real evidence that the missionaries used these supposed resemblances as tools of evangeliza-tion. In general the Andean natives proved more resistant to Christianity, at least in a passive way. This, together with the shortage of clergy, the variety of languages, and geographic isolation, resulted in a strong fusion of pagan and Christian beliefs and practices that remains to this day.

From the beginning there were attempts to give the sons of chiefs and nobles a European education, but there never seems to have been the equivalent of the Franciscan colegio of Santa Cruz de Tlaltelolco. There is little documen-tary evidence concerning the administration of the sacraments by the Francis-cans, at least prior to 1570. After that date all the sacraments except Holy Orders were administered. There is no evidence that the Franciscans in Peru baptized en masse after a negligible preparation as they had in New Spain.

During the first decades of evangelization in the Andean region, the model followed by the Dominicans was that of peaceful persuasion. One of the most prominent missionaries, Domingo de Santo Tomás, was a disciple of Bartolomé de las Casas. At the second Provincial Council of Lima he persuaded the bishops to legislate that religious instruction be given in Quechua, the predominant language of the region. He himself was a student of the language and published a Quechua grammar in 1560. He also participated in the foundation of the first university in Peru and was one of its foremost faculty members.

As time went on, however, and the difficulties of the missionary task became more apparent, there was a stronger tendency to rely on compulsion and constraint. One of these was the reductions, the Peruvian form of resettlement (or congregación, as it was known in New Spain). Another was the move to extirpate idolatry and to present Christianity in a purely European form. This was aided by the civil government, for example the viceroy Francisco de Toledo, because it also reinforced Spanish rule.

By the end of the century the Franciscans and Dominicans were joined by the Mercedarians, the Augustinians, and the Jesuits. The total number of houses and mission centers belonging to the orders was over a hundred by 1600. All the orders tended to keep their men in mission centers, from which they spread out to mission stations in the outlying areas.

The first bishopric, founded at Túmbez in 1529 as reward for Hernando de Luque, never functioned effectively. The first true bishopric was that of Cuzco, founded in 1537 with the Dominican Vicente de Valverde as its bishop. Valverde had come to Peru with Francisco Pizarro and had played an active role in the capture of Atahuallpa, whom he instructed in Christianity prior to his execution. Pizarro had suggested his name for the bishopric. He was later killed in an Indian uprising. The dominant see, however, was destined to be Lima, erected in 1541, to be followed by Charcas in 1552, Asunción in 1560, and Santiago in Chile in 1561.

The first bishop of Lima, Jerónimo de Loaysa (1498–1575) was a Dominican, a member of an important family—a cousin was president of the Council of the Indies. He arrived in the New World in 1530 as a missionary and then was named bishop of Cartagena (1537–1541). After being named to the newly founded see of Lima, he arrived there in 1543 at a time when civil disturbance was still raging. He attempted to reconcile the factions, but with little success. He set about the organization and establishment of the church and to that purpose called the First Provincial Council of Lima in 1551. This mapped a plan for evangelization of the Indians and ecclesiastical organization. In 1567 he convoked the second council, whose primary purpose, like that of its counterpart in Mexico, was to accept and apply the decrees of the Council of Trent. In 1550 he founded a hospital for Indians called Santa Ana, where he also set up a school for the sons of Indian *caciques* (chieftains). He died at Lima in 1575.

The major force in the Peruvian church in the sixteenth century was the monumental figure of Saint Toribio de Mogrovejo (1538–1606). A graduate of Salamanca, he was named inquisitor of Granada in 1574, a position he filled with tact and moderation. He was named archbishop of Lima in 1579, but because he had yet to be ordained priest or bishop he did not arrive there until

1581. Like Moya de Contreras of Mexico, he was deeply concerned with the betterment of the clergy. Far too many priests had come to Peru to become rich or had been corrupted by material gain after arrival. He founded a diocesan seminary and, in accord with the dictates of Trent, made three important visitations of his diocese. It was while he was on the last of these that he died.

## THE THIRD PROVINCIAL COUNCIL OF LIMA

Mogrovejo convoked the third Provincial Council of Lima, one of the most important councils held in the Spanish dependencies during the colonial period. It had originally been planned by Archbishop Loaysa but was delayed by the absence of the viceroy Toledo (who spent most of his term outside Lima) and the prelate's death in 1575. The new archbishop, Mogrovejo, and the new viceroy, Martín Enríquez, entered the city within a few days of one another in 1581. Mogrovejo lost no time in convoking the council for August 1582. Like the third Mexican Council three years later, it lasted for a year and was heavily influenced by regalism. Unfortunately, the council became hopelessly divided over the case of Sebastián de Lartaún, the bishop of Cuzco, whose mercenary and high-handed ways caused people and clergy alike to petition for his removal. Despite this and the bishops' inability to resolve the case, the council drew up a code of laws for the Peruvian church that included the formulation of catechisms in the native languages and a directory for confessors (*confesionario*). In contrast with the Mexican church councils of that century, third Lima decreed the erection of a seminary in line with the decrees of the Council of Trent. Like Mexico, Lima devoted a chapter of its decrees to encouraging defense of the Indians.

## EDUCATION

Beginning in the 1540s, the Dominicans offered courses in philosophy and theology at their monastery in Lima. In 1550 Fray Tomás de San Martín, the first provincial of the Dominican order in Peru, proposed to King Charles I the foundation of a university. He envisioned a full university, modeled on that of Salamanca, the foremost educational institution in Spain. Royal approval was given the following year, but the cédula (royal order) did not arrive in Lima until 1553. The university, with the Dominicans in charge, got off to a modest start because of a lack of funds. The arrangement whereby the Dominicans acted as rectors was an unusual one for Spanish universities of that century, and it did not last long. In 1571 the university received papal approval. Difficulties arose, however, between the Dominican administration and the secular faculty, who resented the predominance of the religious. Viceroy Toledo sided with the faculty and, after appointing a non-Dominican rector, moved the location of the university in 1574. That same year the university was given the name of San Marcos, by which it is still known.

As in New Spain there were serious attempts to provide a European education for the sons of the Indian nobility, in part to divorce them from the Inca past. These were moderately successful but affected only a handful of students. The Jesuits arrived in 1568 to open the colegio de San Pablo. Like all the Jesuit colegios it was a preparatory school with a curriculum that emphasized classical, humanistic education. Jesuit education also emphasized dramatic presentations, poetic competitions, and debates. San Pablo was very successful and the Jesuits quickly established a system of colegios, including foundations in Cuzco (1571) and Quito (1594).

One of the great scholars of sixteenth-century Peru was the Jesuit José de Acosta, who had been born at Medina del Campo in 1539 or 1540. After joining the Society of Jesus in 1552, he studied in his home town until 1557. From 1559 until 1567 he studied at Alcalá de Henares and traveled widely throughout the Iberian peninsula. He was ordained to the priesthood in 1566 and four years later went to Peru as one of the early members of the Jesuit mission. After a year at the Jesuit colegio in Lima, he visited the Jesuit houses in Peru from 1573 to 1574. In 1575 he became rector of the colegio in Lima and in 1576 provincial of the Peruvian Jesuits. In 1581 he relinquished the office of provincial but remained at the colegio. Forced to return to Spain because of ill health, Acosta traveled by way of New Spain, where he stayed from June 1586 until March 1587. He died at Salamanca in 1600. A member of the moderate pro-Indian school, he wrote two major works. The first was the *Historia natural y moral de las Indias*, published at Seville in 1590, which included a great deal of information on Indian religious and social institutions. The other was *De promulgatione evangelii apud barbaros seu de procuranda indorum salute (On promulgating the gospel among the barbarians or on procuring the salvation of the Indians)*, written in 1575–1576 and published at Salamanca in 1588.

There are some interesting similarities in the ecclesiastical histories of New Spain and Peru at this time. Each held three provincial councils during the sixteenth century: in New Spain in 1555, 1565, and 1585; in Peru in 1551, 1567, and 1583. In each the first was a tentative move toward a lasting ecclesiastical organization, the second a rather ineffective affair whose primary purpose was to accept the decrees of the Council of Trent, and the third a crowning success that established a durable code of law and organization, not just for the province but for many areas throughout the Americas and the Orient. The bishops responsible for the last of these councils, Moya de Contreras and Toribio de Mogrovejo, were remarkably similar in many ways. Both were alumni of Salamanca with training in law. Both began their careers as inquisitors. Both convoked highly effective councils that had permanent impact on the Spanish dependencies. Both modeled their episcopal actions on the dictates of Trent and emphasized clerical discipline and pastoral visitations of their dioceses.

In both Peru and New Spain the long-term process of institutionalization and structural strengthening was taking place. An earlier, more improvisatory approach was giving way to the orderly, legal, and rather bureaucratic approach of the Catholic Reformation. While this provided permanence and stability, it also tended to stifle the zeal and creativity that had characterized the earlier missionary approach.

## THE POSITION OF WOMEN

As in New Spain in that century, the number of Spanish women who came to Peru was far less than that of men, though it is almost impossible to arrive at an exact number. The proportion was balanced somewhat in the earlier years because of the high mortality rate among men caused by wars, feuds, and the difficulties of exploration and conquest. Still, there were not enough, and the Spanish men of Peru, like those in the rest of the New World, turned to Indian women and begat a new class of mestizos. Also, as in New Spain, this presented the problem of bigamous marriages, when Spanish settlers lost hope, or interest, in bringing their wives from home.

As noted earlier, a woman in sixteenth-century Spain and the Indies faced two possible futures: marriage or the convent. Marriages were usually arranged by families for the purpose of social advancement and enrichment. The majority of women who arrived in Peru came as members of family groups, not as individual immigrants. Dowries were necessary not only for marriage but also for entrance into a convent. A widow usually had to depend on her family for support, although there are cases of widows who showed skill and initiative in managing their estates.

The woman's function after marriage was to be the head of a household, managing servants and slaves. On the other hand, women were often able to use their dowry goods as a basis for engaging in independent financial activity. This included the ownership of real estate and slaves and discreet moneylending. Women were allowed to have encomiendas in their own right, and these provided both financial security and status. Widows who were encomenderas were theoretically supposed to marry within a specified time, but this was rarely enforced. There was, however, strong social and economic pressure on the widow of an encomendero to remarry. At the lower end of the social spectrum women, whether married or unmarried, functioned as bakers, midwives, and innkeepers. The availability of Indian women to Spanish men lessened the need for a distinct class of prostitutes.

Secondary education was available for the women of Lima. In the earlier days of the Spanish domination upper-class parents hired private tutors for their children, both boys and girls. In the latter half of the sixteenth century there were convent schools to which parents who could afford to do so could send their daughters. By the mid-seventeenth century there were four or five of them in Lima. They were austere institutions. The girls entered around the age of seven and lived there, apart from their families, for six or seven years. They followed a life-style quite similar to that of the nuns. The austerity, however, was lightened by the presence among the nuns of relatives who often served as an extended family and by music and drama. Drama was a basic element in Jesuit education and mission methods, and it had been adopted by many of the convent schools. The curriculum included reading, writing, elementary arithmetic, and practical arts such as sewing, embroidery, and cooking.

CONVENTS

Convents in Peru played the same role they did in the rest of Latin America, serving both religious and civic needs. As in New Spain, they were a source of pride to a city while at the same time assuring the local citizenry that there were centers of prayer and penance nearby. To a certain extent the presence of monasteries and convents relieved the citizens of the need to be overly concerned about their own religious status. Though there were many convents in Lima that were observant of their rule and devotional obligations, that city was burdened with something not found in Mexico: the *conventos grandes*, large convents. These sometimes had as many as a thousand nuns, and as a result they were rarely observant. Civil and religious officials repeatedly complained of their inability to reform these worldly, and sometimes violent, nunneries.

A uniquely Spanish institution was that of the *beata* (literally, "blessed"). These were women, often widows, who lived in a form of pious retirement, either by themselves or with others. They customarily wore a religious habit, often that of a specific order with which they identified or had a formal connection, but they were not nuns or religious in the technical sense of the term. Because they were frequently confused with true religious, bishops often tried to stop the beatas from wearing religious garb; such efforts were usually unsuccessful.

One of the outstanding women of Peru in this period was Saint Rose of Lima. She was born in Lima in 1586, the daughter of Gaspar de Flores, a conquistador who came to Peru in 1548, and María de Oliva. Her baptismal name was Isabel, Rose being a nickname given her as a child because of her beauty. At the age of twenty she joined the third order of Saint Dominic and devoted her life to penance, mortification, and charitable works. She was especially noted for her work with children and the elderly. She died at Lima in 1617 and after her canonization was named the patron saint of Peru.

It is interesting that Spanish South America produced at least three saints—Rose of Lima, Peter Claver, and Francisco Solano—while Mexico had only one, Felipe de Jesús, a Franciscan lay brother martyred in Japan. The recent beatification of Juan Diego of the Guadalupe apparitions may lead to another canonization, but there are serious historical doubts about whether Juan Diego ever existed. It is impossible to assign any reason for this difference between the two regions in this regard.

## THE KINGDOM OF QUITO

The Peruvian missions also encompassed modern-day Ecuador, though the latter was first evangelized from Panama. Although the Indians of Quito had belonged to the Inca empire, it was far enough from the heart of that polity to have retained pre-Inca customs and religious beliefs. The variety that resulted from this retention made the missionary task more difficult. The first priests in Quito were diocesans, as early as 1535. They were soon followed by the religious: Franciscans, Dominicans, and Mercedarians. Until 1546, when it was named a diocese, Quito was part of the diocese of Cuzco. Garcí Díaz Arias was its first bishop. Not much is known of his early life. He was a diocesan priest and a friend of the Pizarro family, though he managed to escape implication in their conspiracies. He proved a capable and zealous bishop and died in 1562.

## NUEVA GRANADA

The first Spanish settlement in what is now Colombia and Venezuela was at Santa Marta, where a Spanish expedition landed on 29 July 1525 and named the area in honor of the saint for that day. The small colony barely survived and did not show signs of permanence until 1529, when García de Lerma arrived as governor, accompanied by twenty Dominicans. The conquest of the area from Lake Maracaibo down to the Orinoco was entrusted to a group of Germans, representatives of the bankers to whom Charles I owed large debts. Twenty Dominicans also arrived with the Germans. In 1531 Santa Marta was made a diocese and the Dominican vicar, Tomás Ortiz, was named bishop. In 1533 the Spaniards founded the city of Cartagena. Because of its strategic importance it was soon made a bishopric (1534), with the Dominican Tomás de Toro as first bishop.

The audiencia, or civil administrative district, of Santa Fe de Bogotá was founded in 1549 and included modern Colombia and Venezuela. Cartagena and Santa Marta were prosperous seaports but were subject to attack by corsairs. As a result Bogotá, with its inconvenient yet easily defended inland position, emerged as equally important. In 1563 it was made an archdiocese, eclipsing Santa Marta. As in other parts of the Spanish colonial world, there were frequent conflicts between the archbishops and the local Spanish governor. In Bogotá these tended to be more frequent and more severe than elsewhere. In 1556 a synod called by Archbishop Juan de los Barrios attempted to moderate the worst excesses of the encomienda. This laid the groundwork for struggles that continued throughout the colonial period. Fierce Indian resistance also continued in what is modern Colombia, almost equaling that of the Araucanians of Chile.

## EXTENSION AND COMPLETION OF THE CONQUEST OF THE SOUTH

### CHILE

In 1548 Pedro de Valdivia returned to Chile, intent on completing the conquest. In 1550 he founded the city of Concepción, which he used as his capital. In 1553 he attempted to subjugate the Araucanians but the latter, under their resourceful chief Lautaro, defeated the Spaniards and killed Valdivia. The Spanish continued the war, but the resistance was so strong that there was sentiment for abandoning Chile altogether. In 1557, however, the Spaniards defeated the Araucanians and Lautaro was killed. Although border skirmishes would continue for some time, the effective occupation of Chile had been completed.

The early days of the church in Chile are obscure. Priests were present there from the first days of the Spanish occupation, but not until 1553 did three Franciscans arrive in Santiago from Lima. Their work prospered enough that in 1571 their mission became an independent province. The Dominicans came four years later. In the sixteenth century there were two episcopal sees, Santiago (founded in 1561 as a suffragan of Lima) and Concepción (1563). Three Franciscans were bishops of Santiago during that century, with Diego de Medellín (1573–1593) considered the true organizer of the diocese. In southern Chile, because of the violence of the Araucanian war, true missions were not developed until the eighteenth century.

### BOLIVIA

Bolivia and the Tucumán, not surprisingly, were penetrated from Peru. As early as 1538 Diego de Rojas had founded Charcas, eventually to become an important administrative center and in the following decade Potosí and La Paz were also established. In 1552 Rome made Charcas into a diocese with its episcopal see at Chuquisaca (modern Sucre) and named the Dominican Tomás de San Martín, who had come to Peru with Pizarro in 1538, as bishop. He died, however, before taking possession of his see and his successor met the same fate. The third bishop, the Dominican Domingo de Santo Tomás, was finally able to take possession in 1563. Charcas was made an archdiocese in 1605. The Peruvian penetration was challenged by the Spaniards of Chile and eventually Bolivia and Tucumán were transferred to their administration. Franciscan missions in those regions were dependencies of Peru, most of them undertaken in the seventeenth century and not really consolidated until the latter half of the century.

### RÍO DE LA PLATA

The initial Spanish penetrations of the La Plata region (what is now Argentina and Paraguay) were plagued by disaster. The first Spanish expedition of 1516 was defeated by the fierce and cannibalistic Guaraní Indians. Later expeditions under Sebastian Cabot, the English explorer then in the employ of Spain, and Diego García Moguer added to the geographic knowledge of the area but provided no lasting settlements. Fired by further rumors of riches and alarmed by the expansionism of the Portuguese in Brazil, the crown sent Pedro de Mendoza in 1535 to establish Spanish hegemony in the area. A man whose life was plagued by disaster and failure, Mendoza succeeded in founding the city of Buenos Aires but accomplished little else. The fierce resistance of the Indians all but destroyed his small colony, and he retired from the scene, leaving an assistant in command. Eventually Buenos Aires was abandoned and its population moved to the newly founded city of Asunción, capital of modern Paraguay. Ultimately the area was consolidated to the extent that Buenos Aires could be refounded in 1580. It did not become a diocese, however, until the following century.

The missionary enterprise was inaugurated by two great Franciscans, Saint Francisco Solano at Tucumán and Luis de Bolaños in Paraguay, who will be discussed somewhat more in detail in regard to the Jesuit reductions. In 1549 three Dominicans went from Potosí in Peru to work in Tucumán. This region remained ecclesiastically dependent on Santiago de Chile until 1577, when the Portuguese Dominican Francisco de Vitoria was nominated first bishop of Tucumán. He did not reach his see, however, until 1581. He immediately fell into a conflict with the autocratic governor, Hernando de Lerma. As in so many other parts of Spanish America, the quarrels were over jurisdiction, including the right of asylum. Vitoria used his attendance at the third Provincial Council of Lima as a pretext for escaping from Lerma, who tried but failed to prevent his return by appealing to the bishops at the council. The audiencia of Charcas eventually deposed Lerma, who died in prison in Spain in 1591.

The bad relations between governor and bishop retarded missionary activity. In the latter part of the sixteenth century, however, both the Franciscans and Mercedarians were able to stabilize the missionary endeavor. In 1585, at the invitation of Bishop Vitoria, the Jesuits came to Tucumán. One of them, Santiago de Estero, acted as the representative of the Inquisition of Lima. The other, Alonso de Barsana, became an expert in the local languages and wrote a grammar and dictionary of Kakan.

Francisco Solano, born in Spain in 1549, was one of the great figures in the missionary enterprise in the region. After studying with the Jesuits, he joined the Franciscans and was professed in 1570. He worked for twenty years in Spain as a teacher and novicemaster. In 1589 he was sent to America with other missionaries who were destined for Tucumán. For a while he was superior of the Franciscan missions in Tucumán and Paraguay. In 1598 he went to Peru as superior in Lima and Trujillo. He died in Lima in 1610 with a reputation for his preaching and charities.

By 1600 the Spanish controlled an immense portion of the New World. The extent of their accomplishment becomes clear when it is remembered that within the space of sixty years they had gained control of the entire Caribbean and of territories extending from modern Zacatecas in Mexico to the southern part of Chile. French Canada and Portuguese Brazil lay outside Spanish domination. So too did unexplored and unconquered areas. Primary among the latter was the area to the north of Zacatecas, sometimes called "the Northern Mystery."

## PORTUGAL IN AMERICA

The first European to touch Brazil was not a Portuguese but a Florentine in the employ of Castile. Amerigo Vespucci, whose name by historical accident would later be attached to the hemisphere, reached the Brazilian coast near the mouth of the Amazon in June 1499. He explored the coastline as far as Cabo São Roque before returning to Europe. The following January Vicente Yáñez Pinzón, who had been captain of the *Niña* on Columbus's first voyage, also touched the coast, as did Diego de Lepe a month later. In April, Pedro Alvares Cabral laid the basis for Portugal's claim to the area. Leaving Lisbon in March 1500 with India as his destination, he swung far into the Atlantic, where winds blew him to Brazil. Realizing that the land lay within the area awarded Portugal by the Treaty of Tordesillas, he claimed it for his sovereign, Manoel I. Before continuing on to India he dispatched a ship to Portugal to announce the new acquisition. In May 1501 Vespucci returned for further exploration, this time in the employ of Portugal.

Despite other voyages of exploration, the Portuguese did not take any immediate interest in Brazil; not until 1531 were the first permanent settlements made. The reasons for the renewed attention lay in the declining East Indian trade and the intrusions of the French, whose pirates and loggers were busy along the coast. Hardwood was the first lure for the Portuguese in Brazil. In 1531 Martim de Sousa was sent to Brazil with a fleet of warships to expel the French and begin colonization. The first he did quickly and efficiently. The second he did at Pernambuco in 1531 and São Vicente in 1532. The Portuguese, however, were disappointed to find nothing comparable to the wealth of Mexico or Peru. As a result the crown tended to give Brazil secondary importance and left its settlement to private enterprise.

In order to attract settlers and entrepreneurs the crown divided the Brazilian littoral into fifteen districts called *capitanias* to be awarded to deserving parties. The recipients were to enjoy extensive feudal privileges and were permitted to exploit the territories for their own benefit. Except for three areas (Pernambuco, São Vicente, and São Amaro), the capitanias proved a failure. Although the geographic divisions remained, the crown decided on a new policy.

In 1549 Thomé de Sousa was appointed governor general and came to Brazil with some colonists, including six Jesuits. They were first to come to the New World, something that is all the more remarkable in view of the fact that the

Society had received papal approval only nine years before. Sousa made his capital at São Salvador (modern Bahia). During the four years of his governorship he laid the foundations for the political and economic life of the colony. His successor, Mem de Sá, was equally successful. During his eighteen-year governorship the colony made progress. Tobacco and sugar became staple products, both for export and for consumption in Brazil. Black slaves supplemented the Indians on the plantations, and the number imported from Africa far outstripped those in the Castilian colonies. The large number of blacks left a permanent imprint on the racial composition of Brazil. After the recovery of Portuguese independence in 1640 Brazilian exports helped sustain the mother country's economy.

In Brazil, the "new Christians"—specifically, the conversos or Jewish Christians—were more important and enjoyed greater freedom than in the Spanish possessions. So deeply involved were they in commerce that the very term *merchant* came to be synonymous with *Jewish*.

## EVANGELIZATION IN BRAZIL

The Portuguese missionary enterprise in Brazil was similar in many ways to that in the Spanish Indies. In both the work of evangelization was under the control of the crown's right of patronage, the patronato for Spanish America, the padroado for Portuguese America. In both areas religious orders played the major role in evangelization, but different orders predominated in each world. Confraternities (called *irmandades* in Brazil) and nunneries had roles similar to those in the Spanish dominions. The Portuguese also followed a policy of concentrating migratory Indians in larger settlements for purposes both of government and evangelization. In Brazil the clergy had great prestige, despite the fact that they did not always live up to their calling. As in sixteenth-century Spanish America, the role of the bishops and the diocesan clergy was more limited in the beginning than it was later on.

There were, however, important differences. The Spanish patronato was more highly developed and uniform than the Portuguese padroado. Portuguese viceroys in Brazil did not have the same power as vicepatrons that Spanish viceroys enjoyed. In Brazil there were missions which were not under the direction of the crown but of the Roman Congregation for the Propagation of the Faith (commonly called Propaganda, from its Latin name), created in 1622 to give the papacy some voice in missionary activity. In the Spanish system the crown was the principal support of the missions to the Indians. In Brazil the preponderance of crown support went to the white Church, with the result that the religious orders came to rely on plantations (*fazendas*) and other sources of income. Although occasional teams of inquisitors went around Brazil to extirpate heterodoxy, the Inquisition as such was never established. Provincial councils, under the leadership of bishops, never played the major role in Brazil that they did in the Spanish dependencies. The missionaries did not use the native languages but rather relied on a form of pidgin or lingua franca developed by the Jesuits and based on the Tupi language. While individual churchmen and some orders, like the Jesuits, defended the rights of the natives against exploitation, here there was nothing comparable to the great Spanish humanitarian movement of the sixteenth century. As in Spanish America, the Franciscans and Jesuits played a major role in the missionary enterprise, but in Brazil four other groups—the Oratorians, Carmelites, Capuchins, and Benedictines—also made a substantive contribution. This was unusual because none of these except the Capuchins was specifically missionary in orientation. In addition, the Brazilian missionaries included a higher number of foreigners than did those in the Spanish domains.

For three decades after their arrival with Thomé de Sousa, the Jesuits were the only Catholic missionaries in Brazil, and they remained predominant until the eighteenth century. At first they worked primarily in the coastal areas. The Jesuits drew many recruits from Brazilian-born Portuguese, so their numbers grew rapidly. In addition to their missions they founded colégios along the coast, which they linked to their missions in the Indian villages or mission settlements. The first Jesuit mission settlement was established in 1553 in the region of Salvador da Bahia, to be followed by others that were also near cities. The Jesuits soon changed this policy to one of placing the missions farther away from the labor demands of the sugar plantations and the Portuguese.

Two of the first Jesuits, Manoel de Nóbrega and José de Anchieta, rank among the major figures in Brazilian history. Nóbrega (1517–1570) had a degree in canon law from the University of Coimbra and entered the Society of Jesus in 1544, a mere ten years after its founding. After serving briefly in Portugal, he went to Brazil. He was an influential adviser to both Thomé de Sousa and Mem de Sá and helped found the Colégio de São Paulo (1544), around which the city grew up, and Rio de Janeiro (1565). He also founded the Colégio de Rio de Janeiro (1567) and was its first rector. He is rightfully regarded one of the founders of Brazil.

Anchieta (1534–1597) also studied at the University of Coimbra. In 1557 he entered the Society of Jesus and, though he was not yet a priest, was assigned to the Brazilian mission two years later. He worked in the capitania of São Vicente and then taught in the Jesuit school at São Paulo de Piratininga. He learned Tupi and wrote grammar for it that was published posthumously. He was ordained to the priesthood in 1566 and named superior of the Jesuit missions in the capitania. He was famous for his zeal and mission work among the Indians and is often called "the apostle of Brazil." After his death many extravagant stories were related about his miracle-working.

The Franciscans arrived in the 1580s and in 1585 began the process of moving along the coastal area from Olinda. They were not so effective or predominant in Brazil as they were in New Spain, and their outlook was certainly less radical. Two other orders also joined the missionary enterprise.

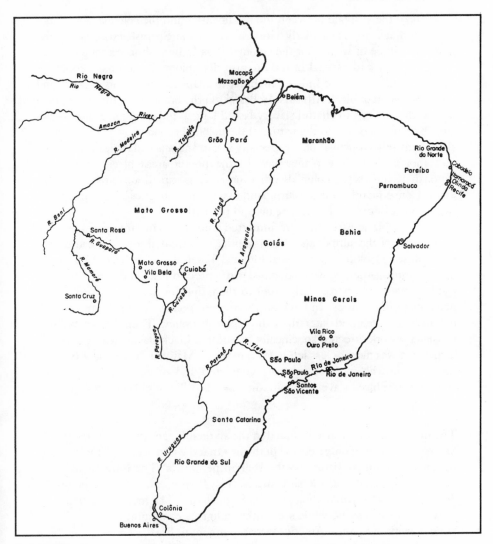

Colonial Brazil

One of these was the Carmelites, a group not usually associated with missions since its primary purpose was contemplation. They arrived in 1580 and began working throughout Pernambuco, Paraíba, Maranhão, and Pará. They were also active in the southern littoral. The other group was the Benedictines, who arrived in Bahia in 1581. Their organization and life-style, based as it was on life in a single, autonomous monastery, was not well suited to the more flexible demands of mission life. Both Carmelites and Benedictines made use of black slaves as a means of supporting themselves.

In Brazil the struggle between the missionaries and the colonists for control of the Indians was particularly virulent. As in the Spanish possessions, the principal source of wealth for the colonials was Indian labor. Although Indian chattel slavery had existed in the Spanish dominions, it died out because of governmental policy, the Indians' inability to adapt to some forms of labor, and the importation of black Africans. In Brazil, on the other hand, the attempts to reduce the Indians to chattel slavery lasted longer and were more intense. In great part this was due to the nature of the colonial economy, which was based almost entirely on plantations, especially sugar. Indians and Africans provided the labor basis for the plantations. In the poorer areas black slaves were expensive, and so the colonials relied on slaving expeditions among the Indians. Consequently, it is not surprising that the missionaries sought to limit or stop contact between the Europeans and the natives.

Although black Africans were imported into Brazil in large numbers, the uncertainty of the supply and the high prices demanded for them caused the Portuguese to look toward the local Indians. The Indians, who lived a nomadic life as hunter-gatherers, were not physically suited to sustained hard labor. As a result, slavery was particularly cruel to them and inevitably involved a high percentage of fatalities. In general, Portuguese policy toward the freedom of the Indian developed later than did Spanish policy. There was never any missionary work directed specifically toward the black slaves, whose religious instruction was more or less left to their masters. Many of the religious (such as the Jesuits, who most strenuously combated Indian slavery) felt no such qualms about black slavery, a contradiction it is difficult today to explain fully.

The missionary enterprise in Brazil in the sixteenth century resembled that of Spain in America, if only because of the fact that the two nations shared, at least partially, a common history on the Iberian peninsula. The differences, however, were as notable as the similarities. The Portuguese did not develop the detailed and effective mission plan the Spanish did. The mendicants were less active than the Jesuits, while some other religious communities that did little mission work in Spanish America were prominent in Brazil. There was nothing comparable to the Spanish humanitarian movement (to be discussed in Chapter 5) in the Portuguese dependencies. In general, the Portuguese enterprise seems to have lacked both the organizational skills and the intensity shown by the Spaniards.

# 4

## FROM CORONADO TO KINO: NORTHERN NEW SPAIN AND THE BORDERLANDS, 1540–1711

### EXPLORERS AND MISSIONARIES

Spanish penetration to the north of Mexico City was irregular. The return of Cabeza de Vaca in 1536 sparked Spanish interest in the north. Although Cabeza de Vaca did not at first embellish his accounts, he and his companions had heard tales of wealthy settlements—probably references to the pueblos in what is now the American Southwest. The Spaniards were eager to believe that there were other kingdoms as rich as Mexico and Peru. In 1539 the viceroy of New Spain, Antonio de Mendoza, commissioned the Franciscan friar Marcos de Niza, who had already traveled over large areas of Spanish America, to go northward on a reconnaissance mission to find the Seven Cities of Cibola, which according to legend had been founded by seven Spanish bishops, refugees from the Moors. Accompanied by Cabeza de Vaca's companion, the black slave Esteban, he reached the Zuñi country of modern New Mexico, where Esteban was killed by the Indians. Niza wrote an enthusiastic report on the pueblos the reliability of which can be questioned. It is possible that Fray Marcos saw the Zuñi pueblos in the setting sun from a considerable distance and persuaded himself that they were truly cities of gold. Whatever the correct version, his report was enough to kindle Spanish enthusiasm for further exploration.

The result was a magnificent expedition outfitted by the viceroy that left Mexico City in 1540 under the command of the young Francisco Vázquez de Coronado. For two years the expedition wandered through the southwestern United States and as far north as present-day Kansas. It discovered the Grand Canyon (to the Spaniards a physical obstacle rather than a natural wonder) but no signs of gold, wealth, or fabulous kingdoms. In great disappointment Coronado and his men returned to Mexico City in 1542, richer only in geographic knowledge. The De Soto expedition at almost the same time proved equally futile. Another bubble had burst.

In 1542 Juan Rodríguez Cabrillo, a Portuguese in the service of Spain, explored the coast of California in search of a passage, the fabled strait of Anián, that would connect the Atlantic and Pacific oceans. He discovered San Diego Bay, but like all Spanish explorers until the eighteenth century missed San Francisco Bay. Cabrillo died during the exploration and was buried on an island in the Santa Barbara channel. Spanish conquest of the Philippines by Miguel López de Legazpi and the subsequent discovery by the friar-navigator Andrés de Urdaneta of a practical route between Manila and Acapulco opened the way for the famous Manila galleon, a trading system that brought New Spain into contact with the riches of the Orient. It also required a port of refuge along the coast of Alta California for reprovisioning and repairs after the long journey. In addition, the upper California area was being threatened by Sir Francis Drake (El Draque to the Spaniards) and Thomas Cavendish. In 1602 Sebastián Vizcaíno, in search of a port of refuge, discovered Monterey Bay but missed San Francisco. He had three Carmelite friars with him on the expedition. The Spanish did not follow up this discovery and the real Spanish occupation of California, and its concomitant missionary effort would not begin until a century and a half later.

What the Spaniards had not realized was that the wealth they sought was much closer to home. Silver was discovered in the Zacatecas area about 1545. Almost simultaneously large deposits of mercury, needed for refining silver, were discovered in the Huancavelica area of Peru. This began a rush to the new riches and led to the settlement of San Luis Potosí, Jalisco, and Durango. It also brought the Spaniards into contact with the Chichimecas— fierce, nomadic Indians who for a long time successfully resisted Spanish intrusion. The Spanish colonists and silver miners demanded that the government undertake a war of extermination or enslavement against them, a demand that was roundly condemned by the bishops and religious of the third Mexican Provincial Council of 1585. Instead, the government made use of the increasingly common presidio-mission method. The crown also utilized Christian Indians, especially the Tlaxcalans, who had been staunch allies of Cortés. They were settled near the hostile or pagan Indians to provide stability and to advertise the advantages of Christianity and Spanish civilization. The system proved successful, especially with the aid of Jesuit missionaries, and peace returned to the northern settlements in the early seventeenth century.

The missionaries followed the explorers; sometimes they *were* the explorers. In general the Jesuits evangelized the western and Pacific-coast regions of New Spain, while the Franciscans served the eastern areas.

## JESUIT MISSIONS IN THE NORTH

The Jesuits inaugurated their missionary work in 1589 in the region of San Luis de Paz. The mission of San Luis de Paz, where they established a residence and small school in 1594, was part of a larger plan to pacify and convert the Chichimecas by peaceful means. In 1591 Gonzalo de Tapia and Martín Pérez set out for Sinaloa to use the same peaceful means for conversions, but this suffered a major setback in 1594 when Tapia was martyred. The mission, and Spanish control, was saved by the firm but diplomatic work of the Spanish captain Diego Martínez de Hurdaide. By the early seventeenth century the process of conversion was far advanced among the tribes of the Sinaloa area. At the time the Jesuits were expelled from New Spain (1767) there were twenty-one missionaries ministering to approximately thirty thousand Indians. Thus began a Jesuit missionary enterprise that came to include Guanajuato, San Luis Potosí, Nuevo León, Jalisco, Zacatecas, Nayarit, Coahuila, Durango, Chihuahua, Sinaloa, Sonora, Baja California, and southern Arizona.

In 1598 the Jesuits began working in Coahuila (which borders present-day Texas), where their mission work spread rapidly. Jesuits under Pedro Méndez moved up the coast of Sinaloa and Sonora from 1604 onward. They were soon ready to move into the valley of the Río Mayo, but the fierce Yaqui Indians did not want to see any further Spanish expansion. By 1610 the Yaqui decided to make peace, so the Jesuits were able to enter the area in 1614. Missionary expansion was such that in 1620 the diocese of Guadiana (Durango) was established, with boundaries that included the Jesuit missions of Coahuila.

One of the most difficult of the Jesuit missions was to the restive and warlike Tarahumara Indians. Conditions on the frontier were so unsettled that regular mission work could not begin until 1630, and even then a number of native revolts resulted in the deaths of missionaries. The missions to the northern Tarahumara in the modern state of Chihuahua, beginning in 1673, were more successful. This, again, was in spite of native uprisings and the murder of missionaries. Less successful were the missions to the Yaquis, one of the fiercest and most independent tribes in Mexican history. These missions had barely begun when the Society of Jesus was expelled from Spanish dominions in 1767. (After their restoration the Jesuits returned to the Tarahumara and work among them today.) The missions in Sonora were much more successful, in part because of one of the greatest of all Jesuits in Mexican and borderlands history.

### KINO ON THE FRONTIER

Eusebio Kino was born near Trent in northern Italy in 1645. While studying at the Jesuit college of Hall, near Innsbruck, Austria, he fell seriously ill and vowed to enter the Society of Jesus if cured. In 1665 he fulfilled that promise in Bavaria and took the name of Francis, in honor of Saint Francis Xavier, the preeminent Jesuit missionary. He was ordained to the priesthood eleven years later. In preparation for going to the Chinese missions he devoted himself to the study of mathematics and astronomy, while at the same time pursuing ecclesiastical studies. In 1678 he was part of a group assigned to the Mexican and Chinese missions. Since the specific destination of each individual was left unclear, he and a fellow Jesuit drew lots. New Spain was to be his destiny. He set out the following year, but because of a delay in Spain did not arrive at Veracruz until 1681. He served as cosmographer and Jesuit superior on the unsuccessful expedition of Isidro de Atondo y Antillón to explore and missionize California in 1683. He also began his career as a mapmaker. Adverse conditions forced the abandonment of the mission in 1685.

Toward the beginning of 1687 his superiors sent him north again, this time to the Pimería Alta, the region with which his name will always be associated. This area straddled present-day Sonora and southern Arizona and was home to the Pima, Pápago, Sobaipuri, and (further north) Yuman peoples. He made his headquarters at the mission of Nuestra Señora de los Dolores. In preparation for his missionary work, he began the exploration of the vast territory committed to the mission. He undertook the evangelization of the Pimas, promoted cattle-raising, and engaged in geographic exploration and cartography. His work caused him to ride thousands of miles through the rugged terrain. In 1689 he was named superior of the mission and arranged for missionaries to visit the towns that had been only partially evangelized.

In 1691 Kino was joined by an almost equally famous missionary, Father Juan María Salvatierra, who was later to explore Baja California. An Italian, Salvatierra, had come to New Spain in 1675 and had come to the Primería Alta as Jesuit visitador. He quickly came under Kino's influence. Salvatierra's presence helped ensure the permanence of a mission threatened by native uprisings. One of the most formidable of these occurred in 1695, in part because of harsh Spanish reprisals for the murder of a missionary, Francisco Javier Saeta. The Pimas rose in rebellion and destroyed several of the mission centers. Kino worked to restore peace, which was finally accomplished in August 1695. Kino rode horseback to Mexico City, some twelve hundred miles, to prevent the abandonment of the mission.

As so often happened with people like Kino, he soon found himself in conflict with some of his superiors, who did not understand either his missionary situation or his life-style. Most of the opposition came from Francisco Javier Mora, the Jesuit superior of Sonora. Accusations of hasty baptisms and failing to live a proper religious life were leveled against Kino. Fortunately, these did not last long and had no enduring effect. He and his neophytes were remarkably successful as ranchers and shipped large quantities of livestock to various missions and villages. He was also responsible for introducing the cultivation of wheat into the area.

Shortly after this, Salvatierra began preparing an expedition to California, with Kino as one of its members. Opposition to losing Kino in the Pimería prevented his joining the group. He did, however, do exploring of his own. In 1698, accompanied by Captain Diego de Carrasco, he followed the Gila River and then crossed it toward the Gulf of California. At the same time he converted some Papago Indians and established a mission at San Marcelo Sinóita. The expedition left Kino convinced that California was not an island, as Spaniards had believed since it was first visited. The following year he returned to explore the outlet of the Colorado River. In February he reached the conjunction of the Colorado and the Gila, where he encountered the Yuma Indians. He explored the Gila as far as Casa Grande.

Kino was responsible for the return of the Jesuits to Baja California in 1697, when Manuel Díaz, joined by Salvatierra, began missionary work in the area of present-day Guaymas. Three years later he undertook two expeditions to prove conclusively whether California was an island or a peninsula. His observations at the mouth of the Colorado River convinced him that it was a peninsula. In 1700, eight years after he first explored the area, he established the famous mission of San Xavier de Bac, outside the modern city of Tucson. In 1702, in two more expeditions, he attempted to reach California by land but was unsuccessful.

In Sonora Kino opened more missions than the Jesuits could staff. Some Jesuits died in the harsh northern conditions, and there was a move to abandon the area. Kino was regarded by many, including fellow Jesuits, as individualistic and unrealistic. The opposition view was that the area was desert, sparsely populated by hostile natives, and a poor missionary prospect. It was at precisely this time that Kino was establishing the financial and social bases of his missions, particularly through cattle-ranching and the instruction of the natives in European crafts.

Kino died at the mission at Magdalena in 1711. By the time of his death the missions of Sonora and the Pimería were already suffering, partly because of economic problems caused by the War of the Spanish Succession. There were conflicts with civil authorities, some of whom were more interested in their own personal wealth than in the good of the natives. More and more mission outposts were abandoned or remained static. Dolores itself, Kino's headquarters, had no missionaries after 1738. Jesuits continued to work in the area, and even farther north, until the expulsion of 1767, but the enterprise lacked its former vigor and extension. After the expulsion the Franciscans took over the missions of both Baja and Alta California.

## FRANCISCANS ON THE EASTERN SLOPE

The Spanish missionary effort in the borderlands was a two-pronged affair. While the Jesuits pushed up through central and northwestern New Spain, the Franciscans evangelized the eastern and northeastern areas. At the end of the sixteenth century Francisco Urdiñola established a colony of Tlaxcalans at Saltillo in order to stabilize the frontier and help in conversions. The real missionary work began in the latter part of the seventeenth century, when the Franciscans entered Nuevo León and Coahuila. The Indians of that area, still called Chichimecas by the Spaniards, were warlike and fierce. The Franciscan work was helped by the establishment in that century of missionary colleges in Querétaro and Zacatecas, which prepared missionaries for work that made different demands than that previously undertaken. (More will be said about these colleges in Chapter 7.) The Franciscans established an outpost at Santiago de Monclova in 1687, which later became a presidio and provincial capital.

The outstanding figure in the history of this missionary work was Fray Juan Larios, who is sometimes called the Founder of Coahuila. He was born in Jalisco in 1633 and joined the Franciscans at the age of eighteen. He was ordained to the priesthood in 1657 and, after working in different parts of Jalisco, became the parish priest in the small town of Sayula. Though his actual stay in Coahuila was brief—only three years between 1673 and 1676—he accomplished a great deal. The crown had tried to evangelize and pacify the area with Tlaxcalan Indians, but they had been massacred. Larios entered the hostile territory, which had already cost some Franciscan lives, and apparently explored as far north as the Río Grande. He earned a reputation as a defender of the Indians. He died in 1676. Unfortunately, neither Larios nor the Franciscan missions in northeastern Mexico have been given the historical study they deserve.

## NEW MEXICO

The Spanish conquest of New Mexico tended to leapfrog the intervening areas. There were a number of reasons for this, despite the disappointing results of the Coronado expedition. The missionaries who had accompanied Coronado were impressed by the receptiveness and character of the Pueblo Indians. The area also seemed to hold promise of mineral wealth. Again, the lure of the fabled strait of Anián drew the Spaniards on, all the more so when rumors circulated that Drake had discovered it. There were some initial probes by unauthorized expeditions that came to nothing. The crown authorized an expedition as early as 1583, but bureaucratic inertia prevented any immediate implementation. Finally, Juan de Oñate, a member of a leading Zacatecas mining family, was appointed to lead an expedition to New Mexico in 1595.

After an incredible series of delays and changes of plan, the expedition set out in January 1598. It was intended as a colonizing as well as an exploring expedition. In March a second party, which included ten Franciscan priests and lay brothers led by Fray Alonso Martínez, followed. Around 1600 Oñate established his headquarters at San Gabriel on the Río Grande, between present-day Santa Fe and Taos. New Mexico proved a disappointment. There was little wealth, much desert, and troublesome Indians. Additional colonists and friars arrived in 1600, but the settlement still seemed precarious. The colony was costly to hold and was a drain on royal finances. One consideration that prevented the authorities in Mexico City from abandoning it altogether was that the newly converted Indians would have been deserted. In 1608 the crown decided to hold onto New Mexico, principally because of the growing success of the Franciscan missionary effort.

The difficulties of the colony, the failure to find the strait, and the bickering of the colonists caused Oñate to resign in 1607. Two years later Pedro de Peralta was named governor. He moved the capital to Santa Fe in order to be closer to the Indian population centers. That city is the third oldest in the United States and has the distinction of being the oldest continuous capital. The church of San Miguel, built soon after, claims to be the oldest continuously used church with at least part of its original construction in the United States. Tlaxcalan Indians were brought from New Spain at an early date to help with the physical labor of construction and to advertise the benefits of Christianity and European life. Though such use of the Tlaxcalans was common in New Spain, this appears to be the only incident of it within the borders of the present-day United States.

The Spanish presence grew gradually, and though towns soon dotted the area they were sparse. As late as 1670 there were only twenty-eight hundred Spaniards in the colony, mostly in the area of Santa Fe. The Franciscan missionary effort was more successful. By the 1630s there were twenty-five missions, serving fifty thousand Indians. As in other mission areas, there was a great deal of conflict between the friars and the civil authorities, mostly over control of the Indians.

The Spanish settlement and evangelization of New Mexico came to a halt with the ferocious revolt of the Pueblo Indians in 1680. New Mexico was never really prosperous and depended on agriculture and livestock, especially sheep. Because of their precarious situation, the Spaniards increased their demands on the Indians. The Franciscans seem to have lacked some of the fire of their predecessors in New Spain. In addition, as throughout all New Spain, later generations of Franciscans did not learn the native languages or become closely identified with the natives. Ironically, one reason for this was pressure from the Spanish officials, who feared that the Franciscans' identification with the Indians weakened royal control. At the same time, the old religious ideas were not dead; many Indians found mission life confining, and the native medicine men were agitating against the Christians. One of them, Popé, had been arrested in a round-up of medicine men in 1675. Although he had been released, he nursed a hatred of Spaniards and their religion. He devised a plan to purge the entire region of the intruders, especially missionaries, and won a large number of chiefs to his side.

The uprising was carefully planned to begin in the entire area at the same time. The Indians had the advantage of surprise and caught the Spaniards totally off guard. At least four hundred Spaniards, including thirty-two friars, were killed—twenty-one Franciscans were killed in one day. The Indians laid siege to Santa Fe and cut off its water supply. The Spaniards, taking advantage of Indian complacency, were able to break out. The Indians seemed content to let them go and did not make a serious attempt to exterminate the survivors. Approximately twenty-four hundred refugees fled to El Paso del Norte on the Río Grande (present-day El Paso, Texas), where they laid the basis for a civilian settlement in what had been until then a military garrison.

Subsequent attempts to probe or reconquer New Mexico were unsuccessful. Finally, in 1688, Diego de Vargas, a farsighted and diplomatic man, was named governor. He began the reoccupation in 1692. His first expedition had an incredible success. With a total force of only one hundred, including three Franciscans and forty professional soldiers, he won over the pueblos with a combination of diplomacy, psychology, and firmness. By the end of the year he secured the allegiance of the majority without bloodshed. By the time he set out with a larger, colonizing expedition in 1693, however, the Indians had again become restive. Vargas decided that only a military venture would succeed, while at the same time trying to use diplomacy. The ensuing war was sporadic and slow. By 1696 most of New Mexico had been recovered, although the Zuñi and Hopi continued to be both independent and hostile.

Located an immense distance from Mexico City, New Mexico tended to develop in relative isolation. As a result there was a continuity in family generations that was lacking elsewhere and a greater sense of relationship to the past. To this day a significant part of the Hispanic population of New Mexico regards itself as Spanish, not Mexican. Even more noteworthy is the fact that some of the original families came from converso or crypto-Jewish back-grounds. Though there is sharp debate among historians concerning the precise extent of Jewish practices and influence among present-day Catholic New Mexican families, research done by Professor Stanley Hordes indicates that they persist to some degree.

The missionary enterprise in northern New Spain and the borderlands proved more formidable and trying than it had to the south. Conditions were harsher, the natives more hostile and tenacious of old ideas; the distances were awesome, and only the hardiest missionaries, like Kino, Salvatierra, and Larios, could cope with the challenge. Despite numerous setbacks, the missionaries did have a measure of success. In some places, like New Mexico, this required the support of Spanish arms. In others, like the Pimería Alta, there was less reliance on force. Not everyone, however, agreed to the idea of coercion of any sort in the propagation of Christianity. In the sixteenth century Spain and its American possessions were rocked by a bitter debate over the nature of the Indians, their capacity for Christianity and European civilization, and the best means of evangelizing them. That debate is the subject of the next chapter.

# 5

## "ARE THEY NOT MEN?"[1]

On the fourth Sunday of Advent 1511, in a small thatched church on Española, a Dominican named Antonio de Montesinos ascended the pulpit. In his hands he held the written text of a sermon he had composed with his two confreres who served the church. All three had signed it and Montesinos was commissioned to deliver it. After stating the text, "I am the voice of one crying in the wilderness," he said a few words about the Advent season. He then launched into a blistering attack on his parishioners and their treatment of the Indians:

> In order to make this known to you, I have come up here, for I am the voice of Christ crying in the wilderness of this island, and therefore you had better listen to me, not with indifference but with all your heart and with all your senses. For this voice will be the strangest you have ever heard, the harshest and the hardest, the most terrifying that you ever thought that you would hear. . . . This voice says that you are in mortal sin and live and die in it because of the cruelty and tyranny that you use against these innocent peoples. Tell me, by what right or justice do you hold these Indians in such cruel and horrible slavery? By what authority do you wage such detestable wars on these peoples, who lived mildly and peacefully in their own lands, in which you have destroyed countless numbers of them with unheard-of murders and ruin. . . . Are they not men? Do they not have rational souls? Are you not bound to love them as you love yourselves? Don't you understand this? Don't you feel this? . . . Be sure that in your present state you can no more be saved than the Moors or Turks, who do not have and do not want the faith of Jesus Christ.[2]

Although Montesinos came down from the pulpit with his eyes blazing and his head held high, the Spaniards were outraged. A contemporary witness said that the celebrant could scarcely finish the mass because of the murmuring in the church.

The Montesinos sermon inaugurated an epic conflict. It was fought out over the course of the century between apologists for Spanish policies in the Indies and pro-Indian humanitarians (mostly, but not exclusively, churchmen). It touched the basic issues of what constituted "humanness," the rights of non-Christian peoples, the nature of sovereignty, the concept of just war, the justice of slavery, and the most appropriate approaches to evangelization and christianization. An obscure friar on a small island in the Caribbean had fired the first shot in what Lewis Hanke aptly called "The Spanish Struggle for Justice in the Conquest of America."[3]

The colonials counterattacked immediately. A delegate went to the governor to demand a retraction of the slanders that the friars had hurled against them. The three Dominicans assured the governor and the colonists that on the following Sunday they would receive a proper explanation of what had been said. Not surprisingly, this turned out to be an even more fiery denunciation of the Spaniards' crimes. Since recourse to the crown for redress of grievances was standard practice in that century, the Spaniards appointed a delegation to go to Spain to resolve the issue. The Dominicans did the same, with Montesinos as one of the delegates.

The principal question, as it was to be throughout the century, was that of forced labor. Despite lurid tales of Spanish cruelty and destruction, the real curse of the colonies was the encomienda. By 1511 this had deteriorated into wanton exploitation, with the Spaniards demanding higher tributes, more labor (especially in the gold and silver mines), with the result that the natives were being rapidly decimated. The Spanish crown was never at ease with the encomienda—and not just for humanitarian reasons. Though it was not a true feudal grant (it did not, for example, grant any judicial rights), it was close enough that the crown, which had spent decades neutralizing the feudal nobility of Spain, was wary of it. After Isabella's death in 1504, however, Ferdinand became regent of Castile and effective ruler of all Spain. The crown needed money for its European adventures, and that money came from the New World. Ferdinand, together with his chief counselor, Juan de Fonseca, the cynical and ambitious bishop of Burgos, was not inclined to stop the exploitation of the natives or alienate the Spanish settlers. As Fonseca put it in a moment of appalling realism after he had been told about the slaughter of thousands of Indians, "How does that concern me and how does it concern the king?"[4]

The two delegations that arrived from Española laid their cases before the crown. Ferdinand turned the matter over to a commission of theologians. The result was an attempt to compromise two apparently irreconcilable principles: the freedom of the Indians and the need for some sort of compulsory labor system. The latter rewarded the conquistadores and provided income for the crown. The resulting compromise was enshrined in the Laws of Burgos, which were issued in 1512 and amended in 1513. In delineating those things that were to be forbidden, the laws painted a horrifying picture of native life and labor in the Caribbean. Worse still, from the reformers' point of view, they gave legal status to the encomienda and constituted it the economic basis of colonial society.

However well intentioned, the Laws of Burgos did not stop the spread of conquest or the numerous slave-raiding expeditions of the Spaniards. The clamor of churchmen against these focused attention on new areas of debate. By what right were Spaniards in the Indies? What was the morality of conquest? What were the bases in law for forcible enslavement? Many of these questions had been asked before, and the answers had always been in favor of the Spaniards. In the case of enslavement Spanish practice, following Roman law, held that such servitude was justified in the case of criminals, rebels, and captives taken in a just war. But what constituted a just war? One opinion held that stubborn refusal to hear the gospel or to admit the preachers of the gospel was one such justification. Rebels were those who refused to accept the rule of Spain, based as it was on the *Inter Caetera*.

Out of this renewed debate came one of the strangest documents in Spanish history, the Requirement, which was probably written by the Spanish jurist Juan López de Palacios Rubios. It contained a synopsis of the history of salvation and the right of Spain to rule, together with a warning to the as yet unconquered Indians that they must accept these or be subject to conquest. Theoretically, the document was supposed to be read to the Indians through interpreters so that they would have the opportunity to submit peacefully and avoid conquest and enslavement. If they failed to do so, then the war against them would be just. It takes little imagination to guess what happened in practice. Bartolomé de las Casas said that when he read the Requirement for the first time, he did not know whether to laugh or cry.

Most Spaniards laughed. Gonzalo Fernández de Oviedo recounted how, during an expedition to South America in 1514 led by Pedrarias Dávila, the Spaniards came upon an empty village, where they were later attacked by Indians:

I should have preferred to have the requirement explained to the Indians first, but no effort was made to do so, apparently because it was considered superfluous or inappropriate. And just as our general on this expedition failed to carry out this pious proceeding with the Indians, as he was supposed to do before attacking them, the captains of many later expeditions also neglected the procedure and did even worse things. . . . Later, in 1516, I asked Doctor Palacios Rubios . . . if the consciences of the Christians were satisfied with the requirement and he said yes, if it were done as the proclamation required. But I recall that he often laughed when I told him of that campaign and of others that various captains later made.[5]

At this point a new figure entered the controversy: a stormy, turbulent, angry man who eventually embodied the most prophetic and extreme elements of the pro-Indian movement—Bartolomé de las Casas.

Las Casas was born in Seville in 1484. His father was a merchant of modest means. The young Bartolomé received his early education in his home city and was old enough to recall Columbus's return in 1493 from the first voyage of discovery. In hope of bettering their fortunes, his father and three uncles accompanied Columbus on his second voyage. When his father returned, he presented Bartolomé with a young Indian slave who was later freed by a royal edict in 1500. In 1501 his father, still trying to better his financial situation, accompanied Nicolás de Ovando, the first governor of Española, to that island and took his son with him. Prior to leaving, Bartolomé received tonsure and thus became a *clérigo*, a member of the clerical state.

The group arrived at Española in 1502. Some four or five years later Bartolomé journeyed to Rome, where he was ordained to the priesthood, though he did not celebrate his first mass until 1512. He also took pride in the fact that he was the first newly ordained priest to say his first mass in the New World. In 1508, the year the Spaniards discovered that Cuba was an island, he was granted an encomienda on Española and became somewhat prosperous. In 1513 he served as chaplain to the expedition that conquered Cuba, during which he witnessed at first hand the atrocities committed by the Spaniards and tried to prevent or moderate them. He was given a large encomienda on Cuba and settled down to the comfortable life of a gentleman farmer and landowning cleric. He always maintained that he treated his Indians well, although he neglected their religious instruction.

Between 1508 and 1515, on both Española and Cuba, Las Casas saw little contradiction between his life as an encomendero and his commitment as a Christian and priest. Once, when a Dominican to whom he wished to go to for confession declined to hear it because he was an encomendero, Las Casas argued vehemently with him. He eventually yielded out of respect for the Dominican's holiness and reputation, but he did not change his way of life. That happened in August 1514, when he was preparing a sermon for the following Sunday. Searching through Scripture for an appropriate text, he chanced on a passage in Ecclesiasticus (now called Sirach), 34:18: "The sacrifice of an offering unjustly acquired is a mockery; the gifts of impious men are unacceptable." A few days of meditation on these words, his memories of the teachings of the Dominicans, and his own experiences brought about a conversion. The following Sunday he announced from the pulpit that he had divested himself of his encomienda and was beginning a life of advocacy on behalf of the oppressed Indians.

In 1515 he joined Antonio de Montesinos on a voyage to Spain, where he intended to lobby on behalf of the Indians at court. He had one interview with Ferdinand, but it availed little. Ferdinand died the next year and the throne passed to his grandson Charles. Until the young king arrived in Spain from

Flanders the country was governed by the regency of Cardinal Cisneros, who was initially favorable to Las Casas. The anti-Indian leaders, including Bishop Fonseca, were fired and a plan formulated for investigating and reforming the situation in the Indies. The investigation was entrusted to three reluctant Hieronymites—Luis de Figueroa, Bernardino de Manzanedo, and Alonso de Santo Domingo—who were sent to Española to gather information on the scene. Specifically, they were instructed to implement a plan for reforming the encomienda, free Indians held by royal officials, and investigate the entire Indian situation—and even to look into the possibility of Indian self-government. Las Casas received the title Protector of the Indians and was to help the Hieronymites in their investigation. While all were still in Spain, however, agents for the colonials began to turn the Hieronymites against Las Casas. As a result he and the three priests sailed for Española on separate ships. Once arrived, relations deteriorated still more, as the three commissioners came under heavy pressure from the colonists. The so-called Hieronymite Interrogatory produced volumes of testimony but accomplished little beyond freeing some Indians from absentee Spanish encomenderos. It was frustrated by the outrage of the colonials, the obstructionism of the bureaucracy in Spain, and the unwillingness of the Hieronymites to take strong action.

For several years thereafter, Las Casas lobbied at court in favor of one of his pet projects, that of colonization and christianization by peaceful means alone. After several years of agitation, he was given permission to establish an experimental settlement at Cumaná on the northern coast of Venezuela in 1518–1519. He hoped to colonize the area with farmers and religious, who together would attract the Indians to a settled, Christian way of life by kindness and good example. Knowing the Spanish love for titles and dignities, he even created a knighthood for the immigrants, the Knights of the Golden Spur. The project failed because the missionaries were dispersed by a storm and because of the hostility of the local Spaniards. In addition, slave-raiding expeditions caused the Indians to resist any further Spanish intrusions. Las Casas later saw that his project had two basic flaws. First, he had not had total control over it. Second, in an effort to make it palatable to the crown, he had promised profits from the experiment; that is, the crown would be the sole encomendero.

This failure caused Las Casas to go through a period of soul-searching and meditation that led him in 1522 to join the Dominican order. The Spanish colonials were relieved by his decision because they believed that he would no longer be in a position to bother them. It was a classic miscalculation. Initially, however, the colonists seemed to be correct. Las Casas spent the next few years studying theology and law, most of it in a way that would support his ideas. He gathered materials for his *History of the Indies*, one of the most valuable sources we have for the early discovery and colonization of the New World. He also began a second history, the *Apologetic History*, a landmark in anthropology. About the year 1530 he began writing a Latin treatise, *De Unico Vocationis Modo*

*Omnium Infidelium ad Veram Religionem* (*The Only Way of Attracting All Unbelievers to the True Religion*). Though only a few chapters have survived, they mark it as one of the most important missionary tracts in the history of the church. Basically, it was a blueprint for his own later missionary experiments: the spread of the gospel by peaceful means alone, the need for understanding of doctrine and clear catechesis prior to conversion, the need to respect and utilize native cultures as part of the missionary enterprise.

In 1536, with Bishop Zumárraga and Bishop Julián Garcés of Tlaxcala, Las Casas drew up some petitions on behalf of the Indians to be forwarded to the pope. Out of these came the landmark papal bull *Sublimis Deus* of Paul III (1537), which proclaimed the Indians truly men and capable of christianization. The bull became a powerful weapon in the hands of the pro-Indian forces, although it was never formally published in the Spanish dominions.

At about the same time the pro-Indian movement was receiving support on a theoretical level. This was due to the most influential Spanish theologian of the century, the Dominican Francisco de Vitoria (1483–1546), holder of the principal chair of theology at the University of Salamanca. A man with a broad humanistic background, Vitoria helped to revitalize scholastic theology, particularly by his emphasis on and use of the works of Thomas Aquinas. In two of his most important lectures, given about 1538 or 1539, *De Indis prior* (first lecture on the Indies) and *De Indis posterior seu jure belli Hispanorum in barbaros* (later lecture on the Indies; that is, on the Spaniards' right to make war against less civilized peoples), he elaborated for the first time a theory of international law, binding on all nations. Strongly influenced by the Scots theologian John Major, who taught in Spain, Vitoria vigorously defended the rights of the Indians, including that of property. He rejected those justifications for conquest that he regarded as unlawful, such as the savage condition of the natives, their idolatry and unbelief, or sins against nature. He denied that the pope or emperor had any authority to judge the Indians for any crimes they might have committed because that right belonged to their rulers. He also denied any right of the pope or the emperor to grant sovereignty over pagan nations to Christian rulers, for they had no temporal power over Indians or unbelievers. Consequently, their refusal to accept the overlordship of either pope or emperor did not justify war against them. He did, however, find reasons that justified conquest. These included the spread of the Christian religion, especially if rulers forcibly prevented their subjects who wished to convert from doing so. He also believed that tyrannical laws and practices that harmed the innocent, such as human sacrifice or cannibalism, justified conquest, a position Las Casas rejected. Vitoria also wrote on just war, helping to advance that theory. He even embraced a theory of selective conscientious objection. He is rightly considered one of the founders of international law, and his teachings were invaluable to Las Casas in defending the Indians. Students of Vitoria and other major Dominican theologians at Salamanca were to be found throughout the New World.

In 1537 Las Casas was given a major opportunity to put his missionary theories into practice at Tuzulutlán in modern Guatemala. The Indians there were hostile, so according to their custom the Spaniards referred to the area as *tierra de guerra* (land of war). Las Casas promptly christened it *tierra de vera paz* (land of true peace). Many Spaniards considered this the perfect opportunity to demonstrate the futility of Las Casas's ideas; he saw it as a providential opportunity to prove the opposite. His methods were truly ingenious. The prehispanic Aztecs had often used traveling merchants called *pochteca* as spies or advance agents of conquest. Las Casas used traveling tradesmen in the same way. He and other friars composed songs in the native language that summarized Christian doctrine and taught these to Christian traders. In the course of visiting the more important villages, after the day's trading was done, the songs were sung as part of the evening's entertainment. When the interest of the non-Christians was aroused, the traders would tell them about the friars who would teach them the rest of the doctrine without demanding anything for themselves. The experiment proved remarkably successful at first, to the chagrin of many a colonial. Ultimately, however, it failed because of the hostility of neighboring tribes, opposition by Spanish colonials, and the deaths of some of the missionaries. By 1556 it was all over, but its memory remains as one of the most audacious missionary experiments of modern times.

In 1540 Las Casas returned to Spain where, with other churchmen and laymen, he began to lobby in favor of the Indians at the court of Charles I. As a result of their agitation, the crown issued the famous New Laws of 1542, a striking combination of political reality and humanitarian idealism. The laws forbade all further enslavement of Indians for any reason whatever. The encomienda, as a private enterprise, was condemned to ultimate extinction: "Henceforth no encomienda is to be granted to anyone, and when the present holders of encomiendas die, their Indians will revert to the crown."[6] The extinction, it will be noticed, worked in favor of the crown, which now set itself up as eventually the only encomendero. For the colonials, the most appalling prospect was that of not being able to leave their encomiendas to their children and hence of being unable to establish family fortunes, something of surpassing importance to Spaniards of that age.

The reactions of the colonials were predictably hostile. In Peru, as noted, a revolt temporarily overthrew royal authority. In New Spain the royal official who was sent to implement the New Laws thought better of it and, invoking a time-honored Spanish tradition, he suspended them. Within a few years the more stringent of the laws were repealed. Still, enough remained on the books to spell the virtual, though not total, end of the encomienda as an important economic institution. The growing capitalist economy of New Spain left little room for the encomienda, from which the majority of later settlers was excluded. In addition, catastrophic epidemics, especially one in 1576 that depopulated entire regions and villages, devalued the encomienda and brought many encomenderos to the poverty level.

Despite the turmoil he had caused, Las Casas did not fall from royal favor. The Council of the Indies sought to make him bishop of the rich city of Cuzco, but he steadfastly refused. Eventually he had to yield to the crown's determination to give him a miter, and he accepted the recently created and very poor diocese of Chiapas in the south of modern Mexico, near the Guatemala border. Not surprisingly, his brief tenure as bishop was not peaceful, as he ordered priests not to absolve encomenderos and launched his familiar attacks on Spanish exploitation. In 1545 he narrowly escaped assassination. After attending a meeting of bishops and church leaders in Mexico City, he returned to Spain in 1547. He would never see the New World again and later resigned his bishopric.

In Spain he found that the controversies over the Spanish conquest and the treatment of the Indians had entered a new phase. The arguments were now to be carried out on a vastly different level from that of the past. The person responsible for this was a famed Renaissance humanist, Juan Ginés de Sepúlveda, the crown's official historian. He was encouraged to enter the fray by Cardinal García de Loaysa, the archbishop of Seville and an opponent of the New Laws. As a result Sepúlveda composed a scholarly Latin treatise in dialogue form called *The Second Democrates or Reasons That Justify War against the Indians*, which circulated in manuscript. Among the reasons cited by Sepúlveda as justifying war were the practice of human sacrifice and cannibalism—the Spaniards, he wrote, had an obligation to come to the aid of the oppressed victims—and the refusal of the natives to accept the universal rule of emperor and pope. Christianity, he asserted, could be introduced by force, the famous *compelle intrare* (make them come in) of the gospel (Luke 14:24) as elaborated by Saint Augustine. Since Sepúlveda was one of the foremost classical scholars of his time, it was only natural that he should also fall back on Aristotle's theory of natural slavery as found in the fifth book of the *Politics*: that some peoples, by reason of their superior intellect and endowments, are naturally fitted to rule while others, because of their brutishness and limited reasoning, are apt only for subordinate or servile roles. What Aristotle actually meant is a matter of dispute today, but there can be no doubt that for Sepúlveda and the Spanish colonials, it agreed perfectly with their concept of the Indians' place in society.

At the basis of Sepúlveda's theories, and explicitly stated in his treatise, was the supposition of Spanish cultural and intellectual superiority (he has been called the first ethnocentric Spanish nationalist). Whether he was the first can be disputed, but ethnocentric and nationalist he certainly was. Sepúlveda did not go so far as to deny the humanity of the Indians—he conceded that they were not quite on the same level as monkeys—but he clearly placed them in an inferior order. This was an interesting position for a man who had probably never seen an Indian.

Las Casas, of course, counterattacked immediately. It was now that his years of selective study of the classics, scripture, the fathers of the Church, and canon and civil law stood him in good stead. He was able to meet Sepúlveda on his own ground.

*The Second Democrates* made the rounds of the universities, where it was almost universally condemned. The uproar that followed caused Charles I to convoke a junta (committee) of theologians to hear the protagonists and arrive at some sort of conclusion. In preparation for this he ordered that all further raids and expeditions into Indian lands be halted. As Lewis Hanke has observed, "Probably never before or since has a mighty emperor . . . in the full tide of his power ordered his conquests to cease until it could be decided whether they were just."[7]

Out of all this came the Junta of Valladolid of 1550–1551. The judges were a panel of fourteen distinguished religious and laity, of whom four were fellow Dominicans of Las Casas. Sepúlveda appeared on the first day and gave a three-hour summary of the doctrine of *The Second Democrates*. Las Casas appeared on the following day and proceeded to read the Latin text of his rebuttal, *Argumentum Apologiae*, for five full days. It was a point-by-point refutation of Sepúlveda's accusations. Even if the Indians were guilty of human sacrifice and cannibalism, he said, that could be explained as a rational step in the development of religious thought. He strongly defended the right of pagan rulers to have jurisdiction in their lands without interference by Christians, ecclesiastic or lay. Peaceful persuasion was the only permissible means of evangelization. If Aristotle believed in natural slavery, then Aristotle was to be rejected. The pope had no right to parcel out pagan lands to Christian rulers. Ruling authority in any nation came from God, but it came through the consent of the governed—no ruler could be imposed on a people against their will. The domestic crimes of a nation, no matter how heinous, were not justification for invasion or subjugation by an outside power.

After that the judges recessed either because, as Las Casas claimed, they were convinced of the truth of his arguments or, as Sepúlveda claimed, they were exhausted. There is some evidence of correspondence among the judges, but apparently they were unable or unwilling to come to a final judgment. So far as is known, nothing specific came from the junta or its discussions. That was a great tragedy. The judges at Valladolid had an opportunity to make a positive impact on crown policy in a matter of surpassing moral importance, and in some ways they failed to measure up to it.

If the colonials had won the battle, at least by default, Las Casas in one sense won the war. *The Second Democrates* was not allowed to be published in Sepúlveda's lifetime—in fact, it did not see print until 1892. And yet in 1552 Las Casas was able to publish his most famous (or perhaps notorious) work, *The Very Brief Account of the Destruction of the Indies*, an angry, inflammatory, exaggerated tract that has provided grist for the Black Legend of Spanish cruelty and exploitation in the New World. Remarkably, it was published without royal license.

Las Casas still had another fifteen years of life. He spent most of that time as a champion and lobbyist at court for the Indians. There is disagreement among historians as to his effectiveness during that time. For some he was a burnt-out comet, a sort of colorful old man humored by the crown but ultimately ineffective. According to this school of thought, the "American reality" and the policies of Philip II spelled the end of the pro-Indian movement. Others see Las Casas at the zenith of his work, still keeping the movement alive and creating a school of followers who would continue his work after his death. Whichever may be the more accurate, it is remarkable that he enjoyed such incredible freedom to criticize the crown and its policies. Despite his alienation from and even hostility to so many of his countrymen, he was never silenced.

Equally notable is the fact that as he grew older, he became more radical. By the end of his life, he was advocating the wholesale withdrawal of all Spaniards from the Indies—unrealistic, but consistent to the end. Sepúlveda was equally consistent. He went to his grave claiming that he had sought only the royal good and been rewarded with calumny and rejection.

Las Casas died at Valladolid in 1566 and was eventually buried in the Dominican chapel of Atocha in Madrid. Unfortunately, his tomb was lost in the course of various reconstructions. In his last will he prophesied divine wrath against his country for its crimes against the Indians. "And I believe that because of these impious and criminal and infamous deeds, so unjustly and tyrannically and barbarously done to and against [the Indians] God will unleash his fury and wrath on Spain . . . unless it does great penance; and I fear it will do it too late, or never, because of the blindness that God, because of our sins, has permitted in great and small alike."[8] He believed that if men ever needed to know the reason for this visitation of divine vengeance, they could find them in his writings.

Las Casas was an extremist; there is no doubt about that. He was a prophetic figure, with all that this implies. He wrote and spoke in superlatives and never gave his enemies credit for good faith. Whether because of or in spite of this, of all the reformers he is the one who has left the strongest impression. In this century alone there have been more than two thousand books and articles about him and the flow shows no sign of stopping. He has become something of a patron saint for liberation theology and other movements that seek to link the gospels to the freedom of indigenous peoples. To use an often-overworked phrase, he was a force of nature and, whether one agrees or disagrees with him, it is impossible to ignore him.

It is a tribute to the Spanish crown and psychology of the sixteenth century that Las Casas and his fellow reformers had such freedom of speech and action. The Spanish concept of kingship was the medieval one of a dispenser of justice rather than an author of legislation. Spanish government was a careful balancing act among pressure groups, and the crown often showed an amazing readiness to alter policy in response to these groups. At the same time it is possible to feel a certain sympathy for the crown, faced as it was not only with differing demands but with a flood of contradictory reports. It is also a tribute to Las Casas's position that he was able to prevent the publication of works by his enemies.

Las Casas, of course, was not alone in his crusade. He has, however, attracted the most attention. A multitude of churchmen and humanitarians fought for the rights of the Indians but often in a more moderate way than the fiery Dominican. Juan de Zumárraga took very seriously his title as protector of the Indians, but his approach was more paternalistic than Las Casas's. Zumárraga opposed the New Laws because he believed that some sort of compulsion was necessary in order to make the Indians work and to have a stable society. Motolinía (Toribio de Benavente), one of the Twelve Apostles of the Franciscans, was a defender of the Indians but an opponent of Las Casas. In 1555 he wrote a scathing attack on *The Very Brief Account* because of its exaggerations and intemperate tone. The fact that Motolinía was a Franciscan and Las Casas a Dominican did not help matters. Gerónimo de Mendieta (1525–1604), a Franciscan with a millennarian and apocalyptic outlook, had an idealized picture of the Indian and saw the New World as a potential terrestrial paradise. He bitterly attacked the exploitation of Indian labor by the Spaniards. Because of his criticisms, his classic work *Historia Eclesiástica* was not published until 1870.

The ongoing strength of the humanitarian movement, as well as its decline, can be seen in the third Mexican Provincial Council of 1585. The mendicants, with the Franciscans in the forefront, condemned Spanish exploitation of Indian labor and the proposal for total war against the Chichimecas. The apocalyptic, millennarian, and unrestrained approach seemed alive and well. Even the bishops, in their letter of 16 October 1585 to Philip II, fell into the same language when describing the labor systems and the situation of the Chichimeca Indians. The impact, however, was blunted by the regalism of the bishops and their absorption of the colonial reality. Their Counter-Reformation approach to important issues, which laid great stress on law, organization, and structure, tended toward acceptance of the status quo.

Part of this acceptance can be seen in their famous decree forbidding the ordination to the priesthood of Indians and persons of mixed blood. The ecclesiastical junta of 1539 had moved toward ordaining Indians because as Christians they had a right to receive that sacrament as well as the others. By 1585 the attitude had changed. The actual wording of the final decree is garbled, in part because of objections raised by Rome, but the clear intention was to reject the ordination of Indians, blacks, or mixed bloods of any sort. One reason was a social reality: such a step would lower the esteem for the clerical state as part of a hierarchical society. Such priests would be socially unacceptable. Again, the Spanish colonial outlook was that to allow the Indian to achieve that role in society would diminish any justification for exploitation.

The Spanish humanitarian movement had no counterpart in the rest of the New World. French, Portuguese, and British America saw nothing like it. In part this was because of the Spanish tradition of constitutionalism and the renaissance of theology in the sixteenth century. It was also due to the place of the Church in Spanish society—an institutionalized conscience. Eventually, regalism and accommodation to the status quo would muffle that voice. Before that happened, however, the movement shone as one of the glories of Spanish history.

# 6

# IBERO-AMERICA IN THE
# SEVENTEENTH CENTURY

In some ways the seventeenth century in Ibero-America is more difficult to describe than the sixteenth. It was certainly a less dramatic period. The age of conquest and initial missionary activity was over. A major part of the missionary task had already been accomplished, at least on a superficial level. The Church in Ibero-America, like its counterparts throughout the Catholic world, was becoming more structured and organizational, in part as a natural consequence of the original evangelization, in part as a result of the Catholic Reformation. In general the century was characterized more by consolidation than by innovation. Numerous new dioceses were established, such as Buenos Aires (which included modern Uruguay) in 1620. There was also a growing sense that the christianization of the natives had not been as profound or permanent as first believed. The reaction of some churchmen was to renew the campaign against idolatry; the reaction of others tended more toward accommodation and acceptance; nostalgic mendicant chroniclers began to view the early years of the missionary enterprise as a golden age. In many areas of the Catholic New World it is possible to sense a certain weariness and decline of fervor in the missionaries.

## FLORIDA

While Florida was safely under Spanish control, the crown had an ambivalent attitude toward it. It was difficult to defend and there were no gold or silver mines to repay the government for the cost of settlement and defense. In 1607 the Franciscans were able to dissuade the government from abandoning Florida altogether. Five years later the Franciscan mission became an independent province, and the Florida missions entered their most active period. In 1647 the Apalache Indians in the north revolted against Spanish exploitation, and three missionaries were killed. The uprising was quelled with great severity, a factor that set back the Franciscan work among the natives. By 1655 there were seventy Franciscans in Florida (including present-day Georgia), ministering, they claimed, to twenty-six thousand Indians. The following year the Timucua and Apalaches, again provoked by Spanish exploitation, revolted, and again the revolt was ruthlessly put down.

By 1674 the presence of the English to the north began to be felt. As they moved their settlements down the coast, they were able to take advantage of the Indian resentment of Spanish exploitation. In the 1680s the Guale Indians went over to the English and abandoned Catholicism. When Florida was turned over to the English by the Treaty of Paris in 1763, the missions had been in decline for some time. The treaty spelled the end. Catholicism all but vanished.

At their height the missions in Florida, which far outstripped in numbers and importance the later Franciscan missions in California, seemed the very model of the enterprise of evangelization. Yet it is possible to question the extent to which the natives were truly christianized. During the periodic revolts, there were large numbers of apostasies from, or abandonment of, Christianity. The Indians to the north readily joined the English, and after the departure of the Spaniards there was little left of Catholicism. The missionaries gave enthusiastic descriptions of the religious lives of their converts, but the facts do not always support them. Unfortunately, the Franciscan missionary activity in Florida was not so well documented as in other parts of the Spanish world, so it is impossible to draw any definitive conclusions about its success or failure.

## NEW SPAIN

In Spain's northern New World possessions the seventeenth century has some-times been called the "colonial siesta," the "silver age," and "the century of depression." All these descriptions have elements of truth, but it is easy to exaggerate them. While it is true that the century was uneventful, at least in comparison with the previous one, it was not altogether somnolent. With regard to the period of economic depression, historians differ in their reading of the evidence. Some see a prolonged period of economic stagnation, others a more progressive and growing society.

In Mexico City in particular, Spanish culture thrived. Silver was the basis of society's riches, at least among the upper classes, and its use was almost universal. Culturally life was dominated by two great literary and religious figures who were also friends, Carlos de Sigüenza y Góngora (1645–1700) and Sor Juana Inés de la Cruz (1648–1695). Sigüenza y Góngora was a priest, a former Jesuit novice, who achieved a high degree of fame as historian, astrono-

*Americae Sive Novi Orbis No Va Descriptio, 1584*

mer, mathematician, ethnologist, and poet. Of strong criollo sympathies and a passionate devotee of Our Lady of Guadalupe, he was a poet, historian, mathematician, geographer, archeologist, and astronomer. He accumulated a vast library that later passed to the Jesuits and then to the University of Mexico. His erudition was exaggerated by admiring contemporaries, but he still ranks as an important figure in Mexican letters. He was also the first to espouse the bizarre theory that the apostle Thomas had preached Christianity to the Indians and then become identified with Quetzalcóatl.

Sor (Sister) Juana Inés de la Cruz was one of the most extraordinary individuals in Mexican history. She was born near Mexico City in 1648, and her family name was Inés de Asbaje y Ramírez. A child prodigy, she was able to read by the age of three and by her teens had mastered Latin. She grew into a beautiful, multitalented woman who was also an early exponent, if not of women's rights, at least of women's basic equality. At the age of sixteen she became a lady in waiting to the viceroy's wife and was thus part of the elite of local society. In 1667, forsaking the prospects of favorable marriage and the rather sterile life of a woman in Spanish society, she entered a convent. Two years later she settled in the convent of San Jerónimo in Mexico City, where she spent the rest of her life in contemplation, study, and especially the composition of superb poetry and drama. In later life she became notable for her charities and died while aiding victims of an epidemic in 1695.

Sor Juana is known in Mexico as the Tenth Muse, and her poetry is regarded as the last of Spain's *Siglo de Oro*, the Golden Age. Some of it was accusatory of contemporary attitudes.

> Stupid men, quick to condemn
> Women wrongly for their flaws,
> Never seeing you're the cause
> of all that you blame in them.
>
> If you flatter them along,
> Earn their scorn, their love incite,
> Why expect them to do right
> When you urge them to do wrong?
>
> You combat their opposition,
> And then gravely when you're done,
> Say the whole thing was in fun
> And you did not seek submission.
>
> . . .
>
> Can you think of wit more drear
> Than for one with lack of brain
> To smear a mirror, then complain
> Since it is not crystal clear?[1]

By the seventeenth century Catholicism was strongly established at all levels in New Spain. The land was filled with religious houses: the mendicants, the Jesuits, the discalced Franciscans, Mercedarians, Carmelites, and others. Every town and almost every village had a church with at least a visiting priest to attend to it. That did not mean that the old ways had died out or that paganism had entirely disappeared. In the frontier areas many prehispanic practices survived, sometimes intermingled with Christian ones. This was particularly true in the Mayan lands to the south, where the tenaciously conservative natives, often at a distance from direct Spanish control, were able to retain some form of their old religion or mingle it with Christianity. This included the identification of various Catholic saints with prehispanic deities. The modern Indian who prays to the rain god before planting his fields or sacrifices a chicken on church steps is heir to this syncretism.

Generally speaking, the bishops of the seventeenth century did not match the quality of their predecessors. One of the baleful effects of the patronato was that bishops tended to become more lackluster, more like government officials than their more charismatic predecessors. The pioneering age was gone; the church was more bureaucratic. The same was also true of the mendicants. Many now accepted the reality of colonial life and had lost some of the initial enthusiasm that motivated the first missionaries. There was a growing nostalgia for the past, a realization that a once-vital period was gone beyond reclaiming. New Spain was no longer a missionary land except in the wild far North.

Although the Council of Trent had decreed the regular celebration of provincial councils throughout the Catholic world, this was not followed in practice. In the Indies, despite a papal concession that declared that such councils should be held every seven years, this was rarely done. In New Spain the very success of the third Mexican Provincial Council of 1585 rendered future meetings superfluous, but other reasons intervened. Archbishop Juan Pérez de la Serna sought to convoke such a council in the first decades of the seventeenth century but was hindered by a shortage of funds and the opposition of many religious and clergy. Mexico did not have another provincial council until the eighteenth century.

The controversies and conflicts of the sixteenth century were carried on into the seventeenth. These included the hostility between the bishops and the mendicants and between the civil and ecclesiastical authorities. Part of the Habsburg policy of ruling was the pitting of one local authority against another as a form of checks and balances, thus preventing an undesirable accumulation of power by any one agency on the local level. Archbishops and viceroys were natural actors in this political drama since their jurisdictions often overlapped. Antagonisms between the two principal leaders of the colony abounded in the sixteenth century but reached the point of violence in the seventeenth.

In 1621 Diego Carrillo de Mendoza y Pimentel, marqués de Gelves, became the viceroy of New Spain. An elderly and authoritarian noble, accustomed to command, he was personally upright, pious, and a reformer. Endowed with a strong sense of the importance of his office, he tried to keep both the mendicants and the archbishop of Mexico, Juan Pérez de la Serna, in their places. Since his appointment in 1613 the archbishop had made himself popular among the people for his kindness and charity, especially toward the poor. Like previous archbishops, he wanted to replace the friars in the doctrinas with secular clergy. The viceroy sided with the religious, and soon he and the archbishop were locked in a struggle over jurisdiction.

Beginning in 1623 as a dispute over the right of sanctuary or asylum in church buildings, the conflict soon escalated over a number of questions, some of them petty or personal. The archbishop excommunicated the viceroy, but the latter, supported by some lay and ecclesiastical authorities, declared the excommunication invalid and counterattacked by levying a fine on the archbishop and decreeing his banishment. Early in 1624 Gelves renewed the decree and attempted to implement it. The archbishop in retaliation placed an interdict—prohibition of all church services—on the capital. A riot broke out among the poorer classes, the archbishop's principal defenders, and a mob attacked the viceregal palace. Gelves was forced to yield. Within a short time New Spain was given a new viceroy and Pérez de la Serna, who returned to Spain in 1624 to defend himself, was later named bishop of Zamora.

In the 1640s this was repeated again in the famous case of Bishop Palafox of Puebla. Juan de Palafox y Mendoza (1600–1659) came to New Spain in 1640 with Viceroy Diego López Pacheco Cabrera y Bobadilla, bringing with him an appointment as bishop of Puebla and a limited commission as visitador of the colony. He soon came into conflict with the mendicants over the doctrinas and with the viceroy over matters of jurisdiction. In 1642 Palafox was appointed interim viceroy and arranged the transfer of power from the viceroy to himself almost in the manner of a palace revolution. He held this position for only five months, but showed himself a just and capable administrator. Though prior to coming to America he had been friendly with the Jesuits, a rift soon appeared between him and the Society in Puebla. The conflict had many causes, but conflict of authority was the basic one. The quarrel soon involved the new viceroy and other religious communities. At one point it looked as if Palafox by himself was ranged against all the civil authority and ecclesiastics of New Spain. This lasted from late 1647 to early 1648, and Palafox was eventually required to return to Spain. He was vindicated when Pope Innocent X found against the Jesuits. Palafox was kept waiting for some years before being given the relatively insignificant Castilian diocese of Burgo de Osma.

These incidents illustrate not only the closed, even hothouse atmosphere of the capital but also the strong sense of personal honor and sensitivity Spaniards of that period, including churchmen, had. It was also part of the balancing act whereby royal government kept its servants plotting against each other rather than against the crown. These servants, including the churchmen, were often strong-minded and turbulent and did not hesitate to take advantage of their distance from the mother country. The tragedy, of course, was that such conflicts deflected the bishops from their true pastoral tasks. Time, energy, and emotion were wasted on something that was both tangential and transient.

## PERU

The early seventeenth century saw a renewed campaign against idolatry in Peru, carried out in two phases. As in other parts of Spanish America there was a growing perception that the missionary task had had limited success. At the head of the first phase was the priest Francisco de Avila, a criollo from Cuzco. There were some positive effects of this campaign, such as renewed instruction and evangelization, but forceful methods, including the burning of at least one apostate Indian, were also employed. The campaign was renewed in 1649 under Archbishop Pedro de Villagómez of Lima, a nephew of Mogrovejo, and continued for nine years. It encountered many obstacles: the difficulties of travel, the fact that diocesan priests would move on to new positions, and the lack of cooperation by the Jesuits, who did not want their missionary work associated with judicial activities. It was even suggested that the Indians be made subject to the Inquisition, a proposal that was not followed.

As in New Spain, there were continued conflicts between bishops and mendicants over doctrinas and between bishops and civil authorities over respective jurisdictions, including the right of asylum. The latter was a consistent source of friction between civil and ecclesiastical authorities. Between 1654 and 1661 there was a serious conflict between Archbishop Villagómez and an official of the audiencia, Juan de Padilla, over the extent to which the prelate was fulfilling his obligations toward the Indians. Unlike the conflict in New Spain between Archbishop Pérez de la Serna and the viceroy Escalona, this one was peaceful and ended in compromise. On a pettier level the archbishop found himself in conflict with his clergy over a ruling he promulgated in 1647 that drastically regulated hair styles, with penalties that included excommunication, suspension, and imprisonment. The matter eventually went to both Madrid and Rome, with the crown moderating the penalties while retaining the regulations.

Unlike New Spain, Peru had two provincial councils after its successful third one. These were held in 1591 and 1601, but because of strong regalism neither one was recognized by the crown. Additional considerations in the Andean region included the difficulty of travel, economic problems, and the opposition of civil authorities, who feared ecclesiastical resistance to the inroads of the patronato.

### SAINT MARTIN DE PORRES

Certainly one of the most remarkable figures in Peru in that period was Martin de Porres (1579–1639). The illegitimate son of a Spanish nobleman and a free black woman, he was apprenticed to a barber surgeon at an early age. After practicing that craft for a few years and earning a reputation for charity, he felt a call to the religious life and asked to be accepted into the Dominicans as a lay helper—he did not feel that he merited to be even a lay brother. After nine years in the community he was accepted as a full lay brother. He gained a great reputation both for his charity and his personal sanctity.

## CARTAGENA

### THE JESUITS IN THE LLANOS

To the east of Bogotá, in the tablelands of Cundinamarca, were the plains or llanos. The Jesuits, who had come to Nueva Granada at the end of the sixteenth century to do educational work, responded to the needs of the natives in the llanos. Two Jesuits, Fathers Medrano and Figueroa, went there but were recalled in 1629 at the insistence of the archbishop and the colonials. Not until thirty years later did the Jesuits return to resume work that was to last until their suppression.

### SAINT PETER CLAVER

Cartagena at the beginning of the seventeenth century was a bustling seaport and one of the richer mercantile cities in the Spanish dependencies. It was also the center for the African slave trade. Thousands of black Africans passed through the city and were sold, after having endured the horrors of the trans-atlantic voyage. Peter Claver (1580–1654) was a Spaniard who had entered the Society of Jesus in 1602. Eight years later he was sent to Cartagena, where his feelings were aroused against the slave trade. In 1616 he went to Bogotá, where he was ordained to the priesthood. Returning to Cartagena, he carried out an intense apostolate among the slaves. He sought to alleviate their sufferings, both by preaching and by physical help. He eventually converted thousands of them and gained a high reputation for holiness.

## THE JESUIT REDUCTIONS

Among the most famous mission enterprises in the New World were the Jesuit reductions of Paraguay. Although probably the best known, they were not unique. Rather, they belonged to the mainstream of Iberian mission methodology together with the policy of congregación, the hospitals of Vasco de Quiroga, the Franciscan missions of California, and the *aldeias* of Brazil. All of these had a certain number of elements in common. One was to bring the nomadic or seminomadic natives together in larger population units (the "congregating" of congregación, the "reducing" of the reductions), where they would lead a form of communal life under the direction of the priests. The villages were constructed according to a set plan. There was a regular routine of religious instruction and the teaching of practical arts. The native was regarded as a minor under the tutelage of the missionary, but with incorporation into European society as the ultimate goal. During this intermediate period the neophytes were kept apart both from pagan Indians and from the whites, who were viewed as a morally corrupting influence or a danger to the Indians' freedom. The villages were ordinarily ruled by elected Indian officials, under the often-strong guidance of the missionaries. If there was a military presence in the village, it could also be called a presidio.

The Jesuit reductions were thus not unique, but they differed from the other systems in that the goal of incorporation into European society was either remote or absent. The reductions were more a parallel than a preparatory society. They were, in addition, remarkably well organized and eventually became strong economic units. Economically, they were a combination of collectivism and limited private property. (The positive and negative elements in this system will be discussed in the conclusions to this study.)

The credit for originating the reductions is often given not to a Jesuit, but to the Franciscan Luis de Bolaños. He was born in Spain about the year 1550 and after joining the Franciscans came to Asunción, Paraguay, in 1575. He then worked among the Indians of Guairá and founded the first reductions. He was not ordained to the priesthood until 1585. After founding numerous reductions, some in close association with the Jesuits, he retired to Buenos Aires, where he died in 1629. He was fluent in the Guaraní language and was the author of a Guaraní grammar, dictionary, and catechism.

The Jesuit reductions can be said to have originated in the early seventeenth century when the governor of Asunción, Hernando de Arias, and Bishop Lizárraga asked for Jesuit missionaries for Paraguay. In 1609 three Jesuits began the first mission at San Ignacio Guazú in southern Paraguay. Between 1628 and 1632 the Jesuits founded fifteen missions in the province of Guairá, thirteen of which unfortunately were within the borders of Brazil. Although Brazil, as a Portuguese possession, was theoretically subject to the crown of Spain, the latter's control over the Brazilians was tenuous at best. In 1627 and 1631 the paulistas—townsmen of São Paulo, also called *bandeirantes*— launched destructive slaving expeditions against the missions. In 1631 the missions and their populations were removed westward to sites in Uruguay and Paraná, within Spanish jurisdiction. When the slave raids continued, the Jesuits secured the crown's permission to form an Indian militia. This later became one of the more controversial aspects of the reduction system. When the bandeirantes struck farther south, the Jesuit–Indian militia stopped them at the decisive battle of Mbororé in March 1641.

The majority of the Indians in the reductions were Guaraní. At the peak of their development the Guaraní reductions numbered about thirty and held as many as a hundred fifty thousand Indians. There were another ten missions among the Chiquito Indians.

The reductions aroused intense hostility. The Spaniards resented the deprivation of Indian labor and the control exercised by the Jesuits. Most of the reductions were self-supporting and the entire enterprise came to be an important economic entity, to such an extent that it has sometimes been termed the Jesuit Empire. Colonials accused the Jesuits of exploiting the natives for their own personal profit. There was also the fear that the reductions, with their autonomous towns and Indian militia, formed a state within a state. Fantastic stories circulated about the power, riches, and motivation of the Jesuits. The expulsion of the Jesuits in 1767 condemned the reductions to a slow death. The natives either reverted to their former ways or were absorbed into colonial society.

The Jesuit reductions still provoke controversy. For apologists, they are a lost arcadia, a socialistic jungle paradise of prosperous, self-sufficient natives under the guidance of men who had a genius for efficient administration. For others they are authoritarian, or at best paternalistic, controling and exploitive of native labor, wrenching the natives from their native culture into a European model. As usual the truth probably lies somewhere in between. The Jesuits' reputation as astute managers has often been exaggerated, though in general their administration was superior to the ordinary haciendas or sugar operations in the Spanish dominions. Undoubtedly the reductions were important in preventing the enslavement of the Indians, especially by raiders from Brazil. At the same time, the life was probably somewhat confining, though Jesuit rule seems to have been mild and exercised through native chiefs. There is no doubt that the reductions were economically important, though stories of vast Jesuit wealth were untrue.

## BRAZIL

Portuguese control of Brazil was limited by a number of factors. One was the absorption of Portugal by Spain between 1580 and 1640. Another was the fact that settlement was confined to the littoral and did not penetrate into the interior except for the gold mines of Minas Gerais. Penetration of the interior was left to the bandeirantes, outlaw bands that explored the interior, carried on trade, and raided Indian villages for slaves. A third factor was the presence of a considerable threat by the Protestant Dutch, who were intermittently at war with both Spain and Portugal.

In the early seventeenth century the Dutch began to turn their attention from the East Indies, where they had founded a trading empire that made the Netherlands one of the richest countries in Europe. In 1621 they turned their attention to the west and established the Dutch West India Company. The industrious and aggressive Dutch sent out trading colonies to the Hudson River, to the Amazon, and to Guiana. In 1624 a large expedition commanded by Jacob Willekens and Piet Hein captured Bahia but were driven out the following year. In 1629 the Dutch began the conquest of a large portion of the Brazilian "bulge." In that year they launched an expedition against Pernambuco and then extended their conquest from the mouth of the Amazon to São Francisco. Taking over the tobacco and sugar plantations of the area, they began an intensive exploitation. In addition, missionaries from the Dutch Reformed Church began working in the area. Like the Jesuits they worked at both christianizing and europeanizing the natives. The Dutch presence, however, did not last long enough for them to leave any permanent imprint. In 1636 Prince Maurice of Nassau, an outstanding administrator, became governor of the area, and it seemed as if permanent Dutch sovereignty was assured. This, however, was not to be. The independence of Portugal from Spain in 1640 awoke a slumbering Brazilian nationalism. The colonials themselves began the war to drive out the intruders. At the same time, the decline of the golden years of the Dutch republic in Europe made it increasingly difficult for them to continue their colonial adventures. By 1654 the Dutch had been expelled and promise of western colonies and wealth disappeared. Portugal was then free to develop its colony. In the seventeenth century sugar became for Brazil what silver was in that same century for New Spain and Peru.

The missionaries began to move inland in the seventeenth century. The Jesuits and Franciscans were joined in this endeavor by two other missionary groups, the Oratorians and the Capuchins. The Oratory, founded in the sixteenth century by the Italian Philip Neri, was not a religious order in the strict sense of the term but rather a grouping of diocesan clergy. Their orientation had not previously been missionary and the Brazilian mission seems to have been the only one in which they were prominent. The Capuchins were an offshoot of the Franciscans, the result of one of the many reform movements that had taken place in the Franciscan order. Prior to 1698 the majority of them in Brazil were French; after 1705 they were replaced by Italians. The Capuchins were also unique in that they were "apostolic missionaries," a term that indicated direct dependence on Propaganda rather than the crown. Both the Oratorians and the Capuchins were active in the interior of Pernambuco. In the seventeenth century the Carmelites, Franciscans, and Jesuits carried on the missions in the Amazon region.

The Jesuits, in particular, sought to isolate the Indians and to provide a protective network against enslavement. When the Jesuits made public a papal bull condemning Indian slavery, they were expelled from São Paulo in 1640. In Ymaranho and Pará, where they were the predominant missionaries, they were driven out by angry colonials in 1661. After a brief return, they were expelled again in 1684. These incidents, and the anti-Jesuit feeling that lingered, laid the groundwork for their eventual expulsion from all Portuguese domains in the eighteenth century.

With regard to the missions the seventeenth century was marked by conflicts between the Holy See and Portugal over the padroado. The papacy was seeking to assert its own control over the missions, particularly by the establishment of the Sacred Congregation for the Propagation of the Faith (more commonly called the Propaganda) in 1622. The conflicts came about after 1640 when Spain refused to recognize Portuguese independence and persuaded the Holy See to do the same. Most of the clashes, however, occurred in the Portuguese East Indies rather than Brazil. One unfortunate effect was that new bishops were not appointed when dioceses fell vacant. In 1668 both Spain and Rome formally recognized Portuguese independence and the situation eased somewhat.

## CONVENTS IN BRAZIL

In view of the fact that the Portuguese outlook toward convents was almost the same as the Spanish, it is surprising that no convent was founded in Brazil until 1677. One reason for the delay was the crown's fear that they would hinder the population growth of the colony. As with the role of women in the Spanish dominions, generalizations about the seclusion and oppression of women in Brazilian society are suspect. Much depended on social class, and women figured as owners of sugar mills and cattle ranches. This usually occurred through widowhood or inheritance. Still, marriage or the convent was the ideal in Portuguese and Brazilian society.

The first convent, Santa Clara do Destêrro in Bahia, was also the only one until 1733. It catered to the upper classes and in many ways offered a life preferable to marriage. As in some Spanish American convents, life was freer, many of the nuns were related, and there were dramas and musical recitals. The convent was also the sole source of female education. Observance was sometimes lax. The convent also had an economic function, especially through moneylending, but it was never so strong or extensive as in the Spanish dominions.

## THE BROTHERHOODS

Like the Spanish cofradías the Brazilian *irmandades* (brotherhoods or confraternities) played an important social and religious role. They were sometimes organized according to race or craft, in which case they had somewhat the character of a guild though some were open to all. Some were also connected with the established religious orders. These were known as third orders (tertiaries), that of the Franciscans being the most famous. The brotherhoods built and endowed chapels and churches and engaged in charitable works. Like the convents, some became wealthy through legacies and shrewd investment and acted as moneylenders. Their patronal feasts were often the occasion for lavish celebrations. The most famous brotherhood in Brazil was the Santa Casa da

Misericordia, which had been founded in Lisbon in 1498. It had branches throughout the Portuguese empire, many of which were quite wealthy.

## ANTÔNIO VIEIRA AND THE JESUITS IN MARANHÃO

One of the greatest churchmen in colonial Brazil was the Jesuit Antônio Vieira. He was born at Lisbon in 1608 of a working-class family with some black ancestry. For the first thirty-two years of his life, Portugal was under Spanish rule. At the age of six he came to the New World with his parents. In 1623, while a student at the Jesuit college at Bahia, he was attracted to the religious life after having heard a hellfire-and-damnation sermon, the sort of apocalyptic preaching that appealed to him throughout his life. Shortly afterward he entered the Society of Jesus and took his vows in 1625. In addition to the ordinary vows of poverty, celibacy, and obedience, he took a special one to work among the Indians and black slaves. To that end he learned at least two of the native languages. Despite his desire to work among the natives and the blacks, he spent a year teaching at the Jesuit college at Olinda. During that time the Dutch, whose war with Spain naturally included Portugal, were campaigning along the Brazilian coast and occupying some of it, with the threat of the establishment of Dutch Protestantism in the area. In these years the Dutch occupied about half of Brazil. Vieira wrote accounts of these campaigns to his superiors in Europe. During his course of studies he managed to give some missions to the Indians near Bahia and to the slaves in a sugar mill in the Reconcavo area.

In 1634 he was ordained a priest and within a short time had earned a reputation as an effective and popular preacher. He played a major role in the defense of Bahia against the Dutch in 1638 and preached the sermon in honor of the Portuguese victory. In addition to celebrating Portuguese Catholic victories, his sermons also denounced corruption in the local administration and the poor condition of the soldiery. In 1640 Portugal reclaimed its independence of Spain and concluded a truce with the Dutch, though the latter retained control of large parts of Brazil. Vieira was chosen to be a member of the delegation that went to Lisbon to pledge Brazil's loyalty to the new king, João IV. The Jesuit soon became very influential with the new monarch, became a close counselor, and maintained an unwavering devotion to him throughout his reign. The king came to depend on him in a special way for advice on Brazilian matters. In addition, he also became a popular preacher in Lisbon. His sermons covered patriotic and apocalyptic themes and condemned abuses in government and society. In 1644 he was named court preacher, and his sermons pictured João IV as the fulfillment of biblical prophecies that foretold the recapture of the Holy Land and the inauguration of a universal Christian kingdom. After the king's death in 1656, Vieira's messianic vision led him to affirm that the king would rise from the dead to begin the fifth biblical monarchy under Portuguese hegemony.

Such eminence and influence were bound to create enemies. In part this was because of his stand on the war with the Dutch (renewed in 1645) and Castile, which had continued since the regaining of independence. Vieira insisted that peace should be made with the Dutch because of their overwhelming economic and naval superiority. He suggested that the king attempt to purchase those areas of Brazil still under Dutch control. As a means of raising the money, he advocated toleration for crypto-Jews and New Christians, some of whom had migrated because of pressure from the Inquisition. When the Portuguese in Pernambuco revolted against the Dutch, Vieira opposed royal support for the rebels. All of these positions were very unpopular in Lisbon. Despite this he retained the king's confidence and in 1646 was part of an embassy to The Hague to negotiate the purchase of Pernambuco with the Dutch. The mission failed.

On a second mission to Holland in 1647 he was captured by English pirates and taken to Dover. After gaining an overview of English life, he made his way back to Portugal. In 1649, in order to finance the war and to protect Portuguese shipping against the Dutch, João IV organized a chartered company for the Brazil trade, making use largely of Jewish capital. This move proved effective but was highly unpopular. Vieira's involvement in politics within the Society of Jesus almost brought about his expulsion, something that was prevented only by direct royal intervention.

In 1650 he went to Rome as part of a secret mission, one aim of which was to weaken Spanish rule in Naples. Again his diplomatic efforts were a failure, and he had to flee Rome to avoid assassination. In 1652 he was allowed to go to Maranhão to reestablish the Jesuit mission, which had been vacant for three years. He spent nine years on the mission, except for one brief visit back to the homeland, and proved himself a zealous and devoted missionary. He strenuously fought the efforts of the colonists to enslave the local Indians for work on the plantations. Shortly before Vieira's arrival the royal governor, Baltasar de Sousa Pereira, had also come with orders to free all enslaved Indians. The result was such an uproar on the part of the colonists that the order had to be suspended. It was at that time that Vieira arrived, armed by the king with extensive authority to organize the missions and Indian labor.

Because of the intense reaction of the colonists, in 1653 the king issued a law that specified the causes for which Indians could legally be held captive. Most of these, such as impeding the spread of the gospel or allying themselves with Portugal's enemies, had already become classic in Iberian law systems. No time limit was given for the captivity, with the result that it became de facto slavery. Needless to say, the colonials had elastic interpretations of the various causes. Vieira returned to Lisbon to lobby against the law, and in 1655 a compromise version was promulgated. Slavery was not outlawed, nor were all the conditions of a just war (the essential element in enslavement) specified. What the law did, however, was even more galling to the colonists. It delegated control over the Indians exclusively to the Jesuits, which in the case of Maranhão meant Vieira.

This law, plus further enabling legislation the same year, incensed both the colonists and the other religious—specifically the friars, who were hostile to Vieira. During the period of his control, the Indians were gathered together in aldeias. The aldeamento or aldeia system was similar to the congregación of New Spain and the Jesuit reductions of Paraguay. They were villages that were simultaneously mission settlements. The Indians were removed, or "reduced" from their nomadic way of life, sometimes by force, more often by persuasion, and gathered in villages that were also mission settlements. There they were instructed in Catholicism, usually twice a day, and taught European ways. One purpose of the aldeias, as with their counterparts in other parts of Latin America, was to keep the neophytes separate from pagans and the Portuguese. There was fear of corruption by both parties and, in the case of the Portuguese, the additional danger of enslavement. By the end of 1655 the Jesuits controlled fifty-four such aldeias. By the end of the seventeenth century, there may have been as many as sixty thousand Indians in the aldeias.

Vieira also kept the king informed of the depredations of the colonists and the corruption of local officials. He wrote that it would be better for the entire colony to collapse rather than be supported by Indian slavery: "For it is better to live by the sweat of one's own brow than by another's blood."[2] He did not, however, have the same radical attitude with regard to black slavery. In the latter case he was more intent on alleviating the abuses involved in it and does not appear to have condemned it as intrinsically wrong.

Vieira's preaching was characterized by an apocalyptic and millenarian outlook, similar to that of Mendieta and the Franciscans of New Spain in the previous century. The Jesuit viewed Portugal as the fifth universal monarchy, which would bring about the conversion of the natives of the New World. For this reason he believed in the justice of colonization, without which evangelization would have been impossible.

As a missionary Vieira had his great success with the Nheengaíbas Indians on the island of Marajó. They had previously been hostile to both Portuguese and missionaries and allied with the Dutch. Vieira was able to overcome this hostility, and they refused to communicate with any Portuguese except through him. Despite this victory for Portuguese control of Brazil, the colonists hated Vieira for his championing of the Indians against slavery and exploitation. The death of King João IV in November 1656 robbed Vieira of his principal supporter. The colonists, who believed that they were condemned to poverty because of Vieira's restrictions on Indian slavery, turned on the Jesuits. A colonial uprising resulted in the imprisonment of most of the Jesuits and some, including Vieira, narrowly escaped lynching. They were deported to Portugal in September 1661.

Vieira's reception at the court in Lisbon was initially favorable, since the widow of João IV, who was then queen regent, supported him. A palace revolution in 1662, however, brought his enemies to power, and the crown prince became King Afonso VI. Because the king was hostile to Vieira, the latter's enemies began to work against him and his pro-Indian laws. A new law of 12 September 1663 undid some of the pro-Indian legislation and returned the situation to that of 1653. The power of the Jesuits was curtailed and Vieira was not allowed to return to Brazil.

The Inquisition, which had been antagonistic because of the Jesuit's toleration of New Christians, arrested him. Although suffering from ill health, he defended himself strenuously during a two-year investigation. Ultimately, he was convicted of Judaism and other errors and sentenced to a loss of his faculties for preaching and to imprisonment in a Jesuit residence. He was soon released, however, when another palace revolution in 1667 brought Pedro II to the throne and returned power to Vieira's supporters.

Though released from imprisonment, he no longer enjoyed the same prestige and authority as before. He went to Rome to plead the cause of the New Christians before the pope. Though he secured a suspension of inquisitorial procedures against them, he was not able to obtain a permanent alleviation of the persecution. He returned to Portugal in 1675, and though his power was not so great as previously, he managed to secure an important victory. In 1680, apparently at his instigation, the crown issued one of the most important pieces of Indian legislation of the colonial period. It outlawed enslavement of Indians for any reason whatsoever. Those who violated the Indians' freedom were subject to arrest and deportation. All Indian slaves were to be freed and, if Catholic, sent to aldeias. Indians captured in just and authorized wars were to be treated as prisoners of war, not slaves. The law, however, did provide for a system of compulsory Indian labor. Unfortunately, it also provided for the sale of five to six hundred black African slaves each year. Finally, the Jesuits were given a virtual monopoly over the missions and the Christian Indians.

The legislation caused a brief revolt in Maranhão, during which the Jesuits were expelled. After it was suppressed, the Jesuits opened the interior to other missionaries and became more cooperative with the settlers in the allotment of Indian labor.

Vieira himself was permitted to return to Brazil in 1681. There he continued to champion the cause of the Indians and to engage in furious battles with the colonists. He died at Bahia on 18 July 1697, at the age of eighty-nine. The Jesuits were able to maintain themselves in the mission without appreciable opposition until 1755.

Vieira's personality was similar to that of Bartolomé de las Casas. Both men were strong and combative. Both were intensely dedicated to the cause of the Indian. Both were alienated from their countrymen over the issue. Both had an apocalyptic and millenarian mentality, Vieira more so than Las Casas. Neither suffered fools gladly, and both were often intemperate in their condemnation of enemies. Both lived long lives and enjoyed the favor of their sovereigns. And both were appreciated more after their deaths than during their lifetimes.

# 7

## THE AGE OF THE ENLIGHTENMENT AND BENEVOLENT DESPOTISM, 1700–1776

### THE AGE OF REASON

The eighteenth century was a time of intellectual ferment throughout Europe known by the global term *Enlightenment*. It was also called the Age of Reason because of its emphasis on reason as the test of all things, and it found its greatest expression in France. Characterized by a rational, critical attitude toward all existing institutions, it spawned a group of reformist thinkers known as *philosophes*. In general they were hostile to what was known as the Old Regime—the governmental organization, the stratified social hierarchy, the economic theories, the religious dogma that had come down from the age of absolutism. Everything was subjected to the test of reason, and most contemporary structures were found wanting. Voltaire satirized the follies of society, Montesquieu inquired into the nature of government, Diderot attempted to synthesize existing knowledge in the *Encyclopédie*, Beccaria advocated rational reform in penology, Beaumarchais satirized the follies of the nobility, and Rousseau exalted the noble savage and total freedom. "Man is born free but everywhere is in chains."

Subscribing to the political theories of the Enlightenment, the monarchs of the eighteenth century saw themselves as benevolent despots, the stern but just fathers who always sought the best good for their peoples. The test of reason was applied to all institutions, even those that had been considered most holy. Science came to enjoy greater prestige, and there was increased interest in public health, scientific observation, and technology. Cartesian rationalism and dualism replaced a decadent scholasticism among the intellectuals. Theology was equated with superstition. These ideas, of course, were confined to a relatively small group of intellectuals, among whom the clergy constituted a large proportion.

Not surprisingly, much Enlightenment thought was hostile to religion, which was regarded as a superstitious relic of the past, closely identified with the Old Regime. There was a special antagonism toward religious orders, which were viewed as useless for the contemporary world. The vows taken by religious, especially the vow of obedience, were considered repugnant to human freedom. The Jesuits, because of their widespread influence and association with the status quo, were the special object of Enlightenment hostility.

The crowned heads of the eighteenth century accepted the Enlightenment, at least in those aspects that fitted their policies. They attempted to apply its principles to government and the good of their states but without accepting all of its criticisms of existing institutions. They accepted technology and progress but kept their grip on power. Thus Catherine the Great had herself vaccinated publicly in order to calm the fears of her subjects, but during her reign the lot of the serfs grew worse. In the Spanish empire there grew an interest in all things scientific, but the major achievements, such as a mass immunization program against smallpox in New Spain, fall outside the chronological limits of this study.

Enlightenment thought came to the New World through the writings of the philosophes. Despite laws against the importation of such books, they appear to have been widespread. By the eighteenth century the Inquisition had lost much of its effectiveness, and in certain areas of the New World it was no match for the economic power of booksellers and importers. Often those charged with enforcing the laws were the ones most sympathetic to the new ideas. In general this thought appealed to and affected a small minority, mostly upper-class criollos and clergy—the latter, surprisingly, becoming a bastion of liberal thought. Yet these were among the most influential classes in the Indies, and they would play important roles in the wars of independence. Membership in Masonic lodges brought together persons of similar persuasion, including clergy, and provided a means of propagating Enlightenment, and eventually revolutionary, thought.

The Enlightenment had less impact in Brazil than in Spanish America. It circulated primarily through intellectual academies dedicated to the study of literary and historical subjects. Partly because of this limited influence, Brazil was to gain its independence and have a history quite different from that of the rest of South America.

In Spain the arrival of the Age of Reason corresponded with a change of dynasty. The Bourbon monarchs who came to the throne after 1701 brought with them the ideas of the French Enlightenment. Paradoxically, in their quest for a more efficient and rational government, they unwittingly violated the social contract with the colonials that had existed since Habsburg times and thus laid the groundwork for the eventual independence of Latin America.

## THE BOURBON CENTURY IN SPAIN

In 1700 King Charles II, the last of the Spanish Habsburgs, died. A tragic result of dynastic interbreeding, he had been all but retarded for most of his life. Simple-minded, superstitious, impressionable, scarcely able to write his name, and totally unable to father a child, he was called *El Hechizado*, the Bewitched, by subjects seeking an explanation for his wretched condition. All Europe knew that with his death there would be a general move to claim or divide his patrimony. The potential for wealth and power seemed limitless. Although Spain had been in a long period of decline and was no longer the formidable power it had been even at the beginning of the century, it still possessed vast territories and wealth. A revitalized Spain, under a new and energetic dynastic, could still play an important role in European affairs.

The pathetic king passed his last days in a nightmarish atmosphere of political intrigue. There were two claimants to the soon-to-be vacant throne. One was Charles of Austria. His claim was the lesser one. The other was Philip of Anjou, the grandson of Louis XIV of France. Charles's candidacy opened the possibility that the empire of Charles V could be revived by a union of the empire with Spain and its possessions. At first that was not a real fear, because Charles was not directly in line to become emperor. Some fortuitous deaths, however, brought him into the direct succession. Equally alarming to European diplomats was the possibility of a union between France and Spain. Spain under the torpid Habsburgs was one thing; Spain under the energetic and modernizing Bourbons would be something else altogether.

The suspense lasted until the very end. As the pitiable king lay dying, a macabre scene in which partisans of each candidate sought to persuade him that his eternal salvation lay in choosing one or the other candidate was enacted. The French faction won, and when the will was read Philip was named king. In one of the most tactless remarks in European diplomatic history, the Spanish ambassador at Versailles is supposed to have said *"Il n'y a plus de Pyrénées"* (There are no more Pyrenees). That was exactly what the major European powers feared, and it became immediately apparent that they would fight to prevent the union. Louis XIV sought to forestall this by a preemptive strike and thus began the War of the Spanish Succession (1701–1713).

The war was long, destructive, and worldwide (in the English colonies it was known as Queen Anne's War). It brought glory to England and its great general Marlborough. It brought near-bankruptcy and near-total defeat to Louis XIV. The Spaniards themselves supported Philip of Anjou, now known as Philip V,

with the notable exception of the Catalans. Strongly under separatist senti-
ment, they supported Charles. A general peace was signed at Utrecht in 1713.
From the point of view of Spain its most important provisions granted the
Spanish throne to Philip (with the proviso that the thrones of Spain and France
could never be united) and awarded Gibraltar to Britain. Thus began the
Bourbon century.

The first two Bourbon monarchs, Philip V (r. 1700–1746) and Ferdinand VI
(r. 1746–1759), sought to revitalize the Spain they inherited, a country devastated by an empty treasury, foreign wars, a sclerotic bureaucracy, and internal
revolt. Philip V approached these problems with vigor and intelligence. In
order to stimulate the economy, he doubled the sailings of the Manila galleon
(from one to two a year) and made Cádiz rather than Seville the port of entry for
the New World. (Cádiz had better harbor facilities.) He also abolished restrictions on the number of ships and the frequency of sailings between Spain and
its New World dependencies. Spain began an economic revival, accompanied
by a modest industrialization in some provinces. As business expanded and
competition increased, prices began to fall and smuggling decreased. Crown
revenue was enhanced both by increased taxes in Spain and by a revived
commerce with the New World. In New Spain there was a dramatic revival of
silver production. Sugar, cotton, tobacco (a government monopoly after 1764),
and dyes constituted the staples of trade between the Indies and Spain. For
Lima, which lost its privileged position in South American trade, the reforms
were less happy. Buenos Aires, strategically more important, became a rival
port. There was, in general, a movement toward a moderate free trade, though
the extent of this has often been exaggerated.

The first Bourbons introduced French governmental institutions and practices. The old administrative system was replaced, at least in part, by the
intendants, a system first devised by Cardinal Richelieu in the previous century. The Council of the Indies was abolished in favor of something closer to a
cabinet system. New Granada became a viceroyalty in 1740, as did the south-
ernmost regions in 1776 as the viceroyalty of La Plata. The sale of public office,
a Habsburg expedient for raising cash, was ended, and all offices were theoretically awarded on the basis of merit. Tax farming, an oppressive practice
based on the letting of private contracts for tax collection, was abolished, and
tax collection became a direct governmental responsibility. The Bourbons
brought a high degree of centralization to government.

These tendencies reached their peak in the reign of Charles III (1759–
1788), generally regarded as the greatest of the Bourbon monarchs of Spain.
Firmly devoted to the ideas of the Enlightenment and to a rational restructuring of government, he introduced an ongoing series of reforms that paradoxically weakened the allegiance of the colonials to the mother country. He and
his ministers saw absolutism as the best means for introducing reform and
governmental efficiency. The solution to Spain's problems lay in an all-

powerful king, unhindered by the social contract and balance of special interests by which the Habsburgs had ruled. This involved extensive changes in colonial government, including the establishment of a standing army for defense. Increased centralization enhanced the power of the state. An important facet of this policy was the total subordination of the church to the state, the final culmination of regalism and the patronato system. Any organization, such as the Jesuits, that stood in the way of that power was ruthlessly eliminated.

In 1764–1765 the crown broke the monopoly of the Cádiz merchants on colonial trade, at the same time opening more ports in the New World to trade with Spain. Some taxes and customs duties were lowered. The cost of mercury was lowered, thus stimulating the silver industry and bringing about a rapid recovery. In 1790, after Charles III's death, the board of trade (*casa de contratación*), which had controlled colonial trade since 1503, was abolished.

Intendants were sent to the Americas to work with and under the viceroys. The viceroyalties themselves were subdivided into intendancies: New Spain with twelve, Peru with ten, La Plata with nine. Their principal task was to improve the financial administration of the intendancy. A regular bimonthly mail service between the colonies and the mother country was inaugurated.

The advent of the Bourbons brought Spain into the vortex of European affairs, including its wars. Although the Treaty of Utrecht forbade the union of the French and Spanish crowns, the Spanish Bourbons became allied with their French relatives by two agreements known as the Family Compacts (1733, 1762). Faced by the rising military and mercantile power of Great Britain (and, in Spain's case, aching to reclaim Gibraltar), the two Bourbon branches fought a series of commercial and colonial wars in the eighteenth century. Britain, in a special way, sought to break Spain's stranglehold on New World commerce. The War of Jenkins's Ear, which began in 1739 and then became part of the War of the Austrian Succession, was fought in both Europe and the Caribbean. The conclusion of the war in 1748 was in reality little more than a truce. The decisive conflict was the Seven Years' War (1756–1763), which actually began in North America, where it was known as the French and Indian War, two years before it did so in Europe. The Treaty of Paris, which ended the war, drastically altered the American scene. France was for all practical purposes eliminated from the New World by the loss of Canada and Louisiana. Spain, which had lost Cuba to Britain in the last years of the war, was able to regain it only by trading it for Florida. At the same time Spain received an uneasy and rather tenuous possession of Louisiana.

These wars made the government of Charles III acutely aware of the need for effective defense of the Indies. New steps were taken in the direction of colonization. As so often happened in the history of settlement, it was foreign pressure that caused the Spanish to send out both colonists and missionaries. Texas and California (where there was the additional fear of Russian penetration) became the foci of the renewed imperialism.

## THE VISITA OF JOSÉ DE GÁLVEZ

In 1765 Charles III sent José de Gálvez to New Spain as visitador-general; that is, with full powers to investigate local conditions and to institute necessary reforms. His primary purpose was to see to the economy of New Spain and the defense of the frontiers, purposes that were interrelated and complementary. Gálvez was a capable and energetic man. He was also, however, ruthless, authoritarian, and totally peninsular in his outlook. His visit, lasting until 1770, accomplished a great deal but also left a residue of bitterness that finally found expression in the first war of independence.

One of Gálvez's principal concerns was the defense of the northern borders of Spain's dependencies. In 1762 Charles III had established a standing army for New Spain, the first such in that colony's history. This army, however, was recruited by a form of conscription, the dread *leva*, which fell most heavily on the poorer classes and was the source of much discontent. It also required additional income, raised by taxes, that fed the growing antagonism toward the mother country. The visitador also instituted a number of reforms into government. He appointed a subvisitador for Guatemala to regain some of the royal control that over the passage of time had slipped to the local authorities, especially the merchants. On his return to Spain he restructured the northern areas into the interior provinces to form a strong buffer against British and Russian penetration.

Vastly more far-reaching in impact and long-term effect were some other instructions that Gálvez brought with him: the expulsion of the Jesuits.

## THE ANTI-JESUIT CAMPAIGN

### THE EXPULSION OF THE JESUITS FROM BRAZIL

The eighteenth century saw an increasing antagonism toward the Jesuits in many parts of Catholic Europe. The reasons were many and encompassed an entire spectrum of political and religious opinion. In seventeenth-century France the Jansenists, proponents of a form of Catholic puritanism, had engaged in full-scale combat with the Society. Blaise Pascal, in his classic *Provincial Letters*, had excoriated Jesuit theology and practices so devastatingly that the Society was never able to mount an adequate answer. In the eighteenth century, as the monarchs of the Enlightenment increased their power and extended it to every level of society, the Jesuits were seen as having too much power. Their work as educators, especially among the upper classes, gave them a strong following of devoted alumni. Since they often held positions as royal confessors, an extremely delicate and powerful post, they were regarded as involved in political and diplomatic matters. Because of their strong internationalism and devotion to the interests of the papacy, they were regarded as inimical to state interests. From Paraguay, where the reductions seemed to be a state within a state, to China, where they ran the royal observatory and were advisers to the emperors, the Jesuits presented the picture of a powerful, supranational establishment. Enlightenment thinkers viewed Jesuit education as antiquated at best, obscurantist at worse. This suspicion and antagonism was shared by many clergy, who resented the privileged position and independence of the Society. Bishop Palafox of Puebla in New Spain had sought to limit the Jesuits but failed. Jesuit theology was often considered "laxist" and detrimental to good morals.

The anti-Jesuit campaign began in Portugal under a prime minister who typified the Enlightenment, José Sebastião de Carvalho e Melo, the marquess of Pombal (1699–1782). He was born near Lisbon and as a young man studied under the Jesuits at Coimbra. For a while he worked for the royal academy of history and throughout the rest of his life often justified political decisions with historical precedent. A posting as ambassador to Great Britain (1740–1744) left him with a combined admiration and dislike for the British. In 1750 King José I (1750–1777) named him Secretary of State for Foreign Affairs and War, but he soon became the dominant personality in all branches of government. He dominated even the king himself. He ran roughshod over his opponents and could tolerate no opposition or criticism. For almost three decades he was the virtual dictator of Portugal and its dependencies.

When Pombal came to power, Brazil was in a depression and revenues to Portugal were declining. Pombal wanted to reinvigorate the economy through reform, efficiency, and centralization. Like the ministers of the Spanish Bourbons, he believed that an absolute monarchy was the only way in which reform and progress could be introduced. As in Spain, an essential part of this was the total subjugation of church to state. A ruthless and ambitious man, his ever-growing hostility toward the Society of Jesus was part of a general plan to subject the Church in Portugal entirely to royal control. It is difficult to trace the personal motives for Pombal's anti-Jesuit policies. For the most part they seem to have been reasons of state. The Jesuits were the most independent of the religious orders and the one most bound to the papacy. As such they were an obstacle to the royal policies of the age of absolutism.

The Jesuits were especially numerous and powerful in Brazil and were to be found everywhere except Minas Gerais. Major landowners and slaveowners (their black slaves were said to have numbered in the thousands), their economic power was formidable. One of their principal enterprises, as in New Spain, was sugar-growing and refining; they had five plantations in Bahia alone. And as in the Spanish possessions, these enterprises were efficient and profitable—all the more so because of special exemptions and privileges the Society enjoyed. Jesuits schools and churches were to be found everywhere. The Jesuits also took a strong stance in favor of the freedom of the Indians (though not for the blacks), a factor that did not endear them to the colonists. In general, their wealth, power, and status aroused a great deal of envy.

In 1750 the Treaty of Madrid between Portugal and Spain brought some of the Paraguayan reductions under the control of Portugal. Under the terms of the treaty Spain was supposed to evacuate the Guaraní Indians on these reductions to Spanish territory. Resisting the forcible transfer, the Guaraní revolted in 1754. This was suppressed two years later by combined Spanish–Portuguese forces. Pombal blamed the Jesuits for fomenting the revolt. In 1755 the Jesuits were deprived of their temporal authority over the Indians in Brazil and total liberty was decreed for the natives. This meant in practice that they were free to leave the reductions, but it also weakened their defenses against enslavement and exploitation. In 1757 Pombal initiated a two-year campaign aimed at restricting the Jesuits' activities and removing them from any influence on public life. An assassination attempt against the life of the king in 1758, some of whose protagonists had Jesuit connections, was used against them. Finally, on 3 September 1759, a secret decree of expulsion was drawn up and communicated to officials in Brazil. The campaign was carried out brutally and with great suffering. Some 670 Jesuits were exiled and their properties confiscated.

The loss of the Jesuits left the Church without any effective defense against the incursions of the state. Pombal carried on a somewhat milder campaign against other orders, such as the Mercedarians. Neither the diocesan church structure, which shortsightedly saw advantages in the expulsion, nor the laity offered any resistance to the move, which seems to have enjoyed widespread approval. Within a few years Pombal had all but detached the Portuguese church from the papacy and made it a state institution. He even went so far as to restrict the number of candidates for the priesthood in order to eliminate competition with the army. In 1768 the crown decreed that its permission was necessary for each admission to the priesthood. Unfortunately, the short-term wealth that came to the crown from the confiscations was not used in a farsighted way. It served to increase many upper-class land holdings and bind their owners to the royal policies; there was no attempt at an equitable distribution or a long-term policy of development. Ultimately, however, Pombal lived to see most of his work undone and himself disgraced.

Pombal's campaign demonstrated the weakness of both the Jesuits and the papacy when faced with a ruthless and powerful adversary. Other states followed his example. In 1764 the Jesuits were declared illegal in France, but the members were not exiled. Three years later it was the turn of the Spanish Jesuits. On 21 July 1773, under pressure from various European rulers, Pope Clement XIV issued the bull *Dominus ac Redemptor*, which suppressed the Society of Jesus throughout the Catholic Church.

## THE EXPULSION OF THE JESUITS FROM THE SPANISH DOMINIONS

A similar campaign was carried out in the Spanish empire and for the same reasons. In 1766 there was a series of riots in Madrid called the "Hat and

Cloak" riots. The favorite minister of Charles III, the Prince of Esquilache (originally Squilacci; he was Italian) blamed the Jesuits. The event was exploited as a reason for removing the Jesuits entirely from all areas ruled by Spain. When Gálvez arrived in New Spain, he carried secret orders for the expulsion. At the same time sealed orders were sent to royal officials throughout the hemisphere to be opened on the same day, 25 June 1767. These mandated the immediate expulsion of all Jesuits and confiscation of their property. The orders were carried out with appalling dispatch and efficiency. Some 220 Jesuits were rounded up and exiled to the Papal States or any state that would accept them. Many, and in some areas the majority, were criollos. In one brutal blow an entire educational and missionary system was deprived of its personnel. Other orders, especially the Franciscans, valiantly attempted to replace them, but their manpower was never sufficient.

In Peru the expulsion was carried out with similar efficiency and ruthlessness under the direction of the authoritarian and sybaritic viceroy, Don Manuel de Amat. The Jesuits left behind some eighteen colegios and several seminaries, another body blow to the colonial educational system.

The Spanish crown experienced a short-term windfall of wealth from the confiscated Jesuit estates, but it never lived up to expectations. Since the Jesuit lands and estates were among the best-administered in Spanish America, the long-term effects were negative. Even more disastrous for Spain was the long-term impact on the criollos throughout Latin America, for whom it was a thunderclap without warning. The reactions of clergy and laity to the destruction of the Jesuits were quite different from those in Brazil. Many were graduates of Jesuit schools and retained a strong loyalty to their former teachers. The criollos were by force of situation and circumstance socially conservative. They now saw the crown not as the protector of their liberties and the font of justice but as a threat to an entire way of life. Particularly in New Spain, the reforms of Gálvez were seen by the criollos as a violation of the implicit social contract between ruler and ruled in Habsburg times. These violations included the standing army and rural militias, both of which required conscription and taxation, burdens that fell primarily on the lower classes; the increased control of the Church, including the absorption of all tithe revenue; the decree on the universal use of Spanish rather than the native tongues; and the increased centralization of authority and the consequent lessening of the power of the criollos, whom Gálvez disliked and distrusted.

Even more damaging to royal interests in the long run was the alienation of the clergy. As in Portugal, the demise of the Jesuits left the Church open to the final triumph of regalism. Most of them were criollos, many were influenced by Enlightenment thought, and many felt their positions, and their Church, to be under attack. In Michoacán in 1767 this led to insurrections, which were brutally suppressed by Gálvez. Some ninety leaders were executed, seven hundred rebels sentenced to life imprisonment, and another hundred exiled. Peace was restored but the memory of the events, with their cries of "Death to the Gachupines [Spaniards]" lived on. It is of great importance that in the year of the expulsion and rebellions, a twenty-four-year-old student, Miguel Hidalgo, was attending the Jesuit colegio in Valladolid (today Morelia), Michoacán. As a criollo, priest, and military leader he would lead the first Mexican war of independence against Spain.

## SPANISH EXPANSION AND EVANGELIZATION IN THE NORTH

### TEXAS

One of the northern areas that Spain now sought to protect was Texas. As in other areas, the method used was to be a combination of missionary work and military force. The first move into the area was at the end of the seventeenth century to counter the French threat posed by the explorations of Robert Cavelier, sieur de la Salle. In 1689 an expedition led by Alonso de León left Monterrey for Texas to locate the French intrusion. With it went a Franciscan, Father Damián Massanet, who left an account of the expedition. It was discovered, however, that the settlement the French had made in Texas had been destroyed by the Indians. Massanet attempted to work among the Hasinai Indians (whose word for greeting was the source of the name *Texas*) but found them too hostile. Another expedition in 1690 went to northeast Texas and established two missions on the Neches River. Texas was made a frontier province the following year, but because there were no further signs of French intrusion, it was abandoned in 1693.

The French threat was renewed in the early eighteenth century. The French governor of the lower Mississippi Valley, Antoine de la Mothe Cadillac, initiated expeditions to the west, partly in hope of opening up trade with Spanish settlers. The Spaniards reacted with alarm and in 1715 made plans to occupy east Texas. An expedition was launched in the following year, with eight Franciscan priests and three lay brothers from the missionary college of Querétaro. The friars were under the leadership of Fray Isidro Félix Espinosa and Francisco Hidalgo. The latter had worked among the Hasinai when Texas was still the short-lived frontier province. These friars were later joined by one of the greatest of the borderland missionaries, Fray Antonio Margil de Jesús.

Margil (1657–1726), who had joined the Franciscans in Spain in 1673, was ordained to the priesthood in 1682. He came to New Spain in 1683 and arrived at Veracruz just after it had been sacked by pirates. In 1684 he assumed direction of the missionary college of Querétaro, which had been founded the year before by Antonio Llinás. Its purpose was to train mobile missionaries to work with Indians who were dispersed over a wide area and to bring new methods to bear on the task. Margil also developed two other missionary colleges, that of Cristo Crucificado in Guatemala City (1701) and that of Our Lady of Guadalupe in Zacatecas (1708). He also worked personally on missions in New Spain and Central America. He was famed for his holiness and zeal, and the cause of his canonization has been introduced.

The Spaniards established a presidio along the Neches and then four mission stations. The Franciscans soon added two more among the Adai and the Ais, both tribes that were close to the farthest limits of the French penetration. In 1718, at the suggestion of Fray Antonio de San Buenaventura Olivares, who was impressed by the location and the docility of the Indians, a mission and presidio were established at San Antonio. The Franciscans worked zealously in east Texas, but progress was slow, primarily because the Indians were nomadic. The Spaniards were not strong enough to enforce congregación, and the results remained meager for the next century.

## CALIFORNIA

Alta California was the last major area to be colonized and missionized by the Spaniards. Again, the reasons were based on military as much as religious motives. The Russians were beginning to establish posts in the northwest, and the British were showing interest in the area. In 1769 Gálvez ordered the occupation of California to forestall these intrusions. Gaspar de Portolá was appointed captain and Fray Junípero Serra (1713–1784), a Franciscan from Mallorca, the president of the future missions. The expedition that set out went in detachments by land and sea. Portolá and Serra went on the second land expedition. In 1769 a presidio and mission were founded at San Diego, although the establishment remained precarious for a number of years because of illness and the difficulty of bringing supplies. Within a year another expedition was sent from San Diego to lay claim to Monterey Bay and protect it from Russian or British intrusion. Soon after a land party discovered a magnificent bay to the north, where in 1776 Juan Bautista de Anza established the mission and presidio of San Francisco. Spanish expansion to the north eventually ran into a determined wall of British resistance. Ultimately eighteen missions were founded by Serra and his successor, Fermín Lasuén (1736–1803).

The California missions have been romanticized far more than any other Spanish enterprise. Contrary to popular belief, they were not founded one day's journey apart. The missions were not established according to any regular chronological or geographic pattern. They were set up where the Indians were. Although they served as hospices for travelers, they were not a chain of motels. The California missions came at the very end of Spanish expansion and evangelization. They were a very small part of the overall picture and numbered less than those that the Spanish had once had in Texas and Florida. Recent controversies surrounding the beatification of Serra have also added to the isolated view of these missions. Unfortunately, they have also overshadowed the work of Lasuén, who deserves as much credit as Serra for the work of the California missions.

## THE BOURBON CENTURY IN SOUTH AMERICA

The Bourbon reforms, especially the economic ones and the expulsion of the Jesuits, had the same impact in South America as in New Spain. In general, however, except for the reductions in Paraguay, this has not been so closely studied. There was nothing comparable to the Gálvez visita. As in New Spain, defense of the frontiers was a dominant concern, but it was directed against the Portuguese in Brazil. In 1724 the crown established the city of Montevideo in a half-hearted attempt to protect the borders from Portuguese expansion. The rivalry between the two powers increased as Spain began its recovery under the new dynasty.

In the area of administration there was some notable reorganization. In 1718 a new viceroyalty, that of Nueva Granada, was formed out of the northernmost provinces of South America. It was abolished shortly afterward and then revived permanently in 1740. It included Panama, Colombia, Ecuador, and Venezuela. In 1776 the crown erected the viceroyalty of La Plata, which covered Argentina, Paraguay, Uruguay, and part of Bolivia. As in the Northern Hemisphere, intendancies were also introduced.

## THE IMPACT OF THE EIGHTEENTH CENTURY

In both the Spanish and Portuguese dependencies the eighteenth century was a watershed. The impact, however, was not the same for both empires.

In both, the century saw the triumph of absolute monarchy. The power of the rulers, at least in theory, was unrestricted. This development was welcomed by reform-minded ministers, who saw it as the most effective way to introduce enlightened reforms and to cure the ills of both mother countries. Hence the first step was the removal of any institution or group that was independent of the monarchy and the second was the further subjugation of those that had already lost their independence. The expulsion and eventual extinction of the Jesuits was a major step in achieving the first goal. The Society of Jesus was numerous, wealthy, and influential. It was a natural target for the reformers of the Age of Enlightenment.

The loss of the Jesuits also meant the loss of the last of the Church's freedom. Throughout Ibero-America regalism was triumphant. Increasingly the last independence of the religious orders was diminished, and they were replaced in the missions by diocesan clergy, whose orientation was historically closer to the civil government. In the gold- and silver-producing regions in Brazil's south (Minas Gerais, Goiás, and Mato Grosso do Sul) all the missionaries in the eighteenth century were diocesan priests.

The impact of regalism and the extinction of the Jesuits was totally different in the Spanish and Portuguese New World. In the Portuguese world the onslaught of benevolent despotism and the Enlightenment was not accompanied, as it was in the Spanish world, by a change of dynasty. In Brazil antagonism toward the Society of Jesus had been festering for years, going back to the Jesuits' defense of the Indians in the seventeenth century. It was aggravated by their economic power, enhanced by special privileges. No tears were shed, either by settlers or the diocesan church structure, over the demise of the Society of Jesus.

It was quite different in Spanish America. The Jesuits were highly regarded for their missionary and educational work. Their alumni tended to remain strongly loyal. The expulsion of the Jesuits was accompanied by, and was almost the culmination of, a series of reforms that brought many criollos and Indians to near-revolt. These included the introduction of standing armies, conscription (which fell mostly on the lower classes), increased taxes to defray the cost of empire, increased centralization, and the triumph of regalism. The ruthless way in which the expulsions were carried out added to colonial resentment. Thus it is not surprising to find clergy in the forefront of criollo thought and even revolution. The two great heroes of Mexican independence, Hidalgo and Morelos, were both priests.

In Brazil missionary endeavor seems to have become somewhat stagnant in the eighteenth century, although generalizations can be suspect. There was further penetration into the back country, but the expulsion of the Jesuits and the overall weakening of the religious orders held back the missionary task. Even prior to their expulsion there had been signs of relaxation and falling interest on the part of the Jesuits. In the Spanish dominions the missions were extended into Texas and California, with apparent success. This, however, was in response to foreign threats and not the result of religious zeal determining public policy.

# 8

# THE MISSIONARY ENTERPRISE: AN OVERVIEW

One of the first things that strikes the researcher into Iberian missionary activity in the New World is the sheer magnitude of the task. That two relatively small nations, more or less on the periphery of Europe, could have done so much over such a large area in a relatively short space of time is nothing less than astounding.

This magnitude arose first from geography. For the Spanish this meant an empire that by the end of the sixteenth century stretched from Zacatecas, some 150 miles north of Mexico City, down to the tip of Argentina. By the eighteenth century the northern boundary had been pushed north of San Francisco and well into Texas. By any standard, the distances that had to be traversed were awesome. By the standards of the time they would appear to have been almost insurmountable.

A second major difficulty in the earliest years of both colonization and evangelization was that there were no traditional or established policies to draw from. Both church and state had to grope toward tactics, processes, and structures that would meet their needs in the New World. When Columbus met Ferdinand and Isabella at Barcelona on his return from his first voyage, no one had any idea what the extent of the new empire would become. Nor was any thought given, beyond immediate needs, to long-range plans for administration and bureaucracy. As a result both Spanish and Portuguese government of the newly conquered lands was improvisory. Although improvisation prevailed briefly, both nations soon came to have a rational and relatively effective colonial administration that, for all its defects, kept their empires together until the nineteenth century. This is all the more remarkable in that for the first century and a half it was done without the benefit of standing armies.

Improvisation also characterized the first missionary undertakings. The New World was the Catholic Church's first great experience in mission work since

120

the conversion of the Slavic peoples half a millennium before. There was relatively little background to draw on, few models to be copied. Again, within a relatively short space of time, the basic missionary program became well defined. In the Spanish dominions this definition came about in New Spain, which was in a real sense the proving ground for missionary methods.

Another factor, one that is perhaps not sufficiently treated in most histories of New World missions, was the crushing financial cost of founding and supporting missions and missionaries. An undertaking so vast required a sound financial base, which only the monarchs could provide. That such a base was established and even proved adequate is one of the wonders of the entire enterprise, all the more so in view of the precarious nature of the Spanish economy in the colonial period. In Spain financial support inevitably became part of the patronato, especially when the crown gained the right to collect tithes. These were redonated to the church according to a complex formula. In addition, however, there were individual grants, called *mercedes*, which were made in response to petitions from monasteries, churches, hospitals, convents, and other religious groups. In Brazil, in a special way, the challenge of supporting the missions and their institutions led to the involvement of the religious in commercial enterprises, such as sugar plantations. A similar process occurred among the Jesuits in New Spain. In exchange for the security and support given by the state, however, the Church gave up its freedom. The domination of the Spanish crown over the Church reached its climax under the Bourbons in the eighteenth century. In Brazil the domination was not quite so total, and there were missionaries whose primary accountability was to Rome, not to Lisbon.

The complexity of the task was aggravated by the bewildering variety of peoples and languages that were encountered: the misnamed Digger Indians of California, the sedentary and agricultural Pueblo peoples, the warlike Apaches and Yaqui, the high civilizations of central Mexico, the stubbornly resistant Mayas of southern Mexico and Guatemala, the centralized and hierarchical empire of the Incas, the formidable Guaraní of Paraguay, and the all-but-unconquerable Araucanians of Chile. These peoples had to be approached in their own languages and with at least a minimal concept of their culture and beliefs. The task of translating Christian European concepts into totally alien tongues and cultures was itself daunting. Indian and European lived on different sides of a major cognitive and psychological chasm. On a superficial level the friars solved this problem by simply incorporating Spanish words, such as *dios, espíritu santo*, or *obispo*, into the native languages. At other times the missionaries adapted native terms to Christian usage, but the result was often confusing. Among many of the New World Indians, for example, the idea of sin as a personal, willful violation of a divine law that merited punishment was incomprehensible. Whereas the Europeans saw the concepts of order and chaos as antithetical, the Aztecs saw them as part of an ongoing dialectical process. This was not confined to the New World. In the late sixteenth century the

Jesuits in China were encountering the same difficulty, one that the institutional Church was unable to handle.

Present-day researchers are showing the impact that translation into a native language had on religious belief. The very fact of using a native word subtly altered the religious concept toward the outlook, mentality, and world-view of the natives themselves. In the case of New Spain this has been called the nahuatilization of Christianity. There is also the implication that the missionaries themselves were affected by these sometimes arcane changes. In the post-Vatican II Church the idea that the evangelizer is to some extent evangelized by those to whom he or she preaches has gained some currency. It seems also to be a valid criterion for measuring the success of the missionary enterprise in Ibero-America.

This gap in understanding between evangelizers and evangelized may have worked in the natives' favor. The latter appeared to have accepted Christianity in its fullness, yet it was often only a veneer. This may have prevented the missionaries from fully understanding the syncretic process whereby Christianity was being mingled with native beliefs and practices, or it may have given them an excessive optimism about the success of their efforts.

The principal agents for the missionary endeavor were the religious. In a special way this meant the Franciscans and Jesuits. Although many bishops were deeply involved in missions and dedicated to their spread, the diocesan clergy as a whole were not, except in parts of Brazil. They belonged to an ecclesiastical system that was essentially postmissionary and presupposed a high degree of structure. The expulsion of the Jesuits from the Spanish and Portuguese domains in the eighteenth century and their subsequent suppression was a devastating blow to mission work in the New World.

By the end of the sixteenth century both the Spanish and the Portuguese had developed similar missionary approaches. Whether called aldeias, reductions, doctrinas, presidio/missions, or congregación, the method required the gathering of the natives, especially those living in small villages or as nomads, into larger and more stable units. In these villages the Indians led a semicommunal existence, learned catechism and European ways, were taught skills and crafts, and were separated both from their pagan brethren and from the corrupting influence of the white man.

The system adopted by both nations required a military presence. Attempts to evangelize hostile Indians without military protection usually ended in martyrdom for the missionaries. This system of presidios was first used on the Chichimeca frontier of New Spain in the late sixteenth century. Usually the garrisons were small, partly because of the financial outlay involved. The presence of the soldiers was a mixed blessing. While it kept the missionaries alive to pursue their work, it also brought the Indians into contact with some of the most corrupting and brutal elements in the Spanish world. Missions were outposts of empire, just as the presidio was the help of the mission. Missions and empire were inextricably intertwined, just as were church and state in Spanish society.

In the Spanish dependencies the regalism of the patronato and the vague and overlapping jurisdictions favored by the Habsburgs as a form of checks and balances on local officials also worked against the missionary endeavor. Persistent conflicts between civil and religious authorities were standard throughout the colonial period. Archbishops and viceroys were natural enemies and rarely worked together in harmony. This was intensified by the factionalism characteristic of Spanish politics and by the excessive sense of personal honor and prestige on the part of all those involved. Far too much energy, time, and work went into these vendettas, to the detriment of the higher work of evangelization.

The very presence of the Spaniard and the Portuguese worked against the missions. The general concept embraced by the mendicants, that contact with the European could only harm the native, was based on fact. Slave-raiding expeditions, incursions for the sake of conquest, labor exploitation, biological contamination, all of these things that were associated with the European turned the natives away from Christianity. It was exemplified in an appalling way by the Mexican Indian who said that he did not want to go to heaven if there were going to be Spaniards there.

In recent times, in part as a response to the beatification of Junípero Serra, this mission method had come under heavy criticism. It has been accused of uprooting native cultures and exposing the natives to European diseases. It has been seen as exploitive in its work demands and cruel in the punishments inflicted on the natives. From the overly romantic view of the missions and reductions that prevailed in times past, the pendulum has swung toward condemnation.

Many of these criticisms are valid. Europeans of the colonial period were unaware of the impact of culture shock. This did not come just from the uprooting of the mission/reduction system. The impact of a jolting removal from a familiar life, language, religion, and society, especially one that was secure and harmonious, caused immense harm. In the sixteenth century, as in the twentieth, conquest by an alien power was traumatic. In New Spain, among a people whose prehispanic laws punished drunkenness, alcoholism became rampant. They were, as Charles Gibson observed about the Aztecs after the conquest, living a life deficient in social controls.[1]

Similarly, one purpose of the missions was ultimately to integrate the natives into European society. This was based on an assumption of the superiority of that society and the need for the natives to enter it. Until that happy day arrived, they were regarded as minors, wards of the crown, under the tutelage of the missionaries. All these systems were halfway houses to a new way of life. A number of factors, including the suppression of the Jesuits, made that goal unattainable. Whether it would ever have been attained is debatable.

In the mission situation the Indians had both private property and a certain level of self-government. Their languages and a vestige of their culture, often syncretistic, survived. The Indians also developed defensive techniques. Often, as in Peru, it was simply getting away from the European. Sometimes it was military resistance, as in Colombia and Chile. At other times it took the form of syncretism, combining the old and the new. Passive resistance and passive-aggressive techniques were also employed. In sixteenth-century New Spain the natives quickly came to appreciate the complexities of Spanish law and manipulated it in their own favor. They were a highly litigious people and were often quite successful in their use of the courts. Contemporary research, using records in the native languages, tends to corroborate the picture of the natives as highly adaptable in their response to subjugation.

The idea of separating the Indian from the European while at the same time seeking to integrate the former into the latter's way of life seems paradoxical and even intrinsically contradictory. And perhaps it was ultimately doomed to failure. It should be noted, however, that whatever the excesses or failures of the mission system, the Indians' situation was vastly better in the missions than it was after the missions disappeared. The expulsion of the Jesuits and the secularization of the California missions left the natives at the mercy of racist and hostile societies: Spanish in South America, American in the United States. For at least part of their history, they were protected.

This leads also to the question of the use of force, physical or psychological, in the process of conversion—an area that still needs further study. There were numerous complaints, for example, that even in the seventeenth and eighteenth centuries the Franciscans of New Spain still maintained jails and stocks for the natives. As late as 1688 it was still customary in New Spain to give the natives five or six blows with a stick when they were late for services or instruction. Certainly this view of punishment and force, a heritage of the reconquista, fitted in with the mentality of the times. There were unabashed apologists for it, such as Juan Ginés de Sepúlveda, who held that the words in Luke's gospel, "force them to come in" (14:24), applied to the Indians and Christianity. The very Latin words *compelle intrare* came to be a code term for some sort of compulsion. This idea was bolstered by the weighty authority of Saint Augustine of Hippo, who had interpreted this passage as supporting the use of compulsion in some circumstances. A sixteenth-century Jesuit, Alonso Sánchez, became one of the leading proponents of the proposition that Christianity could come to the New World only through Spanish domination. He extended this claim to saying that China would be christianized only through force of arms, an idea vehemently opposed by his fellow Jesuit José de Acosta. The very policy of relocating natives into large groupings (congregación, aldeamento) was a form of force. The presence of an armed conqueror who overthrew idols and of encomenderos who endowed churches was also a potent form of intimidation. It can be and has been argued that it is unfair to judge the mentality of the sixteenth century by that of a later, supposedly more enlightened one. This is not entirely applicable to the present question since the longstanding tradition of the Church and a basic theological principle was that faith had to be accepted freely. Many churchmen and missionaries in the New World lost sight of that principle. This was often the result of frustration when gentler methods proved ineffective. In a human way the missionaries blamed their ineffectiveness on the flaws of the natives, shortcomings that needed a firm and authoritarian hand for correction.

The mission situation undoubtedly gave some of the missionaries a taste for power over the docile natives. The accusations of excessive corporal punishment go back to the earliest days of the enterprise and continue down to the nineteenth century. This is a dark, negative thread that runs through mission history. It cannot be denied, but it also must not be exaggerated. The Jesuit reductions, for example, were characterized on the whole by a mild administration.

Against this must be balanced the fervent dedication of the missionaries to their task. The cost of the mission work was not just financial, it was also personal. The number of missionaries who lost their lives in the course of their work cannot be known for sure, but it was exceedingly large. The missionaries endured their own form of culture shock, going into totally foreign circumstances, harsh climates, adjusting to new food, and enduring disease.

As the quincentenary of Columbus's first voyage approaches, more and more voices are using the word *genocide* to describe the European impact on the Western Hemisphere. In truth, the long-range effect was dreadful. Demographic studies have convincingly shown a catastrophic decline in the native populations of the New World. The primary agent of this destruction was the bacterium and the virus. The natives fell in vast number before the onslaught of European diseases—smallpox, typhus, influenza, measles—for which they had no immunological protection. Thousands of years of separation had left them vulnerable, a situation that also occurred in Polynesia. Aggravating this was labor exploitation, culture shock, alcoholism, and despair. The disappearance of the natives of the Caribbean region bears tragic witness to this blot on the Spanish escutcheon.

But is it correct to use the word *genocide*? As elaborated in this century, the term applies to a calculated, deliberate extermination of an entire identifiable people for racial or other reasons. Despite the dreadful consequences of the European invasion of Latin America, there was never any planned or calculated desire to destroy the people as such. After the calamitous mistakes made in the Caribbean, the Spanish colonials realized that the Indian was the basis of their prosperity. Self-interest alone demanded that the Indian be preserved, if not necessarily treated well. There are other terms to describe what happened in the Western Hemisphere, but genocide is not one of them. It is a good propaganda term in an age when slogans and shouting have replaced reflection and learning, but to use it in this context is to cheapen both the word itself and the appalling experiences of Jews and Armenians, to mention but two of the major victims of this century.

The Spanish, and to a lesser extent the Portuguese, were unique among all colonizing and imperialistic peoples in having a formidable movement in favor of the oppressed natives. Unlike the British, and later the Germans and Dutch, the Iberian nations had an institutionalized conscience in the form of a church that had a clearly defined place in society. In addition, Spain enjoyed a rather wide freedom of speech and protest. Clerics, officials, and private citizens wrote to the king (through the Council of the Indies, of course) with amazing frequency. Their letters were noted and evaluated with bureaucratic thoroughness. It is this thoroughness, together with an efficient archival system, that enables us today to reconstruct the great humanitarian movement of the sixteenth century.

The pro-Indian lobby was never an organized, clearly defined group. Some of the protagonists, like Motolinía and Las Casas, were hostile to each other. There were varying opinions about the Indian and how he should be helped. Motolinía and Zumárraga upheld the basic justice of Spanish rule, while Las Casas, toward the end of his life, believed that the Spanish were bound to full restitution, including all the conquered lands themselves. Some held a patronizing view of the Indian, while others exalted him in the best "noble savage" tradition. More important than the differences, however, is the fact that the movement on the whole had an impact, despite setbacks, failures, and the omnipresent "American reality," that is the *de facto* situation that laws and theories could never entirely affect. The frenzied reactions of the colonials demonstrate that quite clearly. Las Casas's missionary experiments failed in the short term but today can be seen as pioneering and farsighted. The New Laws of 1542 were a baffling combination of idealism, practical politics, and centralized government. The fact that many of their specific provisions were quickly repealed does not lessen their impact, for the crown was able to maintain the principle that the encomienda would not create a New World nobility. The Valladolid dispute, despite its disappointing outcome, is remarkable for ever having taken place at all. There is nothing comparable in the history of any other nation. The efforts of the third Mexican Provincial Council of 1585 to lessen the exploitation of Indians in the forced labor service (*repartimiento*) and the textile sweatshops (*obrajes*), together with their fiery condemnation of war against the Chichimeca Indians, are high points in Spanish rule of the Indies. It is essential to remember that Anglo-America never produced a single figure comparable to the great Spanish defenders of the Indians of the sixteenth century or to Antônio Vieira in the seventeenth. Helen Hunt Jackson scarcely belongs in their company.

Because of these efforts, the natives under Spanish rule were surrounded with a network of protective legislation. It is unwise, as many historians insist, to believe that the existence of laws guaranteed good treatment of the Indians who lived thousands of miles from the lawgivers. Still, the very existence of the laws gave both the pro-Indian agitators and the natives themselves a weapon with which to fight oppression. In the history of Mexico these laws were not removed by a conservative, clerical, or colonial government but by the liberal republic of the nineteenth century. In a misguided, and ultimately disastrous, effort to remove the Indians from their minority status and make them equal, the republic left them defenseless before aggressive, liberal, nineteenth-century capitalism. In 1910, as Mexico prepared to celebrate the centenary of its first war of independence and unwittingly prepare for a new revolution, "the millions of rural Mexicans who found themselves in dying villages or subsisting as peones on the nation's haciendas were worse off financially than their rural ancestors a century before."[2]

How successful was the evangelization of the Iberian New World? Opinions vary widely. Some believe that it resulted in a deeply implanted Christianity that remains to this day. Others claim that Christianity was little more than a veneer over a fundamental paganism. A third opinion subscribes to syncretism, a combination of Christian and pre-Christian beliefs and practices. The second opinion is given support by the pessimism that overtook many of the missionaries in the late sixteenth century. They found that in many cases Christianity was merely a veneer and that their peoples were still pagan at heart. This caused many of the friars to look back nostalgically to the early years as a golden age of missionary success.

Given the obstacles that were met and, with varying degrees of success overcome, it must be admitted that on the whole the Ibero-American missionary enterprise was a success. This statement, however, must be taken with great caution and many reservations. It does not mean that the resulting Christianity of the native peoples was all that the missionaries envisioned or that it fit neatly into Western European categories. Adaptation of the new to the old and various forms of syncretism were common ways of adjusting to a change in belief and moral systems. Christianity in the Americas was based on a late-medieval Iberian model and was filtered through the prism of various native American cultures and beliefs. Present-day research, especially that which deals with Aztec-language documents in New Spain, is revealing an unexpected resilience on the part of native cultures. The coping mechanisms of the Indians, especially their manipulation of the Spanish legal system, were stronger than had been previously thought.

Christianity in Ibero-America is in many ways a local and folk religion. It is deeply embedded in the local culture, with the result that its strength is as much cultural as it is religious. In some areas, such as Brazil, Haiti, the Maya country, and the Andean areas, the fusion is such that the old has dominated the new, and the result is neither Christian nor pre-Christian but a mixture of the two. Even where the Catholicism is more identifiable, it tends to be nonclerical, noninstitutional, and nonintellectual. The sacramental system is of less importance, or relevance, than in other Catholic communities. It is significant that sixteenth-century Nahua Indians in New Spain did not speak of attending mass, but of seeing mass. At the heart of worship stands the *santo*, the local patron saint who is the center of grass-roots religious life. The santo, who in some places is identified with a prehispanic deity, is invoked for all needs, his image is a special blessing and is cared for zealously. The cult of the santo frees the individual and community from the control of the clergy and gives direct access to the divine.

Supreme among the santos, of course, is the Virgin Mary. She is the patroness par excellence, whether as Our Lady of Guadalupe in Mexico or the Virgin of Luján in Argentina. In traditional Spanish piety, the Virgin stood between an angry, judgmental Christ and an erring world. She embodied compassion, particularly toward the oppressed and suffering, and gave them hope, if not for this life, at least for the next. In some areas, for example, among the postconquest Mexica, she was for all practical purposes a female deity, the caring and nurturing mother goddess. In both Spain and the New World she was the center of innumerable apparition stories and legends, often for the purpose of giving supernatural approval to a specific shrine or church.

It has often been said that the missionaries deliberately substituted the cult of the Virgin and the saints for preconquest deities and in that way won the Indians to Christianity. That assertion cannot be accepted uncritically. Missionaries of the sixteenth century were highly critical of religious fusion. Their initial policy vis-à-vis native religions tended more toward obliteration than to substitution. In all probability, at some point in the process of evangelization, the clergy came to terms with this syncretism and accepted it, more or less grudgingly. Substitutions did take place, but it was not part of a deliberate missionary plan.

A striking characteristic of Latin American religious practice is a deep concern, almost an obsession, with suffering and death. Such an obsession can be found in preconquest thought, as among the Mexica. It also characterized much of Iberian spirituality, with its bloody crucifix, *memento mori*, physical mortification (also characteristic of preconquest native religions), and realization of the shortness and contingency of life. The realities of the conquest and postconquest life reinforced this for the natives. Life after death was often more real than life before death. Contemporary celebrations of All Souls Day, the Day of the Dead (*día de los muertos*), testifies to the ongoing strength of this preoccupation. Fatalism, an outlook common to both conquerors and conquered, came to characterize the overall view of life.

To what extent was the Church in the new world a wealthy church? Generalizations on this score are difficult and frequently clouded by prejudices and presuppositions. In general, the Church was a major landowner throughout the colonial period. Land was granted by the crown for religious purposes and often left as legacies by individuals. Cash donations for construction and maintenance came from the crown. Donations by individuals established chaplaincies with endowed sources of income. Endowments were also to be found for missions, as in the famous Pious Fund of the Californias. Convents and confraternities often had a significant economic impact through investment in urban real estate and activities as moneylenders. Religious communities often rented their lands or buildings and used the resulting income for their works. The Jesuits were the leaders in entrepreneurial activity, though their corporate genius in that regard has perhaps been exaggerated. The reductions of Paraguay were economically self-sustaining and flourishing. The Jesuit haciendas and sugar plantations of New Spain, the latter often employing large numbers of black slaves, were among the most efficient of the colonial period.

Contrary to a popular misconception, these incomes and possessions did not lay under the "dead hand" of the Church. Much went into circulation through charitable works, purchases, and reinvestment. The Church's holdings also made it a major source of credit in the absence of an established banking economy. Long-term, low-interest loans were made to hacendados, landowners, farmers, and businessmen. Often it was assumed that the capital would not be repaid and so the interest became a form of annuity for religious organizations. This in turn was often plowed back into the local economy. In 1804, as both a reform measure to restrict the Church's activities and as a source of ready cash, the crown decreed the Act of Consolidation, which sequestered the Church's immense charitable funds. This required the Church to call in its mortgages and notes, resulting in disaster for its debtors. This in turn embittered many criollos against the Spanish crown, which was now cast in the role of unfeeling bureaucracy rather than source of justice.

The missionary enterprise in Ibero-America is simply too vast and too complex to be fully described in any single historical study. Fortunately, contemporary scholarship is increasing not only our factual knowledge of this great endeavor but is also shedding light on the fascinating interplay of peoples, beliefs, and institutions that accompanied it. It also is showing the peril of facile generalizations, based on nationalistic prejudices or faddish assumptions about cultures and races. The missionaries accomplished wonderful things but fell short of the mark as far as full christianization of the New World was concerned. It was flawed, like any human undertaking, but still stands as one of the greatest religious and humanitarian enterprises of all time.

**✝ Part II**

# French Catholicism Comes to the Americas

BY ROBERT CHOQUETTE

# 9

# THE BEGINNING OF
# FRENCH CHRISTIANITY
# IN THE AMERICAS

The story of French Christianity in the Americas is the story of a missionary church gradually transformed into an organized institution, a tale that from the beginning mixes heroism and mystic zeal with political and ecclesiastical infighting and with the colonial aspirations and clash of interests among France, England, and Spain. It is a story, too, of a clash of cultures and of the distinctive relationship of the French to the native peoples of the Americas. Finally, it is a story that demonstrates that when forced to choose between their church and their crown, as they were forced to do in both the seventeenth and eighteenth centuries, the French Christians in America, Catholic and Protestant, gave priority to the former.

## CHRISTIANITY IN FRANCE IN THE SIXTEENTH AND SEVENTEENTH CENTURIES

The French experience in the Americas was shaped by the currents and crosscurrents already present in French Christianity in the sixteenth and seventeenth centuries, among them the rupture of the Christian church, the relationship of church and state, and the strong current of mysticism and religious reform that characterized the first half of the seventeenth century.

These currents and crosscurrents in the Church of France were set in the framework of Christendom, that peculiar medieval fusion of the Christian Church and European society that had begun to disintegrate in the sixteenth century. While various European nation-states such as Spain, England, and France were growing in importance at the expense of an increasingly hollow

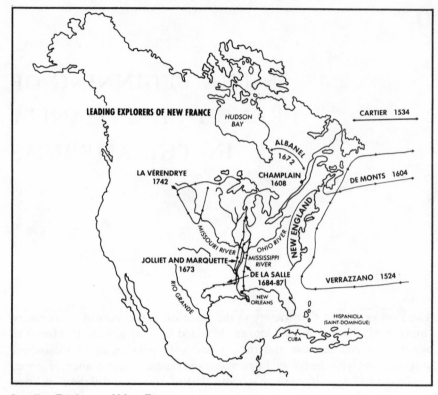

Leading Explorers of New France

Holy Roman Empire, the "Holy, Roman, Catholic and Apostolic Church" was reeling from internal challenges. Indeed, late-medieval reformers like John Wycliffe (1330–1384) and John Huss (1372–1415) had prepared the way for the fifteenth century's conciliar movement that proclaimed the superiority of an ecumenical council over a pope. However, Renaissance pontiffs soon turned the tables on these precursors of church reform. In fact, Alexander VI, pope from 1492 to 1503, not only divided the Americas between Spain and Portugal in 1493–1494 but also prosecuted and executed the Italian preacher and reformer Girolamo Savonarola in 1498. Clearly, church reform was not a healthy occupation at the turn of the sixteenth century.

However, this early-sixteenth-century world of Michelangelo and Renaissance popes like Julius II and Leo X, a world that set the stage for seventeenth-century French Christianity, was also one of profound anguish and insecurity for most European Christians. In France and other European countries these feelings translated into a deepened, sometimes morbid sense of sin, founded on the generalized belief that salvation was reserved for the few while damnation would be the lot of most. Many of the faithful endeavored to purchase tickets to heaven by performing passion plays, earning indulgences, undertaking long and costly pilgrimages, or indulging in excessive forms of asceticism. Indeed, plagues, wars, church schism, and moral abuse had all contributed to a chronic disenchantment with this world among Europe's Christians.

A profound insecurity fostered a heightened sense of sin and guilt for having turned away from a God who was more a harsh judge than a forgiving father. For the theologians of Renaissance France, the world was the devil's playground, and the flesh was synonymous with sin and perdition. The highest state of life was therefore that of the monk, the man who had fled this world for the perfection of an isolated monastic community. This is why Jean-Jacques Olier (1608–1657), the founder of the Sulpician Fathers, an important congregation in the history of North American Catholicism, could write: "Lord, what is the flesh? It is the effect of sin, it is the principle of sin. . . . All the hatred, all the malediction, the persecution that fall upon the devil must fall upon the flesh. . . . Men, angels and even God should therefore persecute us without cease."[1]

Enter Brother Martin Luther (1483–1546), who would launch the Protestant Reformation and a consequent major division in French Christianity. Beginning in 1517, this Augustinian hermit and biblical scholar, driven by a passionate and melancholy temperament, challenged several of the teachings of his Church. For a variety of reasons, other reformers soon emerged, and the Christian Church had the beginnings of a major schism on its hands. While Luther preached fire and brimstone in Germany, the Frenchman Jean Calvin (1509–1564) soon constructed a new theology, and King Henry VIII of England changed wives in spite of papal opposition. Like several of his predecessors, Pope Paul III (1534–1549) responded by condemning and excommunicating. By the mid-sixteenth century, the Christian Church had suffered a traumatic division, for one third of European Christians now claimed to be Protestants, as opposed to Catholics, the latter representing the two thirds that had remained in communion with Rome.

The theology of the Reformers did not, however, substantially change the angst and pessimism underlying all European and French theology in this early modern period. In fact, it reinforced the pessimism by considering that the Christian could not achieve salvation by fleeing into a monastery, for it was the human being itself that was radically corrupt. The only alternative was total escape from reality in the afterlife; meanwhile the Christian could only hope for salvation *in spite* of his or her total depravity. This state of mind of all-pervasive fear and damnation merely confirmed the belief that most people were damned.

It also reinforced the centuries-old suspicion and fear of women, feelings that would prove as important in French Christianity as elsewhere. Thus the reforming Odo (879–942), abbot of the Benedictine monastery of Cluny, states that feminine beauty is only skin-deep and wonders how men can embrace such bags of dung. The Italian poet and humanist Francesco Petrarch (1304–1374) loves the angelic and imaginary Laura while warning against real women who are devils and enemies of peace. While Bernardino of Siena (1380–1444) preached on the necessity of keeping wives busy with house chores so that they would not become distracted with other ideas, the early Jesuit Francis Xavier (1506–1552) wrote of the irresponsibility of women, who were said to be inferior to their husbands. Jean Eudes (1601–1680), the founder of another religious congregation active in Canada, spoke of women as "devil's Amazons" bent on making war on chastity, armed with their curly hair, bare arms and shoulders. The least that can be said is that the time had not yet come for the equality of men and women.

All European countries of the sixteenth and seventeenth centuries had established churches, for religion was considered the most basic foundation of society. Indeed, during the second half of the sixteenth century, the established Catholicism of England was replaced by the established Church of England, Catholics and dissenters being persecuted. In France, the government chose to remain in communion with Rome; it therefore repressed Frenchmen who chose to follow Luther or Calvin (Huguenots).

An important, albeit usually neglected, group of French Christians active in the Americas was the Huguenots. These French Protestants had first been formally organized as a church at the Synod of Paris in 1559. They soon became an important minority throughout the realm, opposed by the Catholic majority led by King Francis II (after 1559) and the Guise family. These wars of religion lasted throughout the second half of the sixteenth century and most of the seventeenth century. They are usually referred to as the Wars of Religion (1559–1598) and the Thirty Years' War (1618–1648). Bloody and savage massacres, rapes, and devastation occurred, some peasants being driven to eat grass or the bark off trees, while some mothers killed and ate their own children. The most infamous incident was the Massacre of St. Bartholomew (1572), allegedly perpetrated in the name of Christ. There was a lull in the fighting when, in the 1590s, King Henry IV converted from Protestantism to Catholicism in order to claim the crown of France. He then issued the Edict of Nantes (1598), decreeing toleration for Protestants in the realm under certain defined conditions.

This French policy of religious toleration ceased to apply once Cardinal Richelieu (1585–1642) became secretary of state to King Louis XIII in 1616, but especially after 1624 when he became president of the council of ministers, and from 1629 to 1642, when he was chief minister and the effective ruler of France. (Richelieu led the royal army that reduced the Huguenot fortress of La Rochelle in 1628.) The Edict of Nantes had practically become a dead letter when it was revoked in 1685. *Dragonnades* (persecution with troops) forced thousands of Huguenots to apostatize, and some three hundred thousand emigrated to Holland, England, Prussia, Switzerland, and America. Some of the latter will number among France's most determined opponents in North America, for within thirty years of the first French settlements in North America, these Huguenots were expelled from the French colonies by Richelieu's Catholic government. Thereafter, until the British conquest of Canada in 1760, France's North-American colonies of Acadia, Canada, and Louisiana, otherwise known as New France, would not welcome Protestant settlers.

The early French Catholicism of North America was the prime offspring of the Catholic Church of France, a church that underwent a profound transformation in the first half of the seventeenth century, just as the colonies of Acadia and Canada were being established. This was when French church leaders decided to implement many of the decisions of the reforming Council of Trent (1545–1563), measures that would include the founding of seminaries for the training of priests, and the appearance of several new religious congregations.

This seventeenth-century French spiritual renewal that would have such manifest consequences in New France was initiated by François de Sales (1567–1622) and Pierre de Bérulle (1575–1629). Appointed bishop of Geneva in 1602, François soon became the foremost leader of French spirituality. While instrumental in founding the order of Visitandine nuns in 1610, he is best known as the author of *Introduction to the Devout Life* (1609) and *Treatise on the Love of God* (1616). While acknowledging the value of austerity and prolonged prayer, François insisted on the possibility of sanctification for Christians in all walks of life through the simple fulfillment of one's duty, providing all is done in the love of God and neighbor. He was thus more of an optimist than most, trusting in the love and mercy of God, an outlook shared by many Jesuits of the day. Francis taught that brewer, baker, soldier, and housewife were all called to Christian perfection and could attain it. The prevalent theology that salvation was reserved for a select few was thereby seriously undermined.

Pierre de Bérulle, founder of the congregation of the Oratory (1611), developed a spirituality rooted in the sovereign majesty of God. While love dominated the teaching of François, adoration and piety were foremost in that of de Bérulle. God's majesty was so far beyond our understanding that the only valid way of salvation was through his Son Jesus. De Bérulle's theology was therefore centered on the Incarnate Word of God. His was a road that required thoroughgoing ascesis and self-denial. The path of salvation proposed by De Bérulle was thus much more demanding and difficult than that of François. The latter would prove more popular.

These spiritual leaders inspired a legion of Catholic reformers in seventeenth-century France. A host of new religious congregations appeared, each endeavoring to implement Church renewal. In French America, the leading male religious congregations were the Jesuits, the Recollects, the Capuchins, and the Sulpicians, all products of the Catholic reform movement of the sixteenth and seventeenth centuries. All of the religious congregations of women active in the Americas were founded in the same period, either in Europe or in Canada.

One of the latter—and one of the first to set foot in Canada—was the order of St. Ursula. It was in 1535 that Angela Merici founded at Brescia (Italy) this earliest and largest teaching order of women. The Ursulines were initially a society of virgins living in their own homes; by 1572 the order had been transformed into a congregation of simple vows and communal living. Beginning in 1612, French Ursulines took to the cloister and solemn vows, a form of life that became the norm for a rapidly growing number of French convents. By 1677 there were more than three hundred Ursuline convents in France. They were accompanied by several groups of nursing sisters and by the teaching sisters of the Congregation of Notre Dame, initially founded in Bordeaux at the turn of the seventeenth century. These were the three foremost congregations of nuns active in teaching and nursing in New France; in fact, these women were the first nuns to leave metropolitan France to work in distant colonies.

New congregations of men also sprang up all across France. While the Oratorians, primarily concerned with the training of clergy, directed forty-three colleges in France by the 1630s, Vincent de Paul (1567–1660) came to personify the evangelization of the countryside and the service of the poor. In 1632 he founded the Vincentian or Lazarist Fathers and, the following year, the Sisters of Charity, both devoted to the ideal of service to the poorest in society.

In both France and the Americas, the Society of Jesus (Jesuits) was the largest and most powerful male religious order. Founded by Ignatius Loyola (1495–1556) in Paris in 1534, the highly disciplined and exceptionally well-trained Jesuits were primarily concerned with reclaiming Catholics lost to the Protestants and with evangelizing the heathen of all lands. Jesuit men vowed particular obedience to the pope, wore no distinctive habit, and were not held to recite the Office in choir. They soon became noteworthy as educators and missionaries in foreign lands, all the while serving as spiritual advisers to the most influential and powerful people in France. At the time of Ignatius' death in 1556, his brotherhood numbered more than a thousand men and was at work in India, Malaya, the Congo, Brazil, Japan, Ethiopia, and China. On the eve of French settlement in North America in 1600, more than eighty-five hundred Jesuits were at work across the globe.

In France their growth was initially slow due to the Wars of Religion and their banishment by parliament in the 1590s. However, beginning in 1603, King Henry IV readmitted the Society of Jesus into the realm, encouraged it to reopen its former colleges, and appointed the Jesuit Father Coton his principal adviser on religious affairs. In 1608 the same priest became confessor to the king, inaugurating a tradition that would endure for two centuries in France. When Henry IV was assassinated in 1610, Jesuits had attained the pinnacle of clerical influence and power in teaching, theological research, and foreign missions. In France, some fifty Jesuit houses sheltered twelve hundred men; by 1640, these numbers grew to seventy houses and two thousand men. Thus, during the first half-century of French exploration and settlement in the New World, the Society of Jesus was far and away the most powerful, influential, determined, and progressive religious congregation in France and the Catholic world.

Another group that would have far-reaching influence in the Americas was the Compagnie du Saint-Sacrement (1627–1665). Established by Henri de Lévis, duc de Ventadour, this society of Christian apostolate, piety, and social service was so secret that not only did most contemporaries ignore its existence, but even historians did not discover it until the twentieth century. Several of the leaders of the Canadian missions were members of the Compagnie du Saint-Sacrement.

While François de Sales and Pierre de Bérulle were renewing French spirituality and religious congregations of men and women were inventing new forms of apostolate and evangelization, others sought to revitalize the training of the clergy, for most acknowledged that the successful reform of French Catholicism depended on good priests. John Eudes (1601–1680), an Oratorian missionary in rural France, began in 1641 by organizing a congregation of women dedicated to "fallen women." Two years later he left the Oratory to found a new congregation of priests whose object was to conduct seminaries. The Congregation of Jesus and Mary, better known as Eudists, would eventually find its way to Canada, as would the congregation of sisters.

The best-known society of priests dedicated to the training of clergy is, however, the Gentlemen of Saint-Sulpice. Founded in 1641 by Jean-Jacques Olier (1608–1657), a member of the Compagnie du Saint-Sacrement, the priests of Saint-Sulpice arrived in Montreal in 1657, took over the island, and were soon involved in far-ranging missions to the outlying areas of New France. They became major players in the Catholic history of the colony, directing the destiny of Montreal and proving to be the foremost rivals of the Jesuits in the Canadian colony. However, Sulpicians exerted most influence in France as seminary directors, for their seminary in the parish of Saint-Sulpice in Paris (1642 and after) became a model for many French seminaries that were founded in subsequent years, including that of Montreal.

By the mid-seventeenth century, the Catholic Church of France was undergoing profound renewal. Although the Christian faith of many Frenchmen still left much to be desired, and while several clerics still led less than admirable lives, the Church of France was decidedly steering a course much closer to that of the gospels. With its missionaries, mystics, and martyrs, the church of Canada would prove its finest offspring.

However, in spite of its manifest zeal, dedication, and holiness, until the British conquest of Canada in 1760 French Catholicism in the Americas was bedeviled by internal disputes over polity, quarrels that were transposition into the New World of perennial French disagreements.

Indeed, French Catholics were not of one mind about the distribution of power within the Catholic Church. Since the second half of the twelfth century when the king of France was granted the title of Very Christian Majesty by the Pope, French kings took a progressively more important role in the direction of French church affairs. When King Louis IX (1214–1270) was declared a saint in 1297 by Pope Boniface VIII, the tendency was reinforced, along with the growing authority of the king as nation-states gradually emerged from the feudal structures of the thirteenth century. The king of France was slowly exchanging his role as suzerain for that of absolute ruler. It was understood that His Very Christian Majesty was chosen by God to command in His name. This gave the king absolute authority over his subjects, although not despotic or capricious power, for the king had to rule according to God's law.

At his coronation, the king of France was anointed and invested with a religious office. He was entrusted with the care of the church, which he swore to defend while exterminating heresy. This mandate was constantly reiterated in the preambles of royal edicts, and kings like Louis XIV (1638–1715) declared that it constituted the king's most important charge.

Over a period of five hundred years various French spokesmen had reiterated and developed these "freedoms of the gallican Church" (libertés de l'Eglise gallicane). While the Sorbonne had always stood for such autonomous rights of the Church of France, fourteenth-century theologians Jean Gerson and Pierre d'Ailly had reinforced the movement, followed by the Pragmatic Sanction of Bourges in 1438 and the Concordat of Bologna in 1516, where the king's right of nomination to bishoprics and other high ecclesiastical offices was acknowledged by the pope. While the decrees of the Council of Trent were not implemented in France (1563–1615), theorists like Edmond Richer (1559–1631) reinforced the gallican movement by minimizing the authority of the pope over national churches and bishops.

This centuries-old autonomist movement within French Catholicism impacted on French Christianity in the Americas in that the movement reached its apogee during the personal reign of King Louis XIV (1661–1715), a time when the Assembly of the French clergy issued its Four Gallican Articles (1682) in response to a conflict between the king and Pope Innocent XI. This representative assembly of French clergy declared that the king was not subject to the Church in temporal and civil matters, and that the pope could not dispense the king's subjects from their allegiance. Infallibility did not belong to the pope individually but rather to the Church, which spoke through general councils. While the pope enjoyed the fullness of apostolic power, he did so jointly with the bishops—whose authority was also of divine origin. Each national church was declared autonomous in disposing of its revenues and property. Rome could not therefore tax the French church without its consent. The French clergy ensured that its autonomy was fully protected by declaring that the ancient liberties of the church of France were inviolable, it being understood that these liberties were never defined. In other words, the French crown and the French courts would decide the extent of Roman authority in church affairs. By the seventeenth century, therefore, five hundred years of French history had reinforced the authority of the French crown over the church of France.

Since the Council of Trent in the mid-sixteenth century, this gallican church of France had been challenged by some French Catholics who believed that the Roman pontiff should be the effective administrative ruler of the Catholic

Church. Indeed, while the term gallican was invented to designate a "France-centered" polity, the term ultramontane designated French Catholics who favored a Catholic authority structure centered in Rome—beyond the Alps. These ultramontanes believed that the Catholic Church should be much more centralized than the loose confederation of national churches allowed in the seventeenth century. Jesuits were the foremost spokesmen of this school of thought, and their numerous and influential colleges served to propagate the movement. The ultramontane–gallican debate was transported to Canada by the arrival of the Sulpician Fathers in 1657.

## ACADIA, THE FIRST FRENCH-AMERICAN CHRISTIAN MISSION

Early French-American Christianity, in either its Catholic or Huguenot traditions, was just as closely bound to its nurturing society as was its mother church in France. Indeed, the welfare of the church was directly dependent upon that of the French state. The latter, after a century of sporadic and indirect contact with North America, particularly through fishermen and commercial entrepreneurs, finally established permanent settlements in the Americas after 1604, first in Acadia, then on the St. Lawrence River. *Acadia* was the name given to the French colony centered on Port Royal, today's Annapolis Royal on the south shore of the Bay of Fundy. The territory of Acadia included all of Canada's maritime provinces and the state of Maine.

The founding of these French colonies and missions of Acadia and Canada was facilitated by earlier French contact with North America—which dated from at least the early sixteenth century, when Breton and Norman fishermen began regular visits to the Grand Banks of Newfoundland, inaugurating a tradition destined to last until the present. While the Irish may have explored parts of the North American continent in earlier times, the Vikings most certainly had around the year 1000; their colonies were later abandoned. This intermittent European presence in North American waters became a sustained one once the French fishermen began their annual visits in the early sixteenth century. This was some fifteen years after Christopher Columbus had rediscovered America in 1492, and a decade after Giovanni Caboto, in 1497 and 1498, bearing letters patent issued by England's King Henry VII, discovered and claimed the North American continent in the name of England. While the Spanish and Portuguese were to give immediate follow-up to these discoveries, England and France were slow to get started.

Given that North America and the continent's Christian missions would later be divided between England and France, it is ironic that both owed their initial claims to Italian explorers. Indeed, while England rested her case for possession on the discoveries of Caboto, France invoked the discoveries of Giovanni da Verrazano, the first European to sail along the North American coast from

Missions in Acadia, 1604–1776

Florida to Newfoundland. Indeed, in 1524, Verrazano sailed under the auspices of King Francis I, seeking a western passage to China and the Indies. He demonstrated that North America was a continent distinct from Africa and Asia. France followed up with the voyages of Jacques Cartier, who discovered the Gulf of St. Lawrence and the St. Lawrence River in 1534 and 1535, designating the north shore of the first as "the land God gave to Cain." Cartier went up the St. Lawrence as far as the rapids alongside the island of Montreal, then wintered near today's Quebec. There may have been two priests on the 1535 voyage. Cartier returned to Canada for a third time in 1541–1542 as second in command to Jean-François de La Rocque de Roberval, who was leading an ill-fated attempt at colonization. Everyone was either dead or back in France by 1543, unaware that the Spaniard Hernando De Soto had just completed an epic crossing (1539–1542) of the territories of South Carolina, Georgia, and Alabama to the Mississippi.

In spite of other ill-fated attempts at colonization in Brazil (1555–1560), in

Florida (1562–1565), on Sable Island off the Nova Scotia coast (1598–1603), and at Tadoussac on the St. Lawrence River (1600–1603), France did not establish a permanent foothold on the continent until 1604. For 150 years thereafter, both the political and ecclesiastical history of Acadia would prove a patchwork of conflicting interests and slow, uneven development.

So it was that in 1604, the explorer and trader Pierre du Gua de Monts (1558–1628), established the colony of Acadia, a region including most of today's maritime Canada and the state of Maine. Due to the poor state of government finances in the early seventeenth century, France entrusted colonization enterprises to individual merchants who undertook to establish specific numbers of settlers in a colony in return for a trading monopoly. Thus it was that De Monts entered into a contract with King Henry IV agreeing to establish sixty settlers per year in Acadia or Canada, two areas the French crown wanted to colonize; Acadia was centered on the Bay of Fundy; Canada was the land surrounding the mighty St. Lawrence River. In addition, De Monts was to win over the Indians to the Christian faith. It was ironic that De Monts, a Protestant, was charged with the Catholic evangelization of Acadia's heathen. In return for his commitment, De Monts obtained the title of lieutenant-general of Canada and Acadia and a fur-trading monopoly in the area. Thus began the story of the Acadian colony.

De Monts organized his expedition, obtained financial support from various merchants, and recruited a work force of various Protestant and Catholic tradesmen. He was seconded by his Catholic lieutenant, François Gravé Du Pont, and by the experienced soldier Jean de Biencourt de Poutrincourt; Samuel de Champlain was the official geographer and cartographer of the expedition, sailing in the company of two priests and an unnamed Protestant minister.

Having sent three ships to trade into the St. Lawrence, as had become customary, in the spring of 1604 De Monts set out with two other ships to explore and colonize Acadia. After exploring along the coast of the Bay of Fundy, his party wintered on Sainte-Croix Island (Dochet Island) in today's Maine, at the southwestern edge of what would become the French colony of Acadia. The group suffered such abject misery from hunger, cold, and scurvy (half of the men died) that they moved camp in the summer of 1605. This is when Port Royal was founded in the Annapolis basin on the Bay of Fundy. France thereby established a permanent base on the North American continent.

If it is ironic that two Italians were responsible for the initial North American discoveries of both France and England, another irony is that France, that "eldest daughter of the church," the realm of His Very Christian Majesty that had fought wars to ensure the dominion of the Catholic Church, was led in its colonial enterprises by Protestants. Indeed, the Brazil colony of Villegaignon and that in Florida directed by Admiral de Coligny were Huguenot undertakings; Roberval, the leader of the 1541–1543 expedition to the St. Lawrence, was also Huguenot. This was also true of Pierre du Gua de Monts, the foremost leader of the French settlements of Acadia and Canada. Given that French Huguenots were prominent in trade, commerce, and finance, and given that King Henry IV had himself been Protestant, it is not surprising to find several Protestants in France's expeditions of the early seventeenth century. Acadia was thus settled by both Catholics and Protestants, the crews of the ships and the leaders of the expeditions being also of both denominations.

While two priests and a minister participated in the journey of 1604, their ministry did not begin under good auspices. Aboard ship the minister and one priest fought so violently over points of doctrine that they came to blows. Champlain records that when both died within the year, the sailors buried them in the same grave to see if they would behave more appropriately in death. The other priest, Nicolas Aubry, managed to get himself lost in the woods in 1604. However, he survived, living off the land for seventeen days, until some of his colleagues happened to find him. Aubry returned to France in 1605.

During these early years of the Acadian story, Christian concerns remained secondary in the minds of the colony's leaders. De Monts had returned to France in 1605, busily fending off rival merchants who were jealous of his trading monopoly. Nevertheless he managed to ship reinforcements and supplies to his colony in May 1606, including the Paris notary and humanist Marc Lescarbot, who would become famous as the author of a general history of New France published in Paris in 1609. In the absence of all clergy in the colony, Lescarbot took over the duties of catechist in Port Royal, spending a pleasant winter (1606–1607) in the company of men like Champlain. However, all was for nought; De Monts lost his trading privilege and repatriated his settlers in 1607, the same year that two English trading companies sponsored the founding of the colonies of Jamestown in Virginia and another at the mouth of the Kennebec River in Maine, a location that would be claimed by France as an integral part of Acadia. De Monts did, however, manage to extend his monopoly for another year, allowing him to establish the colony of Quebec in 1608.

While De Monts was setting his sights on the St. Lawrence, in 1608 his colleague Jean de Biencourt de Poutrincourt managed to obtain royal authorization to continue the Acadian experiment, thereby securing a new lease on life for the tenuous Christian apostolate that had taken place there. De Poutrincourt was able to sail to Acadia only in 1610, but found the station of Port Royal in good order, friendly Indians having seen to its preservation.

For several years Jesuits had hoped to occupy the Acadian mission field, and had even managed to obtain royal orders appointing two of their men to Acadia. However, Jean de Biencourt de Poutrincourt had other ideas. He shared widespread prejudice against Jesuits, believing they were untrustworthy and underhanded. He therefore managed to set sail from Dieppe to Acadia on 25 February 1610 without the Jesuits on board his ships.

However, De Poutrincourt had recruited a secular priest, Father Jessé Fléché, who upon arrival set out to baptize as many Indians as possible, for only then would the De Poutrincourt family, father and son, be able to convince the king's court that Jesuits were not necessary in Acadia. Thus, on 24 June 1610, less than one month after arriving in the colony, Fléché baptized the Micmac chief Membertou and his family; before leaving Acadia one year later, Fléché had baptized some hundred Indians, much to the scandal of the two Jesuit missionaries who arrived in Acadia in 1611.

Indeed, Jesuit fathers Enémond Massé and Pierre Biard had been cooling their heels in France since 1608, awaiting transportation to Acadia, in conformity with royal directives. Widespread hostility to the Jesuits, in addition to the refusal of Huguenot underwriters to authorize the Jesuit mission, led the wealthy and pious Antoinette de Pons, marquise de Guercheville and first lady-in-waiting to the queen, to purchase a share in the De Biencourt commercial interests. The Society of Jesus was then given this share, thereby becoming full-fledged trading partners in the Acadian colony. De Poutrincourt's son, Charles de Biencourt, had no choice but to transport the two Jesuit missionaries with him when he returned to Acadia in the early months of 1611. After an exceptionally long and difficult crossing, their ship anchored at Port Royal on 22 May 1611.

The Jesuits in Port Royal were soon embroiled in a protracted quarrel with the De Biencourt family—especially with Charles, who was in command of the colony after 1611. The priests were accused of meddling in civil affairs after Father Biard sided with a rogue Frenchman accused of the rape of an Indian woman; they then quarreled over the place of burial of Chief Membertou. Various other incidents led Father Biard to excommunicate Charles de Biencourt, who retaliated by forbidding the Jesuits to evangelize distant Indian bands and forbidding their return to France. Charles's father Jean, having returned to France in 1611, was forced to accept an even more important financial partnership with the marquise de Guercheville before being discredited by the Jesuits and their friends. Indeed, in early 1612, the powerful De Guercheville had sent a shipload of supplies to Port Royal with representatives of both parties on board. Each accused the other of disloyalty and incompetence.

At wits' end, De Guercheville planned the removal of the Jesuits from Port Royal and the establishment of a new missionary colony elsewhere. In 1613, she sent a ship to Acadia bearing all the necessities of a new colonial beginning. Commanded by René Le Coq de La Saussaye, the small hundred-ton ship stopped at Port Royal, embarked fathers Biard and Massé, then crossed the Bay of Fundy to drop anchor at Mount Desert Island at the mouth of the Penobscot River, where the priests established the mission of Saint-Sauveur. This is where Captain Samuel Argall of Virginia found them two months later.

Charged with expelling the French from the Atlantic seaboard, Argall fell upon the infant colony of Saint Sauveur in July 1613. Jesuit brother Gilbert Du Thet was one of many killed in the raid, the survivors being treated as pirates. While Father Massé was allowed to leave with Le Coq, fathers Biard and

Jacques Quentin were among fourteen men taken prisoner by Argall, first to Jamestown, then on another raiding expedition into Acadia in November 1613, when Argall destroyed the colony of Port Royal, in the absence of De Biencourt burning and looting everything in sight. The action put a temporary end to the French colony of Acadia. After other misadventures, Biard and Quentin made their way back to France, marking the end of the first Jesuit mission in Canada.

In spite of the squabbling that bedeviled the ecclesiastical history of this first Acadian mission, some elements of North American Catholic missionary policy had already become manifest. First, the Jesuit missionaries established friendly rapport with the native peoples, a characteristic that would become their badge of distinction throughout the forests of North America. One reason for this was the initial Jesuit decision to learn the native languages, a second characteristic that would serve the French well. Third, from the outset, the Jesuits decided to live with the Indians rather than stay isolated in the French posts. Fourth, the Jesuit missionaries refused to baptize Indians who did not have sufficient catechetical preparation or a minimum of understanding of Christian doctrine. All of these policies were manifest in Father Biard's 1611 criticism of the haste with which Father Fléché had baptized dozens of Indians with whom he could not even communicate, not to mention evangelize.

## CANADA, THE CENTRAL MISSION OF NEW FRANCE

It was the settlement of Quebec, at the confluence of the St. Charles and St. Lawrence rivers that would become the main center of both New France and French-American Christianity. This capital of France's North-American empire was founded by the same Pierre du Gua de Monts who had founded Acadia.

In 1608, De Monts sent three ships to establish a colony at Quebec, 120 miles upriver from the trading post and fishing station at Tadoussac. The fishing station, which stood at the mouth of the Saguenay River, had been in operation for several years but, with the exception of the aborted colonies of Roberval (1541–1543) and of Pierre Chauvin (1600–1602), Frenchmen had never wintered in Canada. In spite of the fact that the fur trade was thrown open to all comers in 1608, a fact that threatened De Mont's profits, he decided to continue his infant colony at Quebec under the command of Samuel de Champlain. Champlain had traveled up the St. Lawrence as far as Montreal in 1603 and participated in the Acadian adventure from 1604 to 1607. For the first time, however, Champlain was in command at Quebec, his title being that of lieutenant to De Monts, the head of a French merchant company. Indeed, for the next half-century such commercial companies would exploit New France, enjoying crown-granted monopolies.

No clergymen were among the twenty-eight Frenchmen left at Quebec in September 1608, only eight of whom survived the first winter, scurvy claiming most of the others. Although annual supply ships allowed the tiny settlement to maintain itself from year to year, its existence was tenuous at best. Thus, in 1610, while Virginia's Jamestown boasted five hundred inhabitants, and even cold and rocky Newfoundland had a new colony of forty people, Quebec had a total population of twenty forlorn Frenchmen ensconced in a residence (*habitation*) on the left bank of the St. Lawrence below the escarpment that would later support the fortress of Quebec. Englishmen were also wintering on Hudson Bay and James Bay in 1610, although it would be another half-century before England established any permanent posts in the frigid North. Another chapter was opening in the French–English contest for the control of North America.

It is ironic that Quebec, the town that would later consider itself a new Catholic Jerusalem in the wilds of a Protestant and materialistic North America, had a Protestant as founder. Not only was De Monts a Protestant, but Champlain may also have been of Protestant birth, although he had become a pious and devout Catholic by the time his Canadian career began in 1603. It was this dynamic and enterprising explorer who journeyed up the Richelieu River to Lake Champlain in 1609, paddled up the Ottawa River in 1613 and again in 1615, and wintered with the Huron Indians on Georgian Bay in 1615–1616 after having accompanied them on a raid against their enemies the Five Nations. Not by any means a mystic or a missionary, it was Champlain who invited the Recollect friars to come to Canada in 1615. They would reestablish a Christian missionary presence in French America only two years after the Jesuits were expelled from Acadia.

# 10

## AN AGE OF MISSIONARIES, MYSTICS, AND MARTYRS

The first fifty years of the church in Canada was a period of sometimes heroic missionary activity fueled by mystical zeal. This period was dominated by the activities of members of religious congregations, especially Jesuits, who were often at odds with each other and with civil authorities, all the while writing one of the noblest chapters in the annals of Christian missions.

Upon first arriving in Quebec in 1615, the Recollects found that the ruling trading company, which was owned by Protestants, did not favor the development of Catholic missions. Once the friars had secured the assistance of the powerful Society of Jesus in 1625, both religious orders ensured the unchallenged rule of Catholic doctrine by obtaining from the government of France the exclusion of all Protestants from the colony of New France (1627). Shortly thereafter, it was the Recollects themselves who were forbidden to return to the colony (1632). The Jesuits thereby obtained an ecclesiastical monopoly in Canada that remained unchallenged until the arrival of the Sulpician fathers in 1657 and the first bishop in 1659. During this period of Jesuit hegemony several of Ignatius' followers shed their blood for their faith, while others explored new territories, evangelized new Amerindian nations, and founded a college in Quebec. Meanwhile, Marie de l'Incarnation, the superior of the newly arrived Ursuline sisters, was during a full thirty-three years a pillar of the fledgling colony, an adviser of governors and of the bishop, and one of the Christian church's greatest mystics.

### THE FIRST MISSIONARIES ON THE ST. LAWRENCE

The stage was set for these developments by Cardinal Richelieu's decision in 1627 to ban Huguenots from the colony. The action was initially asked for by

148

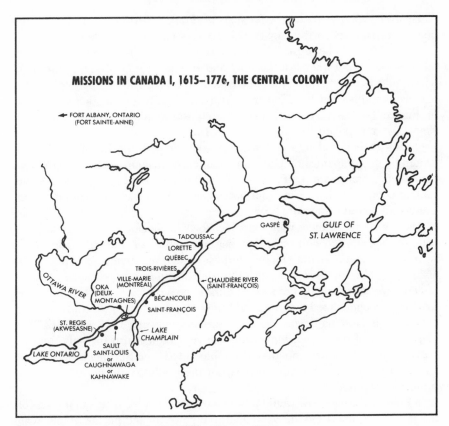

MISSIONS IN CANADA I, 1615–1776, THE CENTRAL COLONY

Missions in Canada I, 1615–1776: The Eastern Provinces

Canada's first missionaries, the Recollects, a group of reformed Franciscans established in the late sixteenth century who would become major players in the Canadian story.

In response to Champlain's invitation, three Recollect priests and one brother shipped out from Honfleur, arriving in Quebec on 8 June 1615: fathers Denis Jamet (superior), Jean Dolbeau, and Joseph Le Caron and Brother Pacifique Duplessis. They lived in a small house near the Quebec trading post until they completed the construction of a new residence and church on the right bank of the St. Charles River in 1621.

The Recollects were primarily concerned with evangelizing the Indians, although their very limited manpower never allowed them to do justice to their dream. Their foremost missionary was Joseph Le Caron who, on arriving in Quebec in 1615, journeyed to the country of the Hurons (Huronia) on Georgian Bay in south-central Ontario, closely followed by Champlain's party. Both men would winter there and return to Quebec in the spring of 1616.

Thereafter, upon spending one year in France (1616–1617), Le Caron became missionary to the Montagnais Indians on the north shore of the St. Lawrence. In 1623 he returned to Huronia for one year in the company of two other Recollects, Father Nicolas Viel and Brother Gabriel Sagard, the man who would later describe in a famous book the land and the people that he observed on this celebrated journey. With the exception of another year spent in France (1625–1626), Father Le Caron remained in Canada until the French were expelled by the English in 1629.

During their initial fourteen years in New France, the Recollects had to contend with companies of merchants frequently unsympathetic to them. On more than one occasion the friars complained to the royal court that successive trading companies hampered and obstructed the work of the Church. Such complaints would eventually bear fruit.

There were never more than four Recollects in Canada at any one time. In spite of their limited numbers, they not only undertook Indian missions and served as chaplains at the Quebec outpost (which numbered sixty people in 1620), they also established a school for Indian children in the same year, an undertaking that struggled to survive during the next few years. However, the Recollects soon realized that they had bitten off more than they could chew, for not only was Huronia devoid of any missionary between 1616 and 1622, but Tadoussac, still the harbor for oceangoing vessels, was also the only mission station during the winter months. Therefore in 1624 the Recollects decided to ask for the help of other missionaries, for their order could not provide any supplementary resources.

In France, the man who would prove instrumental in securing the services of the Jesuits was duc Lévy de Vantadour, the powerful and pious Catholic who would within two years establish the ultrasecret Compagnie du Saint-Sacrement. Lévy had in 1625 purchased from his uncle Montmorency the position of viceroy of New France, an action recommended by Vantadour's Jesuit confessor, Father La Bretesche.

Upon learning of the identity of the new viceroy, the Recollects were enthusiastic, hopeful that Vantadour's well-known apostolic concern would help their Canadian mission. They were not to be disappointed, for it was the powerful duke who managed to obtain the Jesuits to answer the call of the Recollects. In fact, the sons of Saint Ignatius had been praying for such an opportunity ever since fathers Biard and Massé had been forced out of Acadia in 1613. The Recollects were more than pleased, for the Jesuits could provide the money and the men the Canadian mission so desperately needed.

And so it was that in 1625, Father Coton, the superior of the Jesuit province of Paris, designated three Jesuit priests and two brothers to go to Canada: fathers Charles Lalemant (superior), Enémond Massé, and Jean de Brébeuf and brothers François Charton and Gilbert Buret. Having boarded ship at Dieppe on 24 April 1625 in the company of the Recollect father Joseph de La Roche Daillon, the group arrived in Quebec on 15 June. The new missionaries were welcomed by the Recollects—in fact shared their quarters during the next two years, until the Jesuits were able to move into their own residence in the summer of 1627. The new Jesuit house of Notre-Dame des Anges was located across the St. Charles from the Recollect monastery.

Upon their arrival in Quebec, the Jesuits faced the hostility of the trading company owned by the De Caën family, the company that held the Canadian monopoly. They also found that a slanderous Parisian anti-Jesuit pamphlet was being circulated in the tiny outpost of Quebec, much to the delight of the Protestant Guillaume de Caën, who directed the trading company in France. They soon overcame the opposition; they even managed to obtain the services of the interpreter Nicolas Marsolet, who had initially refused to teach the Indian languages to either Recollects or Jesuits.

Rarely to be outdone in strategic and tactical maneuvering, with the support of the Recollects the Jesuits soon assured that Protestants be refused admission as settlers in New France; indeed, in 1627 the Edict of Nantes was revoked in its application to New France. The clergy had managed to convince Cardinal Richelieu that the Protestant-controlled company of merchants was the foremost problem in the colony. On 29 April 1627 the powerful statesman therefore created the Company of New France, usually known as the Company of One Hundred Associates, which supplanted its predecessor.

The founding of the Company of One Hundred Associates (of which Richelieu himself was first shareholder) proved a major turning point in the history of the church in New France. It marked the end of the era when profits were the foremost raison d'être of New France. Thereafter, religious and patriotic motives came to the fore, the crown and church of France now working hand in hand for the good of the colony. Richelieu's charter of 1627 gave the new company full possession of Canada and Florida and granted it a fur-trading monopoly under the following conditions. The company would only allow Frenchmen and Catholics as residents of the colony; some two to three hundred settlers were to be transported to Canada in 1628, another four thousand in the following fifteen years. The new settlers were to be housed, fed, and maintained for three years and were to be granted cleared land and seed or otherwise sustained. During the same fifteen-year period, the company was to pay the costs of worship and provide for the sustenance of three priests in each of the posts that would be established. Finally, Indians who converted to Christianity were to be considered natural-born Frenchmen.

The arrival of three Jesuit priests in Quebec in 1625 did not make the Canadian mission overly strong, for they spent their first winter planning the construction of their residence and learning the Indian languages. Nevertheless, Father Brébeuf did manage to go live among the Montagnais Indians some sixty miles from Quebec; he was there from 20 October 1625 to 27 March 1626. Father Charles Lalemant tried the same thing, beginning on 8 January 1626, but was compelled to return to Quebec after eleven days. Meanwhile, by the fall of 1625 the Recollects were reduced to two priests when Father Nicolas

Viel, returning from Huronia where he had been working since 1623, died while jumping the rapids of the Des Prairies River north of the island of Montreal. Another Recollect, Father Le Caron, had returned to France in 1625. Of the five priests present in Canada, all three Jesuits and one of the Recollects had just arrived in the colony. They collaborated in the ministry to some four dozen Frenchmen in Quebec.

On 29 June 1626, the ship *Alouette* dropped anchor at Tadoussac bearing Jesuit reinforcements. Fathers Philibert Noyrot and Anne de Noüe and Brother Jean Goffestre led a crew of twenty tradesmen hired to build Jesuit installations on land granted to the order by Vantadour. God seemed to be pouring His blessings on the Jesuit mission, for not only were workmen busy building the Jesuit base of operations, but in this same year Jesuits and Recollects decided to reopen the mission to the Hurons. Jesuit fathers Brébeuf and De Noüe and Recollect father La Roche Daillon set off for Georgian Bay, whence Daillon proceeded farther afield to work among the Neutrals farther to the south, in the region of the Niagara River. Quebec was left with three priests.

While the future looked bright for the Jesuits in 1626 and 1627, the reverse was true for the Recollects. Reinforcements did not arrive in either year; they were therefore reduced to two priests in all of New France—one in Huronia, the other at Quebec. Jesuit fortunes soon matched those of the Recollects, for in 1627 the De Caën family refused to allow the Jesuits to ship any goods into the colony, leaving the more than two dozen men of the Jesuit mission without supplies. The Jesuit superior Father Lalemant thereupon decided to ship all his workers back to France, leaving only a skeleton staff in Canada. This included Father Brébeuf in Huronia and fathers Massé and De Noüe in Quebec.

By the end of 1627 the mission of New France that embraced the North American continent from Acadia to the Great Lakes was reduced to five priests (three Jesuits and two Recollects), two of whom were in Huronia. The three priests in Quebec served some hundred white people, the same number as in the English colony of Ferryland on the Avalon peninsula in Newfoundland. At the time, New England boasted two thousand inhabitants, while New Holland on the Hudson included two hundred settlers. So it was that within twenty years of the initial colonization of both New England and New France, the former's population already outnumbered the latter's by twenty to one, a proportion that would remain unchanged. In 1627, the frail colony of Canada was a plum ripe for the picking.

It is symbolic that Richelieu's charter creating the Company of One Hundred Associates was ratified by King Louis XIII in May 1628 at his siege camp outside the Huguenot stronghold of La Rochelle. The attack on La Rochelle induced King Charles I of England to intervene on the side of the Protestants. So it was that the French Huguenot émigré Kirke brothers—David, Louis, Thomas, John, and James—natives of Dieppe, were commissioned by England to make war on New France. Assisted by other French Protestants, David Kirke's squadron sailed to Canada in 1628 in the company of another flotilla that would seize Port Royal. Kirke's three ships dropped anchor in Tadoussac harbor and sent a messenger asking Champlain to give up the fort of Quebec. When he refused Kirke sailed downstream and in the region of the Gaspé, after a brief engagement, seized a fleet of four French supply ships on their way to reinforce the colony of Canada.

This first supply convoy organized by the Company of One Hundred Associates thus came to an inglorious end. The significance of the stroke of luck was not lost on Kirke's underwriters. A second Kirke fleet set out for Canada in March 1629, assisted in its navigation of the St. Lawrence by a Quebec deserter named Jacques Michel. Although the Treaty of Susa, signed in April 1629, had ended the war between France and England, David Kirke was unaware of this. From Tadoussac he ordered Champlain to give up Quebec or face the consequences. Indeed, the sixty people at Quebec were in dire straits, not having received any supplies from Europe in two years. Champlain capitulated on 19 July 1629. Most settlers, all missionaries included, returned to France, closing the first chapter of the history of the Canadian mission.

Like the Acadian mission, the first mission on the St. Lawrence ended ingloriously, but unlike the former, it was destined to be reborn in short order and to do so with a vigor unmatched by its peer. Although the Society of Jesus was not the first religious order active in the Canadian mission field, having been preceded by the Recollects, it had established foundations that would serve it well upon its return to Quebec in 1632.

## FRENCH CHRISTIANITY IN THE CARIBBEAN

Chased out of the St. Lawrence valley by the Kirke brothers in 1629, and barely succeeding in hanging on to one small trading post in Acadia in 1630, France (and its missionaries) developed an interest and founded new colonies in the Caribbean.

The Caribbean islands had remained primarily a Spanish empire since the voyages of Christopher Columbus in the 1490s. However, in the 1630s the French developed an interest in the Lesser Antilles and the Leeward and Windward Islands. Beginning in 1635, important French colonies were founded successively on St. Christopher, Martinique, and Guadeloupe and on seven other islands (including St. Martin, St. Bartholemew, and Grenada) so that by 1685, fifty-two thousand people inhabited ten French islands in the Caribbean.

The original Caribbean native population—including Arawaks, Caribs, and Chibchas—had been decimated within decades of the first Spanish occupation of the islands in the sixteenth century. However, European newcomers were soon outnumbered by Negro slaves imported from Africa. Begun in the fifteenth century, the slave trade grew in importance until its peak in the eighteenth century. Indeed, most Caribbean islands became overwhelmingly black; by 1788, for example, French Saint-Domingue (the island of Hispaniola, shared today by Haiti and the Dominican Republic) was 6 percent white and 94 percent black.

As was the case in the Americas, members of religious congregations, as opposed to secular clergy, were to be the foremost agents of evangelization of the French West Indies. Beginning in 1635, islands such as St. Christopher, Martinique, and Guadeloupe were to be the missionary territories of Capuchins, Dominicans, Carmelites, Jesuits, and only a handful of secular priests. However, theirs was not to be an edifying story, for from the outset they were involved in protracted quarrels among themselves over jurisdiction, property, and the like.

One incident that had far-reaching international repercussions was the case of Jesuit father Antoine La Valette, who after 1746 worked as bursar and then superior of the Jesuit mission in Martinique. He was soon involved in practices forbidden to a priest: trade and commerce on a grand scale. Allegedly to support his mission stations, Father La Valette had invested in real estate, traded in goods, and chartered ships to transport his merchandise and produce to Europe. In 1755, two shiploads of his goods were seized by the English on the high seas; La Valette was ruined. Given the unpopularity of Jesuits in mid-eighteenth-century Europe, after several years of litigation French courts and parliaments held the Jesuit order responsible for La Valette's debts. In 1762, the Society of Jesus was ordered to pay these debts, close its colleges, and disband. Most Jesuits in the Caribbean returned to France, unaware that the pope himself would disband their order in 1773.

It was not in the Caribbean that the church of France was destined to display the best of itself.

## ACADIA

By the Treaty of Saint-Germain-en-Laye, signed on 29 March 1632, England returned to France all its posts in Acadia and Canada.

As was the case in the West Indies, religious congregations dominated the Catholic story in Acadia for the next half-century. After preliminary missionary visits by a handful of secular priests, Jesuits had been first on the scene in Acadia (1611–1613), while Recollects followed six years later. In 1632 Capuchins would also enter the fray.

After the French returned to Acadia in 1630, both their political and their ecclesiastical stories proved as patchy and inconsistent as they had been from the beginning of the colony in 1604 and would remain so for more than sixty years. Indeed, until at least 1670, the political story of Acadia is one of feuding families engaged in a contest to control the sometimes lucrative fur trade and fishing industry of France's Atlantic colony. The names of Biencourt, La Tour, Denys, and Le Borgne are notorious.

Simultaneously, members of several religious orders tried to outdo each other in unalloyed loyalty to one or another of the feuding families, not always remembering that their first loyalty was to the Gospel of Jesus. While the Recollects were earliest on the scene, as they were in Canada, they chose to tie their (and their church's) fortunes to those of Charles de La Tour. The Recollects soon found themselves competing with the Capuchins, another religious order in the Franciscan family, whose first members had arrived in Acadia in 1632. The Capuchins became camp followers of Razilly and of his successor D'Aulnay, the foremost rivals of the De La Tour clan. Recollects and Capuchins dominated the ecclesiastical scene during these fifty years of French presence in Acadia, but they were not alone. Indeed, Jesuits had always had an interest in the area, and continued to do so, although in a limited way. There were even a few chaplains belonging to an obscure order of Penitents active in the fishing station of Canso.

On the political front, when Samuel Argall sailed away from Port Royal in November 1613 he left a devastated settlement under the leadership of Charles de Biencourt de Saint-Just, the twenty-one-year-old son of Jean de Biencourt de Poutrincourt, Pierre du Gua de Monts's associate in the initial founding of the colony. Charles de Biencourt and his settlers spent a hard winter and welcomed the arrival of Biencourt the elder (Poutrincourt) in March 1614. Noting the dire straits of the colony, the latter took most of the settlers back to France the same year, leaving the possession and leadership of the settlement to his son, who until his death in 1623 or 1624 directed a sometimes prosperous fishing and fur-trading business in Acadia, supplied each spring by ships from La Rochelle. However, when he suffered hardship, the French crown refused to come to his assistance; Biencourt was even driven to live with the Indians during his last years.

On the ecclesiastical front, however, Biencourt did manage to secure the services of four Recollect friars between 1619 and 1624. Based in both Port Royal and Miscou Island on the more northerly Baie des Chaleurs, fathers De la Foyer, Fontinier, Cardon, and Sébastien served the tiny French settlement of Port Royal, and various French and Indian bands throughout Acadia, ensuring a priestly presence after six years of clerical absence following the Jesuit removal from Acadia in 1613.

While the Recollects were to bear the standard of Catholic missions alone in New France between 1619 and 1624, they established strong bonds of loyalty with another influential family in Acadia, that of Claude de Saint-Etienne de La Tour and his son Charles. The elder De La Tour had first come to Acadia with De Poutrincourt in 1610. After Argall's raid in 1613, he settled on the Penobscot River in today's Maine. While devoting his time to the fur trade, there it was that he built Fort Pentagouët, a base of operations he occupied until his expulsion in 1626 by raiders from the Plymouth colony.

The capture of Fort Pentagouët in 1626 left only one French post in Acadia, that of Charles de La Tour, the son of Claude. Indeed, upon the death of

Charles de Biencourt in the early 1620s, his colleague and friend Charles de La Tour had assumed the leadership of the colony and moved his base of operations to a new post, Fort Lomeron, sometimes known as Fort LaTour, Cap Nègre, or Cap Sable. The fortified post was located near Yarmouth, Nova Scotia, where Charles cultivated the land and traded in furs with the Indians. When, in 1627 and 1628, he pleaded for assistance, the new and powerful Company of New France sent out four ships, the same ones scheduled to resupply Quebec in 1628; they were seized at sea by David Kirke. One of the passengers taken captive by the English was Claude de La Tour, Charles's father. When Quebec fell to the Kirkes in 1629, Fort Lomeron was the only French post left in North America.

Claude de La Tour then agreed to lead an English expedition to Acadia in order to lay claim to a land that had been granted by the king of England, in 1621, to Sir William Alexander. After several failed attempts, in 1629 Alexander's son succeeded in establishing a short-lived colony on Cape Breton Island on Acadia's easternmost periphery, then another at Port Royal. The first colony lasted two months, until it was wiped out by a French expedition. The second, guided by Claude de La Tour, endured from 1629 to 1632, some seventy settlers struggling to survive in hostile surroundings.

Jesuit fathers Barthélémy Vimont, Alexandre de Vieuxpont, and Philibert Noyrot were part of the French expedition of Charles Daniel that captured the English outpost on Cape Breton Island in 1629. Noyrot drowned at sea, but his two colleagues spent a year evangelizing the native people of Cape Breton from their base at St. Anne's mission near Bras d'Or Lake; they were recalled to France in 1630 in the wake of the Kirke raids.

The same year, however, a ship of the Company of New France landed three Recollects at Fort Lomeron. When Charles de La Tour founded another post, Fort Sainte-Marie on the St. John River across the Bay of Fundy in 1631, the Recollects followed. They soon added a mission station on Miscou Island at the mouth of the Baie des Chaleurs, a traditional fishing haven and a post that would be taken over by Jesuit missionaries in 1635.

The Recollect missionaries of Acadia were reinforced by six Capuchin friars who arrived on board the ships of Isaac de Razilly on 8 September 1632; Razilly was to resume command of Acadia in the name of France. Founded in 1529, the Capuchins were another order of reformed Franciscan friars, renowned during the Catholic Reformation of the sixteenth century as one of the most effective bands of preaching and missionary priests. Wearing pointed cowls, sandals, and beards, Capuchins endeavored to reflect the Franciscan ideals of poverty and austerity. When France repossessed Acadia and Canada in 1632, Cardinal Richelieu wanted to entrust the Canadian missions to one religious order exclusively. He offered the Canadian mission field to the Capuchins, the order to which his confessor belonged. The Capuchins refused, preferring to work in Acadia. So it was that Razilly's expedition of 1632 carried Capuchins to Acadia for the first time. However, as had been the case between the Recollects and Charles de La Tour, the Capuchins soon developed strong ties of loyalty to Razilly, to the point that when the two rival families began feuding, the priests lined up behind their respective friends.

The Capuchins were initially based at La Hève (La Have), an excellent harbor on the south coast of Nova Scotia. There it was that upon arriving in Acadia in 1632, Razilly, experienced mariner that he was, chose to settle his three hundred men, including a dozen families; he built a fortified post and established his headquarters. In December of the same year, he negotiated the takeover of Port Royal from the English captain Andrew Forrester. Thus, by the beginning of 1633, in peninsular Nova Scotia France had posts at Fort Lomeron, La Hève, Port Royal, and a newly established fishing station at Port Rossignol (Liverpool, Nova Scotia) near La Hève. The Recollects ministered in the first station; the Capuchins handled the others.

In 1635, while Charles de La Tour moved his headquarters to his post on the St. John River (Fort Jemseg) in today's New Brunswick, Razilly sent an armed party to regain Fort Pentagouët on the Penobscot River from its English occupants, a station subsequently handed over to La Tour. France had now recovered all of Acadia. The colony's government was bipartite, divided among Charles de La Tour on the north shore of the Bay of Fundy and at Fort Lomeron (Yarmouth), and Isaac de Razilly at La Hève and Port Royal. Both commanders simultaneously exploited the fishing and fur-trading industries, while answering to the Company of New France. Each had a religious order at its service, La Tour owning the Recollects, while Razilly controlled the Capuchins.

The forty-eight-year-old Razilly died in 1635, to be succeeded by his cousin and colleague Charles de Menou d'Aulnay—who commanded in lieu of Razilly's brother, who stayed in France. D'Aulnay moved his headquarters from La Hève to Port Royal and continued to govern both stations.

In addition to the three Recollects based in Charles de La Tour's posts, six Capuchins now worked in the Razilly/D'Aulnay posts at La Hève and Port Royal. In 1633 they founded a boarding school at La Hève, serving Indian and white children.

For more than a decade after 1635, while Acadia's two commanders engaged in continuous quarreling and armed conflict, the Capuchins, stationed in the Razilly/D'Aulnay posts (Port Royal, La Hève, Pentagouët, and Canso), sided with D'Aulnay in denouncing La Tour's allegedly scandalous life. In 1645, the Capuchin monastery at Port Royal sheltered a dozen friars. They not only evangelized white and Indian people, they also taught school to some thirty white children and an equivalent number of Micmac and Abenaki children.

The protracted feuding by Acadia's two leading families continued through the 1640s and 1650s. A third commercial entrepreneur, Nicolas Denys, joined the fray, and then a fourth, Emmanuel Le Borgne. Things went from bad to worse, until the English raider Robert Sedgwick settled the question in 1654 by conquering Acadia in the name of England. (The French would reoccupy Acadia in 1670 in the wake of the Treaty of Breda.)

In this whirlwind of armed conflict, commercial rivalries, and competing nationalisms, it was to be expected that Catholic missionaries could not perform their best apostolate in Acadia. The Recollect friars, present in Acadia from 1619 to 1624 and again from 1630, left the area in 1645 upon Charles de La Tour's defeat at the hands of D'Aulnay. The Capuchins, the foremost group of priests since their arrival in 1632, had four men left in Port Royal when Sedgwick attacked in 1654. Father Léonard de Chartres, the superior of the monastery, was killed in the attack; two other men returned to France; and the fourth, Father Joseph d'Angers, sought refuge with the Abenakis, whom he evangelized until his death in 1667. In fact, Father D'Angers was the only priest in peninsular Nova Scotia during the sixteen years of English rule (1654–1670). In the more northerly Baie des Chaleurs region, the Capuchin father Balthasar spent a decade (the 1650s) working alongside Jesuits. In sum, missionaries were present and active in Acadia, but frequently hamstrung by the commercial feuding.

It has already been noted that in 1635 the Society of Jesus took over the Recollect mission station at Miscou on the Baie des Chaleurs, where a small French colony supported commercial fishing activities. For the next twenty-seven years several Jesuits worked there, in addition to their sporadic presence at St. Anne's mission on Cape Breton Island where fathers Vimont and Vieux-pont had wintered in 1629–1630, to be followed in 1631–1632 by fathers Antoine Daniel and Ambroise Davost.

So it was that between 1604 and 1670 the Christian church in Acadia stumbled along a rock-strewn path, in the wake of oftentimes petty and narrow-minded commercial entrepreneurs whose selfish policies were frequently matched by the unenlightened rivalry of competing religious orders. The latter were allegedly preaching the Gospel. Although Acadia had its missionaries, it suffered a serious shortage of mystics and martyrs.

## CANADA A JESUIT MONOPOLY

While the decade of the 1630s marked the beginning of two centuries of bungling by Catholic clerics in the Caribbean and of some fifty years of largely ineffective efforts by Recollects, Capuchins, and Jesuits in Acadia, it signaled the start of a far nobler story in Canada, one that would thereafter fuel the musings of Canadian Catholic panegyrists. The Jesuit epic in Canada was one of heroes and martyrs.

Upon regaining possession of New France in 1632, Cardinal Richelieu appointed Emery de Caën interim commander of Quebec, for a period of one year, in order to allow him to recover some of the financial losses he had sustained on the Kirke seizure of Canada in 1629. De Caën led the French expedition that took possession of Quebec in July 1632. However, it was Samuel de Champlain who was appointed Richelieu's lieutenant, personal representative, and commanding officer in New France. He arrived in Quebec in May 1633.

When the French reoccupied Quebec in 1632, three Jesuits were included in the initial party. Paul Le Jeune (superior), Anne de Noüe, and a religious brother. Having failed to interest the Capuchins in the Canadian mission, Cardinal Richelieu was left with choosing between Recollects and Jesuits, for he was determined to allow only one religious order into the colony in order to prevent possible quarrels. The choice fell upon the Jesuits, possibly because of the Recollects' reliance on public charity and their refusal to own property, a policy that could be heavy to bear in a tiny colony. The Recollects resented this decision and held the Jesuits responsible for excluding them from the Canadian mission. The seeds of a longstanding animosity between the two orders were sown.

On setting foot in Quebec in July 1632, the Jesuits proceeded to reoccupy their house of Notre-Dame-des-Anges, built in 1626, across the St. Charles River. Constantly optimistic, Father Le Jeune had to renovate the residence built at great expense six years earlier; he proceeded to rebuild with the help of workers imported from France. Four more Jesuit priests arrived with Champlain in the spring of 1633—Jean de Brébeuf, Enémond Massé, Antoine Daniel, and Ambroise Davost—in addition to two religious brothers, François Charton and Gilbert Burel. By 1637 the Jesuit mission in Canada included twenty-three priests and six brothers under the supervision of Le Jeune. It was the beginning of an epic story that lasted for more than twenty years.

While their superior Le Jeune chose to winter (1634–1635) with the itinerant Montagnais hunters in order to learn their language, in the summer of 1634 Brébeuf, Davost, and Daniel accompanied the trading Hurons back to their home in the Lake Simcoe region of today's Ontario, eight hundred miles from Quebec. Simultaneously, other Jesuits established another mission station in the new post of Trois Rivières, upriver from Quebec and halfway to the island of Montreal. The following year the Jesuits had taken over the St. Charles mission on Miscou Island on the Baie des Chaleurs (1635) and were evangelizing along the east coast of New Brunswick and Nova Scotia; they also founded the College of Quebec on land donated by the Company of New France. There they taught catechism and a primary course that would in time develop into a full-fledged classical curriculum.

In 1636, fathers Davost and Daniel returned from Huronia to assist in the founding at Quebec of a seminary for French and Indian boys, an apostolate that became Father Daniel's primary occupation until 1638. Indeed, the Jesuits were learning that it was usually impossible for Indian children to adapt to this European type of education. The failure of the Quebec seminary taught them

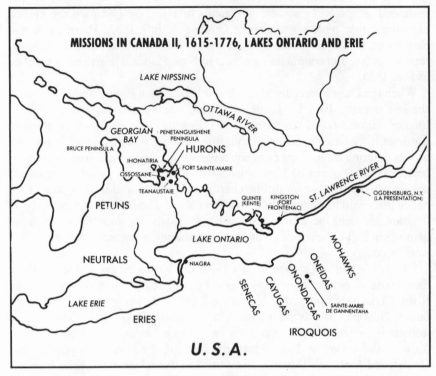

Missions in Canada II, 1615–1776: Lakes Ontario and Erie

that it was preferable to civilize the Indian before converting him to the Christian faith, a lesson French metropolitan authorities would only learn fifty years later (see Chapter 11).

While learning on the one hand that it was necessary to initiate Indians into European civilization if their conversion was to be secured, Jesuits were also coming to realize on the other hand that an overly close association with the French also had its drawbacks. With this in mind, in 1637 the Indian village of Sillery was founded near Quebec. Funded by a pious benefactor in France, Sillery resembled the reductions made famous by the Jesuits in South America. By 1645, 167 Christian Algonquins were living in the village of Sillery on a seasonal basis (these hunters still spent the winter months in the bush). Moreover, every spring, most Indian bands gathered at the seaport of Tadoussac at the mouth of the Saguenay River for the annual fur-trading with Europeans. This traditional harbor for oceangoing ships became a seasonal Jesuit mission in 1640 and remained in the Society's care until 1782.

As the only priests in Canada after 1632 and staffing the wide-ranging mission of Miscou in the neighborhood of the Recollects and Capuchins of Acadia, it was the Jesuit mission to the Hurons that would make the early Canadian church famous and add several names to the Christian church's honor roll of martyrs.

When the Jesuits arrived in Huronia in September 1634 under the leadership of Father Brébeuf, Brébeuf chose to establish the mission of St. Joseph I in the village of Ihonatiria, on the west side of Penetanguishene Bay, in the neighborhood of the village of Toanché (which Brébeuf had occupied from 1626 to 1629). For the next three years Ihonatiria was the only Jesuit residence in Huronia. In June 1637 a second mission, that of the Immaculate Conception, was established in the village of Ossossané, ten miles distant; the mission of St. Joseph at Ihonatiria was then moved to Téanaustaie (St. Joseph II). Each village sheltered some four or five hundred souls.

In the missionaries' cabin, the living area served simultaneously as kitchen, dining room, workshop, office, bedroom, and classroom for the teaching of catechism. The missionaries slept fully dressed on a bed of bark, endured the constant smoke from the campfire located in the middle of the cabin, and subsisted on a more-than-frugal diet. The latter usually consisted of a souplike substance called *sagamité* made of crushed Indian corn boiled in water, sometimes flavored with dried fish; one priest called it glue. They rarely tasted fresh fish or venison.

Their daily schedule was to rise at 4:00 A.M., meditate, celebrate mass, and then receive Huron visitors after eight o'clock. The Hurons were sometimes interested in instruction, but more frequently were merely curious or wanted handouts. The missionaries would sometimes impress the Indians with their prophetic powers, using an alarm clock to predict when the clock's alarm would ring. While one Jesuit taught the children catechism between noon and 2:00 P.M., his colleagues toured the village cabins seeking those at death's door to baptize them in order to save their souls. A brief pause at two o'clock allowed the missionaries to meditate anew and eat their *sagamité* before returning to their visits until 4:00 P.M., when they closed their cabin door. Then followed in sequence the recitation of the breviary, the writing of letters, a discussion of the day's events, language study, and evening prayers.

The missionaries had a thankless task, for not only did they need to learn the ways of the Hurons, but a chain of epidemics of smallpox and influenza in 1634, 1636, and 1639 cut like a scythe into the Huron people, reducing their numbers from thirty thousand to twelve thousand. Contact with the French was proving fatal to the Hurons, who grew progressively more hostile to these white men who seemed to bring death to their nation. When the incantations of the shamans failed to stop the death wave, more and more Hurons held the missionaries responsible for the ongoing death of half of their nation. Their accusations seemed justified, for in three years the missionaries had only managed to baptize children or adults on the verge of death. The baptismal rite therefore appeared to be the coup de grâce delivered by the white sorcerers. Killing the latter should end the dying.

In the fall of 1637, a general council of the Huron bands decided to kill the Jesuits but did not follow up on its decision. The ravages of the disease began to slow in 1638, a year when nine Jesuits were working in Huronia, residing in the two residences of Ossossané and Téanaustaie. This was when Father Brébeuf was replaced as superior of the mission by Father Jérôme Lalemant; however, Brébeuf continued working in the area until his temporary return to Quebec in the spring of 1642, seeking medical care for a broken collarbone.

Newly arrived from France in 1638, Jérôme Lalemant was superior of the Huron mission from August of that year till 1645. He then became superior of the entire Canadian mission until 1650, and then again between 1659 and 1665. He came to Canada with an exceptional record of teaching and administration in the Jesuit colleges of France. Upon arriving in Huronia, he not only organized a census of the Huron people (twelve thousand souls in thirty-two villages) but also inspired and directed a reorganization of Jesuit mission posts. It was Jérôme Lalemant who planned and supervised the construction of Fort Sainte Marie on the river Wye as a central Jesuit mission from which missionaries could evangelize various Indian villages in the area. It was from Sainte Marie (1639–1649) that fathers Brébeuf and Pierre Chaumonot departed in November 1640 to evangelize the Neutral nation on the north shore of Lake Erie. The five-month mission was a failure, the Indians having been forewarned by hostile Hurons that the missionaries were malevolent sorcerers.

Fort Sainte Marie, today fully restored by the Government of Ontario near the town of Midland, was a French oasis in the wilds of Canada. Built in 1639, it came to include a chapel, separate residences for the priests and lay workers, a forge, a workshop, a hospital, a hostel for visiting non-Christians, a cemetery, and a farm with animals and cultivated fields. The outpost was palisaded with two bastions anchoring the defensive perimeter.

The construction of the fort was made possible by another institution of Father Lalemant, the *donnés*, lay workers who contracted to work for the Jesuits in return for no remuneration except their room and board. Lalemant had seen the need for such assistance because not only were Jesuit brothers too few but their status as full-fledged members of a religious order prevented their bearing arms. Since donnés did not make vows of religion, they could defend the post when necessary, while exercising their trades of blacksmith, carpenter, and so on. An indication of their importance in the history of the Huron mission is the fact that in 1649, Fort Sainte Marie included sixteen priests, four religious brothers, and twenty-two donnés.

Fort Sainte Marie became a central base of operations for the missionaries in Huronia. While two or three priests lived there year round, evangelizing the Indians of the immediate area, the others ranged widely, evangelizing a host of nations and bands like the Algonquins, Nipissings, Petuns (Tobacco), and Neutrals. These itinerant missionaries returned periodically to Sainte Marie to rest and revitalize their sense of community.

Strangely enough, this unique and productive French Jesuit outpost was burned to the ground by the Jesuits themselves in 1649. They felt driven to do so by the devastating raids of the Iroquois against the Hurons.

Indeed, the Five Nations of the Iroquois confederacy, inhabiting the region south of Lake Ontario and west of Lake Champlain, had been adversaries of the French and their Huron and Algonquin allies since Champlain had ventured into their land in 1609 with an armed party of Algonquins. Supported by the Dutch and English of New York and the Hudson River, the Five Nations vied with the Hurons in the contest to control the fur trade, which they sought to direct to the English rather than the French. Beginning in 1642, the twenty-five-thousand-strong Iroquois nations, including some twenty-five hundred warriors, became much more aggressive, possibly provoked by the founding in that year of the French colony of Montreal in addition to the nearby Fort Richelieu at the mouth of the Richelieu River. Both posts stood across the usual Iroquois invasion route into Canada. The Iroquois launched a series of murderous raids into the land of the Hurons, among others, and set ambushes along the rivers used by the latter to bring their furs to Montreal and Trois Rivières.

Beginning in 1647, the Iroquois military campaign against the Hurons intensified, leading to the destruction of Huron villages in July 1648, when Father Antoine Daniel was killed. In March of the following year, a thousand Iroquois descended upon Huronia, took the mission of St. Ignace, then that of St. Louis, where fathers Gabriel Lalemant and Jean de Brébeuf were captured. The latter had returned to Huronia in 1644, while the former had only been working in Huronia since the preceding September. The prisoners were taken to the neighboring village of St. Ignace, where they suffered one of the most horrific tortures in the annals of the Christian church.

The donné Christophe Regnault saw the priests' remains shortly afterward. He described how Brébeuf's legs and arms had been stripped of flesh down to the bone; how huge blisters all over his body bore witness to the pouring of boiling water over the victim in mockery of the baptismal rite; how Brébeuf had been wrapped in resin-soaked bark that had then been set afire to inflict serious burns; how a string of red-hot axeheads had been hung from his neck with manifest results; how his lips had been cut off because he constantly spoke of God; how his body was covered with bruises from a severe beating; how his head was scorched and his breast cut in order to remove his heart.

Father Brébeuf died on the afternoon of 16 March 1649, having been tortured for three hours. Gabriel Lalemant's torture then began and lasted until the next day. Their colleagues collected their remains, interred them under the chapel at Sainte Marie, and then transported them to Quebec in 1650.

Indeed, the Iroquois raid of 16 March 1649 served to convince the Jesuits that they could not resist another onslaught, particularly since many of the Hurons had fled the country in panic, seeking refuge with neighboring nations of Indians. The missionaries therefore burned their own station on 14 June 1649 and retired in the company of a few hundred Hurons to St. Joseph Island (Christian Island) in Georgian Bay. There they endured starvation, epidemics, and further Iroquois depredations for a year; on 10 June 1650 some three hundred Hurons along with the French abandoned the Huron country and headed for Quebec—where, the following spring, they settled on Orléans Island, just below the capital. Huronia was no more. The proud confederacy that had held the Five Nations confederacy in check for some thirty years had fallen victim to disabling epidemics, but particularly to the firearms that the Iroquois had at their disposal in growing numbers after 1640. Indeed, while the French only allowed a few Christian Hurons to obtain muskets, beginning in 1640 the English and Dutch of the Hudson River traded firearms with the Five Nations. This sealed the fate of Huronia.

During their sixteen years of uninterrupted missionary activity in Huronia, the Jesuits obtained very uneven results. It took them three years to baptize their first healthy adult (1637); another four years later Father Brébeuf was still reporting only sixty Christian Hurons. Yet, during those seven years of service, some of the Jesuits, Brébeuf in particular, had been beaten, insulted, threatened, and stoned. Nevertheless they persisted, having mastered the Huron language during their first years of residence. A dramatic turnaround in the situation occurred when the Huron nation began to disintegrate before the Iroquois onslaught after 1647. The missionaries then began reporting sudden increases in the numbers of converts; while the latter had numbered only a scattered few since 1634, in 1649 one Huron in two was a Christian. Indeed, they now converted to Christianity in hundreds and even thousands. For example, during the last terrible year in Huronia (1649–1650), the superior of the Huron mission, Father Paul Ragueneau, reported three thousand baptisms.

One modern historian has written: "Conversion to Christianity was essentially a phenomenon of the moon of wintertime, when ancestral spirits had ceased to perform their expected functions satisfactorily and angel choirs promised to fill a spiritual vacuum."[1]

The author is referring to a carol attributed to Father Brébeuf wherein it is said that "twas in the moon of winter time, when all the birds had fled, that mighty Gitchi Manitou sent angel choirs instead."[2] While there can be no doubt that several conversions of Hurons to Christianity reflected an authentic and sincere religious experience, it is equally beyond doubt that these statistics reveal a sudden and dramatic increase of conversions at the time the Huron nation was being destroyed.

On his return from Huronia in 1650 Father Ragueneau became superior of the entire Canadian mission (1650–1653), replacing Father Jérôme Lalemant, who returned to France. Ragueneau, who had officiated at the funeral of Brébeuf and Lalemant at Sainte Marie on 21 March 1649 and who had ordered the transfer of their bones to Quebec in 1650, decided in 1652 to collect pertinent documents relating to the deaths of all the missionaries of New France who were considered by popular opinion to be martyrs. Nearly three hundred years later, on 29 June 1930, Pope Pius XI declared seven Jesuit missionaries and one donné in New France to be saints. In addition to Gabriel Lalemant and Jean de Brébeuf, they were Brother René Goupil and Father Isaac Jogues, who were killed in the country of the Iroquois, the former on 29 September 1642, the latter on 18 October 1646; Jean de La Lande, a donné who accompanied Jogues and who died with him; Father Antoine Daniel, killed in Huronia during an Iroquois attack on 4 July 1648; Father Noël Chabanel, killed in Huronia by an apostate Huron on 8 December 1649; Father Charles Garnier, killed during an Iroquois attack on a village of the Petun nation in Ontario's Bruce Peninsula on 7 December 1649. In 1940, Pope Pius XII proclaimed these same eight martyrs patrons of Canada.


By the 1650s the Church of New France had the blood of martyrs to nourish its soul. Jesuit priests were still the only clergy in Canada, staffing parishes in all settlements, Indian missions, and the College of Quebec. The Jesuit superior at Quebec administered the church of Canada in lieu of a nonexistent bishop; he therefore wielded considerable authority alongside the colony's governor, becoming an official member of the governing council of Quebec after 1647. During this quarter century of Jesuit clerical monopoly, the Jesuit superiors in Canada were successively Paul Le Jeune (1632–1639), Barthélémy Vimont (1639–1645), Jérôme Lalemant (1645–1650), Paul Ragueneau (1650–1653), François-Joseph Le Mercier (1653–1656), and Jean de Quen (1656–1659). The colony they helped govern was in many respects a theocracy.

The collapse of the mission to the Hurons did not, however, discourage the sons of St. Ignatius. In fact, during the next decades, the scattered remnants of the Huron nation often proved the seeds or firstfruits of budding Christian communities among a host of other nations, those of the Iroquois confederacy included.

Indeed, the Iroquoian linguistic group constituted one of the important linguistic families of Indian nations in eastern North America. One of the two components of this linguistic family was the Huron confederacy that had just been destroyed. The other component was the Iroquois confederacy consisting of five nations residing in the area west of Lake Champlain and south and north of Lake Ontario. The Iroquois confederacy was made up of five largely autonomous nations—the Mohawk, the Oneida, the Onondaga, the Cayuga, and the Seneca. In the 1720s a sixth nation, the Tuscarora, joined them from the south.

In 1653, a temporary respite in the French–Iroquois war was the opening so many Jesuits had ardently prayed for. Governor Jean de Lauson, in office from 1651 to 1656, immediately sent Jesuit father Simon Le Moyne as peace ambassador to the Iroquois. Between 1654 and 1662, Le Moyne was to make similar journeys no less than six times, always endeavoring to seal a peace treaty, always at the risk of his life, frequently facing imminent torture and death. On his first journey in 1654, he arranged with the Onondaga nation to send Jesuit missionaries to them.

So it was that fathers Pierre Chaumonot and Claude Dablon worked in Onondaga country, south of Lake Ontario, from September 1655 to March 1656, when Dablon returned to Quebec heralding the opening of the Onondaga mission. Jesuit superior Le Mercier thereupon organized a major missionary expedition to the land of the Onondagas. On 17 May 1656, some fifty French workmen set out in the company of four Jesuit priests (J. Le Mercier, R. Ménard, C. Dablon, J. Frémin) and two brothers (A. Brouet and J. Boursier) to join Chaumonot in Onondaga country on the Oswego River south of Lake Ontario. They planned the construction of a major missionary station similar to Huronia's ill-fated Fort Sainte Marie: Sainte Marie of Gannentaha. The mission had been in existence nearly two years when the French learned that the Indians planned to entrap and massacre them all. In great secrecy they abandoned the post on 20 March 1658, arriving in Montreal on 23 April. It seems that the more easterly Mohawk nation first determined that it was not to their advantage to have a mission among the Onondagas and then convinced the latter to cooperate in eradicating it. The first organized mission to the Iroquois had failed. Over the next three years several visits by Father Le Moyne did not succeed in changing the Mohawks' minds.

The work of the Jesuits in New France is relatively well known thanks to the initiative of Father Paul Le Jeune, the Canadian mission's first superior. Upon his arrival in the colony in 1632, Le Jeune reported to his superiors in France on the journey and the country. His provincial superior in Paris decided to make the report public, starting a tradition of annual missionary reports destined for widespread publication in France; the series of Jesuit *Relations* lasted until 1673. Read in pulpits, convents, and monasteries, their purpose was to elicit spiritual and financial support for the Jesuit mission in New France.

Upon the failure of the Iroquois mission in 1658, only eight years after the collapse of the Huron mission, several Jesuits returned to France. At the time, in addition to the Miscou mission on the Atlantic coast of New Brunswick, there were Jesuit stations at Tadoussac, Quebec, and Trois Rivières. Indeed, the mission at Sillery had failed while the Sulpician Fathers had taken over in Montreal (see below); in fact, even the parishes of Trois Rivières and Quebec were shortly to be handed over to secular priests, leaving the Jesuits with Indian missions only in addition to the College of Quebec.

The nineteenth-century American historian Francis Parkman wrote that "Spanish civilization crushed the Indian; English civilization scorned and neglected him; French civilization embraced and cherished him."[3] Whatever the truth of Parkman's famous dictum, Jesuits were largely responsible for the embrace.

## THE CHURCH OF THE ST. LAWRENCE VALLEY

While the heroic Jesuits were the only male clerics in the colony between 1632 and 1657, they were accompanied by two groups of nuns whose Christian witness was as impressive as that of the more aggressive Jesuits. It was this handful of dedicated women who provided the schooling to young girls and the nursing care to all. The apostolate of the teacher Marguerite Bourgeois, proclaimed a saint in 1984, was closely matched by nurse Jeanne Mance and the mystic Marie de l'Incarnation.

The wave of mysticism that swept through France in the first half of the seventeenth century had direct and immediate repercussions in Canada. In 1635 Marie-Madeleine de Chauvigny de La Peltrie (1603–1671) was a thirty-three-year-old widow drawn to a life of prayer and good works. When she read Father Le Jeune's *Relation* of 1635, she was immediately moved to support the founding of a convent of teaching sisters in Quebec. She consecrated her person and her not inconsiderable fortune to the conversion of New France's native people.

However, Madame de La Peltrie soon fell seriously ill. She then vowed to St. Joseph that if she was cured, she would go to Canada, build a house under his patronage, and devote herself to the care of Indian girls. The very next day, she was as fit as a fiddle. Another obstacle emerged. Her father was determined to marry off his daughter anew and threatened to disinherit her if she refused. The woman therefore organized a fictitious second marriage with a willing accomplice, satisfying her father—who died shortly afterward. Before securing her rights as an heiress, Madame de La Peltrie still had to overcome the objections of other family members; on appeal, the parliament of Rouen declared in her favor.

Her spiritual advisers told De La Peltrie that an Ursuline nun from Tours was also desperate to get to Quebec in the hope of opening a girls' school. She went to Tours, met the woman, and soon came to an agreement with her for a joint project in New France. Indeed, Marie Guyart saw in the young widow the fulfillment of a dream of hers.

Marie Guyart (1599–1672) had an even more colorful story than her new companion. Although drawn to the spiritual life as a young girl, at seventeen she married Claude Martin, a union that did not seem to be blessed in heaven. Two years later she was widowed, bankrupt, and the mother of a six-month-old child. While putting her life back together, she became more and more interested in a cloistered life, particularly after experiencing a "conversion" on 24

March 1620. Nevertheless she continued working in a relative's carriage business, rising by 1625 to the position of general manager of the enterprise. Meanwhile, her mystical experiences continued, confirming her in her determination to seek refuge in a cloister. On 25 January 1631 she left her elderly father, entrusted her twelve-year-old son Claude to the care of her sister, and entered the novitiate of the Ursulines of Tours.

In pronouncing her vows in 1633, the widow Martin chose the religious name Marie de l'Incarnation. Over the next few years a series of dreams showed her a vast country, named it Canada, and instructed her to go there to build a house for Jesus and Mary. The reading of the Jesuit *Relations* clarified the divine imperative, and the meeting with De La Peltrie made it incontrovertible. After adding two other Ursuline sisters to their group, one from Tours, the other from Dieppe, the two mystical and enterprising women set sail from Dieppe aboard the good ship *St. Joseph* on 4 May 1639.

On board the same ship were three nursing sisters belonging to the Augustinian Hospitalers of Mercy (*Hospitalières de la Miséricorde*) of the Hôtel-Dieu of Dieppe. Anne Le Cointre was twenty-nine, Marie Forestier was twenty-eight, and Marie Guenet, elected first superior of Quebec's Hôtel-Dieu hospital, was twenty-two years old. The three women had been recruited by the duchesse d'Aiguillon, a niece of Richelieu and a French benefactress who had secured from the Company of New France, in 1637, a plot of land in the heart of Quebec for the purpose of building a hospital. Arriving in Quebec on 1 August 1639, the three nurses were immediately thrust into caring for the victims of the smallpox epidemic of that year, particularly among the Indians of the village of Sillery. The disease raged for six months, keeping the nuns fully engaged; they thereupon decided, with the assistance of two more women who had arrived in 1640, to establish their hospital in Sillery, according to the wishes of their benefactress. While in Sillery, a short distance west of the town of Quebec, the hospital sisters even taught some classes to a few Indian girls who could not attend the Ursuline school in Quebec. However, Iroquois raids soon forced them back to the town of Quebec, where they occupied a new building in 1646. Quebec's historic Hôtel-Dieu hospital had been born.

Arriving in Quebec on 1 August 1639, the Ursulines (under the leadership of Marie de l'Incarnation) occupied a small house in the post's lower town, awaiting their move in 1642 into a magnificent three-story stone convent on the heights of Quebec. The building measured ninety-two feet by twenty-eight feet. When it burned to the ground eight years later, Marie de l'Incarnation rebuilt, while continuing to cultivate her kitchen garden, exploit her farm, and advise governors, Jesuits, and other leaders of Quebec society.

The Ursulines were teachers and were hard at work within days of setting foot in Quebec. They opened a boarding school for French and Indian girls, fees being paid in kind, given the scarcity of money in the colony. Thus a student's fees often included cords of firewood, pots of butter, pigs, fish, and the like. The initial score of boarders eventually grew to more than a hundred.

The girls were taught reading, writing, and various other skills considered important for a young woman.

Indian girls proved impossible to frenchify, Marie noted, writing in 1668 that of the hundred Indian girls who had passed through the Ursuline convent in Quebec, the sisters had barely managed to "civilize" one. Mother Superior never ceased trying, however. She mastered the Indian languages to the point of writing dictionaries and catechisms in the Algonquin and Iroquois languages. After an apostolate of thirty-three years in Canada, she died on 30 April 1672, at the age of seventy-two, proudest of her son Claude, who had entered a Benedictine monastery in 1641 and become its superior in 1652.

Marie de l'Incarnation's correspondence and writings show her to be one of the Christian church's foremost mystics. Five years after her death, Quebec's Bishop Laval wrote in glowing terms of her virtue and life totally committed to Christ, while France's famous Jacques Bossuet, bishop of Meaux, labeled her the Teresa of Avila of the New World.

While the nuns were busy teaching and nursing in Quebec and the Jesuit missionaries were spilling their blood in the land of the Huron and that of the Iroquois, another handful of pious French Catholics were founding the mission of Ville-Marie of Montreal, a new Jerusalem in the wilderness whose emplacement seriously threatened the Iroquois' river route into Canada.

The 1630s were a privileged time for those in direct communication with God. While the widows De La Peltrie and Martin were being instructed to establish a boarding school in Canada, Jérôme Le Royer de La Dauversière (1597–1659), a humble tax collector in the town of La Flèche in Anjou had a vision instructing him to establish a congregation of nursing sisters. This was in 1632 or 1633. Having managed to do so in 1636, Le Royer enjoyed a second vision advising him to work for the Indians of New France. After obtaining counsel from the Jesuit fathers at the College of La Flèche, his alma mater, the pious father of six journeyed to Paris in order to establish a company capable of directing the foundation of a mission in Canada. There it was that in February 1639 Le Royer met Father Jean-Jacques Olier, a thirty-one-year-old converted man of the world who had also been endeavoring since 1636 to work for the conversion of infidels.

Together Olier and Le Royer planned a Canadian mission, including the purchase of the island of Montreal (August 1640) and the establishment of a company of rich and influential men and women to support their unique project: the foundation of a colony devoted exclusively to the glory of God and the conversion of infidels. The members of the company soon subscribed some seventy-five thousand livres for the new colony. The initiative was facilitated by the fact that both Olier and Le Royer were members of the powerful and secret Compagnie du Saint-Sacrement and were able to obtain the support of its leader baron de Renty.

To lead the colony, they chose Paul de Chomedey de Maisonneuve (1612–1676), a twenty-eight-year-old former soldier who was looking for ways to better devote his life to God. Jesuit Father Charles Lalemant, Jérôme's brother, proposed his name to Le Royer. The two-ship expedition set sail from La Rochelle on 9 May 1641, carrying fifty-six people; arriving in Tadoussac the following August, the founders of Montreal had to winter at Quebec, delaying their Montreal foundation until the spring of 1642.

Aboard Maisonneuve's ships in 1641 was Jeanne Mance (1606–1673), a woman who had long been involved in charitable works in her native Langres in Champagne. She was part of a family of six brothers and five sisters. Upon hearing of the devotion of Jesuits, Ursulines, and Hospitalers, in 1641 Jeanne Mance felt the urge to work in New France. A Recollect priest introduced her to Angélique Faure, widow of Claude de Bullion, former French superintendent of finance. After several meetings, the wealthy Madame de Bullion asked Jeanne to establish a hospital in New France, one that would be paid for by the rich widow, who insisted, however, that her identity be kept secret. Having arrived in La Rochelle, on her way to Canada, Jeanne Mance just "happened" to meet Le Royer in the church of the Jesuits, the Lord allowing them to recognize each other. The pious woman accepted Le Royer's invitation to become bursar and nurse of the Montreal expedition.

Located some 150 miles upriver from Quebec, the island of Montreal had been occupied by Huron Indians in 1535 when Jacques Cartier had visited their village of Hochelaga and named the mountain of Montreal. Indian wars during the second half of the sixteenth century served to depopulate the area; when Samuel de Champlain visited the island anew in 1603 he found it deserted. After founding Quebec in 1608, Champlain returned to the area in 1611, planted wheat, and initiated an annual fur-trading fair with the Indians that would last until 1618, when Trois Rivières replaced Montreal as the site of the annual fair.

When the new arrivals from France resisted the attempts of Quebec's establishment to have them settle instead on nearby Orléans Island, Quebec's governor Charles Huault de Montmagny and the Jesuit superior Barthélémy Vimont visited the island of Montreal in October 1641 and chose the most favorable site for the colony. They returned with the first settlers in May 1642, the governor officially transferring the property into Maisonneuve's hands, while Father Vimont celebrated the area's first mass accompanied by the singing of the hymn *Veni Creator*, followed by the exposition of the Blessed Sacrament. The date was 18 May 1642. The Montreal epic had begun, considered by many a "foolish enterprise" because of the exposure of the isolated colony to the possible depredations of marauding Indians.

Reinforced by another twelve settlers in August 1642, the tiny palisaded colony of some seventy people was almost flooded out in the new year; Maisonneuve thereupon vowed, if deliverance was obtained, to carry a large cross up neighboring Mount Royal and erect it there as a reminder of the Lord's salvation. He did so, accompanied by the colony's two Jesuit chaplains, thus determining the destination of pilgrimages that would last for several years. The priests worked out of a small chapel dedicated to Notre Dame, the patron of the island and the settlement of Ville-Marie.

Activity intensified with the arrival of another forty settlers and soldiers in 1643, accompanied by the first guerrilla raids by the Iroquois, a threat that would continue with little respite for the next quarter-century. The Mohawks in particular were feeling cornered, for the new colony of Montreal came close on the heels of the construction by the French, in 1642, of Fort Richelieu at the mouth of the Richelieu River.

In the fall of 1643 the widow De La Peltrie returned to Quebec, whence she had come with the first settlers eighteen months earlier. Her return to Quebec ensured the survival of the Ursuline convent and school, which depended on her financial support. Meanwhile, Governor Montmagny informed Maisonneuve and Mance that the widow Bullion had made twelve thousand livres available for the construction of a hospital in Montreal; the building was erected in 1644.

For more than twenty years Montreal was a beleaguered outpost, barely surviving constant Iroquois raids. The settlers used trained dogs to detect the presence of Iroquois raiders who frequently lay in ambush in the surrounding forest, waiting to pounce on an unsuspecting victim tilling his field or cutting firewood. Although the raids diminished in 1644–1646 and again in 1655–1656, numbers of French men and women were killed, scalped, or sometimes taken prisoner by marauding parties of Iroquois. Indeed, a family never knew whether a husband and father would return home after a day in the fields or forest.

Nevertheless, Maisonneuve and Mance coped, frequently journeying to France to obtain more money, settlers, and soldiers. The widow Bullion continued to inject large sums of money into the hospital, some of it, loaned to Maisonneuve, serving to hire more than a hundred men who arrived in 1653. They were the colony's salvation.

The reinforcements of 1653 included another young woman who would in turn glorify the annals of Canadian history. Marguerite Bourgeois (1620–1700), born in Troyes, was one of a group of girls associated with the cloistered Sisters of Notre-Dame, although not a nun herself. The nun directing this confraternity was Maisonneuve's sister. Inevitably Marguerite was informed about Canada; she even met Maisonneuve when he was visiting Troyes in 1652. The founder of Montreal accepted Marguerite's offer to come to teach school in the infant colony.

Upon arriving in Montreal in September 1653 and not finding any available school-age children, Marguerite became factotum of the settlers, particularly of Maisonneuve himself. In addition to caring for the governor's household, the pious woman also bore witness to her faith. She it was who organized, in 1657, a collective effort for the construction of Montreal's first stone church, dedicated to Notre Dame de Bon Secours.

She still aspired to teach, however. On 30 April 1658 she welcomed her first pupils into her new school, a stable given to her by Maisonneuve. The school proved so successful that Bourgeois returned to France the same year to recruit other women to help her out. She returned the following year with three new teachers and a female servant. She was thereafter capable not only of teaching school but also of receiving in her house the orphaned girls King Louis XIV sent to New France to serve as mates to the woman-hungry male colony. Some eight hundred of these king's girls (*filles du roi*) were sent to Canada in the decade preceding 1672. In Montreal, they were met at dockside by Bourgeois, taken to her house, initiated into the duties of a housewife and then presented to the numerous settlers desperate for a wife. Indeed, a girl rarely waited more than two weeks before being spoken for.

After ten years of such activities, Montreal's residents referred to the Bourgeois group as the "girls of the Congregation." With Bishop Laval's backing, Marguerite thereupon went to France in 1670, seeking royal letters patent that would ensure the continuity of her band of women. These were obtained in May 1671. Five years later, Bishop Laval acknowledged them as a congregation of "secular" girls devoted to teaching and subject to the local bishop. Widespread expansion of the new congregation followed as a girls' boarding school was founded in Montreal (1676), followed by a housekeeping school and then by a chain of small parish or village schools in the Canadian countryside, the town of Quebec included. Bourgeois resisted the later pressures of Bishop Saint-Vallier of Quebec to annex her group to the Ursuline sisters. Indeed, on 1 July 1698, by making simple vows of poverty, chastity, and obedience, her women became part of a new religious congregation.

However, this Congregation of Notre-Dame was a secular congregation as opposed to a cloistered one, a bold innovation for religious women in the late seventeenth century. The sisters were therefore not bound by the many restrictions imposed on cloistered women; they were free to travel to their widely scattered schools dressed in a habit similar to that of many women of the day. When Bourgeois died in 1700, her followers numbered forty, the beginnings of one of North America's most important congregations of women. The founder was declared blessed by Pope Pius XII in 1950 and declared a saint by Pope John Paul II on the occasion of his visit to Canada in 1984.

On the same ship that carried Marguerite Bourgeois and her helpmates to Canada in 1659 were Jeanne Mance and three sisters belonging to the Hospitalers of Saint Joseph from the town of Laflèche, the congregation founded by Le Royer de la Dauversière in 1636. Jeanne Mance was driven to seek assistance in managing her hospital when she broke an arm and dislocated her wrist as a result of a fall on the ice. She thereupon went to France in 1658 in the company of her good friend Marguerite Bourgeois.

In France all of Mance's wishes were fulfilled. Not only did she recruit three sisters with the help of De La Dauversière, but she also obtained another donation from Madame de Bullion for the support of her Hôtel-Dieu hospital and the care of the sisters. Moreover, while praying in the Sulpician chapel in Paris, Jeanne lay her fractured limb alongside the heart of the deceased Father Jean-Jacques Olier (d. 1657) and was miraculously cured. Wonders never ceased to happen in seventeenth-century France.

In September 1659, when the town of Quebec numbered some eight hundred souls, the arrival from France of more than a hundred new people raised the population of the still-beleaguered town of Montreal from three hundred to four hundred. The Hospitalers of St. Joseph, this first congregation of nuns to work in the colony of Montreal, was seconded by Marguerite Bourgeois's group of women who would soon become nuns themselves. However, the situation was becoming more complex on the ecclesiastical front.

## THE GENTLEMEN OF SAINT-SULPICE

The leading role of Jean-Jacques Olier in the founding of Montreal led Maisonneuve to invite his band of priests to come to work in the colony. The Jesuits had been in charge of the Montreal mission from the outset, as they were of all other Canadian missions. However, Maisonneuve and Mance were dissatisfied with the limited number of priests assigned to Montreal; they also had to contend with frequent opposition to their aspirations by the governors of Quebec, a town that tended to see Montreal as an unwelcome economic and political rival. Given the key role played by the Jesuit superior in Quebec's governing circles, the followers of St. Ignatius were also suspect.

So it was that on the occasion of a visit to France between 1655 and 1657 Maisonneuve obtained the services of the Gentlemen of Saint-Sulpice, a society of secular priests founded by Father Olier in 1641 to serve as agents of the renewal of the French clergy. In 1657 this band of priests was directing seven seminaries in France. By entrusting Montreal to the Sulpicians, the directors of the Society of Montreal, the company that owned the island and the seigniorial rights in the colony, hoped to kill two birds with one stone: They could establish a seminary in Montreal and obtain the appointment of a bishop.

To lead the small band of Sulpicians he was sending to Canada, Olier chose a former classmate and close collaborator, Gabriel Thubières de Lévy de Queylus (1612–1677), a priest who also happened to be a member of the Society of Montreal. He was accompanied by the priests Dominique Galinier and Gabriel Souart and the deacon Antoine d'Allet.

The men sent by Olier were often exceptional in their professional qualifications, not to mention their personal wealth. Indeed the leader De Queylus had become the prime underwriter of the Society of Montreal; his exclusion from Canada in 1661 induced the Society of Montreal, on 9 March 1663, to transfer its seigniorial and ownership rights in Montreal to the Paris Seminary of Saint-Sulpice.

Given De Queylus's long absences from the colony, Father Souart (1611–

1691) proved invaluable as his lieutenant. Upon his arrival in the summer of 1657, the former physician replaced the Jesuits as first pastor of Montreal, oversaw the election of the first board of parish trustees, and became superior of the Sulpician seminary in Montreal (1661–1668; 1674–1676). He also served as chaplain to the Congregation of Notre-Dame and to the Hôtel-Dieu sisters, while teaching school to children after 1668. He was pastor of the outpost during its most difficult years, when two of his priests (Le Maistre and Vignal) were assassinated by the Iroquois (1661) and a great earthquake shook the entire valley of the St. Lawrence (1663). Souart was even more wealthy than his superior De Queylus. He subsidized many religious and charitable institutions, including not only those of Montreal but also the Hôtel-Dieu of Quebec.

Father De Queylus was soon at the center of a protracted ecclesiastical jurisdictional dispute that would bedevil the first ten years of his association with Canada. The question was who was empowered to govern the church of New France. In the early years of the Canadian mission, the Recollect, Jesuit, and Capuchin religious orders were empowered to direct missions by virtue of longstanding privileges enjoyed by their orders. When the Holy See established the Roman congregation *Propaganda Fide* in 1622, the jurisdictional waters became muddied, for while Rome would slowly claim authority over overseas mission lands, countries like France were used to having a national church ruled by French prelates, under the patronage of the crown, with little interference from Rome.

Until the late 1640s, as noted above, Jesuits in Canada worked on the basis of their order's own authority. However, given that most Canadian settlers left French ports in the diocese of Rouen, the archbishop of Rouen had become accustomed to give ecclesiastical faculties and authorizations to departing missionaries. In 1649, he even had done so in favor of the Jesuits, for on 30 April of that year he appointed the Jesuit superior in Quebec his grand vicar in Canada. However, the Jesuits were well aware of the sensitivity of many on this question, for the pope, the crown, and the French church all felt that their rights were at stake; the Society of Jesus therefore kept its Rouen appointment a secret until 1653.

So it was that Father De Queylus sailed from Nantes on 17 May 1657 with an official appointment from the archbishop of Rouen as his grand vicar for New France, an appointment identical to that held by Father De Quen, the Jesuit superior in Quebec. Upon his arrival in Quebec on 29 July 1657 De Quen temporarily accepted De Queylus's overall authority. Once the latter had gone upriver to Montreal, however, a dispute broke out between the two men over the appointment of the pastor of the parish of Quebec. The dispute grew into a comic-opera farce, as both men attacked each other from their respective pulpits; they even ended up in court quarreling over property rights. Thereupon the archbishop of Rouen issued new letters, dated 30 March 1658, making both De Queylus and De Quen grand vicars in their respective spheres, the first in the island of Montreal, the second in the rest of the colony.

The dispute seemed settled, whereupon a new and more serious jurisdictional entanglement appeared, for New France was about to welcome its first bishop.


By the late 1650s, something had changed in the Christian story of New France. For twenty-five years Canada had indeed appeared to be a new Jerusalem, awed by the mystical endeavors of Marie de l'Incarnation, inspired by the apostolic witness of nursing and teaching sisters, and humbled by the martyrdoms of Jesuit missionaries. In the eyes of a seventeenth-century Canadian French Catholic, the Kingdom of God might well be just around the next bend in the road.

However, while Mance, Bourgeois, and others continued their noble endeavors, a new kind of pettiness also seemed to be emerging, as shown in the ecclesiastical quarrel between Jesuit Father De Quen and Sulpician Father De Queylus. The age of heroes and martyrs seemed to be coming to an end.

# 11

## THE ENCOUNTER OF FRENCH
## AND AMERINDIAN CULTURES

While French-American Christianity was slowly putting down roots, painfully in the Caribbean and Acadia, joyously and heroically in Canada, it was all the while encountering a wide range of Amerindian cultures whose very existence would challenge many of the basic tenets of French Catholic Christianity. The problems both parties experienced were compounded by the devastating effects of the brandy trade on the native people and the changing policy of the French statesmen, missionaries, and churchmen regarding the desirability of "civilizing" the Amerindians before evangelizing them.

### THE NATIVE PEOPLE OF EASTERN NORTH AMERICA

In the early seventeenth century, the vast territory stretching from Acadia in the East to the upper Mississippi and Lake Superior basin in the West included a unique mosaic of Amerindian nations, tribes, and bands that is difficult to describe. With the exception of the Inuit (Eskimos) of Canada's far North and the extinct Beothuk of Newfoundland, both of whom constituted distinct linguistic groups, the Amerindians of northeastern North America were divided into two major linguistic groups, Algonkian and Iroquoian. The former occupied most of the territory north of the St. Lawrence River and Acadia, where members of the Abenaki confederacy (Micmacs, Malecites, Abenaki, and others) became lasting allies of the French. Other nations in this Algonkian linguistic group included the Montagnais and the Naskapis on the north shore of the St. Lawrence, the Algonquins in the Ottawa River valley, the Nipissings in north-central Ontario, the Chippewas or Ojibwas on the north shore of lakes Huron and Superior, and the Crees, who occupied most of the land in the Hudson Bay watershed. The Chippewa nation was in turn subdivided into four

176

tribes: the Ojibwas of Lake Superior, the Mississaugas of Manitoulin Island, the Ottawas of Georgian Bay, and the Potewatomis in today's state of Michigan.

The Iroquoian linguistic family occupied lands west of the Richelieu River and Lake Champlain, north and south of Lake Ontario. It included the Five Nations confederacy of upper New York state: the Mohawks, the Oneidas, the Onondagas, the Cayugas, and the Senecas. A sixth Iroquois nation, the Tuscaroras, appeared south of Lake Ontario in the 1720s. The four tribes of the Huron confederacy, located in south-central Ontario, were also of Iroquoian linguistic affiliation, as were the Petun (Tobacco) nation of Ontario's Bruce peninsula, the Neutrals of the north shore of Lake Erie, and the Cat nation (Eries) south of Lake Erie.

With few exceptions, the nations of the Algonkian linguistic family remained allies of the French; those of Iroquoian linguistic stock divided their allegiance to the white man. While the Five Nations supported the English, the Hurons were staunch allies of the French, usually supported by the Petuns and Eries and sometimes by the Neutrals.

The Algonkians were hunting and fishing peoples, nomadic in habitat as they followed game across their vast territories. The Iroquoian nations were more stable, cultivating the land and harvesting such crops as corn, tobacco, and vegetables. They consequently built large villages that frequently sheltered several hundred people and remained in a given location for ten to fifteen years, whereupon the entire village moved because of the inevitable depletion of fish, game, and firewood in the immediate area. They lived in longhouses that sheltered from ten to twenty families. Algonkian bands lived in wigwams that were easily dismantled, and invented ingenious means of transport such as birch-bark canoes, toboggans, and snowshoes. It is from the Algonkians that the French learned techniques for living off the land and surviving in the wilderness, skills that proved indispensable in the fur trade and in the wars against the English.

## INITIAL ENCOUNTERS BETWEEN FRENCH AND AMERINDIAN

From the earliest contact between European fishermen, sailors, traders, and explorers, half-breed children appeared. With few exceptions they were children of white men and native women, were raised by their mothers, and were assimilated into the native bands. While some of this miscegenation resulted from casual liaisons between visiting Europeans and native women, once white men came to Canada to stay, more permanent relationships developed. For example, beginning in the 1650s, a growing number of young Frenchmen and Canadians became *coureurs de bois*, spending most of their time traveling and living in the forests of North America and assimilating into the native way of life. They soon adopted the native custom of being accompanied on their travels by native women who performed most of the chores, carrying burdens, cutting firewood, and "consoling" their men. They had been preceded since the earliest days of the colony by young men like Etienne Brûlé (1592–1633) who, as early as 1610, was sent by Champlain to live with the Algonquins of the Ottawa River in order to learn their language and facilitate trade and communications. Another interpreter was Nicolas Marsolet (d. 1677), accused by Champlain (as Brûlé had been) of sliding into licentiousness and debauchery while living with the Indians. Another such interpreter of the early years was Jean Nicollet de Belleborne (1598–1642).

Although Nicollet managed to emerge from more than a decade of Indian living with his reputation intact in spite of the fact that he may have fathered the child of a Nipissing woman, most of these interpreters "went native," as Brûlé had done, bringing down upon themselves the wrath of the priests in the colony. Indeed, the native life-style and French civilization were poles apart. During the first quarter-century of French settlement, the clash of native and French cultures was minimal, given the small number of French settlers. However, once the French had reoccupied Canada in 1632, devastating epidemics brought the question to a boil.

Before the arrival of the white man, the native people of northeastern North America enjoyed good health. Epidemics were unheard of, and minor illnesses were cured with the use of herbs, ointments, potions, and the widespread use of sweathouses or saunas; gout, fevers, tuberculosis, and rheumatism were unknown. Moreover, the personal hygiene of Amerindians was superior to that of the French, who considered washing immodest and unhealthy. In fact, French medical practices (bleedings and purges in particular) were never renowned for their curative results.

The situation changed dramatically in the wake of regular native–white contact. Tuberculosis, scarlet fever, chickenpox, typhoid, influenza, smallpox, measles, diphtheria—in sum, a wide range of new diseases suddenly cut like a scythe into native nations. Between 1634 and 1640 more than 50 percent of the thirty-thousand-strong Huron confederacy was decimated by epidemics of measles or smallpox. Simultaneously, epidemics were reported among the Montagnais (1635), the Ottawas and Iroquois (1637), the Neutrals, Petuns, Nipissings, and Algonquins (1638), the Abenakis (1645), and the Illinois (1694). Amerindians were not immune to these diseases of the white man. An adversary bent on genocide could not have been more successful in achieving the decimation of the Indian people.

Given their evangelical zeal, French Catholic missionaries were often the first, indeed the only, white men to take up residence among the native people. This also put them at the heart of native concerns, for the epidemics seemed to arrive in the Indian lands on the heels of the missionaries. Brébeuf and his colleagues had been in Huronia less than a year when the native people began to die; the same was true elsewhere. Desperate to find an explanation for the scourge, a growing number of Amerindians began to identify the source of infection with the doctrines, the rites, the objects, or the persons of the evangelical workers. When a missionary hurried into the cabin of a dying Indian in order to baptize him, death frequently followed and the terrified villagers felt that either the rite of baptism, the visit of the priest, or even the holy water or Latin prayers were magical rites that killed. The mass, prayers said behind closed doors, images, blessings, the sign of the cross all became suspect. Catholic spells and charms, cast or carried by the black-robed heralds of death, became symbols of terror in the eyes of desperate Hurons, Montagnais, and Iroquois, most of whom were already grieving the loss of a loved one if not of an entire family. The fact that the missionaries themselves were prone to explain disease and death as punishments from God did not help matters.

What tended to confirm the Indians' conviction that the black robes were to blame for their troubles was that Frenchmen who fell ill tended to recover; Amerindians did not. When the missionaries advised their people not to return to a specific area where an epidemic raged, native people concluded that this proved that the disease was under the control of the priest because he knew where it was located.

The devastating epidemics of the 1630s and 1640s were thus the first episode in the clash of Amerindian and French cultures. When the dust settled, a proud and mighty Huron nation had been ground into political, demographic, and military insignificance; the Iroquois raids of the late 1640s merely confirmed the destruction of the Hurons. Willy-nilly Catholic missionaries participated in this cultural genocide, as did the traders and explorers, all germ-laden carriers of European infections. They usually did not realize that French European civilization was part and parcel of the gospel they preached.

## NATIVE RELIGIONS VERSUS FRENCH CATHOLICISM

The religions of native North Americans were as diverse as the tribes that lived them. More than two score tribes inhabited the immense territory that was part of New France. Each of these nations had its religion (or, better, a world view) that was not limited to "this-worldly" as opposed to "other-worldly" explanations of reality. An underlying assumption of Amerindian religions was that human life was on a continuum with the rest of the natural world, the whole being in equilibrium. The purpose of religious practices or of spiritual interventions was to maintain or restore that balance by combating evil spirits or placating the spirits.

While the spirit world may have been familiar in religions that were part of everyday life, the spirit world was simultaneously extraordinary and awesome. Myths pointed to a primordial time, and there was all-pervasive power inherent in the world. The world was also fundamentally ambiguous, the figure of the trickster or culture hero representing the ambivalence as a powerful hero who sometimes stumbled.

For the Canadian Indian, the spiritual world was inextricably tied to one's nation, which in turn was closely bound to a territory, the land with its rivers and lakes, mountains and swamps, all washed in rain or blanketed in snow, warmed and lit by the sun, the moon, and the stars. All dimensions of reality had a spiritual face in close communion with the life-sustaining and all-encompassing land. Some tribes believed in a pervasive spiritual power (Orenda for the Iroquois, Manitou for the Algonkian) that was sometimes personalized into figures like Gitchi Manitou among the latter. This belief allowed some missionaries to speak of the Great Spirit and proceeded to transform it into a precursor of the God of the Christians. Other Indian nations appeared to have hardly any religion, early European visitors noting that they had no churches, no worship, and no religious ceremonies.

Apart from the extraordinary spiritual powers, Amerindian cultures and religions were peopled by a wide variety of mythological figures, usually represented as animated aspects of the natural world such as the wind, animals, insects, rivers, and so on. Their story was necessarily learned by word of mouth, writing being an unknown skill among Indian people. Morality and spirituality were an integral dimension of these mythologiconatural stories.

Amerindians also expressed their religious beliefs through ritual enactments of masked plays, through prayer, vision quests, hunting and planting rites, and shamanistic performances. Given that they had no sacred texts, written histories, or doctrinal statements, various religious symbols such as medicine bundles, or symbolic actions such as the Sun dance became privileged vehicles of religious meaning. Shamans, sometimes called sorcerers by Christian missionaries, were usually the spiritual leaders of native bands, their foremost function being to heal.

Dreams were often the preferred means whereby Amerindians communicated with the spirits and received insight and instructions. Once a dream was interpreted and understood, its instructions were carefully carried out. For example, an Iroquois traveled several hundred miles to murder his wife, as instructed in a dream.

In accord with their holistic understanding of a world in equilibrium, some Indian nations (the Iroquois, for example) saw nature as the scene of conflict between opposing forces of good and evil, represented in Iroquois mythology as twin brothers, one bent on good, the other on mischief. It does not seem as if one power was necessarily destined to overcome the other.

When French Catholic missionaries encountered these religions, they inevitably sought points of contact with the Christian faith. In addition to transforming Manitou or Orenda into the Christian God, some were inclined to read God and Satan into the dualistic story of the good and evil brothers, while others tried to use the figure of the trickster as prefiguring the "mediator" role of Jesus Christ.

These missionaries were not always aware of the profound difference in the thrust of Indian and Christian religions. The world of the Christian is a provisional "valley of tears" located on a time line that will end with a final judgment day inaugurating eternal life in either heaven or hell—a life of eternal bliss or damnation. Every Christian religious doctrine, rite, or practice is intended to prepare either the individual or the community for this afterlife whose onset is imminent. In contrast, the world of the Indian was already whole, complete and balanced, the purpose of rituals, ceremonies, incantations, and communication with the spirits being to maintain the cosmic balance that was already in place.

While the Christian was urged to repent and change or turn away from this world in order to realize the Kingdom of God, the Indian sought to ensure that everything remain in harmony so that his hunting, fishing, or military expeditions might be successful while his or her self and family continued to enjoy good health and prosperity. While the Christian was driven to change reality, the Indian was driven to maintain it. While the Indian's basic religious symbol was the circle, the Christian's was the cross, both arms of which pointed away from the present and whose story was an eloquent condemnation of this "valley of tears."


One native custom common to most Iroquoian and Algonkian nations was the torture of captives, a practice long denounced as barbaric by white men, although the latter indulged in equally atrocious activities in seventeenth-century Europe. Indeed, while Iroquois, Huron, and Algonkian nations tortured prisoners, Europeans abused, exploited, and frequently killed thousands of slaves, allowed horrible conditions in their galley fleets and prisons, and indulged in wholesale rape and drunken orgies in conquered countries and sometimes in their own. In Europe, judicial torture and capital punishment could be horribly cruel undertakings. Accused sorcerers could be eaten alive by starving rats, dismembered and slaughtered by enraged dogs or pigs, tortured on rack and wheel, beaten in public, hanged, or have their entrails burned before their very eyes. In fact, the sixteenth-century French author Michel de Montaigne considered that the French surpassed the Amerindians in barbarity.

The torture of captives among the Indian people of North America had a religious and social significance. Upon conquering an enemy village, all tribes immediately slaughtered the crippled, the aged, and pregnant women because they would slow the victors' return to their home village. Prisoners were tortured en route because the Amerindians believed that there was a direct correlation between the extent of their cruelty and their success. Their religious belief was to the effect that the reenactment of the victory over the enemy would ensure the repetition of the victory in the future. Upon arriving back in the victors' home village, the prisoners initially had to run a gauntlet of natives armed with knives, sticks, and firebrands. Then the native council decided whether the prisoner would be adopted by a family, made a slave, or condemned to death.

The death penalty was preceded and accompanied by many forms of torture. Fingernails were torn out, the scalp was lifted, skin was peeled off, hot axeheads were hung on the victim, nerves were pulled out, boiling water was poured on the prisoner, belts and collars of resin were set afire on him; in the end, the prisoner's head was cut off, his belly was cut open and/or his heart was cut out, and men, women, and children feasted on parts of the dead body. Many and various refinements were added to these acts of barbarism, the prisoner's sexual organs frequently being the object of particular attention.

The proceedings had a sacrificial aspect, the torturers following predetermined procedures while the victim danced and sang his death song in defiance of the aggressors. Indeed, in spite of the horrors and the excruciating pain, a proud Amerindian never whined or complained under torture. Jesuit missionaries learned to do likewise. It all culminated in a cannibalistic feast so that the tribe's young men could ingest the heroic strength of the victim, for Indians generally believed that the eating of the body of a brave warrior allowed the consumer to absorb the deceased's qualities. There was a disturbing analogy between this barbaric custom and the Catholic belief in transubstantiation for purposes of communing in the body and blood of Jesus in order to absorb His grace. Apart from this religious context, Amerindians rarely indulged in cannibalism.

Other than the flash points of disease and the torture of captives, Amerindian cultures and religions clashed with French Catholic civilization in a host of other areas. For example, the casualness of the Indians about nudity disturbed the French Catholics who, since the fifth century's St. Augustine, tended to identify nudity with sex and sin. The fact that a native woman could give birth to a child with apparent ease, then return to her chores, tended to discredit the Catholic teaching that a woman needed to give birth in pain and suffering as a consequence of original sin. As a rule monogamous, Amerindians could dismiss a partner (wife or husband) with relative ease and marry another, a custom that contradicted the Catholic insistence on the indissolubility of marriage.

Social structures in church and state differed greatly in France and North America. Leadership among Indians tended to rest on spiritual inspiration, vision, or skills in war or the hunt. Among the French, leadership was tied to social class, heritage, rank, and political favoritism. Private property, so important in Europe, was largely unfamiliar to Amerindians, who shared their band's common resources. They could not easily understand the required celibacy of Catholic priests; they found it even more difficult to accept the lack of hospitality shown to them by many Frenchmen since Indians considered themselves bound to be hospitable.

In spite of this clash of cultures, Amerindians were rapidly drawn into dependency on the white man, for they could not resist the iron kettles, axes, guns, blankets, and brandy that the French offered in exchange for the furs of the North American forest. One Indian band after another transformed itself into a nation of trapping servants of the French, for fur-trapping was the only profitable activity for the Indians in the new fur-trade economy. Many gradually abandoned their centuries-old independent and self-sufficient existence and moved into the neighborhood of the French forts, simultaneously becoming progressively more dependent upon French goods and less able to fend for themselves. Every time an Indian accepted an axe, a kettle, or a gun from the white man, he lost a part of himself. He would soon be losing his land— indeed, his pride and identity. Many sought solace in a bottle.

## BRANDY

According to the Jesuit *Relations*, brandy was introduced to New France's Indian people during the English occupation of the country by the Kirke brothers in 1629–1632. Upon reassuming possession of the country in 1632, the French continued exchanging some brandy for furs with the Indians. Only in 1650, however, did the trade become a major problem, for only in that year was a major shipment of brandy traded with the Indians at Tadoussac. In spite of unanimous condemnation by governors Champlain, Montmagny, and others throughout the 1630s, 1640s, and 1650s, the trade grew in importance because French traders soon learned that Amerindians would do almost anything to obtain intoxicating beverages. Brandy had become the most profitable item of trade for the French, many of whom had no scruples about watering down or salting the beverages they sold to the Indians; French traders were often guilty of deliberately intoxicating, when not killing, their Indian suppliers in order to deliberately steal the coveted pelts or obtain them for ridiculously low prices.

The Jesuits and Bishop Laval were soon moving heaven and earth to obtain the banning of the brandy trade with the Indian people. The problem was that with few exceptions, Indian people did not drink moderately. They sought complete intoxication. Having achieved it, they indulged in bestial behavior, killing, raping, murdering, and maiming neighbors, wives, brothers, sisters, children, and themselves. While some fathers drowned or burned their children live, husbands sold their wives, and women and children drank themselves into insanity. The orgies that accompanied the sale of brandy to the Amerindians ended only when no liquor was left; in the meantime, any and every code of moral behavior, French or Indian, Christian or native, was jettisoned. When the drinking Indians recovered from their orgies they found themselves destitute and frequently unable to provide for themselves or their families during the following winter. Starvation and misery followed.

By the time of Laval's arrival in 1659, the evils associated with the brandy trade appeared insurmountable. Nevertheless, within a year of his arrival the bishop issued an excommunication order automatically incurred by any and all who sold or distributed wine or brandy to the Amerindians. He reserved to himself alone the right to absolve transgressors. When newly arrived Governor Pierre Dubois Davaugour reinforced this episcopal directive in September

1661 by forbidding the sale of brandy to Indians under pain of the most severe penalties, the problem seemed well on the way to being resolved. In fact, in October 1661 the governor showed he was serious by ordering the execution by firing squad of two men guilty of having breached his ordinance. A third was whipped in the Quebec town square. The brandy trade with the Indians had suffered a serious setback.

The evil was only in temporary remission, however, for in early 1662 Governor Davaugour withdrew all penalties associated with trading liquor with Indians. He did so because Jesuit Father Jérôme Lalemant had interceded on behalf of a Quebec woman imprisoned by the governor for contravening the ordinance. Miffed at the priest's interference, the temperamental governor peremptorily declared that if it was not wrong for the woman to sell liquor to Amerindians, it would not be wrong for anyone. The previous excesses and crimes were soon a recurring occurrence, prompting Bishop Laval to reiterate his excommunication; the episcopal condemnation was somewhat fruitless, given the governor's authorization to trade. Laval thereupon went to France, obtained the recall of the governor and the appointment of his successor Mézy, who arrived in Quebec in September 1663 in the company of Laval.

The bishop found that the brandy trade had all but stopped, albeit temporarily, the people of New France believing that the earthquake of the preceding months was punishment from God for their evil ways. By 1665, the fat was in the fire once again, Mézy having turned against his clerical friends, gratuitously accusing the latter of indulging in brandy trading in order to enrich themselves. Mézy was recalled and replaced by the new order of royal colonial government led by a governor and an intendant.

The tug of war continued in New France between partisans of the brandy trade and their adversaries. Between 1665 and 1668 Intendant Jean Talon grew progressively more suspicious and distrustful of the clergy. He usually stood against the brandy traders, however, but on the eve of returning to France on 10 November 1668 he obtained from Quebec's governing sovereign council an order authorizing the brandy trade with the Indians while forbidding the Indians to get drunk. This unenforceable ruling marked the beginning of a longstanding policy in New France authorizing the sale of liquor to Indian people. In fact, Talon and most of his followers in the intendant's or governor's office had come to feel that the brandy trade was necessary to the economic well-being of the colony. With slight variations such as a royal edict of 1679 forbidding the transport of liquor to Indian villages, a ruling that was soon disregarded, this policy remained in place until the end of the French regime. Bishop Laval and most priests continued to campaign against the social cancer, but to little avail. In fact, leading civil personages in the colony like Governor Frontenac and Antoine Laumet de Cadillac engaged in the trade for personal profit.

The predilection of Amerindians for alcoholic beverages was merely another, albeit frightening, instance of the loss of their heritage. Some deliberately set out to get drunk in order to facilitate the onset of dreams and the associated contact with the spirits; others wanted to forget their worsening lot, the sweeping dispossession the white man was perpetrating against them; for some, drunkenness was a weapon, because once inebriated, any and all actions were permissible. Many drank out of desperation, as an escape from the growing meaninglessness of life as dependents of the white men. Their world appeared less and less in balance, and they were at a loss to understand the forces that were sweeping them along toward meaningless oblivion.

## EVANGELIZATION AND/OR CIVILIZATION

French Catholic missionaries in New France were soon facing the classical dilemma all Christian missionaries struggled with when sent into countries of cultures different than their own. Was it possible to preach the Christian gospel while bracketing one's culture? Without going back to the numerous cases of the first fifteen hundred years of Christian history, let it suffice to recall the problems encountered by European Catholic missionaries when they attempted to evangelize the people of China, Japan, and India beginning in the sixteenth century. Jesuit missionaries who endeavored to adapt the Gospel to Chinese civilization soon found themselves being accused by other Catholic priests of diluting it. Where was one to draw the line between the Gospel and the culture that bore it? Where did fundamental Christian doctrine end and particular languages and cultures begin? Even if one admitted that the Christian Church could only exist in particular cultural incarnations, how far could cultural adaptation go? The problem was compounded in the seventeenth century by the fact that all Christian churches were national churches, a fact that tended to deny the autonomy of the Christian Church. If the French state held a controlling interest in the church of France, was it consequently necessary to make Amerindians into Frenchmen in order to evangelize them?

From the moment they set foot in North America, French missionaries had to grapple with these questions. Given the powerful sway of the French crown over the church of France, for much of the seventeenth century official French policy was simultaneously to seek the frenchification and the christianization of North America's Indian people. French missionaries—Recollect, Jesuit, Sulpician, Capuchin, or secular—were simultaneously preachers of the Gospel and agents of the French crown. In this respect, the only difference from one missionary to the other was in the priority given to either pole of the dual commitment.

One area that illustrates this dual Christian and French commitment of the missionaries is that of the education of children, a form of apostolate that was centuries old in the Christian Church. Shortly after setting foot in Quebec in 1615, the Recollect friars opened a school for Indian children, in the hope of initiating them to the French way of life and raising them like French children.

The institution was short-lived. The Capuchins did likewise in Acadia beginning in the 1630s, as did the Jesuits in Quebec from 1635, the Ursulines from
1639, and most other religious congregations that came to New France.

Most of these schools eventually developed into successful schools for white
children but were abject failures in the schooling of Indian children. Recollects, Jesuits, Capuchins, Ursulines, Sulpicians all failed miserably in keeping
the presence, not to mention the attention of Indian children. The fact was
grudgingly acknowledged by Bishop Laval, Marie de l'Incarnation, and several
others. The children of the forest simply could not adapt to the disciplined
French program and routine that were taught in these schools. By 1668 at the
latest, French Catholic clergy openly admitted that this attempt at simul-
taneous evangelization and frenchification had failed miserably.

Simultaneously, the missionaries were also trying to evangelize and frenchify
Indian converts to Christianity. As already noted, early missionary treks into
the bush in an attempt to follow itinerant Indian bands had failed due to the
almost impossible conditions of evangelization in such circumstances. Indeed,
it was difficult to say the least to catechize while dragging one's baggage on
snowshoes through the bush, while canoeing down rapids, or while fending off
hordes of mosquitoes or snarling dogs in a smoke-filled wigwam at night. In
addition, when one considered the bad example given Amerindians by French
traders and *coureurs de bois* and the debilitating effects of the brandy trade,
Catholic missionaries soon concluded that the only practical solution was
to establish Christian Indians in distinct villages where a partially sedentary
life-style and shelter from the brandy traders would facilitate the missionary
enterprise.

The first such village was founded by the Jesuits at Sillery near Quebec in
1637. It was followed by others at Lorette (1651); La Prairie (1669), which
became Sault St. Louis (1676); Saint-François on the Chaudière River (1683);
and La Montagne in Montreal (1676), a Sulpician post later moved to Lac des
Deux-Montagnes at the mouth of the Ottawa River. Clearly, then, all Catholic
missionaries in New France soon abandoned any attempt to evangelize Indian
peoples while leaving them in their indigenous settings. They endeavored to
segregate the Christian Indians to protect them from lascivious and greedy
French traders and *coureurs de bois*. Partial segregation was therefore the policy of
the missionaries, who simultaneously acknowledged that the Amerindians
needed to become less itinerant for Christianity to have any hope of taking root.

While field experience in the conduct of Indian schools and missions forced
the missionaries to change their initial policy, the French government continued to preach the merits of French–Amerindian integration until at least 1685,
in spite of mounting evidence of the impracticality of such a policy. Indeed,
French bureaucrats were convinced that the frenchification of the Indians
would solve all their colonial problems. They turned a deaf ear to contrary
advice. So it was that as late as March 1668 both Minister Colbert and King
Louis XIV urged the policy of frenchification on Bishop Laval. The latter

replied that he would do his best to frenchify Indian children by opening a school where they would be enrolled alongside French children. The bishop cautioned that it was a difficult undertaking, given the strong bond between Indian children and parents. He promised to give the project his best effort, although he was skeptical as to its chances of success. Subject to the same pressures, Sister Marie de l'Incarnation wrote:

> It is . . . a very difficult, if not an impossible task to Frenchify or to civilize them. We have had more experience than anybody else, and we have noticed that among one hundred of those who passed through our hands, we hardly succeeded in civilizing one. We find them docile and clever, but when we least expect it, they jump the wall and go to join their parents in the woods, where they find more pleasure than they do amid all the attractions of our French houses. Such is the Indian character. They will brook no restraint. If they are constrained, they become melancholic and ill. Moreover, the Indians have an extraordinary love for their children. When they learn that they are sad . . . we must return their children to them.[1]

In spite of such authoritative advice, and in spite of the growing Jesuit and Sulpician practice of founding segregated Indian villages in the 1670s and 1680s, the French crown continued to press for French–Amerindian integration, meaning assimilation of Indian people into the French culture. Only in 1685 would French officials acknowledge that the policy was a dismal failure.

The arrival of slaves in New France coincided with the demise of the official policy of frenchification of Indians. While a total of eleven hundred black slaves worked in Canada, they were usually prisoners taken in French raids on English settlements, although some came from Haiti and Louisiana. Beginning in the late 1680s, fur traders and Indians began selling other Indian slaves to the French in Canada. A total of some thirty-six hundred of these indentured servants, twenty-five hundred of whom were Indian, worked in Canada during the French regime. They were known as Panis (Pawnees) from the tribe of that name in the Mississippi valley, although Indians of various nationalities were part of the group. Purchased in the marketplace or at auction, they were usually found in the employ of merchants, traders, high government officials, and clergy. So it was that Governor Rigaud de Vaudreuil (1703–1725) owned eleven, while his successor Governor De Beauharnois (1726–1746) owned twenty-seven. Another example is the widow d'Youville, the founder of the Sisters of Charity of Montreal (see Chapter 12), who not only inherited a few slaves from her deceased husband but who also bought and sold others herself during the years when she directed her Montreal General Hospital, which also employed slaves.

\*     \*     \*

French Catholic evangelization of the Indian people of New France had mixed results. Any encounter between two cultures results in positive and negative changes in both. In the wake of the arrival of the French in North America in the early seventeenth century, the Indian people soon found themselves spending an increasing proportion of their time in fur-trapping and less and less time in fishing and hunting. The goods they obtained from the Europeans in exchange for their furs strengthened their own cultures for a time. Both the French and the Indians had gained, the latter remaining largely isolated from the few Frenchmen who resided in small coastal settlements. However, as soon as contact with the white man became more frequent beginning in the mid-seventeenth century, the more advanced technology, the different values, and the diseases of the Europeans soon spelled disaster for the Indians.

There is no doubt that the European presence eventually proved damaging to Amerindian societies, nor is there any doubt that conversion to Catholicism just as inevitably implied the acceptance by the Indian convert of some measure of French culture. All that was in question in the debates of the French was the degree of this frenchification. If one assumes that any and all forms and degrees of assimilation of one ethnic or religious group into another are reprehensible in principle, then the Christian missionary effort in New France must be condemned out of hand. But then, so too must all contact between cultures, because some mutual assimilation always results.

However, a more realistic evaluation has to begin by considering the alternatives that were available at the time. We know that European churches, including that of France, were under the thumb of their respective states in the seventeenth and eighteenth centuries. Although undesirable by twentieth-century standards, some degree of frenchification was therefore inevitable, and unquestioned, in countries evangelized by French missionaries, as anglicization was in countries controlled by the English. In attempting to evaluate the contribution of French missionaries, it would therefore seem more meaningful to assess the French Catholic missionary effort in light of the seventeenth-century context.

One can stand on different platforms in evaluating the Catholic missionary effort in New France, and the choice frequently determines one's conclusions. On one hand, from the point of view of the French Catholics themselves, the only point at issue was the techniques or methods of evangelization; few questioned the underlying assumptions of the missionaries relating to Catholic Christianity as the only true religion or the consequent inferiority of Indian religions. On the other hand, from the point of view of the Indian peoples, what was at stake in the encounter with the French was not fine points of theology or debates on techniques of evangelization. It was rather the global consequences of this encounter on their entire society and way of life and on themselves as individuals. In the matter of religion, their view may well be expressed by a twentieth-century Native American historian of religion. Sam D. Gill condemns the Christian missionary effort in North America, as has become commonplace of late.

> The Native American encounter with Christianity seems to be a rather one-sided affair, one in which native religions have not only been ignored, but also suppressed; one in which Christianity has been the measure and the only acceptable religious presence. It has been a history of oppression, insensitivity, arrogance, and misunderstanding. Certainly from the native point of view, the encounter with Christianity has often been unhappy and frustrating.[2]

There is perhaps a middle ground between the two opposing evaluations of the Christian missionary effort that were noted above for, in retrospect, it is obvious that the stone-age Amerindians were incapable of competing on anything like equal terms with the technologically more advanced European civilization. Given the inevitability that in such unequal encounters the weaker party, if it is to survive, must do the most adjusting to the stronger party, did the French Catholic missionaries help the Amerindians in their inevitable adjustment to the conquering culture, or did they hinder them in their adjustment? Was the inevitable trauma of European-Amerindian contact made more endurable or less endurable by the French Catholic missionaries? Assuming the inevitability of the domination of the more powerful European culture over the weaker Indian cultures, did the French Catholic missionaries use the Gospel as an instrument for the liberation, or for the oppression, of the Amerindians?

It is perhaps best to proceed in comparative terms. Contemporary historians have abandoned Francis Parkman's romantic but simplistic century-old dictum to the effect that Spanish civilization crushed the Indian, English civilization scorned and neglected him, and French civilization embraced and cherished him. Indeed, such a judgment does not take into account the vast differences between the colonial empires of the Spaniards, the English, and the French, differences that conditioned the attitudes of all three European nations toward Amerindians. Specifically, it must be kept in mind that the French empire in North America was primarily a fur-trading empire. While the English of the Atlantic seaboard were primarily engaged in clearing and cultivating the land, in settlement, the French of Canada were primarily engaged in collecting pelts from an ever-widening circle of Indian nations. In 1754, on the eve of the Seven Years' War, there were only fifty-five thousand white people in Canada against more than one million British in the southern colonies. Until 1653 the Indian people not only trapped the animals but also transported the pelts to annual fur-trading fairs on the St. Lawrence River. After 1653, white men journeyed into the interior in growing numbers.

Given the central importance of the fur trade, it was to the advantage of the

French in Canada to facilitate trapping, a policy that was much more acceptable to Indian bands than the English policy of land-clearing and settlement
that inevitably resulted in the destruction of both the hunt and the forest. In
other words, the French had much more in common with the Indian people
than had the English.

The common ground between Amerindians and French Canadians was not
limited to economic and commercial interests. It was usual for the French to
learn to speak the Indian languages, to adapt to the Indian life-style, to learn to
think like Amerindians, to understand and respect them. This behavior remained typical throughout our period of study and through the nineteenth
century. Indeed, although there were major differences in their social values,
there was greater affinity and sympathy between the French and the Indians
than between the Indians and the English or Dutch; this was because both
French and Indians shared personal values like a strong sense of personal
honor, a priority on the enjoyment of life, and less concern than the English
with the accumulation of material goods. The proof was that Frenchmen and
Canadians easily assimilated into Indian society, while Englishmen or Dutch-
men rarely did so. So it was that national character and economic interests
dovetailed to bind most Amerindians and French Canadians into a close
alliance that was only dissolved by force of arms.

Although most Indian people in New France only converted to Christianity
in the "moon of wintertime" when their own cultures were on the wane, the
vast majority of them had become Christian by the end of the twentieth
century. When insulated from liquor, many Amerindians led model Christian
lives in the seventeenth- and eighteenth-century Indian villages of Sillery,
Sault St. Louis, Lorette, Saint-François, and Lac des Deux-Montagnes. The
missionaries usually designated local Indian male and female *dogigues* (cate-
chists) who performed many of the missionary's duties during his absence.
Although the Catholic missionaries of New France never managed to ordain an
Amerindian to the priesthood, some Indian converts lived model Christian
lives. One of the best-known was the young Algonquin–Mohawk maiden
Kateri Tekakouitha (1656–1680).

In 1667, Kateri was struck by the piety of Jesuit missionaries visiting her
Mohawk village. Baptized in 1676, the twenty-year-old woman moved to
the Christian Indian village of St. Francis Xavier near Montreal. There she
spent four years, impressing all by her piety and mortification, until ill health
claimed her life in the spring of 1680. Many have since revered her as a saint,
making pilgrimages to her relics kept in the Indian reservation of Kahnawake
(Caughnawaga) near Montreal. Missionary correspondence throughout
the history of New France tells of several individual Indians who led model
Christian lives. In the eyes of the Christian, their holiness is all the more remarkable in that conversion to Christianity usually required abandonment
of both their native religion and their culture in favor of the religion and
culture of the French.

In sum, while the arrival of European civilization inevitably forced changes—often devastating ones—on the Amerindians, French Catholic missionaries served simultaneously as religious and cultural agents of change. During the seventeenth century most of these missionaries were strongly imbued with a sense of Christian apostolate; French culture was merely a necessary vehicle of the Gospel. During the eighteenth century Catholic missionaries in New France, as elsewhere, were not as highly motivated as their predecessors. Their role as French cultural agents frequently seemed to overshadow their primary calling as preachers of the Gospel.

It is true that Catholic missionaries in New France were leading agents in the repression of the religions of Indian people, religions they considered false and unworthy. The blame for this policy of repression is, however, to be attributed not primarily to the missionaries in the field but rather to the entire European Christian Church and civilization, the source of the condemnatory judgment of Indian religions. Catholic missionaries in New France frequently consecrated their lives to their charges, developing an abiding affection and love for and devotion to their new churches. More often than not, the same missionaries who discouraged Indian religions lobbied, worked, and fought for the economic, social, and educational well-being of their Indian congregations. The Catholic missionary of New France frequently became a trusted friend, leader, and adviser that Amerindians consulted and listened to. Such trust rested on years and lifetimes of devotion and service; many missionaries, particularly in the seventeenth century, cast their lot with chosen Indian bands and spent the rest of their lives with them. The fact that some of these missionaries, Sulpician father François Picquet or Spiritan father Jean-Louis Le Loutre for example (see Chapter 13), also chose to become guerrilla leaders of Indian bands in their wars against the English should not allow us to forget that they had decidedly committed themselves to the welfare of their flocks as they saw it.

While the religions of Amerindians were in fact repressed by the Catholic missionaries of New France, the encounter between Amerindians and Christianity cannot be fairly reduced to a history of oppression, insensitivity, arrogance, and misunderstanding. Such a view is partial and misleading. Given the difficult historical situation for the period's Indian people, the encounter was also fruitful, creative, dynamic, and liberating. While Catholic missionaries in New France can only shoulder part of the blame for the repression of Indian religions, they can take full credit for assisting most bands of Amerindians in their necessary adjustment to the new world of the white Europeans. Few and far between are the traders, *coureurs de bois*, soldiers, or settlers who could make a similar claim.

# 12

# AN EXPANDING
# BUT CHANGING CHURCH

By the late 1650s the age of the martyrs had ended, that of the mystics was ebbing, but that of dedicated apostles like Marguerite Bourgeois, Jeanne Mance, various Sulpician and Jesuit priests, and several frequently unsung Christian lay apostles like Maisonneuve was still in full bloom.

Nevertheless it soon became apparent to these devoted individuals that the church of New France was undergoing profound change. Not only did it begin a century-long process of expansion into hitherto unexplored territory, but it seemed that in the years following the arrival of Bishop Laval in Quebec in 1659 clergymen of all stripes, secular or regular, were less concerned with evangelizing the "heathen" than with ecclesiastical disputes or church-state wrangling. Moreover, the government of France and its colonial administrators were soon engaged in imposing a progressively heavier hand on the church of New France, a church that had enjoyed unparalleled autonomy and indepen- dence under Jesuit auspices. Indeed, the mainstream gallican tradition of church government would soon replace the Rome-centered ecclesiology of the Jesuits in the government of the church of New France.

However, the coexistence and rivalry of two vigorous male religious congre- gations like the Jesuits and the Sulpicians necessitated the presence of a bishop. He would need not only to arbitrate periodic ecclesiastical disputes but also to steer the institutional church through the shoals of church-state relations—while coordinating the pastoral activities of the immense apostolic vicariate of New France. In fact, Bishop François de Laval also supervised the expansion of Catholic missions into distant Indian lands like that of the Illinois nation south of Lake Michigan. In addition, while still resident in Quebec after his retirement, Laval witnessed the founding of the first Catholic missions in the new French colony of Louisiana.

## A Bishop in New France

In 1656, when planning to send the first band of Sulpicians to Montreal, the Society of Montreal and Father Olier also intended to obtain the appointment of Father De Queylus as first bishop of New France. The founders of Montreal had considered seeking an episcopal appointment as early as 1645, but various obstacles had prevented it. They now felt such a step was required.

So it was that in January 1657 the Montreal associates officially presented the candidacy of De Queylus and obtained the endorsement of the Assembly of the French clergy. The Society of Jesus was, however, of another mind. While refusing Regent Anne of Austria's invitation to appoint a Jesuit to the office of bishop of Quebec, they proposed another candidate. Their choice fell on François de Laval (1623–1708).

Laval belonged to the Montmorency family, one of France's most ancient and prestigious clans, which traced its history back to Clovis's pagan Gaul of the late fifth century. For a thousand years the Montmorencys had given France an impressive series of military commanders and churchmen. One of François's two sisters was a nun, while one of his five brothers became a Benedictine monk. Destined for the ranks of the clergy, François was tonsured and donned a cassock at eight years of age, upon his entry into the Jesuit College of La Flèche, a school serving the children of France's leading families. During his ten-year stay at La Flèche (1631–1641) his uncle, who was bishop of Evreux, appointed the fourteen-year-old lad canon of his cathedral. Thereafter François had a meager but secure annual income.

Under the able direction of the Jesuits of La Flèche, Laval grew to appreciate a life of holiness and virtue; in fact, he wrote in 1659 that the Jesuits had taught him to love God. He became a devoted disciple and friend of the followers of Ignatius. After studying theology at the College of Clermont, another Jesuit school, François was ordained a priest in 1647. The following year he was made archdeacon of his uncle's diocese of Evreux and thus compelled to assume diocesan administrative duties. He resigned the position in 1654, hoping to be appointed to the foreign mission field, a longstanding dream of his. Nothing would come of this, although he had already (in 1652) been proposed as a bishop in the Far East.

In 1654, Laval retired into the hermitage of Caën, a house of holiness founded in 1649 and directed by Jean de Bernières de Louvigny, one of France's foremost mystics. There he joined a small community of priests and laymen who endeavored through prayer, austerity, and good works to better achieve salvation. Laval devoted himself to the service of the sick and the poor while serving as administrator and chaplain to two congregations of women. It was at Caën that François de Laval learned that his Jesuit friends had proposed his name as bishop of New France.

The Jesuits had decided to sever their decade-long tie to the archbishop of

Rouen and restore the independence of the church in Canada, which was why they had opposed the episcopal candidacy of De Queylus in January 1657. For some eighteen months thereafter, in utmost secrecy, they promoted the candidacy of Laval before both the French court and the Holy See. With the support of Louis XIV and Anne of Austria, they pressed his case in spite of the reluctance of the Sacred Congregation for the Propagation of the Faith (the Propaganda), the Vatican office in charge of foreign missions, which feared a return to the former Jesuit autonomy in the mission field. That is why the Propaganda suggested a compromise whereby Laval would not be appointed bishop of Quebec but rather vicar-apostolic of New France. This would make Laval an ordained bishop but not the administrator of an autonomous diocese. Such an appointment would protect Rome's direct control over the church of New France while simultaneously severing any ties between the new bishop and the archbishop of Rouen. All agreed. The bulls appointing Laval apostolic vicar of New France were signed in Rome on 3 June 1658. When the archbishop of Rouen learned of the Roman maneuver, he arranged for the Assembly of the French clergy to ask all bishops in France to refuse to consecrate Laval (September 1658) because of the harm such a measure would cause to the church of France. The parliament of Rouen took a similar stand. Since Rome did not accept the jurisdictional claims of the archbishop of Rouen and the French king and queen mother agreed, it was decided to proceed with the secret ordination of François de Laval in a church exempt from the legal jurisdiction of the realm. On 8 December 1658, in a chapel of the monastery of Saint-Germain-des-Prés, the papal nuncio consecrated Laval bishop. The controversy raged for another four months, but with the support of the royal court the gallican party was overcome, and Laval was authorized to sail to Canada.

Having sworn loyalty to the king, Laval boarded ship in La Rochelle on 13 April 1659. His apostolic vicariate included tens of thousands of Indians but only some three thousand Frenchmen; Quebec was still the largest town with some twelve hundred souls in its surrounding area. While seventeen Jesuits worked in the Indian missions and the College of Quebec, four Sulpicians were in charge of Montreal, while six secular priests handled the ministry in Quebec, waiting to take over the parish of Trois-Rivières.

Laval first set foot in Quebec on 17 June 1659 and was immediately embroiled in the complex jurisdictional dispute with Father De Queylus of Montreal, who invoked anew his powers of grand vicar of the archbishop of Rouen. Quick intervention by the crown forced De Queylus to take ship back to France on 22 October 1659. Once in Europe, he managed to obtain Roman authorization to establish a parish in Montreal independent of the authority of Bishop Laval. More controversy ensued until, in the wake of De Queylus's surreptitious return to Canada in August 1660, Laval finally obtained the physical removal of De Queylus in October 1661. This marked the end of the jurisdictional dispute, the archbishop of Rouen grudgingly accepting that he no longer controlled the church of New France.

Meanwhile, other quarrels of protocol and precedence kept Laval busy. Since the late 1640s various priests, churchwardens, seigneurs, and so on had showed their pique and contentiousness in arguing over precedence in processions, the receipt of the Eucharist, and similar matters. One of the plaintiffs was Pierre de Voyer d'Argenson (1625–1709), governor of New France between 1658 and 1661. While faced with constant Iroquois raids he had to come to terms with a bishop who was unwilling to take second place to anyone. The two men therefore quarrelled over a series of issues, insignificant in themselves, whose outcome could establish the order of importance of church and state in the colony. The battle was joined when Laval discovered that Governor d'Argenson enjoyed certain unusual privileges in the church of Quebec. For example, the governor's kneeling chair was located in the church choir's most prominent place; he regularly attended the meetings of the parish's board of trustees and was acknowledged an honorary trustee of the church. The young bishop peremptorily ordered the cessation of these privileges. The governor retaliated in kind. Although such issues of precedence are very important in a hierarchical society, it seems nevertheless that much of the controversy was due to personality conflicts between the two men.

## CONSOLIDATING THE CHURCH IN THE ST. LAWRENCE VALLEY

These power struggles over questions of protocol only served to smear the reputation of a church that deserved better. In fact, it had long been acknowledged that the head of the church in the colony was a full-fledged member of New France's governing elite. Indeed, in 1647, a royal statute created a council, initially three men, to govern the colony, a council that included the superior of the Jesuits as one of its members alongside the governor and the governor of Montreal. It was stipulated that the superior of the Jesuits would occupy his seat only until a bishop was appointed in New France. When the composition of the Council of Quebec was modified in 1657, the superior of the Jesuits was no longer a member.

Upon his arrival in 1659 François de Laval was therefore not a member of the colony's governing council; he became an ex officio member in 1661. However, the constant squabbling between Laval and Governor d'Argenson induced the latter to ask for his own recall in 1661. He was replaced by Pierre Dubois Davaugour, a career soldier who was in turn recalled in 1663 due to general dissatisfaction in the colony over his administration. Bishop Laval played a key role in obtaining his dismissal, because of Davaugour's behavior in the brandy question (see Chapter 11).

The power of Bishop Laval gradually diminished after 1663, the year the administrative framework of the colony changed dramatically. Then it was that Louis XIV obtained abandonment by the Company of New France of its seigniorial rights in North America. The quasiautonomous colony of Montreal was then integrated into the jurisdiction of the Quebec government and a new governing structure established. A two-headed government was put in place, the governor being responsible for military matters and external relations while the intendant handled justice, police, finance, and internal administration. In addition, a Sovereign Council was created to serve as executive and legislative council as well as supreme court. In its latter capacity, the Sovereign Council applied the laws and customs of Paris (rather than those of other regions of France). In spite of the fact that French public servants would now govern the colony, for another ten years the colony's economic interests would be entrusted to another trading company, that of the West Indies. Nevertheless, the crown had definitively taken over in 1663. The church of New France would rapidly be transformed from a primarily missionary church into a French colonial church.

The holy, generous, proud, uncompromising Laval lived a simple life of devotion and good works. Having completed his first pastoral visitation in 1660 and having joined battle with the new governor over the brandy trade, in 1662 the bishop went to France to advance his cause before the king's court. Not only did he obtain royal endorsement of his ban on brandy trading with Indians, but he also obtained the recall of Governor Davaugour and was invited to suggest the name of his successor. Laval chose Augustin de Saffray de Mézy, a pious but reluctant officer; both arrived in Quebec on 15 September 1663.

Mézy soon discovered that the bishop had more real power in the colony than the governor. Indeed, not only had he chosen the governor; he held a permanent seat on the Sovereign Council second only to the governor's. Moreover, Laval's was a lifetime appointment, while the governor was subject to recall and was only appointed for a three-year term. In addition, royal directives made the bishop and the governor jointly responsible for the selection of the other members of the Sovereign Council and for the granting of the large tracts of land known as seigneuries. New France had exchanged an all-powerful Society of Jesus for a just-as-powerful bishop.

While in France in 1662–1663, Laval planned the building of a seminary in Quebec—not an ordinary seminary, however. Like many of his Jesuit friends, Laval believed that church authority needed to be reinforced, both within the church and without, in its relations with the state. He and his ultramontane friends believed in a strong, autonomous, and exemplary church. In keeping with these ideas, Laval planned a seminary that would be much more than a house of training for prospective priests. The Seminary of Quebec would be that, and the headquarters of the Canadian church as well. It would provide a pool of clergy to staff the diocese's parishes and missions; it would collect the revenues generated by parishes and redistribute the money on the basis of need; it would serve as refuge for ill or tired priests and would be the bishop's residence. The bishop exercised his authority over his priests through the directors of the seminary. Although called a seminary, for all practical purposes it was a congregation of secular priests that Laval created by an ordinance dated in Paris on 26 March 1663 and registered in Quebec on 10 October.

More than a year later, on 29 January 1665, Laval affiliated his seminary with Paris' Seminary of foreign missions (*Séminaire des Missions étrangères*) in order to ensure an adequate supply of faculty and financial resources. Paris' *Séminaire* had been founded in 1663 by a group of Laval's friends and received royal letters patent in July of the same year. In fact, since 1658, Laval himself had been involved in the planning of the new Parisian institution whose purpose was the conversion of infidels.

Quebec now had a seminary for the training of priests, a college directed by the Jesuits dispensing general education, and a girls' school run by the Ursulines. In 1668 the bishop added a minor seminary that initially enrolled eight boys destined for an ecclesiastical career and six Huron boys who were to be trained in French ways. The students lived in the minor seminary while studying at the Jesuit college. Laval also founded in neighboring Saint-Joachim an industrial school and an elementary school where children would learn to read and write.

By the same 1663 directive Laval also created the tithe in New France. Traditionally, the tithe was the payment to the church of one tenth of the produce of the land and for a thousand years had been the preferred means of ensuring an income for the clergy in Christian countries. When Laval instituted it in Canada, he ruled that it would correspond to one thirteenth rather than a tenth, a decision endorsed by the king. However, only one month later, the bishop announced that the parishioners of Quebec would be exempt from the tithe for the year 1663 and would have the tax reduced to one twentieth for the subsequent six years. This led many faithful throughout the colony to solicit the same privilege, while withholding payment from their clergy. Once more, the fat was in the fire.

With Governor Mézy supporting the disgruntled faithful, Laval desperately sought some form of compromise solution. Initially he made the Quebec exemption general; then he reduced the tithe to one twentieth of the produce of the land for his entire lifetime; finally, he delayed until 1665 the compulsory payment of tithes. Nevertheless, the people were not paying and refused to do so until 1667, when Lieutenant General Alexandre de Prouville de Tracy, the military commander in New France, in cooperation with the intendant Talon, ordered the tithe set at the rate of one twenty-sixth, the rate that would become permanent.

The arrival in 1665 of Jean Talon, New France's first intendant, marked the beginning of a period of unequaled prosperity for New France. The colony's total population grew from 3,300 in 1663 to 5,870 in 1666, and then 10,000 in 1676.

These years were also those of major new challenges for Laval's church. On his first return voyage to France in 1662 Laval had reported to Rome: "His very Christian majesty . . . has granted me everything that I asked for."[1] Such state generosity was never forthcoming thereafter.

In the spring of 1665, shortly before leaving to take up his new duties in New France, Intendant Jean Talon (1626–1694) received his instructions from Jean-Baptiste Colbert, France's newly appointed comptroller of finances and minister responsible for France's colonies. In the hope of establishing internal peace among the disputatious leaders of the colony, King Louis XIV and his minister decided to ensure that the gallican model of church government prevailed in New France as it did in the mother country. Indeed, Governor Mézy had in turn become embroiled with the Jesuits and Laval over the brandy question. The moment for putting the church in its place was opportune, for not only was a new intendant going to take office, but a new governor was also appointed to replace Mézy, who had died in Quebec on 6 May 1665.

Colbert's instructions to Talon on 27 March 1665 were to ensure a proper balance between temporal and spiritual authorities in the colony, such proper balance being one of dependence of the latter upon the former. The king and his representatives were always to have the upper hand, contrary to the situation that prevailed whereby the Jesuits and the bishop enjoyed too much power; now they were to hold sway over consciences only. Talon was told to observe the situation closely and report to the minister.

While Talon's initial report of October 1665 was not hostile to the clergy, the intendant proved progressively more unfriendly as the years passed. By 1667 he was meddling in church affairs, all the while encouraged to do so by the suspicious and gallican Colbert. In 1668, Talon's about-face on the question of the brandy trade with the Indians was the final insult to the Jesuits and Laval, who had been adamantly fighting any such permission. Actually, Talon was convinced that New France's clergy was overly strict and guilty of holding people in moral bondage.

## CHURCH EXPANSION

In late 1668 Talon went to France, only to return to Canada in 1670; there he remained until his final departure, in November 1672. On board Talon's ship in 1670 were four Recollect priests assisted by two brothers, imported by the intendant to serve as foils to the Jesuits. They were fathers Germain Allart (superior), Gabriel de La Ribourde, Simple Landon, and Hilarion Guénin and brothers Claude François and Anselme Bardou.

The Recollects, first missionaries to Canada (1615–1629), to whom the Jesuits had been preferred in 1632, had long awaited their authorization to return to the St. Lawrence colony. They had even obtained, on 28 February 1635, a Roman decree reestablishing their Canadian mission; however, Richelieu got wind of this, and his Capuchin adviser, Joseph du Tremblay, convinced him that he should not allow the Recollects back into Canada. The pope thereupon withdrew his permission. When they finally managed to reenter the country thirty-five years later, the good friars were more than willing to do the impossible to please Talon. For the next quarter-century they would consequently bedevil both the Society of Jesus and Bishop Laval. Arriving in Quebec in August 1670, the Recollect friars reoccupied their old house on the St. Charles River. Over the next decade, Bishop Laval entrusted them with four missions: those of Trois-Rivières, Percé on the Gaspé peninsula, the St. John River in New Brunswick, and Fort Frontenac, which was about to be founded (1673) on Lake Ontario.

The friars and Bishop Laval soon proved major headaches for each other; a series of conflicts and difficulties characterized the last fifteen years of Laval's administration. First, Laval removed the friars from the parish of Trois-Rivières in 1679. Second, the king had authorized an annual grant of 1,200 livres to the friars on the condition that they abstain from their customary begging, a practice found reprehensible in the colony. They took the money but continued begging. Third, while refusing to allow the establishment of a Recollect convent in Montreal in 1681, Laval dismissed a Recollect preacher in his cathedral, accusing him of using the pulpit to utter indiscreet criticisms of the governor and intendant. Then the Recollects asked Laval's authorization, and obtained royal permission (1681), to build a hospice in the center of Quebec's upper town, exclusively in the interests of their own men. Once the construction of the institution was complete in 1683, the friars were accused by Laval of offering pastoral services to the public, in competition with other Quebec clergy and contrary to their alleged earlier undertaking. A fourth dispute was brewing. More squabbling led to the suspension by Laval of all Recollect priests, an arbitrary act of authority that lasted until 1684, the year of the bishop's return to France. Clearly, these clergymen were not primarily concerned with obtaining the grace of martyrdom. Something had changed in the church of New France.

This lowering of clergymen's horizons also became manifest in the issue of the ecclesiastical status of the church of New France. Shortly after his first arrival in Canada, Bishop Laval realized that it would be advantageous to have his vicariate of New France changed into a full-fledged diocese. While in France in 1662 he began his lobbying and soon obtained the support of the king, who asked the pope to erect the diocese of Quebec. The Holy See was receptive to the proposal until unrelated political problems with the king of France resulted in the proposal being set aside for several years. In fact, Louis XIV demanded that the new bishop of the diocese of Quebec depend on the archbishop of Rouen; this was all that was required to have Roman officials close the file. Meanwhile, Laval constantly badgered the Holy See, explaining that the faithful challenged the apostolic vicar's right to collect the tithe, while the Company of the West Indies argued that Canada was still lacking an ordinary (official ecclesiastical administrator); the company was therefore threatening to import priests, create parishes, and the like. Negotiations between Rome and Paris dragged on until 1669, when Paris abandoned its requirement that the see become a dependency of Rouen.

In 1670, an agreement was imminent on the ecclesiastical status of the church of New France when a new complication arose: Laval could not afford to pay the high fees required by Rome for the erection of his diocese. The bishop begged, pleaded, and prayed for a reduction in the fees. He returned to Europe in 1671, determined never to set foot in Canada again if his diocese was not established. The Holy See finally accepted less money and issued the bulls erecting the diocese of Quebec on 4 October 1674. Laval then swore his oath of allegiance to the king, who had also maintained his right of nomination of candidates to the new see of Quebec. Laval took ship for Canada in May 1675, arriving the following September. The church of New France was now on a more stable footing.

Also in 1675 Louis XIV reorganized Quebec's Sovereign Council, which now included seven councilors in addition to the governor, bishop, and intendant. Indeed, Laval found that the bishop's place was enhanced, marking a return to the situation that existed before Talon. In his ministry, however, Laval was still bedeviled by the brandy question, and a new controversy that centered on the seminary's monopolistic role in the church of New France, another ecclesiastical quarrel that took up much of the energy and time of several clergymen.

When the king endorsed the creation of the Seminary of Quebec in 1663, he approved the payment of tithes to the seminary, and the temporary (rather than permanent) appointment of pastors by the bishop. This latter question was one of fundamental disagreement between gallican and ultramontane Catholics. What was at stake was the autonomy of a *curé* (pastor) in a parish. In the centuries-old European tradition, once appointed to a parish, a pastor enjoyed the protection of the law. A bishop could not dismiss him at will but had to show cause. Given the poor moral and pastoral record of many European priests in the sixteenth and seventeenth centuries, the ultramontane Catholic reformers pressed for the reinforcement of episcopal authority, including the bishop's right to hire and fire curés in his diocese. Otherwise, unworthy priests could not easily be removed from office.

After 1663, this system of parish management was one target of the increasingly arrogant and suspicious intendants and governors, who simply did not trust the Jesuits and Bishop Laval. Only the parish of Quebec had been exceptionally "erected" in 1664—it was the only parish in Canada with a permanent curé in the traditional sense; all other parishes were in fact missions of the Seminary of Quebec. However, in response to local dissatisfaction, in 1679 the king decreed that thereafter tithes were to belong to local pastors who were to receive permanent appointments to their parishes. Although still arguing that Canadian parishes simply did not have sufficient revenues to function in that way, Laval nevertheless implemented the royal edict by erecting seven parishes in 1679 and another six in 1684. Nonetheless, the seminary continued to subsidize the parishes, while Bishop Laval and his associates spent an inordinate amount of time fighting another clerical squabble in the corridors of colonial and court administrators.

Having gone to France in 1678–1679 to fight his battles over the brandy trade and over the erection of parishes, Laval returned to Canada in 1680 and, while undertaking another of his diocesan pastoral visitations in 1681, he began to feel the weight of his years. While surviving a serious illness in 1681, he continued to be engaged in controversy, as he had always been. In addition to the brandy dispute and that over the legal status of parishes, the comic-opera dispute with the Recollect order, his nemesis, continued until Laval's departure for France in 1684. The sixty-one-year-old bishop had decided to resign his see. His quarter-century of episcopal rule had been more concerned with ecclesiastical and court infighting than with evangelizing the heathen. Decidedly, something had changed in the church of New France.

In January 1685, the ascetic and rigoristic bishop proposed as his successor the king's chaplain, Jean-Baptiste de la Croix de Chevrières de Saint-Vallier (1653–1727). Although working at the royal court, this young priest had earned a reputation as an ascetic, devout, and charitable apostle to the sick and the poor. Louis XIV immediately nominated Saint-Vallier. However, political tensions between Paris and Rome resulted in a two-year delay in the issuing of the papal bulls, and he was not ordained a bishop until 25 January 1688. Meanwhile, Laval had appointed him grand vicar and in that capacity Saint-Vallier sailed to Quebec in 1685.

During this initial eighteen-month visit to Canada, Saint-Vallier surprised many with his zeal, stamina, and endurance. After having visited all of Canada's parishes along the St. Lawrence between Quebec and Montreal, in 1686 he set out overland for Acadia, visiting in turn all the French posts either served by or in need of a priest. He preached, catechized, praised, or blamed whenever he considered it necessary. He spent his own money and that of others as if he had an endless supply of it. He was soon known as a difficult, demanding, uncompromising, and stubborn workaholic, although exceptionally generous. When Saint-Vallier returned to France in late 1687, Bishop Laval was hearing protests from several quarters to the effect that Saint-Vallier would not be acceptable as second bishop of Quebec. Laval thereupon tried to secure his protégé's resignation, but the younger man would not hear of it.

On Bishop Saint-Vallier's return to Canada in the summer of 1688, a long dark night descended upon Canada's ecclesiastical affairs. While Bishop Laval had spent most of his time as church administrator fighting the good fight in the corridors of power, he at least enjoyed the support and respect of most of his clergy. This was not to be for Saint-Vallier, a man destined to become the most detested and resented of New France's episcopal leaders. During his nearly forty years in office, not only would the age of mystics and martyrs become a distant memory, but so would that of competent and respected episcopal leadership.

The new bishop's first major battle was with the directors of the Seminary of Quebec. In New France, all members of religious orders, some three quarters of the clergy in Canada, answered to their own superiors rather than to the bishop. Moreover, as noted above, the Seminary of Quebec was established in such a way that with the bishop it controlled most of the secular priests. The bishop was therefore left with little real authority over his own clergy. Within months of his arrival in Quebec in 1688, Saint-Vallier demanded substantial changes in the powers of the seminary and was refused. The battle was joined. It lasted until a royal decision settled the issue in the bishop's favor in 1691, thereby sealing the fate of Laval's unique kind of seminary. Thereafter, the Seminary of Quebec was merely another house of training for priests, albeit an important one.

This was only the opening shot in a protracted series of clerical quarrels that continued, in varying degrees of intensity, for close to forty years. Upon his return from France in 1692 after a year's absence devoted to muzzling the seminary priests, Saint-Vallier proceeded to quarrel with just about everybody in the colony, including Governor Frontenac, Governor Callière of Montreal, the cathedral chapter, the seminary, the Recollects, the Jesuits, the Congregation of Notre-Dame, and the sisters of the Hôtel-Dieu hospital. The bickering was frequently over petty jealousies and disagreements, exacerbated by the bishop's high-handed manner. In fact, Saint-Vallier did not seek or heed the advice of others; he issued decrees and expected any and all to obey on the spot. By 1694 things had reached such a pass that the king ordered Saint-Vallier back to France to justify his actions.

Back in France in December 1694, Saint-Vallier refused to resign, pointing out to the court that in spite of all the screaming by his subordinates, he had managed, within his first six years in the colony, to create Quebec's General Hospital (1692), to begin the construction of a bishop's palace, and to establish Jesuit and Recollect houses in Montreal. By 1697, the bishop was back in Quebec, only to engage in another quarrel with the Jesuits, this time over the missions in the Mississippi River valley.

## THE CHURCH IN ACADIA IN THE
## LATE SEVENTEENTH CENTURY

A remote part of Saint-Vallier's diocese of Quebec was Acadia, a region that displayed a less fractious clergy after the return of the French in 1670. There Catholic missions developed alongside French settlement, the priests rarely having the opportunity to indulge in ecclesiastical guerrilla warfare.

During the second half of the seventeenth century, the Catholic Church continued working in Acadia much as it had in the past: trying to serve a small and widely scattered population with limited resources. In the wake of Sedg-wick's raid on Port Royal in 1654, one priest, the Capuchin Joseph d'Angers was in peninsular Nova Scotia, hiding among the Indians until his death in 1667. Another Capuchin missionary, Father Balthazar, evangelized the Baie des Chaleurs area in the 1650s, while a series of Jesuit missionaries worked out of the Miscou mission until 1662. A decade later, the Jesuits were replaced in the region by the Recollects, who had returned to Canada in 1670 and staffed a mission at Percé, a refuge for fishermen on the Gaspé peninsula, since 1672. Since the formation of the vicariate of New France in 1658, Acadia had been incorporated into Bishop Laval's area of jurisdiction, a legal technicality that did not bring any appreciable change to the area's pastoral services.

In the wake of the Treaty of Breda (1667), which handed Acadia back to France, the crown appointed Hector Andigné de Grandfontaine first French commander of repossessed Acadia. Having taken back forts Pentagouët, Jemseg, Port Royal, and Fort La Tour, Andigné directed arriving settlers to peninsular Nova Scotia, for Intendant Talon had decided to develop Acadia. Not since the 1630s had Acadia experienced such promising developments. In fact, the colony had a long way to go, because the newly arrived settlers of 1670 and 1671 only raised Acadia's total French population to some five hundred souls.

Inevitably, the presence of clergy was modeled on that of settlers. After 1670, Acadia's main settlement of Port Royal became the source of a series of satellite colonies on the isthmus of Chignecto (Beaubassin), and in the Minas basin on the shores of the Bay of Fundy. The contours of the future Acadia were drawn. Bishop Laval thereupon in 1676 sent Louis Petit (1629–1709) to take over the church in Acadia. A former soldier ordained in 1670, Father Petit settled in Port Royal with the title of vicar general of Acadia. While performing his ministry he distinguished himself by establishing a school for girls directed by a sister of the Congregation of Notre-Dame (1685) and another for boys directed by his assistant, the Sulpician Claude Trouvé (1686). In 1687, Petit joined the Seminary of Quebec while continuing to work in Acadia.

In 1684 the Seminary of Quebec was considering following up on the Petit appointment by placing one of its own men in Acadia. Father Pierre Thury (1644–1699) was therefore sent into the region with permission to select the site of his mission. He chose Miramichi, a fishing station of the Denys family on the New Brunswick coast. After working there for three years and noting the impossibility of converting the local Indians, Thury decided, in consultation with Petit, to move his mission to Pentagouët (modern Castine, Maine) near Jean-Vincent d'Abbadie de Saint-Castin's Abenaki settlement. Saint-Castin was a French officer who had come to Pentagouët in 1670, married into the Abenaki nation, and become a powerful commercial and military leader in the area. Thury stayed there for eight years (1687–1695), frequently participating in raiding parties against various settlements in New England, and signifi-cantly contributing to maintaining Indian loyalty to the French. When replaced in Pentagouët by Jesuit Father Vincent Bigot (1694), Thury moved to the Minas basin, becoming in 1698 Bishop Saint-Vallier's vicar general in the area. He died at Chebouctou (today's Halifax) on 3 June 1699.

When Petit arrived in Port Royal in 1676, another priest was already busy in Nova Scotia. Recollect friar Claude Moireau (1637–1703) had begun working in Beaubassin (isthmus of Chignecto) the previous year. While serving the local Acadian population, Moireau visited a number of white and Indian groups on the St. John River in the Gaspé peninsula and in the Minas basin. He was recalled to Quebec on the eve of Bishop Saint-Vallier's visit to Acadia in 1686.

Beginning in 1686, this handful of seminary, Jesuit, and Recollect missionaries was also accompanied by Sulpician priests. The first of these, Louis Geoffroy (1660–1707), newly arrived from France in 1685, was brought to Acadia by Saint-Vallier in 1686 and appointed assistant to Father Petit in Port Royal, where he stayed until his return to Quebec in 1692. The second Sulpician was Claude Trouvé (1644–1704), an experienced missionary who had directed the Sulpician mission on Lake Ontario between 1668 and 1680. After two years at Beaubassin, in 1690 Trouvé was taken prisoner by the English and returned to Quebec, only to come back to his mission of Beaubassin in 1694. For the next ten years he lived among his Acadians and Indians until his death at the French fishing station of Chedabouctou (near Canso, Nova Scotia) in 1704. This station also intermittently welcomed some French chaplains of the order of Penitents.

A third Sulpician stationed in Acadia in the late seventeenth century was Jean Baudoin (1662–1698), a former soldier like Petit, sent to Port Royal in 1688. He soon moved to Beaubassin where, initially in the company of Claude Trouvé, he worked until his 1694 recall to France. After returning to the colony in 1696 and participating in some military expeditions, he died in 1698.

## Missionary Expansion

In the latter third of the seventeenth century, while Catholic missionaries returned to Acadia and the church of the St. Lawrence valley struggled with a variety of internal problems, the Jesuits decided to cast their missionary net farther afield.

This was made possible by a much more aggressive French military policy after 1665, the year of the arrival in Canada of Governor Rémy de Courcelle and Lieutenant General Prouville de Tracy and the Carignan-Salières regiment, a fighting force of more than a thousand men sent specifically to quell and intimidate the Iroquois. After building a chain of forts along the Richelieu River and Lake Champlain, Tracy sent his troops on a punitive raid into the land of the Iroquois, the nations that had for decades terrorized New France with little respite. The first campaign, mounted in the dead of winter, fizzled out before the six hundred-strong army could engage the enemy. A more important raid was organized in the fall of 1666, when fourteen hundred men, assisted by a hundred Algonquin Indians, invaded the land of the Mohawks and destroyed everything in sight. The stage was set for a peace treaty that would last twenty years.

Canada's missionary clergy took advantage of the subdued Iroquois. While the Sulpicians founded a mission station at the village of Quinte at the mouth of the Cataracoui River on the north shore of Lake Ontario (1668–1680), in 1668 the Jesuits opened a mission station in each of the five Iroquois nations (Mohawk, Onondaga, Oneida, Cayuga, and Seneca). As had been the case in early Huronia, the missionaries usually only managed to baptize dying infants. They therefore decided to establish separate villages for Christian Iroquois similar to the villages of Lorette (Huron) and Sillery (Algonquin) near Quebec. So it was that in 1669, Christian Iroquois began to settle around a Jesuit residence at La Prairie on the south shore of the St. Lawrence near Montreal; the village was later moved a short distance away to Sault St. Louis, and named the mission of St. Francis Xavier. As noted in Chapter 11, in 1683 the Jesuits also established a similar village for Christian Abenaki Indians on the Chaudière River south of Quebec. However, once the Iroquois took to the warpath again after 1687, all the Jesuit missions to the Iroquois were closed and remained so until the return of peace in 1702. By this time, fully half the Mohawk nation lived in the Indian villages established by the Jesuits near Montreal, the reservations of Oka and Kahnawake. In the following decades a third reservation, that of Akwesasne (St. Regis) would also appear on the St. Lawrence west of Montreal.

By 1653 the Iroquois onslaught had reduced the supply of furs to the St. Lawrence colony to a trickle, forcing Canadians to begin traveling inland to collect the pelts the Indians did not dare bring down the rivers. The *coureur de bois* was born. Using Indian means of travel—canoe, snowshoe, and so on—a growing number of young men (sometimes sons of Frenchmen and natives) began going upriver into the distant and unexplored lands of the Indians. Two of the better-known of this earliest generation of *coureurs de bois* were Pierre-Esprit Radisson (1640–1710) and Médard Chouart des Groseilliers (1618–1696), who would become prime movers in the founding of the Hudson's Bay Company in 1670. One result of these explorations was an increasing knowledge of the upper country.

This was the setting in the 1660s when the Jesuits' returned to the immense basin of the Great Lakes, a country largely abandoned since the missionaries' escape from Huronia in 1650. Never slow in exploiting a missionary opportunity, in 1660 the Jesuits sent Father René Ménard (1605–1661) on a voyage of exploration into Lake Superior. He traveled in the company of a band of Ottawa Indians who were returning to their homes in today's Michigan. After wintering on the south shore of Lake Superior, Ménard died lost in the forest while traveling to the western extremity of Lake Superior.

Four years later, Father Claude Allouez (1622–1689) took up where Ménard

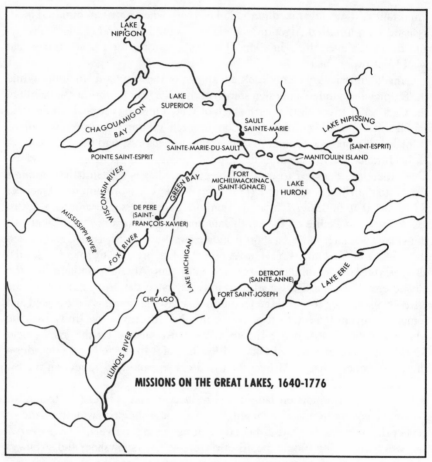

**MISSIONS ON THE GREAT LAKES, 1640-1776**

Missions on the Great Lakes, 1640–1776: Lakes Huron, Michigan, and Superior

had left off. Appointed by Laval vicar general of the area that is today's central United States, Allouez managed to travel to his assigned mission in 1665; he established his base of operations at Chagouamigon, near the southwestern end of Lake Superior near two villages of refugee Hurons and Algonquins who had fled the depredations of the Iroquois. He named his post the mission of the Holy Spirit. The evangelization of the American Midwest had begun.

For twenty-four years Allouez crisscrossed the basin of lakes Superior, Huron, Michigan, and Erie, evangelizing some two dozen bands of Indians. He was one of the giants of early American Christian history. After founding the mission of St. Francis Xavier on Green Bay (De Père, Wisconsin) in 1667, he helped establish two of his Jesuit colleagues there before traveling, the same year, to another new Jesuit mission, that of Sainte-Marie-du-Sault (Sault-Ste.-Marie), located at the junction of lakes Superior and Huron. The residence of

Ste. Marie became the center of Jesuit western missions and Father Allouez' base of operations. When, on 14 June 1671, Daumont de Saint-Lusson took possession of the western country in the name of France, it was Father Allouez who addressed the representatives of the fourteen Indian nations represented at the Sault. The ceremony marked the beginning of extensive French explorations into the West and the Mississippi valley.

Allouez had already ranged further afield. In 1670, in the company of Father Claude Dablon (1619–1697), he had gone beyond Green Bay into the country of the Illinois Indians, southwest of Lake Michigan. The following year, his colleague Jacques Marquette (1637–1675), stationed in the western country since 1668, founded the Jesuit mission of St. Ignatius at Michilimackinac, at the entrance to Lake Michigan. It was from this station, in May 1673, that Marquette set out in the company of the Canadian explorer Louis Jolliet to discover the Mississippi River, which they descended as far as the Arkansas–Louisiana border; they returned via the Chicago River, Marquette deciding to winter at Green Bay. After returning to evangelize the Illinois nation in 1674, Father Marquette became ill; he died in the forest in 1675 while attempting to return to the mission of St. Ignatius.

Having penetrated the land of the Illinois by 1670, the Jesuits continued their work undisturbed until the end of the century. In addition to Allouez, Dablon, and Marquette, other Jesuits active in this vast basin of the Great Lakes in the late seventeenth century included Louis André (1631–1715), Gabriel Druillettes (1610–1681), Antoine Silvy (1638–1711), Jacques Marest (1653–1725) and his brother Gabriel Marest (1662–1714), Henri Nouvel (1621–1702), Etienne de Carheil (1633–1726), and Charles Albanel (1616–1696)—who was appointed religious superior in the area in 1676 at the age of sixty and worked there for another twenty years. This was the same Albanel who had been working in Canada since 1649; he had been the first to travel overland to James Bay in 1671–1672 and again in 1674. Meanwhile, after two short stays in Hudson Bay in 1684 and 1686–1687, his Jesuit colleague Antoine Silvy had returned to that land of snow and ice to minister during six years (1687–1693) in the French outposts centered on Fort Sainte-Anne (Fort Albany, Ontario).

The Jesuit apostolate among the victims of the Iroquois in the American Midwest proved more fruitful than among the Five Nations. It also served to cast a better light on the Christian work of evangelization than did the petty politico-ecclesiastical quarrels of various church leaders.

## The Church of the Mississippi Valley and Louisiana

Another area of church endeavor was the new colony of Louisiana and the upper reaches of the Mississippi River, two regions that were first evangelized at the turn of the eighteenth century. Although some priests in those territories proved outstanding models of Christian living, many more indulged in protracted petty clerical quarrels, aided and abetted by leading church officials like Bishop Saint-Vallier. Their story is no more edifying than that of their peers in the Caribbean or in Saint-Vallier's Quebec.

The country of the Illinois was located to the east of the Mississippi, bounded on the north by the Fox and Wisconsin rivers that led to Green Bay on Lake Michigan and on the south by the beautiful Ohio River. Jesuit missionaries were active in the area after 1670 from bases at Michilimackinac, Sault-Ste.-Marie, Chagouamigon, and Fort Saint-Joseph (1679–1691) on the southeastern shore of Lake Michigan. In the mid-seventeenth century the Illinois nation, including tribes like the Cahokias, Tamaroas, Kaskaskias, Miamis, and Peorias, had taken a severe beating at the hands of the warlike Iroquois; by the end of the century many of them had banded together around the Kaskaskias on the Illinois River, in the neighborhood of Fort Saint-Louis (1683) (today's Starved Rock, Illinois), built by Robert Cavelier de La Salle (1643–1687) while leading his exploratory journeys down the Mississippi.

This is where the Jesuit Jacques Gravier (1651–1708), the "founder of the Illinois mission," found his flock upon his arrival in the country in 1689. Gravier devoted the rest of his life to his Illinois Indians, the Jesuit order appointing him in 1696 superior of the mission to the Illinois, Miamis, Ottawas, and others, while Bishop Saint-Vallier of Quebec had already (in 1690) made him vicar general of the same missions.

Not sufficiently occupied with his numerous internal quarrels in Quebec, Bishop Saint-Vallier initiated another one in 1698 by appointing priests from the Seminary of Quebec to be missionaries on the Mississippi River and by giving their superior the office of vicar general of these missions.

Perhaps Saint-Vallier felt that the Illinois mission of the Jesuits should not extend as far as the Mississippi, because the village of the Tamaroas that would become the main site in contention was 220 miles from the Jesuit mission station of Kaskaskia on the Illinois River (Kaskaskia I on map). Nevertheless, the land of the Illinois had always extended to the Mississippi River. The problem was compounded by the fact that in 1700, the Kaskaskia tribe of the Illinois nation migrated from the Illinois River to establish new homes on the east bank of the Mississippi, between the mouths of the Missouri and the Ohio rivers (Kaskaskia II on map). The French Fort de Chartres was soon built nearby (1718). Moreover, the Tamaroas and Cahokias, two other Illinois tribes, were also established on the east bank of the Mississippi, just below the mouth of the Missouri River in the village of Cahokia.

In sum, by 1700 two bands of missionaries, Jesuits and seminary priests, were each evangelizing the same Indians, the superior of each group being empowered to serve as vicar general of the bishop of Quebec. Given the fractious ecclesiastical climate of the period and the fact that the Jesuits and the priests of the Seminary of Foreign Missions were already at odds over mission-

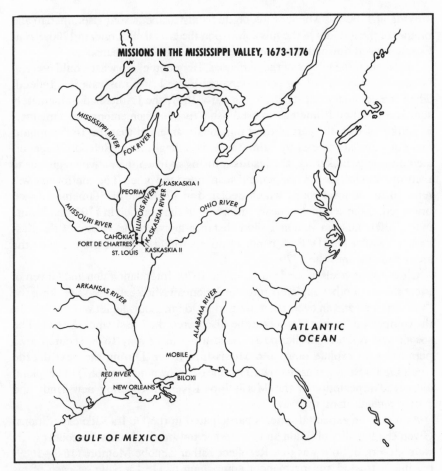

Missions in the Mississippi Valley, 1673–1776

ary policies in the Far East (the Chinese Rites controversy), the stage was set for another fight.

The fight between Jesuits and Seminary priests in the upper Mississippi began when three Quebec Seminary priests (Jean-François Buisson de Saint-Cosme, Albert Davion, and François de Montigny) arrived in the area from Quebec in early 1699. They had left Montreal on 16 July 1698, on their twenty-seven-hundred-mile missionary journey. They traveled in four canoes via the Ottawa River and stopped en route at the Jesuit missions of Michilimackinac and Kaskaskia (Kaskaskia I). De Montigny, the superior, founded his mission among the Tamaroas (near the present Cahokia, Illinois), and by 7 February 1700 had obtained reinforcements in the person of Father Marc Bergier (1667–1707), appointed to succeed De Montigny as vicar general in the area; also arriving in 1700 was Michel Buisson de Saint-Cosme, a young seminarian and brother of the founder of the mission. Upon the arrival of Bergier in 1700, Saint-Cosme moved downstream to evangelize the Natchez Indians.

In Cahokia, the village of the Tamaroas, Bergier took up what would prove to be an almost century-long controversy with the Jesuit missionaries. Indeed, when the seminary priests arrived in early 1699, the Jesuits had immediately sent Father Julien Binneteau to establish a rival mission among the Tamaroas, arguing that this was part of their missionary area and that the 1698 appointment of seminary priests by Saint-Vallier was illegitimate. Relations degenerated into petty bickering, the Jesuits refusing to teach the native languages to their rivals, while each vicar general suspended the other. The controversy was referred to the royal court, which declared in 1701 that the Tamaroa mission belonged to the seminary priests; informed of the decision in 1702, the Jesuits moved their mission station a short distance away, to the village of the Kaskaskias (Kaskaskia II). Both bands of priests would continue evangelizing the area's Indians until the 1770s.

Close on the heels of the Jesuits, in the 1670s Intendant Talon and Governor Frontenac sent other explorers into the American Midwest, always seeking the "western sea" and an eventual route to the Orient. Louis Jolliet was the first. In the company of Father Marquette, he discovered the Mississippi in 1673. The second was Robert Cavelier de La Salle who, on 12 May 1678, secured royal permission to explore down the Mississippi River. During the next decade (until De La Salle was assassinated by one of his own men in 1687) the explorer journeyed repeatedly to the Mississippi River, discovering new lands and Indian nations along the way.

As was to be expected, priests participated in the De La Salle expeditions. Given the hostility of Talon and Frontenac toward the Jesuits, Recollect friars were preferred. So it was that Recollect Father Zénobe Membré (1645–1689) became a trusted and permanent companion of De La Salle on each of his expeditions. During the first, that of 1679–1680, Membré spent several months at Fort Crèvecoeur (now Peoria, Illinois) evangelizing the Illinois Indians and learning their language. It was during his return voyage in September 1680 that his companion, Father De La Ribourde, was killed. Also part of De La Salle's expedition of 1681–1682, not only did Membré bless the cross raised by the explorer at the mouth of the Mississippi, he was also entrusted with the task of reporting to the king on the results of the expedition. Father Membré then spent two years in France before embarking on De La Salle's third and final exploratory journey in the summer of 1684. The resilient friar was present when De La Salle was assassinated in 1687; he then spent another twenty months working at Fort St. Louis, where he in turn was killed on 15 January 1689.

The third Recollect friar accompanying De La Salle in 1679–1680 was Louis Hennepin (1626–1705). He it was who returned to Europe in 1681 and two years later published a famous *Description of Louisiana* wherein he claimed to have made the return journey to the mouth of the river in some thirty days in 1680 and then to have become a prisoner of the Sioux Indians. His book was a best-seller in its day.

De La Salle's ill-fated third expedition, that of 1684–1687, included six priests, two of whom were Sulpicians, and another two Recollects, Membré being one of them. The other Recollect was Father Anastase Douay, who also witnessed the murder of De La Salle. Douay would later accompany Pierre Le Moyne d'Iberville on his voyage of 1698–1699 that resulted in the founding of the colony of Louisiana.

Three Quebec seminary priests canoeing toward the Illinois country in the latter part of 1698 were unaware that they would soon find themselves in the neighborhood of another French colony that was about to be implanted in North America. Indeed, since 1690, King Louis XIV's American policy had become overtly expansionistic in an attempt to contain the English colonies on the Atlantic seaboard. A chain of French posts was planned along the Ohio River, the Mississippi, and the coast of the Gulf of Mexico. A leader was needed to establish the posts that would anchor the southwestern perimeter of New France.

The king chose Pierre Le Moyne d'Iberville (1661–1706), arguably the most dynamic, illustrious, and ruthless soldier Canada has produced, a man who had spent more than a decade making war on the English from Hudson Bay to the Atlantic seaboard.

Chosen by Louis XIV to lead the first French colonizing expedition to the mouth of the Mississippi in late October 1698, D'Iberville left the port of Brest with four ships. After sailing along the Gulf coast, he found the Mississippi delta, built a temporary fort in Biloxi Bay (Ocean Springs, Mississippi), midway between the Mississippi and the Spanish fort of Pensacola, and set off on his return voyage to France on 3 May 1699; he left his brother Jean-Baptiste Le Moyne de Bienville in command of some eighty men at Biloxi.

In January 1700, D'Iberville was back in Biloxi with more supplies and men and proceeded to build a second fort on the Mississippi River itself, loaded his ship with furs, and returned to France. On a third voyage in late 1701, D'Iberville founded the fort of Mobile, at the bottom of Mobile Bay, some fifty-four miles from the open sea, with a view to the military control of the Gulf of Mexico. He left Louisiana in April 1702, never to return. He died of illness in the West Indies in 1706, seven years before the Treaty of Utrecht gave back to England most of D'Iberville's conquests (Hudson Bay, Newfoundland, and Acadia); Louisiana would later suffer a similar fate.

D'Iberville's brother Bienville (1680–1767) became the real founder of Louisiana. Having served under his brother in the military campaigns of Hudson Bay, Newfoundland, and the Atlantic coast, he was also part of the first expedition to Louisiana in 1698. Appointed commander at Biloxi in 1701, on his brother's death in 1706 he became the youngest of the Le Moyne family involved in Louisiana. However, Bienville did not become governor of the troubled colony for several years (1732), although he was appointed military commander of the Mississippi region in 1714. He founded New Orleans in 1718.

The political history of Louisiana during the eighteenth century is mind-boggling. Crown-appointed governors like D'Iberville were followed by commercial companies working in varying degrees of partnership with the crown; then the latter took over once again. Whoever was in charge, the situation was always precarious, for England and Spain were never far away, while various Indian nations sometimes proved hostile. Moreover, few settlers immigrated to Louisiana, its total population being no more than a thousand whites and blacks in 1763; those who did and managed to survive did so at the price of considerable hardship.

The ecclesiastical history of the colony of Louisiana was no more exemplary than its political or social history. The Recollect chaplain Anastase Douay had accompanied the first expedition of 1698–1699, while Jesuit father Paul du Ru was part of the second voyage in 1699–1700, replacing Douay—who couldn't wait to go home. While going up the Mississippi with D'Iberville in February 1700, Du Ru met Father De Montigny, who had come downstream from Cahokia and was evangelizing the Taensa and Natchez Indians. Having returned to Biloxi in April, Du Ru was visited by both De Montigny and Davion, two of the three seminary priests sent to Cahokia the preceding year. Father Du Ru stayed in Louisiana for another year, returning to France upon the arrival of his replacement in 1701; while Davion returned to his Mississippi mission, De Montigny went to France, complained of his lot, and accused the Jesuits of obstructing his missionary work and calumniating him. (This was shortly before the French court judged that the seminary priests rather than the Jesuits were authorized to work in Cahokia on the upper Mississippi.) Petty clerical quarreling and bickering continued between Jesuits and seminary priests until 1704, when the only Jesuit in Louisiana was removed from the area.

The sons of St. Ignatius did not return to the lower Mississippi for another twenty years, a period when seminary priests handled the ministry, assisted for a time (1720–1723) by discalced Carmelites, and then by Capuchins (1722 and after). The wrangling between competing bands of clerics continued, the Jesuits insisting on being assigned a distinct missionary territory; otherwise, the seminary priests might have pulled rank on them, as they had done in the upper Mississippi. The mutual ill will was compounded by Bishop Saint-Vallier, who declared in 1704 that he would never appoint a Jesuit as his vicar general, and by Saint-Vallier's coadjutor-bishop in Paris, Bishop Duplessis de Mornay, a Capuchin who preferred his own kind.

The least that can be said is that the Christian church was not proving very edifying in Louisiana. The quarrels only subsided with the English conquest and subsequent Treaty of Paris (1763), followed by the Spanish takeover of the west bank of the Mississippi in 1769. Evangelizing the heathen had indeed become a distant concern.

## FRENCH-AMERICAN CHRISTIANITY IN THE EIGHTEENTH CENTURY

As suggested above, in the eighteenth century, the story of the church of New France was not so heroic and wonderful as in the mid-seventeenth century. French-American Christianity had put on a different face. The problem was not due to the numbers of clergymen or to the extent of the mission territories; in fact, Catholic priests in the Americas had never ranged over such an extensive area. In 1660, the missions of New France had been limited to one or two fugitive priests in Acadia, none in the land of the Iroquois, and none west of the Ottawa River. Fifty years later, Catholic priests of various orders were working in Acadia, the land of the Five Nations, the basin of the Great Lakes, and the entire Mississippi valley.

In the central St. Lawrence colony, Bishop Saint-Vallier administered a diocese divided (1721) into three parts, corresponding to the divisions of civil government. In 1706, the Quebec region included forty-one parishes serving some thirteen thousand faithful; that of Montreal, twenty-eight parishes including some eight thousand souls; and that of Trois-Rivières, thirteen parishes with two thousand faithful. A generation later, in 1739, the numbers had grown to 22,327 in the Quebec region, 17,423 in the Montreal region, and 3,174 in the region of Trois-Rivières. Of these eighty-two parishes, forty-eight were located north of the St. Lawrence and thirty-four on the south side. They were served by fifty-one priests (1719), many of whom directed several parishes at once. Included in the curé's ordinary duties was that of maintaining the colony's official registers of births, deaths, and marriages. In addition, another eighteen priests worked in the seminaries and colleges. By 1756, the number of parishes had risen to eighty-eight, forty-four of which were financially self-sufficient, while the other forty-four required financial assistance from diocesan authorities. In addition, a score of other mission stations were regularly visited by itinerant clergy.

Moreover, the scarce clergy of New France, male and female, was responsible for most of the social and educational services in the colony. In the eighteenth century, Quebec was served by two hospitals, the first the Hôtel-Dieu, founded in 1639, the second the Quebec General Hospital, founded in 1692 by Bishop Saint-Vallier; the latter was staffed by a handful of nuns who originally came from the Hôtel-Dieu and was then required by the bishop to become an autonomous congregation (1699). Montreal had Jeanne Mance's own Hôtel-Dieu, directed since 1659 by De la Dauversière's hospitalers. The city was given its own General Hospital in 1692, when a local underwriter in the fur trade, having experienced a conversion, decided to devote his life to charitable works. François Charon de la Barre (1654–1719) undertook to found a refuge for old men in need.

Assisted by other pious and generous souls, Charon obtained a gift of land from Montreal's Sulpicians and in 1692 was authorized by the Sovereign Council to begin building his hospice. The first beggar was admitted in 1694. Meanwhile, Charon had founded the Brother Hospitalers of the Cross and of St. Joseph, a congregation of male nurses that would direct the institution; episcopal and royal authorizations were obtained in 1694, the brothers being authorized to admit poor orphaned children, the sick, the handicapped, the elderly, and all other males in need. The Brothers Charon, as they were usually called, soon donned a uniform habit and adopted rules for congregational living. Thereupon the brothers discovered that the king did not want them to become a full-fledged religious congregation; indeed, he forbade them to make vows and to wear a uniform habit. After the death of François Charon in 1719, his successors proved less skillful in managing his hospital. By 1747, only three aged brothers remained, living in a largely empty and decrepit building.

In a colony that had benefited from the earlier work of the widows De la Peltrie and Guyart, it was fitting that a young widow should salvage the work of Charon and make the Montreal General Hospital into one of North America's most important health-care institutions. Marie-Marguerite Dufrost de Lajemmerais (1701–1771) was born in Varennes, Quebec, into one of New France's foremost families. Having moved with her family to Montreal, in 1722 Marguerite married François d'Youville, who gave her two surviving sons before his death in 1730. The marriage had not been a happy one, the husband's death signaling a second chance at happiness for Marguerite. While becoming very active in religious confraternities and charitable works, Marguerite joyfully witnessed both her surviving sons entering upon studies that would lead them to the priesthood. In 1737 she associated with a handful of other like-minded women in devoting their lives to caring for poor and sick women, some of whom were admitted into residence with the "sisters." By 1745, the five women formally undertook to live together, share their property, and devote their lives to the care of the poor.

Given the moribund condition of the General Hospital, the Gentlemen of Saint-Sulpice recommended to the governor of New France that he entrust the hospital to the widow Youville and her band. This was done in 1747, when Marguerite moved into the debt-ridden hospital with six companions. Thereafter the Montreal General Hospital would admit patients of both sexes, in addition to "lost women." Overcoming several administrative and financial obstacles put in her way, including a disastrous fire in the 1760s, the widow Youville proved an excellent administrator, as many businesswomen were wont to do at the time. By 1755, her band of sisters adopted the name of Sisters of Charity of the General Hospital, although many continued to designate them "gray nuns," from the French adjective *grises* (tipsy), an epithet coined in the

1730s in commemoration of the widow Youville's late husband's alcoholism, bootlegging, and brandy-trading.

Beginning in the mid-nineteenth century, a hundred years after their founding, these Sisters of Charity would become one of North America's most prolific congregations, founding hospitals and schools all across the continent. The congregation, which today comprises some four thousand Gray Nuns scattered over four continents, attained a pinnacle of honor when, on 9 December 1990, Marguerite Dufrost, the widow Youville, became the first Canadian-born Christian to have her name entered onto the Roman Catholic Church's calendar of saints. Her canonization, only six years after that of Marguerite Bourgeois, indicates the Church's new insistence on social service.

Education was also a privileged form of apostolate in New France. Girls were served by the Ursulines in Quebec (from 1639) and Trois-Rivières (after 1697); by Marguerite Bourgeois and her Congregation of Notre-Dame in Montreal (from 1658), Trois-Rivières (from 1664), and Quebec (from 1686); and even occasionally by hospitalers. Boys of the Quebec region enjoyed the schooling of the Jesuits in their College of Quebec (from 1635), and of the seminary priests who staffed elementary schools by the end of the seventeenth century. In Trois-Rivières, the Recollects directed elementary schooling while they were in charge of the parish in 1671–1683 and 1693–1777. In Montreal, Bourgeois's first school admitted both boys and girls until 1668, when Sulpician father Souart opened a school for boys, a service that the Gentlemen of Saint-Sulpice continued to provide until the British conquest of 1760. A number of rural schools also existed, more often than not established by the local pastor.

While the founding of the Sisters of Charity bore witness to a continuing dynamism and vitality in eighteenth-century Canadian Catholicism, the story of Canada's bishops proved less edifying. The controversial Bishop Saint-Vallier had gone to France in 1700 determined to bring the Jesuits to heel in the controversy over the Cahokia mission and then over the Louisiana mission. While in France, he published a rigoristic and pessimistic catechism and a book of diocesan ritual, both of which were denounced by the Jesuits, provoking another controversy. Having settled these disputes to his satisfaction, Saint-Vallier took ship for Canada in 1704 but was captured on the high seas, taken to England, and held prisoner until 1709. Once liberated, he discovered to his dismay that the French court refused to allow him back into New France. However, the stubborn bishop refused to resign and managed to get himself back to his diocese in 1713; he had been absent since 1700. In Quebec, the unloved bishop took up residence in the General Hospital, displaying an even greater austerity while denouncing the mediocrity of both clergy and faithful; he even considered that the end of the world was at hand. His own demise was forthcoming on 26 December 1727.

The unpopular Saint-Vallier was succeeded in the see of Quebec by Louis-François Duplessis de Mornay, the court-appointed coadjutor-bishop of Quebec since 1713. The Capuchin De Mornay had always resided in Paris, whence he refused to depart to take up his duties in New France; however, he did collect the revenue paid to the bishop of Quebec. De Mornay immediately obtained the appointment of a coadjutor-bishop to administer the see of Quebec in his place. Pierre-Herman Dosquet (1691–1777) was a Sulpician on loan to Paris's Seminary of Foreign Missions, who had served as chaplain to the Congregation of Notre-Dame in Montreal (1721–1723).

Dosquet arrived in Quebec in September 1729, accompanied by a retinue of servants. He soon proved just as unpopular as Saint-Vallier, trading accusations and insults with the diocesan chapter and the congregations of nuns. Lacking in tact and diplomacy, he had to administer his see without the benefit of the revenues that were being collected by Bishop De Mornay in France. After three years in his unhappy situation, he returned to France in late 1732, obtained the resignation of De Mornay, and was back in Canada in August 1734. Aware of his growing unpopularity, he returned to France the following year and spent the next four years traveling while negotiating a generous settlement from the French court that sought his resignation (1739).

Dosquet was succeeded by François-Louis de Pourroy de Lauberivière (1711–1740). Having set foot in Quebec on 8 August 1740, the new bishop died twelve days later of an epidemic that had broken out on board ship. The see of Quebec that had suffered from absentee bishops for twenty of the previous forty years was vacant once again. With the arrival on 29 August 1741 of Quebec's sixth bishop, Henri-Marie Dubreil de Pontbriand (see Chapter 13), the situation improved.

## CHRISTIAN LIFE IN EIGHTEENTH-CENTURY NEW FRANCE

The generosity of the widow Youville's Gray nuns and the profiteering, selfish, petty, or arrogant episcopal administrators of the eighteenth-century church were two opposite poles in a church of New France that cannot be identified with one or the other.

The church of New France was not rich. While colonial administrators took advantage of the fact that the crown provided some 40 percent of the church's revenue, the balance was generated by the income from the land owned by various ecclesiastical institutions; in fact, church-owned property increased from 10 percent of the seigniorial land in 1663 to 25 percent by the end of the French regime. Another source of income was of course the contributions of the faithful, in the form of tithes and otherwise. State subsidies covered the deficits in the operating budgets of church-administered social services. In addition to the hospitals and schools noted above, these included the bureaus of the poor established in Montreal, Quebec, and Trois-Rivières, offices that served as relief centers and employment agencies.

During the period of Jesuit monopoly in New France (1632–1657), the governors of the colony usually legislated in support of the moral teachings of the priests. So it was that on 29 December 1635, notices and prohibitions were placed on a pillar in front of the church in Quebec, announcing penalties against drunkenness, blasphemy, and failure to attend mass and religious services on holy days. An iron collar was attached to the same pillar alongside a wooden horse for the punishment of delinquents. Father Le Jeune reported in 1636 on the punishment of some blasphemers and drunkards in January 1636.

When the proud, stubborn, devout, and ascetic Laval was succeeded by the equally ascetic but uncompromising Saint-Vallier, the church of New France was not priest-ridden by any stretch of the imagination, given that only fifty parish priests were serving more than eighty parishes. Indeed, in 1683, the Intendant De Meulles reported that most of the people did not hear mass more than four times a year, that several died without the benefits of the sacraments of the Church, and that most had little understanding of Christian doctrine.

Both Laval and Saint-Vallier regularly denounced various abuses, real or alleged, in the colony. For example, on 26 February 1682, Bishop Laval roundly accused many women of vanity and scandalous luxury in that they appeared in church indecently dressed, showing bare arms, shoulders, and throats, in addition to curling their hair and baring their heads in church.

While in France in 1702, Saint-Vallier published his catechism and ritual, books that would be the only authorized texts in the diocese until 1777. The bishop had been preparing them since 1688, for his diocese had no uniform catechism, various French ones being in use since the colony's inception. Molded in the spirit of the Council of Trent, the catechism's Christian doctrine was grouped under five headings, those of faith, hope, charity, sacraments, and justice. Nine commandments of the Church were listed, including the obligations to attend mass on Sundays and holy days, to confess one's sins annually, to receive the Eucharist at Easter, to fast during Lent and on the eves of holy days, to abstain from eating meat on Fridays and Saturdays, to pay the tithe, and to avoid weddings during the liturgical seasons of Advent and Lent.

Among the moral strictures found in Saint-Vallier's catechism are those condemning blasphemy, dancing, attendance at the theater, balls, and masquerades. Confessors were forbidden to absolve women who confessed to having shown bare throats or shoulders, even in their own homes, while the same priests were urged to bend every effort to eradicate lewd or suggestive behavior.

The harsh condemnations and warnings uttered by various bishops suggest that the moral behavior of the colonists in New France may have been particularly reprehensible. However, other indications suggest that the people of New France were not any more immoral than others. For example, the several hundred *filles du roi*, marriageable girls who were sent to Quebec between 1659 and 1673, were not women of easy virtue, as some have suggested. Moreover, the birthrate of illegitimate children in New France was low in the seventeenth century, although it did increase in the eighteenth.

A most telling testimonial to the piety and religious behavior of the Canadians is that of Peter Kalm, a Swedish botanist and agriculturalist who toured eastern North America in 1748–1749. After visiting the New England colonies from September, 1748, Kalm went up the Hudson River and into Canada via Lake Champlain. Kalm was a careful observer who, on 19 July 1749, boarded a boat that regularly plied the waters between Fort St. Frederick (Crown Point, New York) and Fort St. John at the northern extremity of Lake Champlain, where Kalm arrived on 20 July 1749:

> The French, in their colonies, spend much more time in prayer and external worship, than the English and Dutch settlers in the British colonies. The latter have neither morning nor evening prayer in their ships and yachts, and no difference is made between Sunday and other days. They never, or very seldom, say grace at dinner. On the contrary, the French here have prayers every morning and night on board their shipping, and on Sundays they pray more than commonly: they regularly say grace at their meals; and every one of them says prayers in private as soon as he gets up. At Fort St. Frederic all the soldiers assembled together for morning and evening prayers.[2]

Continuing his five-month visit to Canada, Kalm compared the women of Canada and New England, the former emerging as "handsome, well-bred and virtuous, with an innocent and becoming freedom," while the latter he judged slothful and lazy.

Between 2 and 4 August 1749, while traveling down the St. Lawrence from Montreal to Quebec, Kalm described several churches along the way, adding:

> There are several crosses put up by the road side, which is parallel to the shores of the river. These crosses are very common in Canada, and are put up to excite devotion in the traveller. They are made of wood, five or six yards high, and proportionally broad. In that side which looks towards the road is a square hole, in which they place an image of our Saviour, the cross, or of the holy Virgin, with the child in her arms; and before that they put a piece of glass, to prevent its being spoiled by the weather. . . . They put up about . . . [those crosses] all the instruments which they think the Jews employed in crucifying our Saviour. . . . A figure of the cock, which crowed when St. Peter denied our Lord, is commonly put at the top of the cross.[3]

Having arrived in Quebec on 5 August, Kalm described the town's several stone churches, those of the cathedral, the Jesuits, the Recollects, the Ursulines, the Hôtel-Dieu hospital, the bishop's chapel, and the lower-town church of Notre-Dame-des-Victoires. The latter had been built in 1690, in thanks for deliverance from an English invasion. With Saint-Vallier's permission, he visited most of the town's religious institutions and proceeded to compare Jesuits and Recollects, heaping praise on the former while deriding the latter:

> The Jesuits are commonly very learned, studious, and are very civil and agreeable in company. In their whole deportment there is something pleasing; it is no wonder therefore that they captivate the minds of the people. They seldom speak of religious matters; and if it happens, they generally avoid disputes. They are very ready to do any one a service. . . . Their conversation is very entertaining and learned, so that one cannot be tired of their company. Among all the Jesuits I have conversed with in Canada, I have not found one who was not possessed of these qualities in a very eminent degree. . . . Everybody sees, that they are, as it were, selected . . . on account of their superior genius and qualities. They are here reckoned a most cunning set of people, who generally succeed in their undertakings, and surpass all others in acuteness of understanding.[4]

Having noted the fine large residences of the Recollects in Quebec, Trois-Rivières, and Montreal, the Swedish traveler wrote:

> [The Recollects] do not endeavour to choose cunning fellows amongst them, but take all they can get. They do not torment their brains with much learning. . . . At night they generally lie on mats. . . . They have no possessions here . . . and live chiefly on the alms which people give them. To this purpose, the young monks, or brothers, go into the houses with a bag, and beg what they want. . . . Sometimes they go among the Indians as missionaries. In each fort . . . the king keeps one of these monks instead of a priest, who officiates there. . . . On board the king's ships are generally no other priests than these friars, who are therefore looked upon as people belonging to the king.[5]

In sum, the Catholics of New France were probably no better or worse than other Catholics of the day. On the one hand, their bishops frequently complained, but that was part of their job. On the other hand, a learned and widely traveled observer like Kalm painted a possibly overly romantic picture of the piety and devotion of Canadians, some of whom still believed in witchcraft and sorcery, while others went on annual pilgrimages to the shrine of Sainte-Anne de Beaupré, downstream from Quebec.

More prosperous and happy than the European peasant, the Canadian *habitant*'s numbers grew rapidly after 1650. The one thousand colonists of that year had tripled their number during the 1650s and tripled them again during the 1660s, assisted by important migrations from France. Thereafter, the increase of the colony's population was almost solely due to a phenomenal birthrate among the Canadians, who more than doubled their numbers every twenty-five years, reaching a total of fifty-five thousand in 1754. Beginning in the late seventeenth century, they were encouraged to do so by a governmental baby-bonus system that awarded families with more than ten children state grants of three and four hundred livres per year. Thereafter the typical French-Canadian family included ten or more children, and would continue to do so until the 1940s. A new nation had been born.

As the eighteenth century progressed, French-American Christianity continued to change, as did the social, political, economic, and cultural situation. A major cause of this latter change was the growing power of England and the resulting increased threat to the security of New France. The colony's church had a new cross to bear.

# 13

## A NEW CHURCH IN
## A NEW STATE

Centered on Quebec, French-American Christianity was a full partner in New France, a colony that stood at the peak of its power and influence at the beginning of the eighteenth century. Indeed, the French crown held most of the North American continent in fee, from Hudson Bay in the north to the Gulf of Mexico in the south, from Acadia in the east to the Illinois country and the vast Northwest. The only rival English enclaves were those of Newfoundland in the North Atlantic and the colonies of the Atlantic seaboard. The former was a colony of negligible force; the latter were powerful, rich, and compact settlements whose population was sixteen times larger than that of New France. Historians are still amazed by the fact that New France managed to hold the latter in check for so long.

Between 1710 and 1763 occurred the unraveling of the French empire in the Americas, with inevitable consequences for the church. The tragedy for New France began to unfold with the conquest of Acadia by England in 1710, but especially with the Treaty of Utrecht of 1713 whereby France gave away to England its North American holdings because of the French crown's military losses in Europe. Indeed, the significant military gains made by D'Iberville and his peers were traded away to buy peace from the English. Beginning in 1744, however, another European war soon escalated into one whose stakes were nothing less than the control of North America. Once the dust settled and England had emerged triumphant in 1760, the conqueror discovered that his own upstart colonies on the Atlantic seaboard sought their own independence from the mother country. Indirectly, the French-American church was again involved.

By definition, a Christian church is an institution aimed at adapting the Christian faith to a specific society and culture. The several changes of government in North America meant that the church of New France had to adjust rapidly to the new political conditions in Acadia, Canada, and Louisiana. The undertaking was fraught with pitfalls, for a French and Catholic people was endeavoring to adapt to an English and Protestant power.

## THE ACADIAN TRAGEDY

As was to be expected, Acadia, that Palestine of North America, was first to bear the brunt of the English assault on New France. After 1710, the year the English conquered peninsular Nova Scotia, French Catholic missionaries had to decide where their loyalties lay, either with the occupying English forces or with their own French fellow subjects who still occupied the neighboring Ile Saint-Jean (Prince Edward Island), Ile Royale (Cape Breton Island), and today's New Brunswick. Their dilemma was ultimately settled for them by the ruthless deportation of the Acadians by the English (1755 and after), and the definitive conquest of the fortress of Louisburg on Cape Breton Island in 1758.

During the first half of the forty-year (1670–1710) French occupation of peninsular Nova Scotia, the colony had enjoyed the most prosperous period it had ever known or would know for a long time afterward. However, when hostilities broke out anew between England and France in 1690, things took a decided turn for the worse in Acadia. For another twenty years (1690–1710), while France largely neglected its colony, guerrilla raids, acts of piracy, and finally a full-scale assault on Port Royal by a Boston fleet bearing thirty-four hundred British soldiers led to the conquest of Port Royal and of most of Acadia by Britain.

When the Treaty of Utrecht (1713) ended the War of the Spanish Succession, it also tolled the death knell of New France, particularly of Acadia. Hudson Bay, Newfoundland, and peninsular Nova Scotia passed into English hands, France retaining Prince Edward Island (Ile Saint-Jean), Cape Breton Island (Ile Royale), and the islands of Saint-Pierre and Miquelon off the coast of Newfoundland. The French also continued to claim and occupy the north shore of the Bay of Fundy and the isthmus of Chignecto, where the settlement of Beaubassin was located. At the time, in peninsular Nova Scotia the Acadians numbered some fifteen hundred people, most of whom inhabited Port Royal or the neighboring Minas basin, while a few hundred were at Beaubassin. Forty years later, on the eve of the deportation, the number of Acadians had grown to some eighteen thousand; they faced a New England population of more than a million.

By the terms of the Treaty of Utrecht, the Acadians were to enjoy the free exercise of their religion to the extent allowed by the laws of Great Britain. The English permitted French priests to continue serving in Acadian parishes. In addition, France began occupying unpopulated parts of French Acadia, specifically Cape Breton and Prince Edward islands. Although they only settled on the latter after 1719, and only in small numbers, they built the major fortress of Louisburg on Cape Breton (following 1717).

Priests were part of these new colonies. In addition, from bases on or near Cape Breton, France also sent missionaries to the Micmac and Abenaki Indians in English Nova Scotia. The seeds of ongoing conflict were there, for these missionaries to the Indians were appointed and paid by the French crown, to which they answered.

In order to understand the convoluted ecclesiastical story of Acadia in the first half of the eighteenth century, one basic fact must be kept in mind: that two different groups of clergy were at work there. The first group consisted of the priests assigned to the Acadian parishes; the second group was made up of the missionaries to the Indians. With few exceptions, members of the first group showed unalloyed loyalty to the British crown and were instructed to do so by the bishop of Quebec. This was the case for Sulpician fathers Jean-Pierre de Miniac, Claude-Jean-Baptiste Chauvreulx, Charles de La Goudalie, Jean-Baptiste de Gay Desenclaves, and others who were pastors of Acadian parishes from the 1710s to the 1750s. These men frequently had cordial relations with several British governors.

This parish clergy in eighteenth-century Acadia usually belonged to either the Society of Saint-Sulpice or to the Recollect order. Although Quebec seminary priests had been in charge of Port Royal until 1702 when the last of them, Father Abel Maudoux, was recalled, it was the Recollect friar Felix Pain (1668–1741) who was assigned as his successor in the post of chaplain to the garrison. Pain worked in Port Royal until the English occupation in 1710, whereupon he moved to the parishes of Minas (Wolfville, Nova Scotia) and Beaubassin (Amherst, Nova Scotia). In 1725, Pain left Nova Scotia to work another six years (1725–1731) at Ile Saint-Jean (Prince Edward Island) and a final two years at Louisbourg (1731–1733), whereupon he left the ministry. Another Recollect was appointed pastor of Port Royal and vicar general of Acadia in 1704. This was Justinien Durand (1667–1746), who worked in Nova Scotia until 1726, becoming involved in the Acadian resistance to the English requirement that they take an unconditional oath of allegiance to the British crown.

We have already seen that in addition to their evangelical duties, members of the second group of clergymen, the missionaries to the Indians, were also in the employ of the French government, and worked as political agents of the French crown.

In their capacity as missionaries to the Indian people, the Jesuits belonged to this second group. When the Treaty of Utrecht was signed in 1713, the disciples of Saint Ignatius directed a mission to the Abenaki on the Penobscot and Kennebec rivers in today's Maine, and another mission at Meductic, New Brunswick, on the St. John River. The latter had been founded in 1701 for the Malecite Indians, friends of the Abenaki. This was territory claimed by both England and France; the Treaty of Utrecht was unclear as to the border between the two colonies.

The mission on the Kennebec had been established in 1694 by Jesuit Father Sébastien Rale (1657–1724) at Narantsouak or Norridgewock, today's Old

Point, South Madison, Maine. Rale was soon involved in the fighting between the Abenakis and the French on the one hand and the English on the other. For the next quarter-century he inspired his Abenaki against the English, ultimately being killed in an English raid on his mission in 1724, when his scalp was taken and sent to Boston for bounty.

Between 1701 and 1763, it was at the mission of Meductic on the St. John River that successive Jesuit missionaries such as Joseph Aubéry, Jean-Baptiste Loyard, Jean-Pierre Daniélou, and particularly Charles Germain simultaneously evangelized the Indian people and kept them loyal to France in an ongoing guerrilla war against New England.

These missionaries worked under the supervision of the Canadian Antoine Gaulin (1674–1740), the priest entrusted with the Indian missions in Acadia at the time. Sent to Acadia by the Quebec seminary in 1698, four years later Gaulin was promoted vicar general of Acadia. Initially based on the Penobscot River, Gaulin was fully committed to the French cause, contributing to keeping the Indians loyal to the French. In the wake of the Treaty of Utrecht and France's construction of Louisbourg (1717 and after), Father Gaulin established a new mission for his Micmac Indians near today's Antigonish, Nova Scotia, some fifty miles northwest of Canso and Cape Breton Island. While succeeding in settling many Indians there, he failed to induce many Acadians to migrate to Cape Breton's rocky coves. Thereafter he spent five years (1726–1731) as pastor of an Acadian parish at Minas, Nova Scotia, and another at Annapolis (Port Royal), before retiring to Quebec in 1732.

In addition to vicar general Antoine Gaulin and Jesuit father Charles Germain, the most notorious missionaries to the Indians were Jean-Louis Le Loutre and Pierre Maillard. While both of the latter belonged to Paris's Seminary of the Holy Spirit, both were on loan to Paris's Seminary of Foreign Missions.

Chosen to work in Cape Breton's Micmac missions, Maillard (1710–1762) set foot in Louisbourg on 13 August 1735. He had soon so mastered the Micmac language that he was publishing books in it and inventing a syllabic alphabet. Based on Chapel Island (Sainte-Famille island) south of Cape Breton's Lake Bras d'Or, Father Maillard toured the various Indian missions, including those on Prince Edward Island and peninsular Nova Scotia. Frequently denouncing the brandy trade with the Indians, beginning in 1742 he was involved in a quarrel with the Recollects who staffed the parish of Louisbourg; the latter were accused of being overly accommodating and derelict in their duty in not denouncing the many moral abuses manifest in Louisbourg.

Within a few years of his arrival, Maillard had become indispensable to the French in ensuring the loyalty and military commitment of the Micmac. Beginning with the outbreak of war in 1744 and throughout the 1750s, he participated in most raids conducted by the Micmacs against the English. Upon the fall of Louisbourg in 1758, he sought temporary refuge with a band of fugitive Acadians at Miramichi on the New Brunswick coast. Then he joined his beloved Micmacs at Merigomish, Nova Scotia, until he accepted a peace settlement offered by the English in November 1759. Thereafter, until his death on 12 August 1762, Father Maillard was a salaried English Indian agent, working for the pacification of the Micmacs, a task he fulfilled successfully. He was colorful even in death, for he asked for and obtained the religious assistance of Anglican minister Thomas Wood and was then given a solemn funeral service organized by the government of Nova Scotia, the same government that had outlawed Catholic priests four years earlier.

Jean-Louis Le Loutre (1709–1772) was another missionary who was larger than life. Arriving in Louisbourg in the fall of 1737, two years after Maillard, within the year he was stationed at a Micmac mission on the Shubenacadie River, near today's Truro, Nova Scotia, in the geographic heart of Nova Scotia. On a renewal of hostilities between France and England in 1744, Le Loutre became fully committed to the French cause. The British put a price on his head. Absent in France from 1746 to 1749, Le Loutre was back in Acadia in the latter year; he was stationed near Sackville, New Brunswick, at Pointe-à-Beauséjour, for Shubenacadie was too close to the enemy. From this contested borderland, Le Loutre continued to incite his Micmacs to war against the English, becoming thereby the nemesis of the British forces. When Fort Beauséjour was taken by the English on the eve of the deportation of the Acadians in 1755, Father Le Loutre slipped out of the colony, made his way to Quebec, then took ship for France. Captured at sea by the English, he was held prisoner in England for eight full years, until the signature of the Treaty of Paris (1763).

The ongoing power struggle between France and England was the setting that determined the behavior of priests like Le Loutre and Maillard. For their part, the British authorities had been trying since 1713 to get the Acadians to swear an unconditional oath of allegiance to the British crown. The wily Acadians always set conditions to their swearing such an oath—that they not be required to bear arms against France and that they be left free to practice their religion. The Acadians wanted to be treated as neutrals, because they were tired of always being caught in the middle of the constant wars between France and England.

By 1754 and 1755, Governor Charles Lawrence of Nova Scotia was no longer inclined to be tolerant. Constantly harassed by Micmac and Abenaki raiders who were aided and abetted by the French, the British decided to stop pussyfooting on the matter of the oath of allegiance. In collaboration with Governor Shirley of Massachusetts, Lawrence organized military raids on the French Fort Beauséjour on the Chignecto peninsula. The latter fell on 19 May 1755. One month later, Nova Scotia's governing council decided to expel all Acadians from the region in order to give their lands to English settlers. In July, in the wake of British general Braddock's military defeat at Fort Duquesne

(Pittsburgh), the council told an Acadian delegation that their only options were either to take an unconditional oath of allegiance or be expelled from the colony. They refused the oath; the British deported them.

The Catholic faith would prove the spiritual mainstay of the beleaguered and persecuted Acadians, people who for the next hundred years would have very little else to nourish their hope in a better future. Indeed, theirs was a tragic fate for, beginning in the fall of 1755 and for a period of eight years, most Acadians were deported from their country, some sixteen thousand people altogether. Between 1755 and 1757, while fifteen hundred fled through the forest towards Quebec, seven thousand men, women, and children were hunted down, arrested, and forced aboard British ships and dumped on the shores of Massachusetts, Connecticut, Pennsylvania, New York, Delaware, Virginia, the Carolinas, and Georgia. In the following four years (1758–1762), another thirty-eight hundred were shipped to France, while Massachusetts turned away shiploads of another fifteen hundred. These latter victims came from English punitive raids of 1758 and 1759 in the lower St. John River valley, Cape Breton Island, and Prince Edward Island. Finally, another two thousand Acadians emigrated to France over the next quarter-century. It was from all these points of the compass that several thousand refugee Acadians eventually found their way to Louisiana in the second half of the eighteenth century; others simultaneously came back to their beloved homeland, settling in the more inaccessible reaches of the upper St. John River, the Madawaska River, and the Baie des Chaleurs in today's New Brunswick. The contours of nineteenth- and twentieth-century Acadia were drawn.

To ensure the success of his deportation, Governor Lawrence had begun by arresting Acadia's parish priests in August 1755. Sulpician father Claude Chauvreulx had since 1749 been the only pastor in the Minas basin, residing in the parish of St. Charles at Grand-Pré and serving three thousand faithful. In 1749, he had taken the oath of allegiance to the British crown and had advised his parishioners to do likewise, much to the displeasure of Father Le Loutre. At the time, his fellow Sulpician Jean-Baptiste de Gay Desenclaves, pastor of Annapolis Royal, had also recommended to his flock the swearing of the oath. Also arrested in August 1755 was Father Henri Daudin, newly arrived pastor of Annapolis Royal and successor to Desenclaves, a militant pro-French priest in the Le Loutre tradition. A third arrested priest, Father Lemaire, was mentally deranged at the time and not entrusted with any pastoral office. All three priests were shipped back to Europe. Desenclaves, who had retired in August 1755 was later (1758) arrested on Nova Scotia's south shore.

By August 1755 all priests had disappeared from peninsular Nova Scotia, for while the parish priests were arrested, the missionary Le Loutre fled the country.

Some clergy were still active in French Acadia, however, for Father Maillard retired to Louisbourg before hiding in the woods of New Brunswick, while Father François Le Guerne continued working with the fugitive Acadians in the forests along the Shepody, Petitcodiac, and Memramcook Rivers of southern New Brunswick. Le Guerne spent two years in the bush (1755–1757) surviving in the company of two hundred Acadian families, all the while hunted down by British troops. In addition, Jesuit missionaries were still active on the St. John River. There it was that during the year 1755–1756 Jesuit Father Charles Germain was assisted by his colleague Jean-Baptiste de La Brosse, who gave special care to fugitive Acadians.

Another priest active among New Brunswick's Acadian fugitives was the Recollect Bonaventure Carpentier (1716–1778), who began his ministry among the Indians and Acadians of the Miramichi River in 1758. When British troops destroyed his parish in September 1758, Father Bonaventure fled with his flock toward the Baie des Chaleurs region, where he took up residence at Bonaventure, Quebec. However, by 1767 Bishop Briand was hearing allegations that Carpentier had sired a child with an Indian woman. Briand thereupon ordered the missionary to come to Quebec and explain himself; when the latter did not comply, the bishop suspended him from the ministry. The rebel priest eventually (1769) made his way to Quebec and was partly reconciled with his bishop.

When Father Maillard was employed by the British between 1759 and 1762, he was the only priest active in peninsular Nova Scotia after the deportation until the arrival in 1767 of Charles-François Bailly de Messein. The primary mission of both clergymen was the pacification of the Micmac Indians, the Acadian nation having been decimated.

Moreover, while deporting its Acadian population, the colony of Nova Scotia had introduced anti-Catholic legislation, in conformity with the laws of Great Britain. Indeed, in the mother country, Roman Catholicism had been illegal since Elizabeth's sixteenth-century reign, a tradition reinforced by the next century's Corporation Act (1661) and Test Acts (1673, 1678). So it was that in 1757, in preparation for the election of its first legislative assembly (1758), the Nova Scotia Council determined that "no Popish recusant" could vote in the elections of 1758. Not to be outdone, the newly elected assembly of Nova Scotia legislated in 1758 that:

> Every Popish Person, exercising any ecclesiastical jurisdiction, and every Popish priest or person exercising the function of a Popish priest, shall depart out of this province on or before the twenty-fifth day of March, 1759. . . . [If not] he or they shall, upon conviction, be adjudged to suffer perpetual imprisonment.[1]

Nova Scotia's anti-Catholic legislation merely served to add another burden to the already overly heavy cross that the Acadians were forced to bear.

In 1771, Acadians numbered some twelve hundred souls in Nova Scotia, in addition to another thousand on the more northerly coast of New Brunswick and on Prince Edward Island. The ordeal that had been imposed upon them by the British, and that had torn their nation asunder, ironically also served to bind the Acadian people to their Catholic faith, a stance that would become manifest in the painful resurrection of Acadia in the nineteenth century.

## THE CHURCH AND THE SEVEN YEARS' WAR

As had been the case from the earliest days of the colony, during the eighteenth century Catholic missionaries continued to work in close cooperation with the French crown in the exploration and development of the vast territory of French America.

In spite of the Treaty of Utrecht (1713), so disastrous to its interests, France had continued to explore the continent in the eighteenth century. Having moved its primary western base from Michilimackinac to Detroit (1701), and while endeavoring to move up the Mississippi from Louisiana, the colony of New France had not abandoned its plans to discover the western sea that would lead to the riches of the Far East. It was with this in mind that Jesuit father Pierre-François-Xavier de Charlevoix (1682–1761) was appointed to report on the possible direction in which this hypothetical western sea was to be sought. Charlevoix toured New France between 1720 and 1722, traveling via the St. Lawrence, Michilimackinac, and down the Mississippi River; he then published his findings and observations, thereby fueling renewed interest in western exploration.

Father Charlevoix had recommended going up the Missouri River and founding a mission among the Sioux; such a mission was attempted in 1727–1728 but failed. Charles de Beauharnois (1671–1749), the governor who had ordered the failed mission, shortly thereafter authorized the western explorations of Pierre Gaultier de Varennes et de La Vérendrye (1685–1749) and his sons. These pathfinding journeys of the 1730s, 1740s, and 1750s into northern Ontario, the Canadian prairies, and the American plains continued the tradition established by Champlain, Jolliet, La Salle, and others.

These voyages were usually made in the company of a Jesuit. For example, Father Charles-Michel Mésaiger accompanied La Vérendrye on his first journey in 1731; he was replaced in 1735 by Father Jean-Pierre Aulneau who, after visiting the upper Missouri River, was murdered by Sioux Indians at Lake of the Woods on 8 June 1736.

It was the Seven Years' War (the French and Indian Wars), that decisive confrontation between France and England in North America, that would seal the fate of New France and profoundly transform the destiny of the French–American church. Although the war only began officially in 1756, fighting between France and England had already broken out two years earlier at Fort Duquesne on the Ohio River and in 1755 in Acadia; in fact, hostilities had rarely ceased since the 1740s, the British endeavoring to put a stop to New France's growing prosperity. Bloody skirmishes and battles were fought in the regions of Lake Ontario, the valley of the Ohio, Lake Champlain, and the St. Lawrence valley. When the dust settled, the British had taken Quebec (September 1759) and then Montreal (September 1760), sealing thereby the fate of New France. All of North America had become British territory.

In Canada, the Sulpician father Picquet took on the role so colorfully played out in Acadia by missionaries like Le Loutre, Germain, and Maillard. Although primarily active in and around Montreal, the Gentlemen of St. Sulpice had from the time of their arrival in Canada always shown a sustained interest in missions. In addition to their work in Acadia and around Montreal, they hoped to convert the Iroquois Indians, those perpetual enemies of the French. That had been the purpose of the Quinte mission on Lake Ontario (1668–1680). It was also the purpose of Sulpician father François Picquet (1708–1781).

After five years of parish work (1734–1739) in Montreal, Picquet had been stationed for ten years (1739–1749) at the Sulpician mission of Lac des Deux-Montagnes (Oka). Having become well acquainted with Indian ways and languages, Picquet took it upon himself to become the "apostle to the Iroquois." With the support of the intendant and governor of New France, in 1748 Picquet headed for Fort Frontenac (Kingston, Ontario) on Lake Ontario in order to select a site for another village for Christian Iroquois Indians. He chose a site on the right bank of the St. Lawrence below the Thousand Islands, today's Ogdensburg, New York. There it was that in June 1749 Father Picquet directed twenty-five Frenchmen and a handful of Indians in the building of Fort La Présentation, which within the year sheltered some three hundred Indians of Iroquois, Huron, and other origins. The priest's main objective was to gain for France the loyalty of the Six Nations.

After visiting France in 1753–1754, Picquet became a leading participant in the Seven Years' War. He was not only a chaplain but also a counselor—indeed, a soldier. Leaving his mission in the care of other Sulpician priests, particularly Pierre-Paul-François de Lagarde (1729–1784), Picquet would even have been worth ten regiments, according to Governor Duquesne. Indeed, in 1756, Picquet was part of the French attacks on Fort Bull (east of Lake Oneida, New York) and on Fort Oswego (Oswego, New York). He led his Indians in the famous battle of 8 July 1758 at Carillon (Ticonderoga, New York), where a French, Canadian, and Indian army of thirty-six hundred men routed invading British General James Abercromby's army of fifteen thousand.

Thereafter, the fortunes of war fell to the British. On the eve of the capitulation of Montreal, Father Picquet escaped down the Mississippi to New Orleans (1760–1761), stayed there for two years, then returned to France. Picquet's fate was that of New France.

In spite of the leading military role played by priests like Maillard and Le Loutre in Acadia and Picquet in Canada, it remained unusual for priests to become guerrilla leaders in New France, even during the protracted fighting of the Seven Years' War.

The Canadian church began to see the effects of the advent of British rule when the two-month bombardment of Quebec in 1759 left few buildings unscathed; one-third of the town's houses were completely destroyed, while many others had to be torn down in the aftermath. Given that most of the religious institutions were located in the upper part of town alongside the fortifications, most of them took a severe pounding. Completely destroyed were the cathedral, the seminary, and the parish rectory, the chapel of the bishop's palace, and the church of Our Lady of Victories; partially damaged were the chapels of the seminary, of the Recollects, of the Ursulines, and of the Jesuits. Outside town, in the wider Quebec region, few churches suffered extensive damage, although the damage to property was extensive along the south shore of the St. Lawrence downstream from Lévis. The story was similar elsewhere, for only one of the twenty churches in the region of Trois-Rivières was destroyed, while only four of forty-eight churches in the Montreal area were damaged.

The effects of conquest on the church became more manifest when, after having occupied Quebec in September 1759, the British army took over both the Hôtel-Dieu hospital and the convent of the Ursulines to serve as extra hospitals for the troops while repairing the Ursuline chapel, which then served for Anglican worship during 1759–1760. Thereafter (1760–1796), it was the Recollect chapel that housed the Church of England, the Ursulines having also taken back their convent in 1760. Moreover, the Jesuit college had closed in 1759, the English transforming it into a central military warehouse.

Quebec's teaching and nursing sisters had fled the bombardment by moving into Quebec's General Hospital, which was located some distance away from the town center. The institution became the refuge for all nuns and for a number of families fleeing the fall of shot and shell, not to mention the patients being treated there. Of the 113 nuns sheltering there in 1759, thirty-five were Ursulines, forty were Hospitalers from the Hôtel-Dieu, and thirty-eight belonged to the General Hospital itself. With few exceptions, these nuns were natives of Canada. When added to the Montreal nuns (the Congregation of Notre-Dame, the Sisters of Charity of the General Hospital, and the Hospitalers of the Hôtel-Dieu), the total number of nuns in Canada numbered 190 in 1764, roughly divided into two groups of equal numbers located in Quebec and Montreal. Fourteen Ursulines were also at work in Trois-Rivières in 1764.

Although not so numerous as were the nuns, Canada's male clerics would bear the brunt of Britain's mistrust of all things Catholic and French. In 1759, in addition to just under a hundred secular priests, there were twenty-four Recollects, thirty Sulpicians, twenty-five Jesuits, and five Quebec Seminary priests. Five years later there were fifteen fewer men in religious congregations, most of whom had gone back to France. Indeed, with the exception of the unloved Recollects, who were 70 percent Canadian, all the other members of male religious orders were native Europeans, and fully 80 percent of the secular clergy was Canadian. Moreover, all positions of leadership in the

Canadian church were held by Frenchmen, a fact that served to fuel a growing Canadian nationalism among the secular clergy.

Finally, the difficulties wrought upon the French-American clergy by the British conquest of Canada culminated in the fact that they no longer had a bishop after 1760. In fact, shortly before the British occupied Quebec in 1759, Bishop Henri-Marie Dubreil de Pontbriand (1708–1760) fled to Montreal and took up residence at the Sulpician seminary, where he resided until his death on 8 June 1760, two months before the capitulation of Montreal. So when Canada became British in 1760, the Canadian church had no bishop.

## A French-Catholic Church in a British-Protestant Land

The status of the Canadian church after 1760 is defined in three official documents: the Articles of Capitulation of Montreal (8 September 1760), the Treaty of Paris (10 February 1763), and the instructions of Lord Egremont to James Murray (13 August 1763). In the Articles of Capitulation of Montreal, in effect those of Canada, articles 27 to 35 dealt with the status of the church. This temporary agreement between British commanding general Jeffrey Amherst and defeated Governor Vaudreuil of Canada provided for the free exercise of the Catholic religion without molestation of any kind, and the maintenance of the nuns and secular clergy in their rights and functions. However, the continuance of the tithe and that of the rights and privileges of male religious orders (Jesuits, Recollects, Sulpicians) was said to depend on the king's pleasure, although all religious communities without exception could preserve their property.

On 10 February 1763, Britain, France, and Spain signed the Treaty of Paris. Article 4 succinctly dealt with the Canadian church, stipulating that Britain would allow "the liberty of the Catholic religion" to the sixty-five thousand Canadians. Catholics would enjoy freedom of religion "according to the rites of the Romish church, as far as the laws of Great Britain permit." Six months later, instructing James Murray, Minister Egremont wrote that he must keep a close watch on the Catholic clergy in Canada, for the crown feared that the priests might endeavor to maintain a political connection with France. This was not to be tolerated. Egremont then explained that the wording "as far as the laws of Great Britain permit" in the treaty meant exactly that. In other words, the laws of Great Britain "prohibit absolutely all Popish hierarchy . . . and can only admit of a toleration of the exercise of that religion."[2]

In addition to these legal documents, London occasionally sent further instructions to Murray relative to religion. This was the case on 7 December 1763, when Murray was instructed to carefully apply the clause of the treaty pertaining to religion and not to admit any Roman ecclesiastical jurisdiction in Canada. In addition:

> To the end that the Church of England may be established both in principle and practice, and that the said inhabitants may by degrees be induced to embrace the Protestant religion, and their children be brought up in the principles of it, we do hereby declare it to be our intention . . . [that] all possible encouragement shall be given to the erecting [of] Protestant schools in the said districts . . . by . . . allotting proper quantities of land for that purpose, and also for a glebe and maintenance for a Protestant minister and Protestant schoolmasters; and you are to consider and report to us . . . by what other means the Protestant religion may be promoted, established and encouraged in our province.[3]

London's policy was clear. The implementation of this policy proved to be another matter, for it so happened that the two first British governors of Canada, James Murray and Guy Carleton, soon became sympathetic to the king's new subjects and chose not to oppress Canada's Catholics.

The soldier James Murray (1721–1794) was appointed commander of the Quebec garrison in October 1759, governor of the Quebec region one year later, and governor of the province of Quebec on 21 November 1763, although the civil government he led was only implemented in Canada on 10 August 1764. He left Canada on 28 June 1766 but maintained his official title of governor of Canada until 12 April 1768. His successor was Guy Carleton (1724–1808).

During Murray's tenure as military and then civil governor of Canada, one of the foremost problems faced by the Canadian church was that of obtaining a bishop to succeed the deceased Pontbriand. Upon the latter's death in June 1760, in conformity with the rules of the Council of Trent, administrative responsibility for ecclesiastical affairs had automatically become that of the Chapter of Quebec, a group of twelve senior priests residing in Quebec. During the vacancy of the see, the chapter decided to entrust the church's administration to three vicars general, each resident in one of the colony's three regions (Quebec, Montreal, Trois-Rivières), and to three grand vicars entrusted with the more distant parts of the diocese of Quebec. Heading this company of lieutenants was canon and vicar general Jean-Olivier Briand (1715–1794), the head of the Quebec region.

Once Canada was definitively given to Britain by the Treaty of Paris, Briand and his colleagues began working in earnest to obtain the appointment of a bishop. The challenge was daunting, for not only was Roman jurisdiction outlawed by the crown, but any French cleric was perceived as an alien by British officers. How then was a French Catholic bishop to be appointed in a French Catholic country governed by an English Protestant monarch? Faced with this impasse, Quebec's chapter decided to revert to the old French custom, abandoned in 1516, whereby the chapter elected the bishop of a diocese. On 15 September 1763, the canons chose Sulpician father Etienne Montgolfier (1712–1791), superior of the Montreal seminary; the latter thereupon went to Europe, where he obtained the required authorizations from Rome and London, but before being consecrated bishop, he learned that Governor Murray did not want him as bishop; Canon Briand would be preferable. The Sulpician thereupon came back to Canada and submitted his resignation (9 September 1764) as the chapter's bishop-elect.

Briand was then elected by the chapter (11 September 1764), and went to London where he was held up for more than one year. He finally was told by British officials that British law did not allow them to approve of his consecration, but if Briand slipped out of the country discreetly and got himself consecrated in France, the British government would be inclined to accept the fait accompli and acknowledge him as superintendent of the Romish Church in Canada. Rome accepted the compromise and issued bulls in favor of Briand; he was consecrated in a private chapel in Paris, returned to London to swear an oath of allegiance to the British crown, and was back in Quebec on 19 July 1766. The Canadian church had overcome one of its major hurdles.

In addition to the challenge of reconstructing church buildings in the town of Quebec, Briand had to establish a satisfactory working arrangement with the British governor. During the five years (1759–1764) that he had dealt with Murray, the two men had come to respect each other. Briand's prime concern had been to have the British accept a separation of church and state, in order not to have the Protestant civil administrators interfering in internal church affairs. The Quebec clergy knew that it had to be pliable and conciliatory while working toward greater autonomy. So it was that the priests accepted, sometimes grudgingly, various vexatious measures by the British, such as the occupation of some churches, the burial of Protestants in Catholic cemeteries, and the governor's intervention in the appointment of some pastors and of the bishop. In return, Murray did not insist on implementing all the instructions he had received regarding the church.

Bishop Briand frequently accepted the direct political and/or financial support of British colonial authorities. Beginning in 1762, Murray's government paid a twenty-pound annual gift to Father Briand in recognition of good behavior. Once a bishop in 1766, Briand was paid an annual salary of two hundred pounds sterling, a stipend that would be continued to his successors and increased to a thousand pounds in 1813. In addition, Catholic missionaries to the Indians were also salaried by the crown. Moreover, Briand also found the crown useful in enforcing his episcopal authority. For example, when he was disputing the possession of Quebec's rebuilt parish church/cathedral with the board of trustees of Quebec's Notre-Dame parish, it was the civil secretary and lieutenant governor of the province of Quebec, Hector-Theophilus Cramahé, who facilitated the bishop's victory over the rebellious trustees (1774).

Briand's policy of conciliation rested on solid theological ground, for Catholic theology acknowledged the right of a legitimate sovereign to the loyalty of his people. Briand reminded his flock of that teaching; he even inserted prayers for King George III into the canon of the mass, in addition to complying with

Murray's request to have a *Te Deum* sung in Quebec churches to celebrate the signing of the Treaty of Paris.

Nevertheless, at the risk of appearing overly submissive to the British, after a few years Bishop Briand succeeded in making the governors dependent on him in all ecclesiastical affairs. Given that neither Murray nor Carleton ever showed any inclination to meddle in doctrinal or moral questions, Briand was in fact accepting their influence in disciplinary matters in exchange for church independence in doctrinal and moral matters.

Guy Carleton, another career soldier, took over as lieutenant governor and administrator of Canada in 1766 and was promoted governor in 1768. He continued the policy of his predecessor, befriending the Canadians and striking compromises with Bishop Briand. For example, in spite of opposition in London, Carleton approved the appointment of a coadjutor bishop of Quebec, a step earnestly desired by Briand in order to ensure the episcopal succession in the see. In doing so, however, the governor ensured that only a candidate he approved of was appointed. The candidate chosen by Carleton and consecrated in 1772 was the Canadian priest Louis-Philippe Mariauchau d'Esgly (1710–1788), who was five years older than Briand.

So it was that by 1772, Canada's Catholics could claim considerable gains in their relationship with the British conqueror. Bishop Briand was in place, as was his coadjutor, and a positive and constructive relationship had been established between the bishop and the colonial government.

Surprisingly enough, Bishop Briand's major challenges proved to be internal ones. One challenge was the limited authority the bishop enjoyed within his diocese. Indeed, the bishop's authority was limited, given that both the Quebec seminary and the Montreal seminary had always been largely autonomous.

A more important threat to the well-being of Briand's church was the fact that the British government refused to allow the Jesuits and Recollects to recruit new members, thereby sealing the fate of both orders. In fact, the Society of Jesus was disbanded by the pope in 1773, thus ensuring its disappearance from Canada, although the colonial government allowed surviving Jesuits to continue in office until their deaths. The last Jesuit died in 1800, the last Recollect in 1813. Sulpicians were facing the same fate until several refugee French royalist Sulpicians were allowed into Canada after 1790, ensuring the survival of the Gentlemen of Saint-Sulpice. Nevertheless, the recruiting of clergy for the diocese of Quebec was seriously threatened.

This threat was also reflected in the diminishing number of secular priests. Indeed, by 1766, the number of secular priests had dropped alarmingly, since the lack of a bishop coupled with the closing of the Seminary of Quebec (1759–1765) had interrupted the ordination of new priests. The 180 priests, secular and regular, of 1758 had become 138 in July 1766. During the first decade of Briand's administration the situation worsened; he declared in 1774 that, since his arrival in 1766, he had ordained twenty-five priests but thirty-two had died, while two others could no longer work. Nine years later, it was said that seventy-five parishes had no pastor.

While the congregations of nuns maintained themselves, the male religious withered on the vine, and the secular clergy dwindled, Bishop Briand faced disciplinary problems with his clergy and his flock. The dispute over possession of the parish of Quebec has been noted. Several of the diocese's clergy were admonished by Briand during his first decade in office. They were chastised for a wide range of faults including gossiping, nonobservance of fasts, and meddling in politics, a score being accused of serious disciplinary offenses such as drunkenness, avarice, or social indiscretions. Some of the faithful practiced marriages *à la gaumine*, a custom whereby a couple who wanted to marry but did not want to submit to church controls and fees simply attended mass together and, unbeknownst to the priest, pledged themselves to each other before witnesses. The bishop was very harsh in his judgment of the quality of his flock's Christian life, declaring that Canadians wanted to run the church themselves all the while believing that, in matters of religion, they were more knowledgeable than the priests and bishops.

Quarrels were rife in the diocese of Quebec, sometimes leading to open rebellion of the faithful against a pastor or the bishop. People fought over the site of the parish church, the construction of the rectory, the paying of tithes, the morals of the priest, or the autonomy of the parish board of trustees. Briand replied in kind, threatening, cajoling, warning, excommunicating. Occasionally, he claimed that Canadians were Christians in name only, praying the Lord while denying the faith in their behavior. Sometimes depression seemed to set in, when he wrote that he was unloved as bishop; at other times, he seemed less pessimistic, judging his flock in more moderate terms.

## The Church, the Quebec Act, and the American Revolution

While Bishop Briand endeavored to govern his frequently fractious people, in August 1770 Governor Carleton entrusted the country to Cramahé and went to England determined to obtain constitutional changes for his colony. Four years later he had obtained the adoption of the Quebec Act by the Parliament of Great Britain, a piece of legislation that constituted a milestone for Canadians, a threat for Canada's newly arrived English merchants, and a red flag for rebelling settlers in the English colonies of the Atlantic seaboard. Conscious of the growing discontent in Britain's more southerly colonies, Carleton wanted to ensure the loyalty of Canada.

The Quebec Act made major concessions to Britain's new Canadian and Catholic subjects. The boundaries of the province of Quebec were extended to the fishing grounds of the Grand Banks on the east and to the junction of the Ohio and Mississippi rivers in the West. The colony was to be administered by the governor, assisted by a legislative council rather than an elected assembly. The policy of anglicization in place since the royal proclamation of October 1763, was abandoned, although in fact Quebec's governors had always administered their province in French, as had their officers. Britain now accepted Canadian laws and customs as they had existed at the time of the conquest; in civil law, this meant the official recognition of the custom of Paris. Criminal law would be English. Catholics were henceforth eligible for public office, and the payment by Catholics of tithes to the Church of Rome was acknowledged. Nevertheless, the colony's government was empowered to legislate with a view to establishment of the Church of England in Canada.

Indeed, a series of private and secret instructions sent to Governor Carleton in 1775 tended to negate this policy of openness toward Canadian Catholics by continuing the previous policy of establishment for the Church of England. The instructions of 1775 forbade any episcopal correspondence with Rome, limited the bishop's authority to what was necessary to the free exercise of religion, and required the bishop to obtain a special license from the governor for the performance of various episcopal duties such as ordinations and confirmations. Moreover, the governor was to make all appointments to parishes and became the official visitor of seminaries, while all priests were to be free to marry. Carleton chose to disregard these instructions of 1775, treating them as mere suggestions. It was the Quebec Act that was binding in law. The bishop of Quebec was more than content. Briand intensified his collaboration with his good friend Carleton.

Canadian Catholics could indeed rejoice, for they had achieved constitutional recognition and civil equality more than half a century before their English co-religionists would do so in England. In fact, England began to relax its anti-Catholic legislation in 1778 by adopting the Relief Act, which permitted Catholics to buy land and removed the penalty of perpetual imprisonment of priests. Adoption of the Emancipation Act in 1829 granted full religious and political equality to English Catholics. The colonies of Nova Scotia, Prince Edward Island, and New Brunswick tended to follow the English timetable for liberating their Catholic citizens. In Quebec, the threat of secession in the South, the influence of Guy Carleton, and the skill of Bishop Briand secured liberation sooner.

Upon returning to Quebec in September 1774, Governor Carleton proceeded to reinforce his own authority in the colony by not reconvening his legislative council after 1775. He simply did not implement the instructions regarding the anglicization and protestantization of Quebec. Instead he reinforced his ties with Bishop Briand.

The first American Congress (1774) protested the Quebec Act, noting its surprise at the English Parliament's granting of legal emancipation to a religion that had allegedly bathed England in blood and spread hypocrisy, murder, persecution and rebellion throughout the world. These were fighting words to the bishop of Quebec. When the same Congress then appealed to Canadians, urging them to join the rebels and cast off the yoke of British oppression, all the while promising to respect their religion, many were less than convinced of the trustworthiness of their American neighbors.

The leaders of the Canadian church were forced to choose sides in the spring of 1775 on the outbreak of hostilities between British troops and American settlers at Lexington and Concord, Massachusetts. Rebel troops having captured British forts at Crown Point and Ticonderoga, New York, in May 1775, Governor Carleton was concerned. He asked Bishop Briand for his support; the latter in turn asked Father Montgolfier, his vicar general in Montreal, to lend a hand. The Sulpician wrote a model sermon for the priests in the Montreal district, arguing in favor of supporting the British government and opposing the American invaders. He also supported Carleton's later decision to reestablish the Canadian militia. Bishop Briand did likewise in June 1775, publishing a mandamus read from all pulpits, reiterating the Canadian Catholic's duty to support the crown. The bishop spoke of the pernicious design of a band of rebel subjects of Canada's legitimate sovereign. The singular goodness and gentleness of George III's government was praised, including its recent generous legislation in the Quebec Act. Catholics were told that both their oath of loyalty and their religion required that they give every support to their country and their king.

An American army succeeded in taking Montreal on 13 November 1775; it occupied the town briefly while another American army led by Benedict Arnold and Richard Montgomery assaulted Quebec at the end of December. Montgomery was killed and Arnold wounded during a disastrous attack on the fortress.

The tide had turned. While Montgomery's siege troops were decimated by an epidemic and a rigorous winter, after four months of intermittent bombardment of Quebec they only managed to kill one boy, one cow, and one turkey in the Canadian capital. The arrival of a small British naval squadron in May 1776 was sufficient to chase out the demoralized Americans, who retreated to Montreal. Within the month they were facing superior British forces at Trois-Rivières and Montreal. By the end of June 1776 the American armies were back across the border.

While most Canadians remained neutral, many Canadians tended to support the Americans at the beginning of hostilities in 1775; by 1776 many had changed their minds and wanted a victory for British arms. Although the majority still remained neutral, unmoved to fight on the side of the army that had conquered their country only fifteen years earlier, one reason for the change was the unalloyed support of the clergy for Carleton's government. Canadians who helped the invaders were excommunicated and made to bear the church's harshest penalties; they were only readmitted to the sacraments after having made a public apology for their treason.

## FRENCH-AMERICAN CHRISTIANITY IN 1776

When the United States declared its independence in 1776, New France was no more. The crown of France still ruled a number of islands, such as Saint-Pierre and Miquelon off the coast of Newfoundland, and especially the Caribbean islands of Saint-Domingue, Guadeloupe, and Martinique. However, the main French colonies of Acadia, Canada, and Louisiana were now either British or Spanish. Indeed, by a secret arrangement in the Treaty of Fontainebleau (1762), all the French territory on the west bank of the Mississippi, in addition to the city of New Orleans, was ceded to Spain. When France, Britain, and Spain signed the Treaty of Paris in 1763, Britain took over the east bank of the Mississippi, while Spain gained control of the west bank.

The advent of British control meant that Protestants were no longer outlawed as they had been in New France. Indeed, British law favored Protestants and outlawed Catholics. In fact, in the late eighteenth century, in spite of strong anti-Catholic feelings in the British population, English aristocrats and governors tended to be more tolerant of Catholics. This resulted in the variegated, at times contradictory situation reserved for Catholics in France's former North American colonies. While Nova Scotia outlawed its Catholics, it paid salaries to Catholic priests working with the Indians; while the British monarch swore a coronation oath against Catholic doctrine and ruled a country that had outlawed Catholicism, King George III nevertheless signed into law the Quebec Act that granted civil equality to Canada's Catholics; while British policy required the establishment of the Church of England in Canada, governors Murray and Carleton paid an annual salary to the Catholic bishop of Quebec.

Beginning in 1760, in spite of the close cooperation between the British governor of Canada and the bishop of Quebec, the longstanding adversarial relationship between England and France served to weld together the interests of the Catholic church and the Acadian and Canadian people. On the eve of the British conquest of 1760, tensions existed between French and Canadian members of the Catholic church in Canada. The former occupied all positions of leadership in the church and accounted for all the members of the Jesuit and Sulpician orders. Canadians represented 70 percent of the Recollect membership and 80 percent of the secular clergy. The French tended to look down on the Canadians, considering them second-class priests and unworthy of their French peers. Obviously, Canadians resented this.

When the British refused to allow male religious orders to continue recruiting members, they condemned the all-French Jesuit order, the all-French Sulpician band, and the majority-Canadian Recollects to extinction, although the Sulpicians managed to survive. Canadian priests must have taken some satisfaction from such a measure, because the French clergy that had never treated them as equals disappeared. The feeling was reinforced when both Murray and Carleton insisted on the appointment of Canadian priests only to parishes;

the same rule applied to episcopal candidates. No Frenchmen need apply. The British governors were concerned with removing any potential political threat represented by French aliens. Simultaneously they were helping Canadians take over their own church. Ironically, the British were unknowingly facilitating the subsequent emergence of a powerful French-Canadian nationalistic movement within the ranks of the Canadian clergy.

The military and political takeover by the English Protestants also served to drive the French North American clergy closer to its flocks. Although such a fusion of interests became apparent only in the nineteenth century, it began with the British conquest and was reinforced every time an English administrator created or represented an obstacle to the development of Acadian or French-Canadian interests. From the outset, governors Murray and Carleton both realized that it was in their best interests to work with, as opposed to against, the church. The people soon came to realize that the church was the only Canadian institution whose officers were born and raised in Canada, used French as its native language, and was deeply rooted in all parts of their country. In sum, the British conquest laid the foundations of the powerful Acadian and French Catholic Canadian nationalism of the nineteenth and twentieth centuries.

Inasmuch as piety and devotion were concerned, it has already been noted that Bishop Briand did not consider his flock or his clergy particularly holy. In keeping with the mood of the eighteenth century, most Acadians and Canadians were not especially prone to falling on their knees. The same may be said of many priests. This situation was only reversed in the mid-nineteenth century.

In sum, while citizens of the United States of America were undertaking a new beginning in 1776, French-speaking Christians in North America were also starting anew. The difference was that the former had seized political control of their country and were building a new nation. The latter, Acadians and Canadians especially, had to rebuild a collective identity in the shadow of a sometimes hostile, sometimes benevolent foreign government. They did so increasingly with the support of their church.

# 14

## THE WATERSHED OF
## FRENCH-AMERICAN
## CHRISTIANITY

Although troubling in some respects, the story of French-American Christianity is of great interest and considerable significance. The preceding chapters have outlined how French Christians, both Protestant and Catholic, initially set out to establish commercial enterprises in America, in the company of clergymen whose presence was at first tolerated at best. However, once the dynamic and aggressive Jesuits entered the fray, in both Acadia and Canada Catholic–Protestant confrontations resulted, for the powerful Jesuits were determined not to take second place to the Huguenot entrepreneurs who initially held the French-American commercial monopolies.

While the story of the Acadian missions is all too frequently one of bungling, pettifogging, and dependence on selfish rascals, all set in a political context that was never overly healthy, the story of the Canadian church is far more encouraging and admirable. It was in the Canada of the mid-seventeenth century that was written one of the noblest pages in the annals of the Christian Church. These missionary men and women faced the daunting challenge of evangelizing dozens of North American Indian nations, all too frequently stumbling over cultural hurdles that were not always evident to them.

Beyond the 1660s, French-American Christianity changed. While Catholic missions spread to the American Midwest and eventually to both the upper and lower Mississippi River valley, the zeal that had distinguished the founders of the Canadian mission became less and less apparent. Church leaders gradually became more and more mired in protracted and petty ecclesiastical quarrels while claiming to fight the good fight on the brandy trade. The end came on board British warships.

The English Protestant conquest of a French Catholic country provided the

Catholic Church with a new challenge: that of serving as intermediary between a new but legitimate sovereign on the one hand and a suspicious but benevolent people on the other. Bishop Briand succeeded in laying the foundations for the all-powerful Canadian Catholic church of the mid-nineteenth to mid-twentieth centuries.

The American experience shaped the subsequent Catholic church of Canada in a number of ways. The strong missionary heritage provided by the seventeenth and eighteenth centuries later became the touchstone for the equally amazing nineteenth-century missionary epic of French and Canadian Oblates in Canada's North and West. Indeed, the Oblate missionary who was canoeing down the more-than-a-thousand-mile-long Mackenzie River in an effort to evangelize the Arctic's Inuit knew that he was continuing the tradition set by so many Jesuit missionaries of New France.

French-American Christianity also left the heritage of a committed, hands-on church whose clergy knew only too well that they needed to roll up their sleeves and get their hands dirty if they wanted to succeed in their evangelical endeavors. When establishing a new mission station or parish, priests knew that they needed to clear the forest, fell the trees, build the chapel and cabin, and sometimes even depend on their own hunting and fishing skills to feed off the land, for church supervisors were rarely able to subsidize them. Such a practical attitude became a badge of distinction of Canadian Catholic missionaries; they wore it proudly in the tradition of the priests of New France. For them it meant becoming a settler with the settlers, just as the missionary of old had assimilated into the Indian life-style. This was the meaning of the theology of the Incarnation as it applied in French America.

This practical missionary church was conscious that it was nourished by the blood of martyrs, the foremost factor that reinforced a strong Christian spirituality in French-American Christianity.

French-American Christianity was also one where women played a role as important as that of men and had done so from the outset. Indeed, the honor roll of heroes and leaders of the French-American church contains as many powerful and influential women as it does men. Suffice it to recall the names of the most celebrated of these: De La Peltrie, Guyart, Mance, Bourgeois, Youville. They established a strong tradition of social service by women in French America, a tradition that would continue (indeed, grow in importance) beginning in the nineteenth century.

The close ties between French-American church and state had advantages and drawbacks. On the positive side of the ledger, it meant that the Christian church was intimately involved in the establishment and development of French America from the inception of the colonies of Acadia, Canada, and Louisiana. Indeed, French-American Christianity was not restricted to monastic walls or to the sanctuaries of churches. On the contrary, the church, and by extension the Christian faith, was part and parcel of daily life in French America. This included the enjoyment of state support for various meritorious Christian social services, such as schools, colleges, hospitals, and orphanages. It also included the recitation of public prayers on ships, at military forts, and at roadside crosses.

The obverse side of that coin was the extent of church accommodation to political and national interests. While the established church of French America enjoyed state support in a number of ways, it also had to bear its share of the opprobrium of resentment and opposition to state policies. This was particularly evident in the English conqueror's refusal to allow male religious orders to recruit in Britain's new province of Quebec. Indeed, Jesuits, Sulpicians, and Recollects were suspect largely because of their French identity. The perennial missionary question emerges: How far can a church go in adjusting to a particular culture, before compromising the Gospel of Jesus?

Ironically, it was this Catholic church that had always been led by Frenchmen that was taken over by Canadians and became the key instrument in reconciling the new British masters of Canada with its French and Catholic inhabitants. In the process, the church moved progressively closer to its faithful and away from its roots in France. In less than a century, under the aegis of a clergy closely bound to the rank and file of its people, the church of Canada would be poised to assume the leadership of French-Canadian national aspirations. In fact, during the nineteenth century, while European Christians were putting more and more distance between themselves and their church, French America's Catholics were moving closer and closer to their own.

Is it possible to assess the impact of French-American Christianity on the church of France, or on the international Christian Church? Yes, but only in the most general terms. In the short term—during the second half of the eighteenth century—the troubled and/or bland history of both the church of France and of the international Roman Catholic Church seems to indicate that the nobler and edifying face of the French-American Christian experience was largely forgotten. It is the self-serving motivation and limited horizons of some French-American Catholic clergymen that seem to be perpetuated in the mediocre and lackluster Catholicism of both France and Rome before the turn of the nineteenth century. However, when one considers the new dynamism that characterized French and international Catholicism during the last three quarters of the nineteenth century, a renewal built on the strongest discipline, the multiplication of religious vocations (especially of women), and an unprecedented international and North American missionary crusade, one may explain it as resting on the fallow ground that was first broken by the heroic missionaries of New France.

# ✝ Part III

# Christianity Comes to British America

BY CHARLES H. LIPPY

# 15

## RELIGIOUS CURRENTS
## IN REFORMATION EUROPE

A quarter of a century after Christopher Columbus and his crew came ashore on land they presumed to be India a religious revolution erupted in Europe. Known ever after as the Protestant Reformation, this religious upheaval was to have great significance for the shape of Christianity in the Americas, particularly in the area that was first to be part of British America and then the United States.

The beginnings of the Reformation are inextricably intertwined with the towering figure of Martin Luther and the movement he led in Germany in the sixteenth century. But many of the ideas associated with Luther had antecedents in earlier religious movements that had been classified as heretical. In England, for example, in the fourteenth century the followers of John Wycliffe called for significant change in the character of English Christianity as well as in the structure of the political order. While Wycliffe was condemned and his followers (known as Lollards) persecuted, the views they espoused did not die out, and many came to the fore again with the Reformation in the sixteenth century.

Even on the European mainland, there were foreshadowings of the shift in focus of Christianity to which Luther would give direction. Of these, the one of greatest import for later developments that would have an impact in America was the Hussite movement in fifteenth-century Bohemia (part of modern Czechoslovakia). There Jan Hus, whose movement also had both religious and political ramifications, echoed many of the concerns articulated in England by Wycliffe. Hus too was declared a heretic and burned at the stake in 1415. But like English Lollardy, the Hussite movement resurfaced when Reformation currents swept Germany a century later.

In time the Protestant Reformation altered the character of Christianity in much of Northern and Western Europe, including Scandinavia—and, of course, Britain. The forms these Protestantizing forces took outside Germany showed considerable variation, often adapting to particular local or regional circumstances. In time, too, most of these variants were to have counterparts in British colonial America.

To understand the shape of Christianity in British America, one must appreciate all these varieties of Protestant Christianity for several reasons. First, the vast majority of immigrants who came to territories that were part of the British colonial empire were Protestants, who brought with them the religious styles of European Protestantism. Second, many of these Protestants came to the colonies in the New World because they were discontent with the religious situation at home, though religion was never the only motivation for colonization. Frequently what these Protestants saw as basic to Christian belief and practice did not reflect the Protestantism dominant or legally established in their homelands. Some, like the Puritans, hoped to complete the work of Reformation in a setting unencumbered by the trappings of European Christianity; others sought a refuge from outright persecution at the hands of other Protestants. Third, many of the Protestants who emigrated maintained ties with co-religionists in Europe and saw their religious institutions as extensions of or complements to what they had left behind. A transatlantic dimension marks much of colonial Protestantism. Fourth, religion itself was related to the quest for empire that dominated Protestant and Catholic Europe alike. Hence another strand in the tapestry of colonial Christianity is the political rivalry between Catholic and Protestant nations in Europe and the desire to claim part of the New World for the form of Christianity each perceived to be true. There are other reasons, but this summary should make clear that colonial Christianity reflects so many facets of European Christianity—primarily European Protestantism in the case of British America—that the story must begin in Europe.

## THE LOLLARD AND HUSSITE "HERESIES"

John Wycliffe (1328–1384) emerged at the center of a movement in fourteenth-century England that itself had roots stretching back at least a century, when anticlerical sentiment became a strong undercurrent in English Christianity. Simply put, anticlericalism in this context challenged the authority of both pope and clergy as the sole mediators of salvation through the Church. To critics like Wycliffe the role the priesthood assumed was the role reserved for Christ alone in the scheme of salvation. As well, Wycliffe and his Lollard followers were incensed at the notion that the Church alone, through its priesthood, could properly interpret Scripture. That position seemed to erect a barrier between the Word of God and the humanity to which it was addressed. Wycliffe's own study of Scripture, which was to result in a translation of the

Bible into the English vernacular so Scripture would be directly accessible to the people, also led him to question some of the doctrines vital to the medieval Church. Wycliffe, for example, felt that the doctrine of transubstantiation, formally adopted by the Fourth Lateran Council in 1215, lacked adequate scriptural basis for its claim that at the time of consecration the bread and wine of the Mass were literally transformed into the actual body and blood of Christ. Wycliffe had also questioned the legitimacy of clerical celibacy, the practice of confession, the value attached to pilgrimages, and more importantly the priority medieval Christianity gave to the sacramental system over preaching of the Gospel.

But Wycliffe's movement had important political ramifications. The Church itself, with its system of parishes and monasteries, controlled a vast amount of land in England. The peasant folk who resonated to his call for change were to Wycliffe not only religiously subservient to an unscripturally structured priesthood but in many cases economically subservient as well. Thousands were trapped in a near-feudal labor arrangement, working the lands owned by the Church and watching the Church reap the bounty of their efforts. In the end, the potential for economic upheaval and revolt may have led as much to Wycliffe's condemnation as his religious protest against certain doctrines and practices. Labeling the movement a heresy, however, did not eradicate Lollardy; it merely went underground and continued to flourish in several areas in the southeastern region of England. When Luther mounted his protest in Germany in the sixteenth century, many of those who harbored Lollard sympathies eagerly welcomed his teachings.

As church authorities were attempting to suppress this perceived heresy, many kindred notions were garnering support in Bohemia in the teaching of Jan Hus (1369–1415). Hus, too, questioned the authority exercised by popes and priests and even Church councils, arguing as Wycliffe had that the Bible alone was the sole authority in matters of faith and practice. The primacy of Scripture was later to become a hallmark of the Lutheran Reformation in Germany. Another key ingredient of the Hussite movement was its challenge to the practice of offering only the Eucharistic bread to laity in communion and reserving the wine for priests. Hus and his followers felt that practice lacked any scriptural precedent. Just as the Lollard movement in England appealed to the peasantry, so too did the Hussite movement in Bohemia, for it also posed a threat to the economic control the Church exerted over much of the population and carried the potential for a popular revolt. By the middle of the second decade of the fifteenth century, the possibility of revolt seemed imminent.

In 1415, an important church council was meeting in Constance, one that would ultimately enhance the power of the papacy by paving the way for the pope again to be headquartered in Rome rather than in Avignon in France. That council sought as well to address the problem in Bohemia and ordered Hus to appear to respond to charges that his teaching reeked of heresy. The council offered Hus "safe conduct," assuring him that he would be permitted to return peaceably to Bohemia regardless of the council's verdict. That promise, however, was soon forgotten, and once the council became convinced of the dangers posed by Hus, it ordered him burned at the stake. The Hussites were far from unified as they too became an underground movement, but the core of Hus's teaching was preserved by the Bohemian Brethren, who were to achieve rapprochement with Luther's followers in 1542. Much later, some of the spiritual heirs of Jan Hus from Moravia (the geographic base of the Bohemian Brethren) were to seek refuge in Germany after a generation of displacement because of the ravages of the Thirty Years' War (1618–1648) to their homeland. Clusters of these Moravians would in time make their way to British North America.

Wycliffe and Hus were not the only ones to question the teaching of late-medieval Christianity. One might also add, for example, the Waldensians of the Savoy and Piedmont regions of the Italian peninsula. But Wycliffe and Hus stand out because many of their views—especially those about the role of the Bible and the authority of priests and popes—found powerful expression in the Protestant Reformation of the sixteenth century.

## THE LUTHERAN REFORMATION

Born in 1483 in Eisleben, in modern Germany, Martin Luther was the son of a coal miner. Hans Luther, the father, attempted to steer his son toward the law and had him begin legal studies at the University of Erfurt. But after a dramatic religious experience during a thunderstorm, Martin abandoned the study of law and entered the monastery of the Augustinian friars in Erfurt, much to his father's dismay. (Indeed, relations between father and son were never to be pleasant thereafter.)

Luther's spiritual pilgrimage as a young friar was tortuous. Although he was ordained in 1507, he had no more inner peace as a priest of the Church than he had as a law student. To some extent, Luther magnified the image of Hans, the human parent he had let down, and fashioned a notion of God as a heavenly parent who also stood in judgment over a humanity that seemed always to fall short of expectations and therefore remained unworthy of divine favor and salvation.

Despite his inner turmoil, Luther pursued academic studies, receiving a doctorate in theology in 1512 and appointment as professor of Bible at the recently founded university in Wittenberg. The introspection and melancholy that marked these years were to remain with Luther throughout his life. But even before he began his teaching career, other religious matters were beginning to plague him. In particular, the popular practice of buying indulgences greatly troubled Luther, for he not only disagreed with the theology behind them (the idea that one could purchase merit in God's eyes), but he also recognized that the profits gained from the sale of indulgences sustained other abuses in the Church.

Luther's personal spiritual crisis moved toward resolution in 1516–1517 as he prepared a series of lectures on Paul's letter to the Romans. Pausing over the apostle's quotation in the first chapter from the Hebrew prophet Habakkuk to the effect that the righteous shall live by faith, Luther found his own thinking transformed. He became convinced that faith, simple trust in God's righteousness, was the key to a personal experience of God's saving Word and that this divine righteousness meant that God always looked graciously on the sinner, accepting all who repented not on the basis of their merit but on the basis of their trust alone.

This conviction rested behind Luther's attack on indulgences that marks the beginning of the Protestant Reformation. On 31 October 1517, in time-honored fashion, Luther posted a series of ninety-five theses (propositions for debate) on the door of the castle church in Wittenberg. If Luther expected to engage in a simple academic exercise, he was mistaken. Within two months, church authorities who recognized the ramifications of his position took steps to have Luther recant his teaching or be silenced. Opposition merely fueled Luther's attacks. By 1520 he had broadened his assault to include the authority of both tradition and pope within the Church in a move reminiscent of both Wycliffe and Hus before him. Thanks to the efficiency of the recently developed printing press, pamphlets that set forth Luther's position were quickly and widely distributed. When Luther's excommunication became official in 1521, German Christianity had been irrevocably divided.

Several features of Luther's thought and the movement he spawned were to have profound impact on later developments. The first is Luther's insistence that the final authority for matters of Christian belief and practice is the Bible, the Word of God. *Sola Scriptura* (Scripture alone) became the rallying cry of those who denounced the authority of tradition, church councils, priests, and pope. By translating the Bible into vernacular German Luther also challenged the role of the Church as sole interpreter of Scripture. People should be able to read the Scriptures themselves and allow the Bible to speak to them the word of faith that had come to Luther as he studied Paul's letter to the Romans. The centrality of the Bible both to the fledgling Lutheran movement and to Protestantism generally was to mean that Protestant Europeans who flocked to British North America were a people of the Word.

A second aspect of enduring significance in the Lutheran Reformation was Luther's conviction that personal religious experience was central to the Christian life, though his own spiritual heirs in Germany were soon to forget it. Experiencing the righteousness of God was not something one person could do for another; it was a matter of the inner life where belief and feeling merged. Virtually every strand of Protestant Christianity to take root in what became the United States in some fashion built on Luther's sense of inner appropriation of the promises of God found in Scripture.

Third, Luther saw the political order as an ally of the Church and hence did not challenge as much as some would have liked the intricate connections between church and state that had prevailed in Europe since the Middle Ages. Essentially, Luther saw church and state as two distinct spheres through which God ordered human life. The proper role of government was in a sense to regulate the common life of all the people, not just those who had an experience of salvation. Hence Luther called on the German princes to crush the Peasants' Revolt of 1524–1525 so that order might prevail and accepted the support of political rulers to protect the Church. Luther insisted, however, that it was not the province of government to dictate to the Church matters of belief and practice.

Luther's willingness to work with the political sphere is evidenced in the arrangement that brought an age of religious conflict to a temporary end in Germany in 1555, nine years after Luther's death. The Peace of Augsburg decreed that the ruler of each German state would decide whether to be Catholic or Protestant (Lutheran); all the inhabitants of the states were to follow suit. Individual religious choice was not an alternative. Most of the other Protestant strands rooted in Reformation Europe were to assume that there should be some connection between church and state; many of them brought that belief with them to the New World. But in time, even in Lutheran Germany, the notion of a state church became problematic, for critics insisted that state support of a church sapped the vital piety essential to true religion.

Luther's protest unintentionally became a prototype for other movements calling for religious change. If scripture alone is the ultimate religious authority, whose interpretation is to prevail? If tradition and popes have no absolute power, should not all human authority be questioned? Since Lutherans did not revamp all of Christian practice, did they not retain too many trappings of a corrupt Catholicism? After all, the German mass of Luther still bore striking resemblance to that of Roman Catholic Christianity; Protestant bishops continued to exercise authority in Lutheran polity; ties between Protestant leaders and political powers—church and state—remained as strong in Lutheran areas as in Catholic regions. The range of answers offered to these questions suggests that built into the Lutheran Reformation were the seeds of pluralism, the recognition that many religious approaches had validity. Nowhere was that pluralism to emerge more fully than in the British colonies in North America.

## THE SPREAD OF LUTHERANISM

Part of the success of the Lutheran movement in Germany no doubt derived from its appeal to nationalist tendencies. Hence it is no surprise that within a few years after Luther began his protest, similar currents began to appear elsewhere, especially where German communities existed in mercantile cities. Indeed, the beginnings of Lutheranism in Scandinavia is attributable largely to the presence of such communities in major metropolitan areas. Within a decade after Luther had posted his propositions for debate, the Danish church had pretty well severed ties with Rome and had been transformed into a state church under firm government control. About the same time, through German influence, the Lutheran message was taken to Norway. The scales tilted in favor of Lutheranism there, however, when an already-Lutheran Denmark established its power over Norway in the late 1530s. Because of the association of Lutheranism with a resented Danish power, a residual Catholicism remained strong for some time. Nonetheless, in Norway a Lutheran state church became official. In Sweden, Catholic religious authorities were able to resist an encroaching Lutheranism somewhat longer, though there the association of King Gustavus Vasa (reigned 1523–1560) with Protestant forces paved the way for a strong national Lutheran church to develop within a century. About the same time, immigration to the New World by Scandinavians, particularly from Sweden, introduced yet another strain of Lutheranism to what became British North America.

Lutheranism also reached into the Netherlands, though there the situation was much more complex. The southern region remained firmly within the Roman Catholic orbit, while in the northern area Lutherans soon began to vie with Protestants more identified with John Calvin than with German reform for pervasive influence. By the beginning of the seventeenth century, when Spanish domination of the Netherlands had ended, Reformed views of the Calvinist stripe had carried the day. But the enormous energy Calvinists devoted to the struggle for independence from Spain and the presence of numerous enclaves of Protestants of other persuasions thwarted efforts to impose Calvinist views universally. Hence the pragmatics of the situation created a context in which an uneasy toleration of a range of Christian approaches existed for a time. When the Dutch began their ventures in the New World in areas ultimately incorporated into British North America, however, the Calvinist Reformed perspective gained an important foothold in the mid-Atlantic area, although at the same time the toleration that prevailed at home provided a refuge for a smattering of other Protestant groups encountering difficulties in their native lands. Among the most important of these for British North America later were the Separatists, whose staunch Calvinism rendered them unwelcome in an England where a moderate Protestantism emerged victorious once the religious upheavals of the Age of Reformation had faded.

## JOHN CALVIN AND THE
## REFORMED MOVEMENT IN SWITZERLAND

The year after Luther launched his reform efforts in Germany, Huldreich Zwingli (1481–1531) assumed priestly duties at the Great Minster in Zurich. In close cooperation with civic authorities, Zwingli quickly began the process of religious reform there, though his efforts and beliefs provoked controversy. As long as Zwingli had the support of the German princes, the movement maintained momentum. But when he and Luther reached an impasse in trying to reconcile their divergent views of the Eucharist, Zwingli lost that support. Swiss cantons that remained loyal to Rome then undertook military reprisals against Zurich, leading to Zwingli's death at the battle of Kappel in 1531.

By the time of Zwingli's death, John Calvin (1509–1564), the figure who was to dominate Swiss reform, was studying at the University of Paris, where he encountered the writings of Martin Luther. Around 1533 Calvin underwent an intense personal religious experience that soon led him to abandon Roman Catholicism and leave his native France. Settling first in Basle, he began work on the first edition of what was to become a classic systematic statement of Reformed belief, his *Institutes of the Christian Religion*. In 1537, the year after the *Institutes* first appeared, Calvin determined to settle in Strasburg, but circumstances required him to detour through Geneva en route. There Calvin met Guillaume Farel, who invited him to remain in Geneva to help stamp a Protestant character on the religious life and culture of that city.

Always somewhat controversial because of his vision of a holy commonwealth in which all persons—not just those of Christian affirmation—would follow the guidance of the church, Calvin ran into serious confrontations with the citizens of Geneva. Expelled from Geneva in 1538, Calvin finally did go to Strasburg, where he became associated with another Reformation figure, Martin Bucer. Called back to Geneva in 1541, Calvin again set about the task of creating a holy commonwealth where the rule of the saints would prevail. Calvin's efforts were never entirely successful and were often resisted, but his grip on the city remained firm. His association with Bucer meant that his views gradually came to influence much of Rhineland Protestantism.

Later generations remember Calvin primarily for his doctrine of predestination, the belief that God before all time determines who will be elected to salvation and who will be condemned to everlasting damnation. For Calvin, this belief epitomized the absolute dependence of humanity on God's grace, not the capricious God picking and choosing persons for salvation and reprobation that later critics found in the doctrine. A careful reading of Calvin's work suggests that the doctrine of God, particularly those aspects concerning the sovereignty and providence of God, lies at the heart of Calvin's formulation of Protestant theology. Central to Calvin's scheme was also a high regard for Scripture, the Word by which the Spirit demonstrated God's sovereignty and providence to the individual.

In a larger sense, Calvin's significance lay in his overall ability as a systematizer and organizer in all arenas, not just in matters of religious thought. Because Calvin regarded the church as superior to the state in the sense that the state should not have control over church teaching and practice, he devoted considerable attention to developing the system of church polity that later became known as presbyterian. Indeed, the priority Calvin gave to the church

in the social order meant that he and his followers assumed it was the prerogative of the church to offer guidance to the state to assure that policy reflected
scriptural precept and for church members to control government.

The practical consequences of Calvin's thought are as important as the
theology itself. Ascertaining God's will in Scripture and adherence to the moral
demands of a righteous God require a disciplined life. One must diligently
study Scripture to learn what it says. That same discipline, as Max Weber
argued decades ago, went hand-in-hand with emerging capitalist economics to
produce precisely the type of human being who would achieve economic
success. As well, the human face of predestination came in looking for signs
that one was among the elect. While inner experience might testify to one's
own election, there was no more effective public sign of God's favor than
material success. But this discipline also meant that Calvinists became cadres
of deeply committed people who could transfer the discipline of the religious
life to that demanded to resist political oppression, false teaching, and the like.
Calvinism was primed for ready expansion in Europe, even where conditions
required that expansion be an underground movement.

## REFORMATION COMES TO BRITAIN

When the Lutheran protest began to shake the foundations of continental
Christendom, and even when Calvin began to erect his holy commonwealth in
Geneva, England remained entrenched in the Roman Catholic fold, at least on
the surface. Its Tudor monarch, Henry VIII (r. 1509–1547) relished the title,
Defender of the Faith, bestowed on him by a grateful pope for a treatise Henry
had published in 1521 attacking Luther's doctrine. But the seeds of discontent
with a pope-centered Catholicism based in a distant Rome had, of course,
been planted by an anticlerical movement in the thirteenth century and nurtured by John Wycliffe and his Lollard followers in the fourteenth century.

What led to England's break with Rome and released these hitherto pent-up
urges to bring the Reformation to the English church was not at first as much
religious as political. Desperate to father a male heir to succeed him as king,
Henry sought papal dispensation to divorce his wife, Catherine of Aragon, the
mother of Henry's daughter Mary Tudor. Approving the divorce seemed impossible to papal advisers, for it meant both revoking a previous dispensation that
had made the marriage possible and alienating Catherine's Spanish kin, the
real power pulling papal strings at the time and Catholicism's most strident
political proponent. With his paramour, Anne Boleyn, pregnant, Henry could
not risk an illegitimate birth that would render a son ineligible for the crown.
Thus, in 1534, Henry severed administrative ties with the papacy, proclaiming
himself head of the church in England.

Although the child Anne bore was a daughter, Elizabeth, Henry was not
about to realign the Church of England with the papacy. There were simply

too many other advantages to retaining royal control over the church. Even before this formal break, Henry had ordered the dissolution of English monasteries and thus taken over much valuable land that greatly augmented his power and his financial resources as monarch. But Henry personally remained comfortable with the fundamentals of Catholic doctrine and refused to entertain blatantly Protestant shifts in basic belief and practice. Indeed, the Six Articles Henry issued in 1539 reaffirmed basic Catholic belief within the Church of England. The only significant gesture Henry made toward those of more obvious Protestant sympathies was allowing the publication of an English translation of the Bible in the realm. Nonetheless, behind the scenes many church leaders (in some cases building on foundations laid by Wycliffe) were quietly tilting toward Protestantism and hoped to stamp a more distinctly Protestant character on the English church.

Their day came when Henry was succeeded in 1547 by his son Edward VI, a sickly twelve-year-old. With effective governmental power in the hands of advisers, religious leaders like Thomas Cranmer (1489–1556) seized the opportunity to move the Church of England in a more Protestant direction in both doctrine and liturgical practice. The *Prayer Book* that became the only legal basis for worship under the Act of Uniformity of 1549 was essentially based on Lutheran principles and attempted to combine elements of tradition with Reformation theology. The revisions promulgated in 1552 were more radically Protestant, incorporating into the liturgy statements that reflected the Swiss Reformers' view that the Eucharist was merely a memorial of Christ's sacrifice. So, too, the Forty-two Articles of Faith proclaimed in 1553 reflected more the views of the Swiss reformers than those of Luther. What was clear, however, was that the English people were deeply divided, with some dissatisfied with the new trends because they abandoned much popular Catholic practice and others disgruntled because they were not more thoroughly Protestant.

But protestantizing moves came to a halt when Edward died in 1553 and Mary Tudor became queen. Mary was a fervent Catholic both by preference and by necessity. Her legitimacy (and therefore her claim to the throne) depended on repudiating the divorce that had generated her father's break with Rome. Hence Mary embarked on a program to restore papal authority in the English church. Many of those most committed to Protestantism fled to the Continent, where they were to come under the spell of Calvinism and Rhineland Protestantism. Somewhere between two and three hundred prominent Protestants who did not flee or publicly abandon Protestant belief and practice were burned at the stake. Mary's harsh efforts generated considerable resentment among her people, even among those inclined to Catholicism. That resentment mushroomed when Mary married Philip II of Spain, a vigorous defender of Catholicism and the papacy, who no doubt regarded the union as a way to expand the Spanish empire.

Mary died in 1558 and was succeeded by her half-sister Elizabeth I. Elizabeth's personal preferences in religion still remain something of an enigma, but her claim to the throne did require her to revoke the ties Mary had established with Rome. After all, her legitimacy depended on acceptance of Henry's divorce from Catherine of Aragon. But Elizabeth also recognized the danger to national unity of any religious extreme, Protestant or Catholic. Although she replaced Catholic religious leaders appointed under Mary with others of Protestant persuasion, Elizabeth was inclined to promote a middle way, the *via media* for which the Anglican tradition has become well known. Under Elizabeth episcopal polity remained intact, the *Prayer Book* adopted in Edward VI's reign revised and restored, overt Catholic practice prohibited, and at least genteel conformity with the arrangements of the Church of England expected. Elizabeth was always alert to the potential dangers, religious and political, of the Catholic minority in England whom the Spanish and French covertly urged to attempt to depose her so that a Catholic might again accede to the throne.

That situation was exacerbated when Calvinist religious reform came to England's northern neighbor, Scotland. John Knox (1505–1572), who called Geneva "the most perfect school of Christ that ever was on earth since the days of the Apostles,"[1] returned to Scotland in 1559 after studying with Calvin in Geneva. He immediately launched a powerful Reformation movement there. Blending nationalism and attacks on a corrupt Catholicism in Scotland, Knox quickly became such a symbol of national identity that when the Catholic Mary, Queen of Scots herself returned to Scotland from France, she was powerless to stop the movement. Indeed, Mary shortly found herself in exile in England, where she became a symbol of Catholic opposition to Elizabeth until her execution in 1587. But Knox etched such an abiding Calvinism into the religious life of the nation that historian A. G. Dickens could proclaim that "in no other country did Calvinism mould so forcibly the powers and the limitations of a people."[2] Scottish influence was strong in Northern Ireland as well after an influx of Presbyterian Scots there early in the seventeenth century, and a century later the Scots-Irish would account for the largest single group of people emigrating to the part of British North America that became the United States, bringing as part of their baggage the staunch Calvinism of John Knox.

But religious turmoil to the north and the presence in England for nearly twenty years of a potential Catholic rival to the throne were only one challenge to Elizabeth's hopes for conformity to the Church of England. More significant opposition came from the Marian exiles who began to return to England after Bloody Mary's death. In both Geneva and the German Rhineland these so-called Marian exiles had profoundly absorbed the doctrine and practices of the Calvinists, including Calvin's vision of a state ruled by saints. This intense exposure to Calvinism had also engendered hostility to the trappings of Catholic belief and practice that they felt remained in the Church of England. High on their agenda was the desire to remake the English church in much the same way John Knox had refashioned the Church of Scotland. Knox had been extraordinarily successful; the Puritans (as many of these returning exiles became known) were less so until they abandoned their efforts to reshape the

Church of England and with their growing followers embarked on their "errand into the wilderness" to erect the prototype of a holy commonwealth in New England.

In the minds of many interpreters, however, these Puritan efforts to eliminate the vestiges of Catholicism marked the real Reformation in the Church of England. The major targets of criticism were religious ceremonies thought to be without scriptural warrant and a polity based on episcopacy, another corruption of pure religion thought to lack scriptural support. At first those who attempted to "purify" the church further (hence the name) worked from within the church structure, and at the outset they had considerable support from within Parliament. In addition to the required services following the *Prayer Book*, Puritans frequently held supplementary gatherings for teaching and biblical exposition. These highlighted the Puritan desire for inner experience, a passion to know within whether one was numbered among the elect. Through study of Scripture and intense introspection, Puritans could apply scriptural precepts to the conduct of life, covenant with God to pursue the way of holiness, and evaluate whether there were sufficient signs through which individuals could discern for themselves whether God had elected them for salvation. As well, a millennialist streak permeated Puritan thought, for many were convinced that England was itself an "elect nation" that, once the church was fully reformed, was destined to have a pivotal role in God's coming reign.

So long as Puritans outwardly conformed to the Church of England, Elizabeth was reluctant to move against them. Hence, during her reign there was an ever-expanding religious subculture within the religious establishment. Only a small proportion felt that the Church of England was so hopelessly corrupt as to constitute a false church on par with Rome from which one must separate completely lest one's own spiritual life be polluted. But these Separatists also had qualms about some of the Puritan agenda; for example, they rejected both the episcopal polity of the Anglicans and the presbyterian polity of the Puritans as unscriptural, insisting that only a strict congregational polity reflected the patterns of New Testament Christianity.

Elizabeth was also reluctant to take direct action against those who remained firm in their affirmation of Roman Catholic belief and practice so long as there was outward religious conformity to the Church of England. But Catholicism and treason remained nearly synonymous in the popular mind, since even after the execution of Mary, Queen of Scots the assumption prevailed that all Catholics—even those of prominent families—were in league with England's traditional Catholic enemies, France and Spain, not only to overthrow Elizabeth but also to conquer England itself. Called Recusants because of their refusal to accept the authority of the established church, English Catholics also became part of an underground religious movement, with priests smuggled into the country, kept in hiding by wealthy Recusant families, and offering the mass and other rites of the church in secret chapels.

Under James I (r. 1603–1625), son of Mary, Queen of Scots and successor to

Elizabeth I, came concerted efforts to eliminate all dissenters from the Church of England, especially those who were most vocally Puritan. Even so, most Puritans refrained from separatism, while those who did join with the Separatists sought refuge in the Netherlands, where there was a broader tolerance of religious nonconformity, before emigrating to British North America in 1620. Puritan hopes were raised briefly when James I authorized a new translation of the Bible into the vernacular (the well-known King James Version). But these hopes for the church's and England's combined future and for ultimately succeeding in their reformation efforts quickly faded when Charles I became king in 1625. Charles aroused Puritan suspicions when he appointed William Laud archbishop of Canterbury in 1633. Laud was a virulent non-Calvinist of high-church preferences who was eager to see Puritanism quashed. Charles's situation was not helped by the fact that he was overtly tolerant of Roman Catholicism; after all, he had married a Catholic queen. Many Puritans, non-Separatists and Separatists alike, began to look to the New World as the only hope for translating from vision to reality their ideas of a pure church and a pure state. Thus began the great Puritan migration to the shores of New England in British North America that marked the 1630s.

Events in the 1640s again fueled Puritan hopes for England's divine mission. Political dissatisfaction with Charles I was growing, largely because of his attempts to rule without the assistance of Parliament. During the era of the Long Parliament, so called because Charles refused to summon Parliament or authorize new elections from 1629 to 1640, much of the political dissent coalesced around the Puritans. By 1642 civil war had erupted. When some antiroyalists not necessarily identified with the English Puritans entered into an alliance with Scots Presbyterians, it became clear that a Christianity rooted in the Calvinist Reformed perspective was on the ascendancy. Puritans controlling Parliament succeeded in having the hated Archbishop Laud executed in 1643, the same year religious divines convened as the Westminster Assembly. Out of the Westminster Assembly, which met through 1645, came striking changes designed to replace the middle way of the Church of England with doctrine, practice, and polity grounded in Calvinist ideology. Among the most significant of these changes were the abolition of episcopacy as the mode of church government; the adoption of the Westminster Confession, a statement of doctrine destined to have enduring influence on Congregationalists, Baptists, and Presbyterians in British colonial America; and preparation of catechisms for instruction in the faith that reflected Puritan-Calvinist belief.

The period of Puritan control of government also witnessed a deterioration in the situation of English Catholics, for the Puritan parties were more virulently anti-Catholic than they were anti-Anglican. Especially after the execution in 1649 of Charles I, who had been baptized a Catholic just before his death, Catholics were increasingly confined to the periphery, where they always remained suspect. Indeed, it was not until 1778 that any relief came to English Recusants by way of reducing the disabilities they suffered because of their religious faith. Little wonder, then, that some Catholics looked to colonial ventures as a way to escape the situation in England. And during the Puritan regime, even those who remained faithful to the doctrine and practice of the Church of England were suspect, both because of their religious perspective and because of their identification with the defeated royalist cause. Hence many Anglicans began to look to the colonies under British control in the New World as offering greater possibilities than England for the middle way.

Internally, however, Puritanism itself was also divided. The emphasis on purity in faith and practice virtually carried within it the propensity for some to define purity more rigorously than others. Hence the Puritan age was also an age of sectarian development in English religious life. Baptists, for example, accounted for a minute number of Puritan Independents at the start of the seventeenth century, and while they had gained some numerical strength by the outbreak of the Civil War, they grew rather quickly during the war years, when it was virtually impossible to impose religious discipline. Another group that gained strength were the followers of George Fox (1624–1691), known as the Society of Friends, or Quakers. As Sydney Ahlstrom aptly wrote, the Quakers signal "the relentless movement of the Puritan-Reformed impulse away from the hierarchical, sacramental, and objective Christianity of the Middle Ages toward various radical extremes in which intensely individualistic and spiritual motifs become predominant."[3]

Following Calvin, most Puritans maintained a significant role for the church and the clergy in the process of salvation, for it was church and clergy together that offered instruction in pure doctrine, set standards of proper moral behavior, and guided individuals in their quest to ascertain whether God had elected them to salvation. Fox and the Quakers went further in claiming that the Holy Spirit granted individuals direct, immediate access to God. Not even the church was necessary as a mediating agent. Because of this extraordinary emphasis on the individual and the concomitant denial of any human authority in matters of religion, the Quakers came across as a threat to all order, civil and religious. To rely on individual apprehension of the Spirit through the "inner light" was to sanction chaos. Such fears were confirmed when the direct apprehension of God's grace issued in ecstatic experience, sometimes with physical manifestations (hence the name), or when Quakers would disrupt worship services to condemn the corruption of a religion that placed church, clergy, and even Scripture between God and believers.

Hence Puritans and Anglicans alike tried to quash the Quaker movement. It is not surprising then that as early as the 1650s, some Quakers began to look to Britain's North American and Caribbean colonies as providing a more hospitable environment for seeking the truth within. But there too they frequently encountered hostility and disabilities that matched those imposed in England until 1681 when William Penn (1644–1718) obtained a charter for a proprietary colony where he could launch a "Holy Experiment" in which Quaker principles would inform government, but toleration would be offered to any who affirmed simple belief in God.

The dominance of Puritans in English religion and politics was to be short-lived. The death in 1658 of Oliver Cromwell, who had headed the government during the era of the Puritan Commonwealth, revealed such disarray in the Puritan ranks politically that in 1660 the monarchy was restored. With restoration, even though the new King Charles II was himself a Roman Catholic, came the re-establishment of the Church of England, the return of episcopacy as the form of church polity, and a reaffirmation of the middle way of Anglicanism. Once again Puritanism became relegated to the role of dissent, where it would remain for generations. Only gradually was toleration (not religious equality) to become the norm in Britain, when legislation passed following the Glorious Revolution of 1688 required both that the monarch be a member of the established church and that a modicum of toleration be extended to all Protestants.

## OTHER CONTINENTAL MOVEMENTS

Other currents in European religious life also shaped the coming of Christianity to British colonial America. Many resulted from movements that emerged in reaction to Lutheran developments or from the expansion of both Lutheranism and Calvinism in new regions. For example, even in the sixteenth century there appeared groups that thought Luther and other reformers had not gone far enough in restoring Christianity to its New Testament foundations. Some became known as Anabaptists because, convinced that Catholic ways were corrupt, they rebaptized followers. The roots of this left wing of the Reformation lie as much in Switzerland as in Germany, but it grew rapidly in many areas of Europe where Protestant currents took hold. Regarded as radical not only because of the practice of rebaptism but also because of their convictions regarding nonparticipation in the social order and their emphasis on a love ethic that challenged the distribution of wealth, Anabaptists encountered virulent opposition everywhere. In Germany, a strident millennialism became part of the Anabaptist thrust and led to outright persecution in 1534 when Anabaptists took control of Münster. As religious persecution in Europe waned, surviving Anabaptists gradually assumed a less aggressive posture. For example, those who followed Menno Simons (1496–1561) preferred to withdraw from society quietly, content to pursue their vision of New Testament Christianity from the margins of society. Though numerically small, before the close of the seventeenth century spiritual heirs of Menno Simons began to migrate to British North America, particularly to Pennsylvania, where they were known as Mennonites.

By the end of the seventeenth century, discontent with the religious status quo in Lutheran Germany began to emerge, though this discontent ultimately infected most of Protestantism on the European continent. The identification with the state had brought an arid quality to the vitality that spurred the first generation of Reformers. As well, continuing conflict with Roman Catholic Christians led Protestant thinkers to draw up credos and statements of doctrine that seemed to replace Luther's emphasis on simple trust in the righteousness of God with a near-Scholastic dogmatism. Because this movement attempted to restore Luther's stress on personal faith, it became known as pietism. Centered initially around the work of Philip Jacob Spener and August Hermann Francke, pietism breathed fresh life into German Lutheranism in the late seventeenth and early eighteenth centuries. It had an enduring influence in England through John Wesley and others associated with the Methodist revival, which was to have a multidimensional impact in British colonial America. Pietism also helped shape the Moravian community, those spiritual heirs of Jan Hus who came to pietist strongholds in Germany because of the Thirty Years' War.

In France, Calvinism had made such inroads that in 1598, to end an epoch of religious strife between Catholics and the Calvinists known as Huguenots, the Edict of Nantes granted certain privileges to those of Protestant persuasion. But when the Edict of Nantes was revoked in 1685, the Huguenots faced an intolerable situation. Thus began an exodus from France of some of the nation's wealthiest people, an exodus that took some elsewhere on the Continent (particularly to Holland and Germany), some to England, and some to British America.

## LOOKING TO BRITISH AMERICA

All these variegated styles and forms of religious expression, from those of the Lutheran Reformation in Germany to those of the Puritans of England, wrestled with common issues. What was the appropriate religious experience for one who sought to be a Christian? Was it what was nurtured by ritual and devotion, as in Anglicanism and Catholicism? Was it the experience of election promoted by the Calvinists? The inner light of the Quakers? The idiosyncratic view that combined pietism with particular ethnic and folk cultural patterns of the German sectarians? All these approaches and more would find advocates and a place in British colonial America.

Another common concern was the proper relation between religion and government, between church and state. Should there be only one established church? If so, which one? Should the state have power to control the church, or is the church superior to the state? Or perhaps the two should be totally separate, each dealing with concerns germane to its own sphere without interference by the other. Proponents of all these positions, each with roots in Reformation Europe, would find a place for themselves in British America.

The sheer variety of responses offered to both these issues by those who left Europe behind to make a home in the New World meant that, however one answered the questions, pluralism would prevail. From the start, British colonial America was peopled by colonists from a diversity of ethnic, national, and religious backgrounds. Even those who wanted to impose their own way on the folk around them because they were convinced that they and they alone possessed the truth of salvation were unable to do so. In a word, they often found that their neighbors shared equally strong but very different and sometimes contradictory convictions about things religious. The dilemma was compounded because many of these groups felt that implementation of their version of Christian truth would set the stage for the coming of God's ultimate rule in human history. Hence, how to convince others of the truth in a pluralistic setting (in other words, how to propagate the faith) was also a matter of concern.

But in every case, the truth that came from Europe and the dreams of constructing in the New World the ideal setting for that truth to prevail found themselves transformed by the conditions colonists confronted once the European invasion and conquest of the Americas got under way.

# 16

## PURITANISM COMES
## TO BRITISH AMERICA

Of the many currents of Christianity that eventually found a home in British colonial America, none was destined to have more significant and enduring impact than Puritanism—especially in those colonies that eventually became the United States. Yet Puritanism itself came in many guises. All who were drawn into the Puritan orbit reflected the influence of Calvinism and the Reformed movement in continental Europe. Reformed Christianity's emphasis on the absolute sovereignty of God and the depth of human depravity had particularly profound influence on the shape of all strains of Puritanism, along with the concomitant necessity to maintain strict moral discipline to keep the control of evil in check. Most of the Puritans who came to the New World filtered that influence through the prism of the Church of England and the experience of attempts to effect changes in the Church of England that would bring its belief and practice in keeping with the perceived principles of New Testament Christianity.

Determining precisely what changes were needed and how best to implement them brought considerable variety to Puritanism. Three clusters of Puritans, each with different responses to these concerns, made their way to British areas of the Americas in the seventeenth century. One cluster included those who were generally content with the Elizabethan settlement that stamped a broad Protestant character onto the Church of England. For them, the thrust of Reformed influence rested primarily with the individual pursuit of holiness and the discipline that quest required if one hoped to have a clear sign of election to salvation. Another group believed that reformation efforts in England had ground to a halt. Thus the Church of England itself became for them a barrier that thwarted their spiritual journey. The largest group, however, remained convinced that the seeds of pure Christianity had been planted in the Church of England but required careful cultivation if they were to blossom. Simply put, these Puritans believed that reforming Christianity in England had an unfinished agenda that must be completed for the Church of England and the nation itself to realize the destiny intended by God.

Puritans of the first stripe first became part of the colonial venture in Virginia, but ultimately were to be found throughout Britain's American empire. Those who despaired of their ability to effect needed reform in the Church of England made up the bulk of those who established the colony known as the Plymouth Plantation. The third group built its first settlements in the Massachusetts Bay Colony, though in time Puritans of this ilk were to absorb the Plymouth Colony, launch other colonial ventures in New England and elsewhere in British North America, and leave an enduring mark on the character of religion and society in virtually every British colony in the Americas.

## PURITAN IMPULSES IN VIRGINIA

As Sydney Ahlstrom has noted, "religious motives were hardly primary for the London merchants who supported" the first British colonial settlement at Jamestown in 1607.[1] Indeed, those who invested in the Virginia Company were far more interested in gaining commercial profit, perhaps even on the magnitude that England's longstanding national rivals, the Spanish, were reaping in Mexico. But religious motives lurked beneath the surface. On the one hand, a successful settlement would plant Protestantism in the New World and thus counter the growth of Catholicism there that the Spanish promoted. As well, the charter for the new colony granted by James I emphasized the need to evangelize the native Indians who "as yet live in darkness and miserable ignorance of true knowledge and worship of God."[2] Suffice it to say that these endeavors met with limited success.

Perhaps the necessity of fostering the discipline that was necessary to build a colony from scratch prompted the formal religious life of Virginia early on to assume a character that resembled that of the more overtly Puritan colonies to the north a few years later. For, although the Church of England was legally established at the outset of the colonial venture, the first written legal code of Virginia, enforced by Governor Thomas Dale (who arrived in 1611) and therefore popularly dubbed Dale's Laws, had a distinctly Puritan cast. Even when the first colonial legislature, the House of Burgesses, repealed *The Lawes Divine, Morall and Martiall* in 1619, the new legislation retained the most obviously Puritan aspects of the old. For example, immoderate or extravagant dress was prohibited, Sabbath observance and attendance at worship twice each Sunday required, idleness and other conduct deemed reflective of moral lapse punishable. As well, clergy were granted authority to admonish the morally negligent. On paper at least, these ordinances differed little from what John Calvin had urged on Geneva nearly a century earlier in his labors to erect a holy commonwealth there.

But an ingredient was missing in Virginia that was to abound in Puritan Massachusetts Bay and in Plymouth: There simply was not the same degree of religious zeal among the Virginia settlers that was to mark those who came to New England. As well, the leadership of the Virginia Company that remained in England, though it included people of distinct Puritan sympathies such as Sir Edwin Sandys, ran afoul of James I. Consequently, in 1624 the company's charter was revoked and Virginia became a royal colony. As such, its religious life came more directly under the control of the established church and the Puritan impulse that had basically dominated the early years of the colony began to wane. After William Berkeley, a staunch supporter of the established church, became governor in 1642, measures were enacted to curtail Puritan and other nonconformist influence in the colony even as Puritans at home were gaining power during the Civil War and the Puritan Commonwealth.

## SEPARATISTS COME TO PLYMOUTH

In early November 1620, the *Mayflower* arrived off Cape Cod, having missed Virginia, its intended destination, by several hundred miles. Those aboard represented the second cluster of Puritans to settle in British North America. They had long before abandoned hope that true reformation could come to the Church of England and had become convinced that the only avenue to recapturing authentic Christian belief and practice lay in separating from the established church (hence sometimes they are known as Separatists).

Their roots go back to the larger Puritan movement that had been growing in England since Elizabeth I had come to the throne. Although many local congregations within the Church of England were dominated by Puritans, most had acquiesced to the status quo under the Elizabethan settlement, hoping that fresh opportunities to purify the English church would emerge after Elizabeth died. When James I failed to support Puritan initiatives, several congregations concluded that separation was the only recourse. But given that the Church of England could call on the coercive power of the government to enforce conformity, organizing separate congregations entailed potential risk, though numerous groups managed to do so.

One such congregation that formed in 1606 in the Nottinghamshire town of Scrooby in retrospect seems to have experienced greater despair at the prospects in England of what they believed to be genuine Christianity. Under the leadership of Separatist pastor John Robinson, the Scrooby congregation relocated in 1609 to Leiden in the Netherlands, where greater toleration of religious diversity prevailed. But within a decade, fresh discontent had emerged. Satisfactory employment opportunities did not materialize, leaving these Separatists without a solid economic base. The lure of Dutch culture was also seen as a threat, for though these folk harbored serious misgivings about England and its brand of Christianity, they retained a distinct pride in their English cultural heritage. Then, too, some of the congregation had found other religious alternatives flourishing in Holland more attractive than the austere simplicity of the Separatists. Once the English colonial settlements in Virginia had a modicum of stability, migration there offered to those remaining in the Separatist fold the possibility of achieving economic security in an English environment where they would have the freedom quietly to practice their form of pure Christianity.

After surmounting numerous difficulties in securing financial backing and other support for their venture, just over a hundred sailed from England in the early fall of 1620 with their vision fixed on Virginia. Arrival at Cape Cod only momentarily forced rethinking plans. Now, instead of joining an already functioning colony, the Separatists would have to build their own civilization in the wilderness, a task compounded by a severe winter after their arrival that saw half the colony's population die. But the Separatists' religious ideology provided a basis for a common life in which the good of the whole would prevail over individual needs and desires. Before disembarking, the men joined together in a covenant (a phenomenon of especial significance to all Puritans) known to later generations as the Mayflower Compact.

Fortunately, one layman who was part of the enterprise, William Bradford (1590–1657), possessed extraordinary leadership abilities and an abiding commitment to the radical Puritanism of the Separatists. In *Of Plymouth Plantation*, his history of the struggling colony, Bradford became the first to label these Separatists "Pilgrims." The term is an apt one, for the Plymouth settlers were engaged both in a pilgrimage to create a new civilization and in a spiritual journey to nurture a simple, unadorned Christianity that they found consonant with the New Testament.

In sectarian fashion, the Pilgrims at Plymouth remained as aloof as possible from the larger colonial world developing around them. The colony remained numerically small until it was joined with the larger Massachusetts Bay Colony in 1691. But the Pilgrims in some sense found in the New World what they had been seeking when they emigrated to Leiden. They did have the freedom for a time to pursue their own religious quest. Their sense of discipline, integral to all strains of Puritanism, gave them a modicum of economic stability and early on allowed them to repay their English creditors. And, though always skeptical about the direction England itself was taking, they were able to maintain their English cultural traditions with minimal dilution by those around them. The relative isolation that made all this possible, however, was not to be part of the story of spiritual cousins of the Pilgrims who came to Massachusetts Bay.

## THE PURITANS OF MASSACHUSETTS BAY

The third cluster of Puritans who peopled British North America in the seventeenth century were perhaps the most optimistic and the most visionary group, but ultimately the most frustrated when reality whittled away at their optimism and caused their idealism seemingly to come apart at the seams. Unlike the Separatists who wound up in Plymouth, these Puritans believed that the transformation of the Church of England in the sixteenth century had launched English Christianity on a new course—indeed, on the right course. It was just that the job remained unfinished. By working within the established church, many Puritans were convinced that the work of truly reforming the church, of bringing it in line with New Testament precepts, could be accomplished. Setbacks that caused Separatists to despair only increased the resolve of other Puritans to work harder to make the essence of the Church of England a beacon of authentic Christianity.

Why then did those who saw such potential within the Church of England wind up leaving their homeland for the New World? If dreams of profit propelled those who came to Virginia and dreams of faith inspired the Pilgrims to compact and form a holy commonwealth at Plymouth, a mixture of circumstances and motives prompted the Puritans who settled Massachusetts Bay. On the religious side, foremost stand two phenomena: the marriage of Charles I to a Catholic queen and the rise to power within the Church of England of William Laud (1573–1645), the bishop of London appointed archbishop of Canterbury in 1633. Charles's marriage to Henrietta Maria of France aroused the antipapal sentiment endemic to Puritanism; Laud's Arminian bent and fondness for ceremony grated against the Calvinism and antiritualism of the Puritans, and his high-handed style reinforced the Puritans' conviction that a congregational polity, not episcopacy, was the most authentic replication of New Testament church structure. On the political side was Charles I's ineptness in dealing with Parliament and his seeming inability to contain the growing influence of Catholic France in European affairs. Both combined to shatter the Puritan vision for the England of the future, an England that would be the model of God's rule on earth. On the economic side was the hope that a fresh start in the New World would reverse the disabilities associated with religious dissent in England. On the personal side was something akin to the herd mentality; many began to ponder emigration to the New World simply because family and friends had already determined to be part of the enterprise.

Those who resisted leaving a revered homeland did so because they shuddered at abandoning a nation with England's potential. Those who left did so in part so that a godly remnant could create in the New World what had been thwarted in the Old. By 1628, when Charles I was clearly moving in the direction of more absolute rule, several nonseparatist Puritans secured controlling interest in the New England Company (later the Massachusetts Bay Company). Although this group included persons of means for whom the profit motive might have been expected to have been paramount, the Puritan stockholders spearheaded a move to make colonization the chief aim of the company. They were no doubt inspired in part by the settlement of some of their fellow Puritans in Salem (Massachusetts) late in 1628. Then, in a bold move, the stockholders determined to transfer the entire company to Massachusetts Bay, taking the charter with them and designating John Winthrop (1588–1649) governor. Some four hundred, including Winthrop, set sail for the New World in the spring of 1630. An additional six hundred were to follow before the year's end, and within a decade nearly twenty thousand had made the move to New England.

From the start, these Puritans perceived themselves as part and parcel of the Church of England. Before leaving England, Winthrop and several other key figures in the move to emigrate had written: "We . . . esteem it our honour to call the *Church of England* . . . our dear mother . . . ever acknowledging that such hope and part as we have obtained in the common salvation we have received in her bosom and sucked it from her breasts. We leave it not, therefore, as loathing that milk wherewith we were nourished there; but blessing God for the parentage and education, as members of the same body, shall always rejoice in her good."[3] But this devotion did not mean that the Church of England would simply be transplanted to New England. Rather, the colonial venture provided the Puritans with the opportunity to fashion the church into what it was supposed to be, a church shorn of vestiges of Catholicism and rebuilt on the principles of New Testament Christianity.

The Puritans recognized the import of their move, for they believed that they stood on the brink of bringing into reality their dream of reforming the church completely and thereby being poised to construct both a model church and a model civilization. They would be what England was destined to be. Evidence of this keen sense of mission is found in John Winthrop's oft-quoted address aboard the *Arbella* before the colonists disembarked in June 1630: "For the work we have in hand, it is by mutual consent, through a special overruling providence and a more than an ordinary approbation of the churches of Christ, to seek out a place of cohabitation and consortship, under a due form of government both civil and ecclesiastical . . . therefore we must not content ourselves with usual ordinary means. Whatsoever we did or ought to have done when we lived in England, the same must we do, and more also where we go. . . . Thus stands the cause between God and us: we are entered into covenant with Him for this work; we have taken out a commission, the Lord hath given us leave to draw our own articles. . . . We shall find that the God of Israel is among us, when ten of us shall be able to resist a thousand of our enemies, when He shall make us a praise and glory, that men shall say of succeeding plantations: 'The Lord make it like that of New England.'. . . For we must consider that we shall be as a city upon a hill, the eyes of all people are upon us."[4]

Winthrop directly or indirectly called attention to several ideas vital to the Puritan commonwealth in Massachusetts Bay in these words: mutual consent and covenant, providence, proper organization of church and state, and an abiding sense of mission ("city on a hill"). In so doing, he highlighted both the ideological base of the Puritan enterprise and also the arenas where problems would emerge to challenge this grand vision. In order to appreciate the forces that would test the ability of the Puritans to erect a true Christian commonwealth, one must examine the implications of Puritan ideology.

## THE PASSION FOR PURITY

The Puritans who came to New England frequently drew analogies between their experience and that of ancient Israel—witness Winthrop's reference to the "God of Israel" in the quoted passage. On a conscious level, they drew on Israel's experience of becoming a people, especially the experience of Israel's wandering in the wilderness, to make sense out of their own common life in the New World. In a sense, they were reliving what had transpired in ancient Hebrew history, for they were in the process of creating a new nation in a new wilderness. Yet it was not ideology alone that enabled Puritans to link their venture with that of Israel. Equally important were the Puritans' own encounters with both the land in the New World and with the Native Americans whose civilizations were thriving on the land. From their perspective, since the accoutrements of civilization had been left behind in England, the land of New England was very much like a wilderness and became an extension of the biblical wilderness through which the Hebrew tribes had wandered while being forged into a people. At the same time, the presence of the Native Americans, always regarded as both friend and heathen foe, enhanced the comparison, for here were peoples who functioned like the Canaanites who had inhabited Israel's promised land. Alluring yet alien, the Native American civilizations reinforced the conscious conviction of the Puritans (indeed, of many other Protestants who came to the New World) that they were replicating the experience of God's chosen people.

This parallel with Israel also operated on an unconscious level. Just as the covenant between Yahweh and the Hebrews called Israel into being as a holy people, so too the Puritans had a sense of being called to holiness. They had a passion for purity in every aspect of life, individual and corporate. In ancient Israel, this sense of holiness led to the creation of a detailed code of law, of rules and regulations to govern even the trivial dimensions of daily life, so that the whole of existence might be hallowed. The popular image of Pilgrims and Puritans as dour folk who were, in H. L. Mencken's words, "in constant dread that someone somewhere might be happy" clearly misrepresents the dynamic of New England Puritanism, but it does highlight the passion for purity that undergirded Puritan life.[5]

Anthropologist Mary Douglas, in her book *Puritan and Danger*, convincingly argued that any group captured by a passion for purity must draw boundaries. It must seek diligently to distinguish between that which will promote the pursuit of holiness and that which endangers such a pursuit. It must avoid contamination at all costs, lest pollution infect and ultimately destroy true purity. For those with John Winthrop aboard the *Arbella* and the thousands who followed them, concern for boundaries was very real. Hence Winthrop's concern for a "due form of government, both civil and ecclesiastical" was a means of erecting structures that would facilitate the pursuit of purity and minimize potential contamination from external sources.

Where did one find the guidelines for erecting such structures? In true Reformed tradition, the Puritan response would be the Bible, the Word of God that set forth what was required of those who would be a pure people, a holy nation. Hence Scripture was of paramount importance to the Puritans. Scripture was explicated in sermons that often lasted two or three hours and always placed emphasis on the practical application of Scriptural precepts to daily life. But Scripture was also to be studied by ordinary folk, not just explained by the clergy. Hence the passion for purity also engendered an abiding commitment to education. Only those who could read and understand Scripture would be able to scrutinize their own lives both to see how far short they fell from the ideals of holiness and whether there were signs that God had elected them to salvation. The Puritans were not fundamentalists in the late-twentieth-century sense, but they were biblicists in the sense that all they did was to be judged by the standards found in the Bible.

For the Puritans, this commitment to building both church and society on a scriptural base was not constraining or restrictive. Rather, from the outset Puritan preachers and politicians spoke of liberty, the freedom to construct a pure church and a holy commonwealth unfettered by the tainted ways of the Old World. Genuine liberty was the freedom to live the life of purity that God intended for God's people; it never meant "anything goes." Hence when Massachusetts Bay first codified its laws in 1641, the name given to them was *The Body of Liberties*. Nathaniel Ward (1578–1652), who became pastor in Ipswich after he came to Massachusetts Bay in 1634, gave testimony to the way that Puritan liberty was also a means of drawing boundaries in his treatise *The Simple Cobler of Aggawam in America*. "I dare take upon me to be the herald of New England," he wrote, "so far as to proclaim to the world, in the name of our colony, that all familists, Antinomians, Anabaptists, and other enthusiasts shall have free liberty to keep away from us; and such as will come to be gone as fast as they can, the sooner the better. . . . I dare aver that God does nowhere in His word tolerate Christian states to give toleration to such adversaries of His truth, if they have power in their hands to suppress them. . . . If the devil might have his free option, I believe he would ask nothing else but liberty to enfranchise all false religions and to embondage the truth."[6] Liberty, then, was the freedom to pursue the path of holiness outlined by Scripture; never was it blanket toleration.

That all of life was to be holy is also seen in the Puritans' understanding of and use of space. Mircea Eliade, in his classic work *The Sacred and the Profane*, called attention to the ways that religious persons sacralize some space, another dimension of creating boundaries. As James P. Walsh has shown, the New

England Puritans on the surface rejected the notion that some space was more sacred than other space. That was a false notion inherited from Catholicism. Rather, since all of life was to be holy, all space must be equally holy. On a practical level, this hallowing of all space meant that Puritan meetinghouses (not called churches at first) were constructed in a simple architectural style— what later generations would call the Protestant Plain Style. They lacked altars or other accoutrements that would give the impression that some space was especially sacred. As well, the meetinghouses would be used as gathering places for the community to discuss common concerns, not just places of worship used on Sundays. That practice would also collapse the distinction between sacred and profane and integrate all of life around true purity.

The Puritans did perhaps unwittingly sacralize space, but they did so as a sign of their commitment to building a total way of life devoted to holiness. In any new settlement, the meetinghouse was the first structure to be erected, and meetinghouses were in theory carefully located in the center of a town. The familiar grid pattern intended for New England towns, with the meeting-house centrally located, symbolically demonstrates the subordination of all life to pursuit of purity, for in the meetinghouse the way to holiness was pro-claimed. Of course, in actuality, most New England towns developed in a more haphazard fashion, and rarely did meetinghouses wind up in the precise geographic center. Nonetheless they remained the symbolic center, the *axis mundi* of the town (to use Eliade's term), and thus served as a visible sign of the community's commitment to holiness.

## THE ROLE OF COVENANT IDEOLOGY

Perhaps the most important practical expression of the Puritan commitment to holiness lies in the notion of covenant and the way covenants of one sort or another formed the basis for public and private life in New England. The reliance on covenant ideology has led to the designation of much Puritan thought as "federal theology," from the Latin *foedus* (covenant). That cove-nants were central to the biblical way had a long heritage, antedating the Puritans. Calvin occasionally wrote of covenants; Heinrich Bullinger, who succeeded Zwingli as the Reformation leader in Zurich, placed much emphasis on covenant ideas. Reformed thinkers in the Rhineland and in the Netherlands were particularly taken by covenants as the primary expression of God's proper dealing with humanity. In England, Puritan theologians at Cambridge Univer-sity, with which many of those who migrated to Massachusetts Bay had association, expanded covenant thinking considerably. Among these was Wil-liam Ames (1576–1633), one of the theologians most carefully studied and most frequently quoted by New England Puritans.

At the core of covenant thought was the conviction that predestination of some to salvation and some to eternal damnation did not represent the work of a whimsical deity whose decrees operated impersonally. Rather, God's eternal decrees were part of a scheme of grace, rooted in the covenant God made with Abraham (recounted in Genesis 17) and especially in the covenant God made with Jesus Christ to effect human redemption. But the Puritan reading of Scripture dealing with covenants revealed that God always took the initiative in establishing this special relationship with human beings. That action alone made the covenant a gift of grace. Those whom God called into covenant relationship must respond in faith. Yet faith itself was impossible without God's prior action in prompting a total commitment to the way of holiness. The rub, of course, was whether human beings themselves played any direct role in the process. Puritan thinkers were reluctant to grant a sinful humanity any part in the scheme of redemption; to do so would be to usurp God's prerogative, to challenge God's absolute sovereignty. But they were also convinced that humans were unlikely to experience God's call to election apart from preparation. Simply put, those who obligated themselves to the pure life, to following scriptural precepts, were more likely to discern signs of their election that would culminate in a discrete experience of regeneration.

What set the New England Puritans apart from others captured by federal theology was the way in which they pushed covenant thought to its logical limits. Covenant should determine not only an individual's relationship with God. It must also be the infrastructure undergirding social relationships (government), the religious community (church), and even the family. Covenant was never just a matter between God and an individual; it bound people to each other through mutual consent to form both a true church and a true society. When covenant thinking combined with the commitment to purity, an implication of tremendous consequence for New England life became apparent: to protect those who were in covenant relationship with God, only those who could testify to their own election should determine public policy. While all might be part of the social covenant, only the regenerate should govern or even make laws, for only they understood the way to implement biblical guidelines in a society that included many who were not of the elect. Nowhere was this more blatant than in the New Haven colony and the settlements along Long Island Sound that looked to New Haven for leadership. There, under the direction of the Rev. John Davenport and Gov. Theophilus Eaton, who had spearheaded the move to New Haven of a congregation of London Puritans in 1637, Scripture precept was to be "the only rule to be attended unto in ordering the affairs of government."[7]

Thus once settled in the New World, Puritans began to require individuals to testify to an experience of election in order to qualify for church membership, a more stringent test for membership than had been expected in England. There the standard among Puritans remained basically a commitment to Puritan belief and the pursuit of holiness. Once public testimony to regeneration had been given and accepted as legitimate, the individual not only became a member of the church but also, if male, received the right to vote and have a voice in public affairs. Thus church covenant and social covenant became intertwined. But the result was not the "theocracy" that earlier generations of historians proclaimed it; rather, church and state were both to be under the authority of those who had entered into covenant with God because of their experience of regeneration and therefore best understood what Scripture decreed for the ordering of the commonwealth.

Imbedded into covenant thought was thus a sense of hierarchy within equality. No elect person held superior status to another elect person in any absolute sense. God simply called some to special tasks for the good of the whole. It followed that deference was owed to those so called—so long as they faithfully executed their divine charge. Clergy rarely held public office; that was not their calling. But reminding political officials (Puritans were fond of calling them magistrates) of their duty was a legitimate ramification of their oversight of the spiritual well-being of the people. Likewise, magistrates did not have authority to determine church practice or belief, though it was within their calling to enforce the moral guidelines that followed from religious belief and to help resolve religious controversy for the social well-being of the people.

The same mind set determined Puritan notions of the proper ordering of family life. While the Puritans adhered to the distinctions in gender roles endemic to the seventeenth century, they did so not because of the belief of later generations that one gender was innately superior to another. Rather, men and women, husbands and wives, were in a covenant relationship with each other. Therefore by mutual consent each had a divine calling to particular responsibilities within the family just as each had a duty to church and to society. As well, it was within the context of the family that children could best be taught the necessity of pursuing the path of holiness and precisely how one might discern signs of election and be prepared to assume the obligations of covenant relationship in church and society. Indeed, to a great extent, the structure of the family for the Puritans and for many others of a Protestant bent was the model for the structure of both church and society since it was in the family that children received their first exposure to covenant relationships, to hierarchy of responsibility, and to the pursuit of holiness. If the covenant operative within the family gave precedence to the male as husband and father, in actual practice it gave women as wives and mothers much de facto power for it was through their role in rearing children that new generations would come to understand the ways of God. It should therefore come as no surprise that although the formal apparatus of Puritan culture was male-dominated, women accounted for the majority of those who owned the church covenant. Indeed, throughout British colonial America, more women than men were church members.

If covenant ideology formed the basic framework for the Puritan venture in British colonial America, it also had profound impact on how Puritans understood the role of the individual in both church and society and on how the Puritans interpreted their corporate experience. Each must be examined in turn.

## PURITAN INDIVIDUALISM

Puritan thinking always maintained a tension between the individual and the community. By its very nature, covenant ideology was community-oriented. After all, covenant required mutual consent between the parties submitting to it. The social covenant bound together all those who would be part of the public community; the church covenant bound all those who had experienced election to each other as well as to God. But in the insistence that the individual must have some direct, discrete experience of election prior to owning the church covenant lies the source of tension between the individual and the community endemic to New England Puritanism.

How were individuals to know that what they had experienced was a genuine sign of God's electing them to salvation? On the surface the answer seems simple: When individuals recounted their experience before the congregation or before the pastor (in the case of women), congregation and pastor could compare what was said with what others had related before. As might be expected, in time this process led to accounts of conversion taking on something of a stock character. Persons learned the vocabulary of election from those whose personal narratives allowed them admission to the church covenant and then applied them to their own experience.

But two problems remained. One was the role of the individual in the whole scheme of salvation. If election was God's work, did not humans have to respond? If people had not yet experienced God's grace in election, could they not prepare themselves so that when the regenerating work of the Spirit did come, they would indeed recognize it? The other problem is a question of authority. Who was to say that the Spirit might not work in different ways in different people? Should not individuals be the final arbiters in determining whether God had effectually called them to salvation? After all, part of the impetus for Puritanism in England had been the rejection of the authority of bishops and parliament to determine religious affairs, the rejection of human meddling in the work of God. By the end of the colonial period this strain of individualism was also to have profound implications among those who rejected the authority of king and parliament in the political affairs of colonies and thus played into the move for independence in those colonies that became the United States.

In response to the first problem, there developed on the one hand an elaborate scheme of "preparation for salvation" based on the conviction that faithful attendance on the means of grace (reading of Scripture, attendance at worship, prayer, and the like) would lead to recognition of God's work—if not nearly guarantee that God would elect those who were prepared. On the other hand, there remained those who were reluctant to endorse preparation, lest doing so be construed as coercing God's sovereign will through human endeavor, but nevertheless saw the practical value in maintaining order and preserving the path of purity from pollution in having all who were part of the commonwealth attendant on the ministrations of the church. Nonetheless, Puritan diaries are replete with accounts of individuals searching their souls for signs of God's regenerating power at work, alternating between anxiety that their human frailty precluded them from saving faith and rejoicing that assurance had come that God had indeed numbered them among the elect. The second problem, the matter of authority, brought seemingly endless debates over polity to determine precisely how authority should be expressed in the church and where its limits rested. It also issued in some specific conflicts that threatened to undermine the New England Way. Simply put, within the first decade of Puritan settlement in New England, as we shall see, the various responses that could be offered to all these questions were to reveal the impossibility of fully implementing the theory and ideology of Puritanism into viable structures for both church and society.

## COMMUNAL SELF-UNDERSTANDING: PURITAN MILLENNIALISM

The corporate implications of covenant ideology endowed the Puritans of New England with an abiding conviction that the people as a whole had been called of God to a specific mission, that of building a society and a church according to biblical precept. Underlying this conviction was a subtle millennialism: Should the Puritan mission succeed, then not only would the world have a living example of what God intended for the ordering of human life, but all would also be ready for the culmination of history in the full and final reign of God over all creation. The millennial age would dawn.

Puritan millennialism found early expression in John Winthrop's sermon aboard the *Arbella*. The image of the "city on a hill" is clearly a millennial one. But it also recurs in countless sermons of numerous Puritan preachers, particularly in those laments known as jeremiads in which preachers bemoaned the ways in which New England was ever straying from its high calling and urged recommitment to the Puritan Way. The millennial streak in Puritan thought appears in especially bold relief in the interpretation of New England history penned by Edward Johnson (1598–1672). Published in London in 1654, Johnson's *Wonder-Working Providence of Sion's Saviour* proclaimed New England as "the place where the Lord will create a new heaven and a new earth in, new churches and a new commonwealth together."[8] The parallel with the vision of John on Patmos in the New Testament Apocalypse is unmistakable.

Not just individual Puritans were numbered among the elect; the whole of New England was perceived as an elect nation, as Israel had been. But where Israel had faltered, God's redeeming work in Jesus Christ could permit New England to be the beacon pointing to God's ultimate rule. As Mark Noll has argued, this millennialist thrust had vital consequences for the communal self-understanding that permeated the Puritan colonial enterprise, for it "encouraged harmony in social relationships, a willingness to forego private good for the public welfare, and a contentment with one's own position in the body politic."[9] If this millennialism engendered zeal for the commonweal, it could also breed an arrogance and self-righteousness in dealing with those who did not share the passion for purity or who were otherwise excluded from participation in the New England Way. Puritan relationships with the Native American Indians, for example, reflect this smug, hypocritical self-righteousness, for many a New Englander saw the hand of God at work whenever Indians suffered defeat in struggles with the colonists despite the quiet efforts of a few missionaries to bring the natives into the Puritan fold.

But like the individualism that periodically threatened the New England Way, so too did Puritan millennialism carry within it an implicit danger. If dissension rather than harmony prevailed, was such a sign of God's disfavor with New England as biblical accounts suggested it had been in ancient Israel? Did God withdraw providential support during hard times? What could be done to prevent the people from abandoning their high calling and turning to worldly pursuits that would destroy the elect nation? Just as controversy surrounded the ever-present tension between the individual and the community, controversy ensued as those who first settled in New England and their heirs sought to answer these troubling questions. Many times the two went hand in hand.

## CRACKS IN THE PURITAN FOUNDATIONS

Within a decade of the settlement of the Massachusetts Bay colony, conflict and controversy had become common. While much conflict was inherent in the idealism that framed Puritan ideology, some also emerged simply because of the impact of events in England. The great migration, noted above, that got under way as England teetered on the brink of civil war brought with it a host of difficulties. While many of the thousands who migrated shared Puritan belief in its broad contours, they also lacked the zeal for erecting a holy commonwealth more characteristic of the first settlers. Then too, increasing numbers simply meant that the motives for coming to the New World of some who arrived on New England shores would be antithetical to Puritan ideology. The larger the number of new colonists, the greater the possibility of diversity and varying degrees of commitment to the path of purity. As well, the task of incorporating large numbers of new arrivals into what was really an embryonic social order at best was a sociological challenge of great magnitude. And while upheaval in England continued, there would be little guidance forthcoming from Puritans at home—if such guidance were wanted. New England would have to confront the cracks in the foundations of its ideology on its own. Each challenge was to reveal that despite the ideology that presumably bound Puritans to one another and to God as part of a single whole, diversity and pluralism were present from the start.

Among the earliest controversies was one that ultimately prompted Thomas Hooker (1586–1647) and much of his congregation to leave Massachusetts Bay starting in 1634 to build a separate holy commonwealth in the Connecticut valley, with its major settlement at Hartford. While the need for more land to accommodate a growing population was doubtless a major factor in the move, religious differences also played a part. Hooker locked horns with another towering figure in early New England history, the Reverend John Cotton (1584–1652), who was pastor of the church in Boston. Their disagreement centered around one of the dilemmas already noted: whether individuals should or even could prepare themselves for regeneration. Hooker was far more inclined than Cotton to view preparation for salvation as axiomatic to the work of the Spirit. Thus the Connecticut colony tended to be less rigorous in insisting on a discrete experience of election for admission into the church covenant and more open to granting the franchise to persons who were not yet church members. At the same time, though, Hooker and his followers were deeply committed to their understanding of the New England Way. A reading of the *Fundamental Orders of Connecticut* (1639), which provided the basis for the formal structures of both church and state in the new colony, reveals that the same vision and ideology that undergirded the Bay Colony, the same dedication to the path of purity, prevailed there. Ironically, if in the context of the seventeenth century Hooker's colony seemed less concerned about establishing strict boundaries to protect the Puritan Way, Connecticut was destined to become the colony where Puritan principles remained most deeply ingrained.

More disconcerting was the controversy that surrounded Roger Williams (1603–1683) almost from the time of his arrival in Massachusetts in 1631. Williams was so committed to the pursuit of purity that he declined the pastorate of the Boston church because the church still regarded itself as part of the Church of England, albeit a manifestation of the established church that was more in line with New Testament Christianity. To remain linked to a church that was itself corrupt was for Williams to sanction impurity. Other aspects of the Puritan commonwealth in Massachusetts troubled this seeker. Williams was convinced that the state had no authority over the church, not even the authority to enforce orthodoxy. Just as the pure church must be separate from a corrupt religious establishment, the church must also be totally separate from the state. Williams also questioned the ethics and the legality of the colony's simply taking over land belonging to the Native Americans. He did not accept the argument that charters issued by kings made such action moral and legal, since kings themselves had not acquired the land by proper means.

Williams for a time settled in Plymouth; he had mistakenly expected to find greater sympathy for his views among the Separatists there. But when he returned to Massachusetts in 1635 as pastor of the church in Salem and called for the congregation to separate from the other churches in the colony, he appeared to both religious and political authorities as a threat to good order. To allow one congregation to go its own way would undermine the manner in which covenant ideology bound all together in a single commonwealth. Thus in October 1635 the Massachusetts General Court decreed that Williams be deported. Instead, in January 1636 Williams and five followers fled from Salem, ultimately purchasing from the Indians the land that became Providence and in time the colony of Rhode Island and Providence Plantations.

But Williams had not abandoned covenant principles. He simply regarded the covenant between God and Israel as applying in his time only to the relationship between the individual and God. The covenant that undergirded society and government was entirely a secular matter that had no bearing on an individual's ties with God. God covenanted only with persons, not nations. Thus in 1638, when Williams and twelve others joined together to give their secular undertaking a formal foundation, they provided for what later generations would call complete "separation of church and state" and for freedom of conscience in matters of religion. Williams was to make a classic argument for religious freedom, rooted in his understanding of authentic Puritan ideology, in his *The Bloudy Tenent of Persecution for the Cause of Conscience Discussed*, published in London in 1644 while its author was in England to secure a government patent for the colony to assure that it would not be under the authority of Massachusetts. Both separation of church and state and religious liberty were reaffirmed in a document adopted in 1647 to provide for government structures under the new patent. That compact clearly demonstrated that the people of Rhode Island regarded the social covenant that pertains to all to have no connection with individual conscience or religion. Witness its conclusion: "These are the laws that concern all men, and these are the penalties for the transgressions thereof, which, by common consent, are ratified and established throughout the whole Colony. And otherwise than thus, what is herein forbidden, all men may walk as their consciences persuade them, every one in the name of his God. And let the saints of the Most High walk in this Colony without molestation, in the name of Jehovah their God, for ever and ever."[10]

If Roger Williams was a thorn in the flesh to the leadership of the Bay Colony, Anne Hutchinson (1591–1642) was even more so. A nurse and midwife, Hutchinson had been a member of John Cotton's congregation in Boston, Lincolnshire, before Cotton migrated to Boston, Massachusetts Bay. Cotton's preaching and exposition of Puritan theology, particularly his insistence that salvation was wholly the work of God, completely captured the mind and heart of this mother of fifteen. Hence when Cotton removed to the New World, Hutchinson and her family soon followed. About the same time the General Court was deciding what to do with troublemaker Roger Williams, Hutchinson also came to the attention of authorities. Hutchinson had begun holding meetings in her home, purportedly to explain and discuss Cotton's sermons. Hutchinson, however, took Cotton's emphasis on inner experience of regeneration to its logical extreme. If grace came only through the work of the Spirit, then nothing humans could do—including preparation for salvation—made any difference. Preparation and even the moral actions that were seen as signs of God's grace in the lives of the elect were to Hutchinson mere works of no value at all. When crowds began flocking to Hutchinson's home to listen to her discourse on the unconditional, direct work of the Spirit in election, the religious and political leadership of the colony smelled danger. To them, Hutchinson's position demolished the moral basis of the commonwealth. It smacked of dreaded antinomianism (hence the later designation of this controversy as the Antinomian Crisis), and it seemed to undermine the authority of the clergy in affairs of the soul. Of course, the fact that Hutchinson had overstepped the boundaries of accepted behavior based on gender roles also was integral to the concern of her detractors.

In 1637, both the General Court and a church synod took action against Hutchinson. Thomas Hooker returned from Hartford to preside over the synod, which found more than eighty points of her presumed teaching to condemn. The General Court then held a trial that, according to Edwin S. Gaustad, "stumbled between absurdity and farce,"[11] until Hutchinson recounted receiving personal, direct revelation from God not mediated through any ordinary means of grace. This apparent fanaticism, when added to other charges, led the court to order her exiled from the Bay Colony. Excommunication from the Boston church followed, and Hutchinson departed for Rhode Island in 1638 with her family and a substantial number of followers. Four years later, Hutchinson, now a widow, and six of her children left Rhode Island for New Netherland, settling in what is now Westchester County [New York]. There, about a year later, she and five of the children lost their lives in an attack by Indians.

But banishing Anne Hutchinson did not seal all the cracks in the Puritan foundation. In 1639 spiritual cousins of the Puritans now known as Baptists established the town of Newport, in Roger Williams's Rhode Island. These Baptists traced their roots to Separatists who migrated to the Netherlands about the time the Pilgrim Separatists made their move there and, influenced by Dutch Mennonites who practiced adult believers' baptism, formed a Baptist congregation near London, England, in 1612. The major figure in the Newport settlement was Dr. John Clarke. Clarke and his followers used Newport as a base to carry Baptist views first to Plymouth and then to the Bay Colony. Perhaps because they shared the heritage of English Puritanism, the Baptists made some inroads in Massachusetts. Nevertheless, official opposition remained strong. The Baptist insistence that government should have no association with the church and especially should not use tax money to support clergy and churches challenged both the ideology and the practice of Massachusetts.

Authorities were never able to quash the Baptist presence the way they had done with Anne Hutchinson, though they tried. Clarke and two others from

Newport were arrested in 1651 in Lynn, Massachusetts, for holding an unauthorized religious gathering (even though Lynn residents had invited them
to the town). Such moves did little to thwart Baptist expansion. Indeed, the
Baptists were to remain a vocal dissenting presence amid the New England
Way, always objecting to their having to pay taxes to support churches they did
not attend and clergy whose ministrations they refused until all legal disabilities were removed long after the colonial period had ended. Occasionally,
Baptists gained allies from unexpected quarters. For example, Henry Dunster,
while president of Harvard College in the 1650s, espoused Baptist principles
and was forced to resign. That Baptist views had penetrated New England
Puritanism's major institution for training of clergy suggests the degree to
which pluralism would prevail, despite the penchant for uniformity inherent in
Puritan ideology.

Part of the dilemma for leaders of the Bay Colony was that there were also
disagreements brewing within the orthodox fold, not just challenges from
those of the ilk of Roger Williams, Anne Hutchinson, and the Baptist followers of John Clarke. Some of these internal problems were actually exacerbated by the Puritan ascendancy in England during the time of the Civil War.
Especially divisive was determining how the various churches within the
colony would be related to one another. In England, Puritans who opposed
the established church (and ultimately the crown as well) were divided
between those who advocated a presbyterian form of polity and those who
advocated "independency." Both positions granted considerable autonomy to
individual congregations, but differed when it came to considering how much
authority synods should exercise over those congregations. Those favoring the
presbyterian approach saw synods as having direct authority over individual
congregations, for such would enable the churches together to move effectively in dealing with a problem church. Independents, however, insisted
that synods or any body beyond the local congregation had only advisory
authority over the churches (hence the label *congregationalism*). Synods might
suggest policy or a course of action, but they had no enforcing power.
Presbyterians demurred.

In Massachusetts, the matter did not become a subject of debate until the
controversy surrounding Anne Hutchinson provoked the calling of a synod of
clergy to condemn her theology. By then, the situation in England leading to
civil war was escalating. At first, presbyterians were dominant in that struggle, but the general unsettledness of the age saw many making claims for
positions far more radical than independency. Polity had become a central
matter. In the early 1640s, colonial presbyterian sympathizers called for
adoption of their form of church government as normative for New England.
By the fall of 1646 the debate had spread throughout the Bay Colony, leading
the General Court to acquiesce to the urging of some clergy and call a synod
to resolve the matter. By the time the Cambridge Synod adjourned (after

having three separate sessions), the tables had turned in England and the independent cause had triumphed. So, too, in the Bay Colony. The Cambridge Platform, adopted by the synod in August 1648, firmly endorsed congregationalism.

Perhaps the clergy framing the platform recognized that congregationalism had the possibility of pluralism or at least toleration built into it. If individual congregations had complete autonomy, each would be free to go its own way— even to lapse into teaching and practice antithetical to the New England Way. As a check on extremism, the synod did call for the state to enforce uniformity and insisted that the doctrine in the Westminster Confession would be the standard for acceptable belief. But a door that could never be completely closed again had been opened.

Other challenges that would even reveal the limits of Roger Williams's brand of toleration were to come with the arrival of Quakers in British North America. Like the Baptists, the Quakers are spiritual cousins of the Puritans for they, too, have from their beginning been suspicious of hierarchical church order and liturgical worship, but adamant about the primacy of individual experience in religion. George Fox (1624–1691), the founder of Quakerism, around 1648 had an intense personal religious experience—a direct inner apprehension of Christ—that was not dependent on church, clergy, or even Scripture. Fox did not deny the authority of Scripture as a means by which God might communicate with humanity. But he did insist that the revelation contained in Scripture must be inwardly experienced by each individual. Fox zealously proclaimed his gospel message in England, reaping much public abuse as well as frequent arrest and imprisonment. His individualism was simply too extreme for the Church of England to countenance; it dangerously undercut church and sacrament alike. In time it was too extreme for New England Puritans and even Roger Williams to countenance.

Little wonder then that Quakers began to look to the New World as a more viable arena in which to preach the "inner light" of salvation than old England. Prior to the founding of Pennsylvania as a haven for persecuted Quakers, Barbados became an important center for Quaker missionary work in the New World. From Barbados in July 1656 came Mary Fisher and Ann Austin, the first Quakers to attempt to settle in New England. Word of their presence aboard the *Swallow* reached authorities as the ship lay at anchor in Boston harbor. At first confined to the ship and then imprisoned, the two women were deported to Barbados after five weeks. But two days after their departure, another eight Quakers arrived. They too were imprisoned and then deported to England, but they did gain one convert to their cause, Nicholas Upsall, who in turn sought refuge in Rhode Island.

Because the Quakers were branded as enthusiasts who would disrupt the religious order of the colony, the Massachusetts General Court quickly passed legislation that not only banned Quakers from settling there but also fined shipmasters who brought Quakers to the colony. Hence Quakers looked to tolerant Rhode Island as a place of entry to British North America. Despite protests from other New England colonies, Rhode Island refused to deny Quakers entry and, despite beatings and imprisonment, Quakers persistently ventured from Rhode Island to Massachusetts Bay and to Plymouth. By the time Massachusetts enacted harsher laws that ultimately saw four Quakers hanged between 1659 and 1661, Quaker meetings had already been established in scattered areas in the southern part of Massachusetts. Nevertheless imprisonment and deportation continued, though royal decree prohibited further hangings.

That there would continue to be a Quaker "underground" in Puritan New England was assured after founder George Fox visited the colonies in 1672. Coming to Rhode Island, Fox held a number of meetings in private homes and elsewhere where, as he wrote in his *Journal*, many "were mightily affected with the meeting, and there is a great desire amongst them after the Truth."[12] Fox's visit stirred the usually tolerant Roger Williams to propose a public debate in which Williams hoped to argue that Quakers did deny the authority of Scripture. While the debate with Fox did not occur, Williams and Fox did engage in a brief literary jousting that probably served more to give wider currency to the Quaker perspective than it did to halt its advance. Barbados and Rhode Island were to remain important centers of Quaker activity, along with enclaves throughout New England and in New York until they were eclipsed by William Penn's "holy experiment" in Pennsylvania. Their enduring presence signaled that the cracks in the foundations of the Puritan holy commonwealths had become deep indeed.

Another episode internal to New England Puritanism also reveals the way the vision of John Winthrop and his associates was fading. That concerned a decline in the numbers of those who presented themselves to offer a confession of God's redeeming work in their lives and own the church covenant. The problem was especially acute among the second generation of New England Puritans, those who had been brought to the church for baptism by parents who were full members of the church. Such persons were by Puritan standards prohibited from sharing in the Lord's Supper, from presenting their own children (the third generation) for baptism, and from having the franchise in public affairs—even if by virtue of their own baptism they were under the care of the church. While the drop in the numbers of full members was worrisome to clergy, in retrospect it should not have been unexpected. After all, the second generation had been nurtured in a culture shaped by Puritan ideology. For them the Puritan way was not an alternative to an established church thought corrupt, and an experience of election not a sharp contrast to religious complacency. The Puritan world was simply the way things were. Puritanism was the norm, not the exception.

Hence fewer and fewer of the second generation, however devout, in scrutinizing their souls found the same signs of regeneration that marked the first migrants to the New England wilderness. The problem became more acute for the third generation. Unless their parents owned the church covenant, children of the third generation could not be baptized and would remain outside the watchful eye of church and state alike. Many clergy saw a crisis brewing that could ultimately destroy the whole Puritan enterprise. In 1657, clergy from Connecticut and Massachusetts met to ponder what to do, but the formal response came in 1662, when the Massachusetts General Court called a synod of clergy to propose concrete action. The result was what scholars have labeled the Half-Way Covenant. Simply put, the Half-Way Covenant permitted upstanding parents who had been baptized but who had not owned the church covenant to present their children for baptism and thus bring them under the ministrations of the church (though those baptized under this scheme would still be barred from the Lord's Supper and from voting). Rather quickly, Half-Way standards became the norm in both Massachusetts and Connecticut and then even in more strict New Haven when that colony was joined with Connecticut later in 1662.

But the Half-Way Covenant itself became a source of controversy. Opponents believed it compromised the path of purity and undermined the whole ideological foundation of Puritanism. Others believed it reinforced the rigorous standards for church membership, since confession of personal faith remained necessary for admission to the church covenant and the Lord's Supper. The Half-Way Covenant also bears the marks of what anthropologist Anthony F. C. Wallace called a "revitalization movement," for it was an attempt to preserve and give new life to the Puritan Way in a social context radically different from that which gave birth to Puritanism. At least it had the advantage of promoting social unity. For some, the Half-Way Covenant became an avenue to rethink other aspects of Puritan theology. Solomon Stoddard (1643–1729), grandfather of Jonathan Edwards and for fifty-seven years pastor of the church in Northampton in the Connecticut River valley, was one of those. An enthusiastic advocate of the Half-Way measures, Stoddard broke with tradition and began to admit all baptized persons—not just full church members—to the Lord's Supper on the grounds that the sacrament itself could be a "converting ordinance," one that might well confirm for believers that God had indeed elected them to salvation.

Puritan ideology demanded total commitment to a rigorous path that allowed in theory for no deviation if true faith were to flourish and the holy commonwealth move toward its divinely ordained destiny. But the debates over precisely how the Spirit might work that led Thomas Hooker to Hartford, the concern for radical purity of Roger Williams, the presumed antinomianism of Anne Hutchinson, the presence of Baptists and Quakers who simply could not be silenced, differences over polity that led to the adoption of the Cambridge Platform, and the perceived declension that brought about the Half-Way Covenant were all signs that pluralism would prevail. But pluralism would always be unsettling. Still other signs of unsettledness came from changes transpiring across the Atlantic in Britain.

## PURITAN COLONIES RESPOND TO CHANGE IN BRITAIN

Many of the cracks in the foundations of New England Puritanism appeared at a time when Britain itself was undergoing a period of turmoil. The civil wars that led to the beheading of Charles I in 1649 and the establishment of the Puritan Commonwealth led by Oliver Cromwell meant that Puritan New England was pretty much left to its own devices to sort out its problems and resolve them. But in 1660, with the restoration of the monarchy, crown and parliament gradually began to seek ways to exert firmer control over British colonies everywhere. Some control came in the form of restrictions on colonial trade; some in greater regulation or elimination of colonial legislative assemblies. For New England, the latter came in 1685 when the Puritan colonies were joined with New York and New Jersey in the Dominion of New England, a scheme of colonial governance that lasted only until the Glorious Revolution brought William and Mary to the throne.

While New England Puritans pondered the extent to which political change in Britain would affect if not infect their holy commonwealths, matters closer at hand brought additional turmoil. The expansion of the New England population, with its attendant need for more land, helped fuel confrontations with the Indians. New Englanders had long had ambivalent feelings toward their native neighbors; missionary efforts of those such as John Eliot and Experience Mayhew designed to gain Indian converts to the Puritan Way received only half-hearted support. The Puritans could never decide whether Indians should be welcomed into the fold of believers or regarded as dangers to the advance of God's commonwealth—an indecision that was also to mark religious dealings with Africans forced to migrate as slaves. When armed conflict with the Wampanoags erupted in 1675–1676, bringing serious destruction to more than half the settlements in Connecticut and the Bay Colony, the devout were convinced that Indians were more enemies than potential converts and the ravages of war a sign of God's displeasure. Add to that the devastation of fires that struck Boston in 1676 and 1679, and one can well understand the conclusion of a synod of Massachusetts clergy in 1679 that "God hath a controversy" with the people of New England. Reform and rededication to the pure way of the first Puritan settlers were desperately needed, argued the clergy.

On the political front, the dismantling of the Dominion of New England in 1689 brought some hope that the old ways might be revived. But the new charter for Massachusetts Bay granted in 1691 was a signal for all New England of what lay ahead. Massachusetts was to be a royal colony with an appointed, not elected, governor. In addition, the franchise was to be based on property, as it was in England, not on church membership. More disturbing in the long run was the requirement that Massachusetts (and ultimately all British colonies in North America) would have to allow the same toleration (albeit a limited toleration) of Protestant Christianity that prevailed in England. No longer would Baptists and Quakers or even members of the established church who adhered to Anglican ways be subject to overt persecution.

Reaction and response to these changes came in many forms. Perhaps the most well-known and also the most difficult to explain and interpret centers around the witch trials in Salem Village (now Danvers, Massachusetts) in 1692. In February that year, a group of female adolescents became subject to convulsions which they attributed to the bewitching power of a slave woman from Barbados named Tituba and to two older village women of dubious repute, Sarah Osborn and Sarah Good. The girls experienced convulsions again when authorities interrogated the three women, leading Tituba to confess to being a witch and to claim that in addition to the three accused, there were at least seven more witches in the village. The girls continued to accuse others, whose guilt was often presumed since the girls evidenced convulsive behavior whenever they were around those named. Those who confessed were usually released from prison if they repented. But those who did not were sentenced to death. Some twenty persons were executed before the hysteria abated in the fall of 1692.

Some interpreters have put the Salem witch trials in the context of the popular belief in witches characteristic of the period and the more widespread witch craze that struck continental Europe in the seventeenth century. Some have argued that the convulsions and delusions of the adolescent women resulted from the ingestion of fungus on rotten bread. Others claim that their bizarre behavior exhibited qualities of psychopathy as well as the ecstatic behavior associated with demon possession. Still others have seen the fascination with witchcraft as part of an experimentation with the occult. Then, too, some analysts have treated the accusations of witchcraft as signs of rebellion against an ideology that fostered social repression in the name of total dedication to purity.

But trying to identify a specific cause for the episode may well be less significant than understanding what gave plausibility to these claims at this particular time in New England history. Historians of religion have long recognized that outbursts of ecstatic behavior may be linked to epochs of broadly based social change and transition. When the cultural patterns and beliefs long accepted as normative cease to provide a basis for social cohesion, what seems bizarre in comparison is likely to emerge. In this view, it may well be that the gradual changes to the New England Way planted by Pilgrims and Puritans of the first generation had simply created a social environment where the ideological underpinnings of Puritan ideology no longer supported the structures erected on them. The Salem witch craze was simply an extreme reaction to the erosion of the Puritan Way that was evident to all in the new order mandated by the Charter of 1691.

Less titillating, but equally a sign that a new day was dawning, was the organization in 1699 of the Brattle Street Church in Boston, the symbolic center of Puritan New England. Perceived as dangerously liberal and therefore a source of contamination of the Puritan Way, the Brattle Street Church offered full membership to all who professed Christian belief, not just those who could testify to the work of regeneration in their lives or even to those baptized under the terms of the Half-Way Covenant. But economic factors may have also played a part in giving birth to this "broad and catholick" congregation.[13] The founders of the church counted many wealthy Boston merchants in their number, including John Leverett and the brothers Thomas and William Brattle. The Puritan ambivalence toward wealth as a sign of God's favor as well as a potentially damaging preoccupation with things of the world did not speak to the situation of a class for whom economic well-being was now assumed. Nor did the seeming narrowness of Puritan theology sit well with a class whose thinking revealed influences of the Enlightenment. The establishment of King's Chapel in Boston, to provide for Church of England ministrations for the royal governor and other appointed officials, was another signal that neither church nor state could enforce conformity to the hallowed New England Way.

## Toward the Eighteenth Century

By the close of the seventeenth century, currents of change were evident everywhere in Puritan New England. If John Winthrop and his compatriots had hoped to establish a "city on a hill" that would be both a beacon to the world and a precursor of God's final reign on earth, their descendants had seen how reality could alter the vision of even the most committed. Pluralism had indelibly transformed the ideal of a holy commonwealth. But, as Mark Noll has reminded us, "the New England of 1700 was a stable land where many indeed could still be found who honored the same God as the forebears, in much the same way, with at least some of the same zeal."[14]

# 17

## ANGLICANS AND CATHOLICS
## COME TO BRITISH
## COLONIAL AMERICA

If Puritans ventured to British colonial America to carve a total civilization grounded in their variant of Calvinist ideology, those settlers who organized the movement to conquer Virginia and other Southern areas that were to become part of the United States (as well as numerous islands in the Caribbean) were far more oriented to commercial profit. Simply put, the London merchants behind various colonizing schemes—and probably the majority of those who actually crossed the Atlantic—hoped to extract from the New World wealth that would rival what the Spanish, Britain's traditional foe, appeared to be reaping from their burgeoning colonial empire. Religious motives were clearly secondary for the 105 men who came ashore at the James River on 24 May 1607, as they were for those who planted the royal flag at St. Christopher, Barbados, Nevis, Providence Island, Monserrat, and Antigua between 1624 and 1633.

But religious motives were not entirely absent. Along with the hope to gain riches equal to Spain's was the desire to thwart the advance in the New World of dreaded Roman Catholicism that the Spanish crown was dedicated to protecting and promoting. Existing in theory more than in practice, though formally noted in nearly all the British colonial charters, was another religious rationale for conquering lands in the New World: the conversion of the American Indians to Protestant Christianity. As in Puritan New England, Anglicans in the Southern and island colonies remained ambivalent about their relationship, religious or otherwise, to the Indians. Such ambivalence became even more pronounced and complex after slave ships arrived in Virginia in 1619, bringing from Africa the first forced migrants who would work the tobacco fields of the South and the sugar plantations of the West Indies.

## PLANTING THE CHURCH OF ENGLAND

At first in the Southern and island colonies, oversight of religious affairs was left in the hands of the merchant companies that organized the settlements or of the governors of the colonies themselves, though technically the Anglican bishop of London held titular authority over these areas. In Virginia, for example, Anglican cleric Robert Hunt conducted services according to the *Book of Common Prayer* shortly after the colonists arrived. Hunt had been appointed by the colony's president, and in this case, the appointment had been approved by the archbishop of Canterbury, Richard Bancroft. But the practical problems encountered in erecting a viable colony, along with numerous changes in the formal leadership of the Jamestown settlement and squabbles among factions in the Virginia Company in England, meant that organized religion in Virginia was not the top priority that it was for the Puritans who peopled Massachusetts Bay. Even though the ways of the Church of England were expected to be implemented, many of the early provisions for religion revealed a distinct Puritan cast, as noted in the preceding chapter.

Founded in 1619, the year the first slave ships arrived, the Virginia House of Burgesses for a time assumed much legislative responsibility for the colony, including general authority in religious matters. Soon, however, continuing internal disagreements meant that the Virginia Company was basically disintegrating, a matter of grave concern to James I and his advisers. Violent conflict with the Indians in 1622, which resulted in the deaths of nearly one-sixth of the Virginia population, added to the instability of the day. A royal commission appointed in 1623 exposed many weaknesses within the Virginia Company and recommended more direct royal involvement. Hence in 1624 the crown revoked the Virginia Company's charter, and Virginia became a royal colony with a crown-appointed governor who would be required as a condition of appointment to be a member of the Church of England. Only from that time forward was there in actuality a formal Anglican establishment in Virginia. Even so, as we shall see, colonial establishment was rather different from establishment in the mother country for a variety of reasons.

The situation was somewhat similar in the island colonies in the Caribbean when they were settled. There, too, in the early years Puritan sentiment was strong, though on St. Christopher, services according to the *Book of Common Prayer* were held as early as 1626, about two years after the colony's founding. But the fortunes of the Church of England were unsteady at best. Colonial rebellions in 1641, largely the result of dissatisfaction among the Puritan colonists, brought considerable upheaval to St. Christopher, though after they were put down, the Church of England for a time became more influential. Roman Catholics, many of French extraction, also made their way to St. Christopher, and Jean Destriche (popularly known as Father Strich) was celebrating mass covertly by 1650. St. Christopher, like many of the other island colonies, was something of a pawn in the power struggle among the French, Spanish, and British for dominance in the Caribbean. Hence in 1666 the French were able to seize control of the colony and remained in power until they were again expelled by the British in 1689. During that epoch, the Anglican church remained in disarray.

In 1625 Barbados was discovered, and within two years the first British settlers had arrived. However, there is no surviving evidence regarding religious life on Barbados prior to 1629, when the island was divided into six parishes. It is not known whether there was clergy in the colony to serve them. On Barbados, the Church of England did receive legal establishment—but on the authority of the governor and council, since there was no representative assembly until 1639. This establishment received confirmation in 1651 when Barbados formally submitted to the control of king and parliament. By then there were in theory around a dozen parishes, thanks to the earlier efforts of Governor Philip Bell, an Anglican with strong Puritan tendencies.

Around 1632 Montserrat was first settled by Europeans, including Irish Roman Catholics who had intended to go to Virginia but were denied the opportunity to remain there on religious grounds. By 1636, when Montserrat was generally recognized as English territory, the Anglican church had established its presence on the island. Two years later, a decree issued by the governor and council required observance of the Lord's Day as in England. But throughout the seventeenth century, on Montserrat Roman Catholics outnumbered Anglican settlers six to one. Priests evidently came to minister to them, for several were expelled by English authorities prior to 1650. Nevertheless, the Church of England retained the prerogatives of establishment until the French captured Montserrat in 1667.

The pattern was to be repeated in the seventeenth century throughout the Southern colonies on the North American mainland and areas in and around the Caribbean while the British remained in control: the Carolinas, Providence Island (lost to the Spanish in 1641), Antigua, Surinam (lost to the Dutch in 1667), Anguilla, Jamaica, Barbuda, the Bahamas, the Leeward Islands, the Virgin Islands. But the way Anglican establishment worked in the New World differed considerably from the way the Church of England operated in Britain and from the way Puritanism dominated both public and religious life in New England.

## THE NATURE OF ANGLICAN ESTABLISHMENT

In the mother country, the meaning of legal establishment was theoretically clear: The Church of England was the only religious body recognized by crown and parliament and as such received its financial support from the government. Under establishment, no other religious groups had any legal standing. But from the time of Elizabeth I, conformity to the Church of England in a practical sense had denoted tacit acceptance of worship according to the liturgy of the *Book of Common Prayer*, of the doctrine encapsulated in the Thirty-Nine Articles of Faith, and of an episcopal polity that vested leadership in bishops and archbishops. Outer conformity, however, never required inner commitment. Hence from the later sixteenth century on, considerable latitude existed even within the one established church when it came to matters of personal belief, interpretation of doctrine, and the like. So long as outer conformity prevailed, religion would buttress social cohesion. This "broad church" approach in the sixteenth century had appeared the only viable one, for popular religious sentiment spanned the gamut from Roman Catholicism to Calvinism. Indeed, the expectation that outer conformity sufficed enabled Puritanism to gain such a strong following and hence revealed a potential weakness within the framework of establishment. Diversity and dissent, while never formally acknowledged, would remain undercurrents within the established church.

More than agreement on nuances of doctrine, since such never existed, what actually held the Anglican establishment together was adherence to the *Book of Common Prayer* and the episcopal polity of the church. From the perspective of colonial developments, the latter was of special significance. Bishops officiated at the ordination of priests for the church and confirmed individuals as full members of the church. Bishops and priests controlled parish life, including the use and maintenance of church property. Bishops represented the interests of the church to parliament and the crown, placed clergy in parishes, and supervised the work of the various auxiliary agencies of the church. Bishops also were responsible for assuring conformity to the religious establishment and had at their disposal the coercive power of government, if needed, to secure that conformity. Bishops were thus an essential component of religious establishment in Britain.

On a local level, the Church of England had taken over the parish system from Roman Catholicism. Parishes denoted not only individual churches but geographic districts as well. The rationale behind the parish system was to assure that the ministry of the church extended to all people in the land. Hence the land was divided into units (the parishes), each with its own church and its own clergy. All people living in the geographic area served by a parish were presumed to be communicants of its church; it was also assumed that a parish would include enough families to provide through assessments or endowments adequate financial support for the clergy and church. Even those who did not personally subscribe to Anglican belief and practice were counted among the parish and expected to give tacit allegiance to the church.

When the Church of England was planted in the New World, however, establishment assumed a different cast. Many persons came to the Southern and Caribbean colonies who were nominal Anglicans but harbored Puritan sympathies; some were Roman Catholics who hoped distance would minimize the necessity of even outward conformity to the Church of England. The undercurrent of diversity and dissent ever present in the mother country would be accented in the New World. In addition, placing oversight of colonial religious life under the jurisdiction of the bishop of London, rather than designating bishops who would themselves be resident in the colonies, made it impossible to duplicate the structure of the Church of England so that the advantages of an episcopal polity were lost and all the disadvantages revealed. The parish system that seemed so logical a way to organize the church at home proved less than adaptable to the colonial environment. As well, events in Britain, particularly the civil wars of the 1640s, that brought upheaval to the established church had many ramifications for colonial Anglicanism, some of which were markedly different from effects in the mother country.

## THE DISSENTING PRESENCE IN COLONIAL ANGLICANISM: THE EXAMPLE OF VIRGINIA, BARBADOS, AND MARYLAND

Virginia's colonial charter mandated that the "ecclesiastical laws of England" govern the formal religious life of the settlements there.[1] In theory, such remained the case throughout the colonial period, but reality was somewhat different. The Puritan influence that pervaded early legal codes and the Puritan inclinations of some of the early clergy have already been noted. But in the early decades of settlement, Virginia clergy, unlike their counterparts in New England, made no effort to challenge those ecclesiastical laws, even if their personal theology tilted toward the Calvinism that undergirded Puritan theology. A good case in point is Alexander Whitaker, perhaps the most astute clergyman in early Virginia. Whitaker's father, a Cambridge theology professor, openly espoused Calvinist teaching that Whitaker himself absorbed. His *Good Newes from Virginia*, published in 1613, castigated many of the colonists for their inattention to matters of the soul, particularly their failure to seek signs of election and reconciliation with God through attendance on the means of grace. But Whitaker remained a priest of the Church of England and adhered to the *Book of Common Prayer* when leading worship.

But it is also clear that settlers came to Virginia who were not at all sympathetic to the Church of England and did not wish to conform even outwardly to its norms. While one cannot identify precisely how many dissenters came to Virginia in the seventeenth century, they were present in sufficient numbers for the House of Burgesses to feel compelled to pass legislation against certain forms of dissent and for colonial officials on occasion to take action against some individuals and groups. For example, in 1629 George Calvert, the first Lord Baltimore and father of the Baltimore who would a few years later spearhead the founding of the Maryland colony, and a handful of other Roman Catholics were denied the right to settle in Virginia because they refused to take the Oath of Supremacy that acknowledged the monarch (not the pope) as supreme governor of the Church of England. In 1643, the number of Puritan nonconformists (independents) had grown so significantly that a colonial law ordered them to leave the colony. The law had little effect, however, since that same year three independent churches attempted to call New England Puritan clergy to serve as pastors, although they were denied the opportunity to come to those congregations.

But Virginia during this period was also feeling the effects of developments in Britain that eventuated in civil war. Despite the Puritan ascendancy in the mother country, royalist sentiment and its corollary—at least token support for the Church of England—remained relatively strong in the colony. Hence many English Royalists or Cavaliers sought refuge in Virginia. They were, however, joined by a significant number of Roundheads, the derisive label given to the Puritan-dominated Parliamentary Party in the upheaval. Though Anglican establishment remained in place during the age of Cromwell, the Roundheads were to prove a thorn in the flesh in proprietary Maryland to the north, where a greater degree of religious toleration existed by law.

After the restoration of the monarchy, Virginia again moved to curtail religious dissent. In March 1662, for example, the House of Burgesses enacted legislation that banned both Baptists and Quakers from Virginia. In the case of the Baptists, the move seems a response to a perceived threat rather than a real one, for there is no evidence that there was a single Baptist congregation in Virginia at any time in the seventeenth century. The Quakers offer a different story, for by the 1650s—almost as soon as George Fox began preaching in England—numerous Quaker colonists were found in Virginia, particularly along the coast, where a regular meeting was organized by 1662, the year the law banning them was passed. But the law apparently was ignored since George Fox included Virginia on his colonial tour in 1672 and recorded in his *Journal* enthusiastic accounts of speaking at several meetings organized by Friends or those sympathetic to the Quaker cause.

The situation on the island colony of Barbados was more complex. Although the Church of England was the legal establishment, from the outset Barbados had a population that included not only Anglicans but also a significant number of Puritans and Roman Catholics and, in time, even some Sephardic Jewish settlers from Brazil (who organized a synagogue in 1644). This accepted diversity in the midst of establishment was confirmed in policies adopted by the Committee for Foreign Plantations in 1646 that assured reasonable liberty of conscience. Such made it possible, for example, for New England Puritan pastor James Parker that same year to assume spiritual leadership of an Anglican church in Barbados without challenge. But this grass-roots toleration had its limits. In 1647 a public act demanded all colonists to conform to the established church because "divers opinionated and self-conceited persons, have declared an absolute dislike to the Government of the Church of England, as well by their aversion and utter neglect or refusal of the Prayers, Sermons, and Administration of the Sacrament and other Rites and Ordinances thereof, used in their several Parish-churches; as by holding Conventicles in private houses and other places; scandalizing Ministers, and endeavouring to seduce others to their erroneous opinions, upon pretence of an alteration of Church-government in England."[2]

With the Puritan ascendancy in England that led to the inauguration of the Commonwealth, many royalists (the Cavaliers) came to Barbados and other British colonies in the Caribbean as they had to Virginia. Because they were supporters of both monarchy and the established church, the Cavalier colonists in Barbados sought even stricter conformity to the Church of England. What had been lost in the Old World would be cemented in the New. Thus in 1650, a proclamation issued by the governor directed that all religious services conform to the *Book of Common Prayer* and recognized the Church of England as the only legal religion on the island. But such a policy was both unworkable and inconsistent with the mores of the colony. Two years later, while retaining established status for the Church of England, Barbados again guaranteed liberty of conscience to all persons provided their beliefs were not "inconsistent with civil government."[3] After the Restoration, there would be some efforts to enforce conformity to the established church, particularly the payment of taxes for church support, but the spirit of toleration did not die.

Perhaps it was this climate of toleration that turned Barbados into something of a Quaker refuge within a few years. In 1655 Mary Fisher and Ann Austin, who were to attempt to carry the Quaker gospel to Puritan Boston, arrived in Barbados. They and their fellow Friends rather quickly gathered a significant following that encompassed many who were, in Carl and Roberta Bridenbaugh's words, persons "of piety, probity, and principles." But Quakers were not always readily accepted. Some fled to Jamaica in 1658 because of persecution for their refusal to pay taxes to support the established church and serve in the colonial militia. From Barbados Quakers also made inroads on Nevis and Antigua, where persecution only gradually gave way to grudging toleration. George Fox's colonial tour brought him to Barbados in 1671. Fox's visit greatly revitalized the community of Friends there and throughout the Caribbean. But that renewed vitality brought fresh controversy, since one consequence of Fox's visit was an increase in Quaker efforts to bring Christianity to the slaves. Indeed, the Quakers were the first Christians on Barbados to show any concern for the spiritual life of the growing slave population. A 1676 law prohibited black slaves from attending Quaker meetings, but even with renewed persecution, the Friends steadfastly refused to abandon their ministry among the slaves. Hence, while the Church of England was formally established, dissent remained strong.

Yet a different situation was to emerge in Maryland. The story of Maryland's beginnings is intertwined with the delicate relations that existed between high-ranking Roman Catholics and Anglicans in Britain. While many English Catholics gave lip service to religious conformity, they continued Catholic worship and practice covertly. While all Catholics were politically suspect and frequently subject to abuse and persecution, some had personal ties to James I and then to Charles I. Among them was George Calvert, the first Lord Baltimore, who was the secretary of state at the time he converted to Catholicism in 1625. Eager to provide a haven for his fellow Catholics, Calvert used his connections with James I to secure a charter for what was essentially a feudal barony carved out of the existing colony of Virginia.

Calvert died before the settlement of Maryland began, but under his son Cecilius, the second Lord Baltimore, plans were laid to undertake development of the proprietary colony. While the first colonists included a score of Catholics from the ranks of the nobility and some two hundred of lesser station, it was clear from the start that the colony would have to attract non-Catholics if it were to succeed. Aware of the hostility toward Catholics prevalent among English Protestants of all stripes, Baltimore embarked on a policy of religious toleration that would for a time include failure to recognize any church as a legal establishment. If anything, Baltimore erred on the side of caution, for his initial instructions to the colony not only urged Catholics to worship in private and refrain from discussing religion in public, but also to "suffer no scandal or offense to be given to any of the Protestants, whereby any just complaint may hereafter be made."[5]

A tumultuous early political history combined with expediency to advance religious toleration in colonial Maryland. Although two Jesuit priests, the renowned Andrew White and John Altham, were among the first colonists who had some success in winning both Protestant English settlers and Native Americans to Rome, Catholics quickly became a minority in the Maryland population even if they retained influence in the colonial assembly and through the proprietor. Indeed, within a decade after initial settlement, persons of Puritan sentiment were undoubtedly in the majority. As early as 1639 an ordinance promoted religious toleration, paving the way for the more famous Act Concerning Religion (or Act of Toleration, as it is popularly known), passed by the Maryland Assembly on 21 April 1649. That law made clear what had long been Maryland policy: "noe person or persons whatsoever within this Province . . . professing to believe in Jesus Christ, shall from henceforth bee any waies troubled, Molested or discountenanced for or in respect of his or her religion nor in the free exercise thereof."[6] Nontrinitarians, however, were still subject to the death penalty.

Subsequent religious developments in Maryland in the seventeenth century may be seen as both reverberations of events in Britain and signs of growing discontent with seemingly high-handed rule. Puritan aspirations for a greater voice in Maryland affairs came to the fore during the Interregnum when the Protestant governor, William Stone, left the colony in 1651, naming a Roman Catholic Royalist to serve in his stead. A Puritan near-revolt in the colony led Parliament (then controlled by the Puritans) to attempt to take control of Maryland. Local discontent led a Puritan-dominated Maryland Assembly in 1654 both to revoke the 1649 Act of Toleration and deny the Calverts' proprietary rights. The following year Maryland Puritans, joined by Roundheads who had come to Virginia, took successful military action against Governor

Stone and forces aligned with the proprietor. The victorious Puritans then made Roman Catholicism illegal in the colony and ordered all priests to leave. Only after Lord Baltimore two years later submitted to demands for a Protestant governor were proprietary rights restored.

Even then, religious hostility and dissatisfaction with proprietary government ensued. But it was not only Maryland Puritans who were discontent; after the Restoration the few Anglicans in Maryland began to express their displeasure with the religious situation in the colony. In 1676, the year one of several antiproprietary revolts occurred, one of the three Anglican priests in the colony, John Yeo, penned a plaintive petition to the archbishop of Canterbury detailing the sorry condition of the Church of England in Maryland. Action to elevate Anglicanism to the status of religious establishment in Maryland, however, awaited the age of the Glorious Revolution. In 1689, a coalition of Protestants, the so-called Protestant Association, seized control of the Maryland government and remained in power until 1691, when king and parliament rechartered most provinces (including Maryland) as royal colonies. Although the next year the colonial assembly passed an "Act for the Service of Almighty God and the Establishment of the Protestant Religion" designed to give the Church of England legal privilege, the law and three subsequent ones with the same end were disallowed since they were so narrow as to violate Parliament's own Act of Toleration that had extended some recognition to most Protestants even if the Church of England alone received legal establishment. Indeed, not until 1702, when the colonial assembly grudgingly accepted a law framed by the board of trade, did Anglicanism become the official religious establishment in Maryland. Though the number of Anglicans in Maryland was small even then, some thirty parishes were designed and lay vestries organized in just over two-thirds of them. But the record also shows that there were only nine Anglican priests to minister in them.

## THE DILEMMAS OF ANGLICAN COLONIAL ESTABLISHMENTS

Maryland's apparent shortage of Anglican clergy was a common problem wherever the Church of England was established in British colonial America, a problem that would endure throughout the colonial period. But one cannot appraise the significance of that shortage without considering other dilemmas confronting the established church in the colonies: a lack of episcopal supervision, the considerable power exerted by lay vestries, the geographic size of parishes (especially on the North American mainland), and the popular perception that many Anglican priests who did serve in the colonies were incompetent, immoral, or both. These dilemmas are so intertwined that it is difficult, if not impossible, to discuss each in isolation from the others.

From an organizational perspective, the lack of episcopal supervision seems paramount. All through the colonial period, devout Anglicans and priests alike bemoaned the failure of the Church of England to designate a bishop or bishops who would be resident in the colonies and the policy that placed Anglican religious life in the colonies under the jurisdiction of the bishop of London. While this policy may merely be the religious concomitant of the broader British colonial policy that always in theory saw colonies as adjuncts to or extensions of Britain itself rather than as entities in their own right, it had a deleterious effect on colonial Anglicanism because of the centrality of the episcopacy to the organization of the established church.

In England, bishops had an automatic entrée to government and hence could promote the welfare of the church at the highest levels of power. Such was not the case in the colonies, where the church even when legally established lacked such direct advocacy. As well, technically, confirmation into membership in the Church of England required laying on of hands by a bishop. More to the point, so did ordination to the priesthood. Hence any colonist who desired ordination would have to journey to the mother country both for formal training for ministry and for proper ordination. The cost and time involved no doubt deterred many from seeking holy orders and returning to the colonies as priests of the church. There are some cases where individuals actually served in the colonies without having been ordained. When Sir Richard Dutton came to Barbados as governor in 1681, for example, he found one man who had been serving as an Anglican priest there for twenty-four years without ever having received holy orders, though in Barbados the shortage of clergy was less acute than elsewhere in British colonial America.

The net result was that the bulk of Anglican clergy came as immigrants like other colonists, creating the unfortunate impression that those who did settle in the colonies were men who could not find satisfactory positions in England or who were deemed unsuited for a respectable living in the mother country. Criticism of parish priests as lacking necessary intellectual abilities, pastoral skills, and moral character abounds. In the oft-quoted words of one Virginia planter, Anglican priests were simply "black cotted raskolls" given to idleness and luxury. While there is some evidence to support these contentions, on balance the vast majority of Anglican priests in the colonies were deeply dedicated men forced to minister in circumstances that must have appeared extraordinarily difficult when compared to the situation of their counterparts at home.

It was not only the absence of direct episcopal supervision and support that hindered the effectiveness of Anglican clergy in the colonies. More to the point may be the unusual power wielded by colonial lay vestries. In Barbados, for example, vestry control of parish life was established by 1637, a decade after initial settlement. In Virginia, colonial law in 1643 recognized the right of the vestry not only to oversee parish affairs and property but also to secure and support the priest. In England lay vestries also existed, but their power was largely restricted to oversight of parish business and did not involve designating a priest to serve the parish or determining his salary. In those matters, bishops had considerable authority, and appointment of a priest by a bishop to a particular parish or other living was generally a lifetime proposition. In the colonies, because there was no resident bishop, much of this power or influence devolved on the lay vestries.

Virginia provides a good example of how lay vestries extended their power in a way that was replicated in other Southern colonies. By the time Virginia vestries became self-perpetuating bodies (1662), they had simply assumed the prerogatives both of setting the annual salary of the parish rector and "presenting" him a living. Such formal action would have granted life tenure and hence job security and a guaranteed salary to the rector. Instead, in a practice that would endure throughout the colonial period, vestries frequently invited a priest to serve on a temporary basis, without ever formally presenting him a living. This way, salaries could be kept low or used as a means to control rectors (and hence make sure that rectors' beliefs, behavior, and ministry conformed to the wishes of the vestry). Any priest who wished even a modicum of security would hardly dare challenge a virtually all-powerful vestry. Estimates suggest that in as many as nine out of ten cases in colonial Virginia, vestries refrained from formally presenting rectors with a living. As well, low salaries generally meant that clergy often could not devote full time to pastoral ministry but had to seek outside means of financial support for themselves and their families.

Given this state of affairs, it is more a wonder that dedicated clergy were willing to serve the colonial established church than that a few were unqualified or of questionable moral character. But it may also be the case that vestries found an advantage in claiming clergy incompetence or immorality even where such did not exist, for then they would have some acceptable rationale for withholding a living or for keeping salaries abysmally low. Hence the vestries themselves may have had reason for promoting a perception of the quality of the clergy that only occasionally meshed with reality.

Topography and economics were also to have a profound impact on the effectiveness of the colonial Anglican clergy and on the fragile influence of the Church of England in colonial society throughout British America, but especially on the North American mainland. Since economic factors were among the more compelling reasons for the colonial settlements in Virginia and the Caribbean, of paramount importance was finding a source of profit for investors in the colonial scheme and a means of livelihood for the people themselves. In Virginia, the cultivation of tobacco quickly dominated economic life once settlers discerned that conditions there were ideal for its production. In the Caribbean, sugar plantations became the economic base of the colonial enterprise. Both soon became almost totally dependent on African labor, the toil of slaves forced to come to the New World. As Sydney Ahlstrom noted in the case of Virginia, "Gradually, the colony's social structure and every major feature of its life began to be conditioned by the presence of a rapidly growing slave population."[7]

Just as New England Puritans were ambivalent in their attitudes toward both native Indians and Africans, so too were the Anglican planters of colonies to the South. The policy early on was to regard slavery as a permanent condition. But two fundamental questions plagued the planters: Did they have a religious duty to attempt to convert the slaves to Christianity and did conversion and subsequent baptism of slaves mean an end to involuntary servitude and acceptance of Christian Africans as free and equal to the white slaveowners? By and large, planters were disinclined to provide any religious instruction for African slaves until well into the eighteenth century, in part because of their own tepid religiosity and in part because of their aversion to engage in any public activity that might have dissolved the distance between owner and slave. Much the same applied to the feeble efforts to proselytize among the Indians.

Among Anglicans, this unconcern for the religious life of the slaves and Native Americans was compounded by the shortage of clergy to minister to the religious needs of even the planter class. Only in Maryland, where Jesuit missionaries worked among the Patuxents and the Piscataways, and in Barbados, where Quakers actively ministered to the slaves, were there any real efforts to bring non-Europeans into the Christian fold and nurture them in the faith. But Jesuit missions were hampered by the arrival of increasing numbers of European colonists who pushed the native Indians from their lands, and Quakers in Barbados were frequently persecuted for their ministry among the slaves.

The question of the status of slaves who did become Christians was resolved by legal rather than religious means. The Virginia House of Burgesses in 1667 enacted legislation that declared forthrightly that "Baptisme doth not alter the condition of the person as to his bondage or freedom."[8] This position was to prevail throughout the colonial period and became imbedded in the slave codes of other Southern colonies.

The tobacco culture of the mainland and the sugar culture of the Caribbean, once slavery was introduced, led to the creation of large plantations often at some distance from each other. The plantation system meant that the population was rather widely dispersed—more so on the mainland of North America than on the island colonies of the Caribbean. In Virginia, for example, this scattering of the population on plantations that dotted the rivers of the Tidewater created major difficulties in organizing the parish system basic to the Church of England. A single parish could often encompass a territory of several hundred square miles. The sheer size of the parishes made it difficult for the few available Anglican priests to tend to their flocks, let alone engage in evangelistic work among the slave population. In the Caribbean colonies, the smaller land areas of many of the island colonies meant that parishes were generally not as huge. But the plantation arrangement—and dearth of clergy—nevertheless complicated the establishment of the parish system. In Jamaica, for example, it has been estimated that near the close of the seventeenth century fully one-third of the population was not reached by the ministry of the established church.

The contrast with the Puritan experience to the north is instructive. With the meeting house the symbolic center of the Puritan town and the notion of covenant as a binding force to link people together, organized religion promoted a strong sense of community in Puritan colonies. Religion was a basic factor in providing the social cohesion that marked the New England colonies, at least in theory. Slavery and topography in the Southern and Caribbean colonies undermined the effectiveness of the church in advancing a sense of identity with the whole and made it virtually impossible for the religious establishment to function as an agent of social cohesion.

The net result in Virginia at least was to bring an identification of the established church with social privilege. Where the church existed, it was controlled by the planters who dominated the powerful vestries and also the colonial assembly (which had considerable authority over the church by law and tradition). This awkward situation created innumerable difficulties in trying to organize the church properly and diminished the influence of Anglicanism in the colony. Nowhere in British America in the seventeenth century did the Church of England come close to having the powerful role in the social order that Puritanism had in New England. Anglicanism may have been established by law in Southern and Caribbean colonies, but establishment did not necessarily bring either prestige or power.

## TOWARD THE EIGHTEENTH CENTURY

All the dilemmas and problems confronting the Church of England in the New World were becoming increasingly evident by the close of the seventeenth century. Try as some colonies did to assure that dissent was minimal and the established Church of England the only recognized body, pluralism became more and more the practical reality. Puritans, Catholics, and Quakers were too persistent and too resilient to be snuffed out. Before the seventeenth century ended, yet another group was beginning to gain a foothold. Francis Makemie (1658–1708), Irish-born, received a commission in 1681 from Scottish Presbyterians to go to the British North American colonies as a missionary. Makemie proved a tireless evangelist for the Presbyterian message, preaching in Barbados, the Carolinas, Virginia, New York, and New England before founding the first Presbyterian congregation in North America in 1684 at Snow Hill, Maryland. Soon the Presbyterian brand of Calvinism would be a force to be reckoned with.

In newer colonial settlements where the Church of England was to receive formal establishment, religious matters rarely received high priority. Developments in the Carolinas are a case in point. Early attempts at settlement of the area south of Virginia by New England Puritans and by a group from Barbados had both failed. Permanent settlement was to await the granting of a proprietary charter to a group of royal intimates in 1663. But these proprietors demonstrated little interest in religious affairs; their goal was in reality to found a feudal barony. In 1669, the first group of colonists sailing under proprietary aegis left England, establishing Charles Town in 1670 after stops in Barbados and Bermuda. For pragmatic purposes, the proprietors offered liberty of conscience to any who came to their colony. But the sparse and scattered population and the haphazard government of the proprietors made it difficult for any group to organize congregations. Quaker George Fox's visit in 1672 and Presbyterian Francis Makemie's tour just over a decade later were two of only a handful of efforts to attempt to bring a religious presence to the area. Indeed, in the northern district (later North Carolina) even the token establishment of the Church of England did not come until the eighteenth century. In the southern district (later South Carolina), Anglicanism fared somewhat better. In 1681, St. Philip's in Charleston became the first parish organized, but in South Carolina, too, formal establishment of the Church of England and legislation demanding conformity to its ways would await the early years of the eighteenth century. Clearly religion attracted little notice among either proprietors or colonists in the Carolinas for the first three or more decades of British settlement.

But near the close of the seventeenth century, two men came to British North America whose work was ultimately to bring fresh life to colonial Anglicanism. James Blair (1656–1743) arrived in Virginia to serve as rector at Henrico in 1685; Thomas Bray began a four-year ministry to Maryland in 1696. Blair's significance rested in his relentless efforts to point out the weaknesses in Virginia's established church, Bray's in two organizations he founded after his service in Maryland that would in time considerably extend the influence of the Church of England in the North American colonies and elsewhere.

Blair pastored Anglican churches in three Virginia settlements: Henrico (1685–1694), Jamestown (1694–1710), and the colonial capital, Williamsburg (1710–1743). But his labors extended well beyond the borders of his parishes after 1689 when the bishop of London designated him "commissary" (or administrator/overseer) of the Church of England in Virginia. Although his formal authority as commissary was minimal, Blair attempted to exercise almost the same prerogatives that a resident bishop would have, frequently coming into conflict with colonial governors and local vestrymen who saw his work as intruding on their domain. But Blair did attempt to respond to popular criticism of the quality of the clergy and the ongoing problem of morale among priests ministering in the colony. In 1690, for example, he presided over a meeting of Virginia clergy in order to provide what a later age would call a network of support and sharing of concerns. Out of that gathering came what would be Blair's most lasting achievement, the call for founding a college to serve the colony. In 1693, the College of William and Mary received its charter, and Blair added its presidency to his other responsibilities, serving until his death. William and Mary lacked the level of popular support New England Puritans gave to Harvard in its early years, and during Blair's tenure as president the college's story is one of struggle for survival more than of dazzling success. But it did serve as an important symbol, for now colonial Anglicans who might seek ordination would at least have a place to begin to obtain the necessary education even if they still had to journey to the mother country for holy orders. But as far as Blair was concerned, the founding of William and Mary was a vital first step in upgrading the religious life of colonial Virginia and the state of the established church. Nonetheless, in 1700 Blair noted that more than half of the Anglican parishes were without ordained ministry.

That situation would change in the eighteenth century, in part because of the work of Thomas Bray. Bray shared many of Blair's concerns over the tepid condition of colonial Anglicanism during the four years (1696–1700) he served as commissary of the Church of England in Maryland, particularly the concerns for a properly trained professional clergy and the extension of the church's ministry. Although Bray actually spent only a few months "on the job" in Maryland in 1700, he worked tirelessly on behalf of colonial Anglicanism in England both before his departure for the New World and after his return. In March 1699, nine months before he set sail for Maryland, Bray presided at the first meeting of what was to become the Society for Promoting Christian Knowledge (SPCK). An unchartered voluntary organization, the SPCK had as its mission the establishment of libraries both in the colonies and in the mother country. More than thirty libraries were set up in British North America, with the largest located in Annapolis, Maryland. Although these became semi-public lending libraries, their aim was to provide appropriate literature for the edification of both clergy and laity.

More significant in upgrading the quality of colonial Anglicanism was a second society for which Bray secured a royal charter a few months after his return to London following his brief sojourn in Maryland. This was the Society for the Propagation of the Gospel in Foreign Parts (SPG). Until American independence, the SPG was to be the mainstay of the established church in North America. With enthusiastic support from the Church of England hierarchy, the crown, and leading political figures, the SPG sought to identify highly qualified men who would go to the American colonies as missionaries to extend the ministry of the Church of England—among colonists, Indians, and slaves. It also provided much-needed financial support for clergy already serving parishes in the New World.

The SPG, through carefully coordinated efforts, used its financial resources well. Its work, moreover, was not restricted to the colonies where the Church of England enjoyed formal establishment, although there the SPG accomplished much by way of providing dedicated, well-trained clergy for many parishes which could not or would not support a professional ministry. It was also the SPG that influenced the moves in the Carolinas early in the eighteenth century to grant legal establishment to Anglicanism and that joined other philanthropic efforts that led to the founding of Georgia in the 1730s. As well, SPG missionaries brought the Anglican message even to Puritan New England, with no small degree of success in gaining prominent converts to the established church and founding numerous parishes.

In the seventeenth century, Anglicanism may have dominated the religious life of the Southern and Caribbean British colonies. But it did so more because it had a legal relationship to the government than because it had either the deeply committed laity that enabled Puritanism to flourish in New England or a strong, aggressive clergy. Indeed, in many areas church membership was more nominal than a sign of vital religious experience, and, as we have seen, religious dissent (both Protestant and Roman Catholic) was always an important feature of overall religious life. But thanks to the work of individuals such as James Blair and Thomas Bray, the eighteenth century would witness a revitalization of Anglicanism in much of British North America. Yet many of the ancillary forces that contributed to that renewed vitality also strengthened dissent. Ultimately, as in New England, in the eighteenth century pluralism would more and more become the mark of Southern religious life.

# 18

## ETHNIC AND RELIGIOUS
## PLURALISM COME TO
## BRITISH COLONIAL AMERICA

Before the close of the seventeenth century, Great Britain had extended its colonial empire in North America to include areas initially settled by Dutch, Swedish, and German folk. The area that was in time to encompass New York, Pennsylvania, New Jersey, and Delaware revealed a remarkable diversity in both the national and ethnic backgrounds of those who carved out a European presence. It also became home to a variety of forms of Christian expression, albeit mostly Protestant.

This diversity had several consequences for the development of Christianity in what became the "middle colonies" in British North America. To the northeast, the region's New England neighbors had an initial cohesiveness resulting from a common affirmation of the Puritan Way. Despite the differences that were to develop in New England over precisely how covenant ideology should work and the many cracks in the structure of belief and practice that Puritans were constantly striving to mend, the widespread support for its broad contours did help create a common culture and grant a homogeneity to the region. The middle colonies were never to reap the benefits of such a homogeneity.

On the North American mainland to the south, where the Church of England enjoyed at least nominal establishment, religious ideology was less a factor in providing a regional identity. But what religion did not do an economy based on tobacco cultivation and a slave labor system to some extent did. By contrast, the middle colonies did not develop that same kind of regional identity. While a mercantile economy did emerge, it did not provide the same degree of shared vested interests that the tobacco culture gave to the Southern colonies.

As well, the political history of the middle colonies also meant that diversity would characterize the region. New York began as a Dutch colony, but when English control was established in 1664, it for a time became a proprietary colony under the authority of James, duke of York and brother to Charles II. But by the century's end, yet another change in political structure came in the era of general colonial rechartering that followed the Glorious Revolution. New Sweden, in the area now known as Delaware, only briefly functioned as a Swedish colony per se. Within two decades of its founding, Fort Christina had been destroyed by the Dutch in New Netherland, but when the British defeated the Dutch there, they regarded the short-lived New Sweden as part of Pennsylvania until the early eighteenth century, when Delaware was separately chartered. While the Jerseys were technically proprietary colonies under grants dating as early as 1648, West Jersey had strong ties to Pennsylvania and East Jersey to the Puritan colony in New Haven once colonial settlement got under way in the 1660s. When the two were unified as a royal colony by decree of Queen Anne in 1702, they already had somewhat distinct identities. Pennsylvania, of course, began as a proprietary venture, but early on there was considerable dissatisfaction with proprietary government that was complicated by internal tensions within the Quaker majority in the colony. This maze of types of government in the seventeenth century worked against creating a sense of political loyalty to either a specific colony or to the crown and reinforced the natural divisions resulting from the varying national, ethnic, and religious backgrounds of those who came to settle in the middle colonies.

In terms of chronology, European colonization of the region began in New Netherland, following Henry Hudson's exploratory voyage in 1609. New Sweden (Delaware) was the second area to become home to Europeans, with the arrival of Swedish Lutherans in 1638. The first permanent European settlement in the Jerseys did not come until 1666, though the Dutch had attempted to extend their influence in the region between the Hudson and Delaware rivers in the 1630s and again in the 1650s after they had eliminated Swedish control along the Delaware. Pennsylvania, the most carefully planned colonial venture in the area and unwittingly the paradigm for the religious pluralism that would finally dominate British colonies on the North American mainland, was the last to be settled—after William Penn received his proprietary grant in 1681. We shall look at the coming of Christianity to each of these colonies in the order of their settlement.

## FROM NEW NETHERLAND TO NEW YORK

At the dawn of the seventeenth century, the Netherlands was on the brink of becoming a major commercial force; indeed, for a time it was to serve as the hub of European commerce and banking. Poised for such expansion, the Dutch also looked not only to the Americas but also to Asia as likely places to

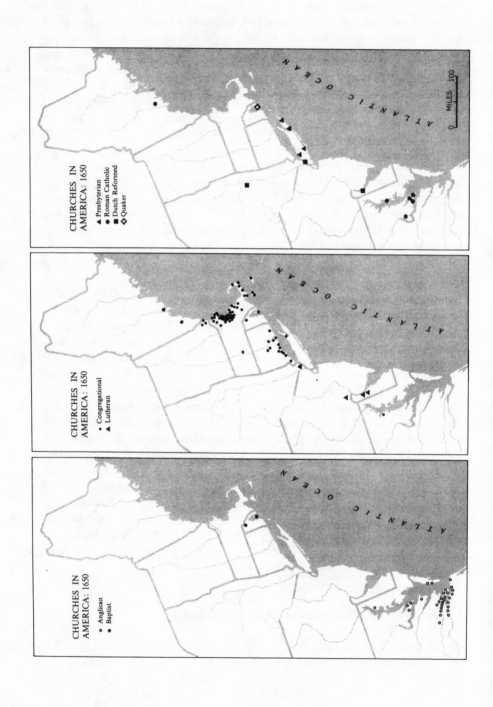

CHURCHES IN
AMERICA: 1650

▲ Presbyterian
● Roman Catholic
■ Dutch Reformed
◇ Quaker

CHURCHES IN
AMERICA: 1650

● Congregational
▲ Lutheran

CHURCHES IN
AMERICA: 1650

○ Anglican
● Baptist

MILES  100
0

ATLANTIC OCEAN

ATLANTIC OCEAN

ATLANTIC OCEAN

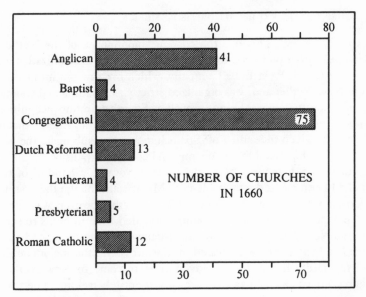

Number of Churches, 1660

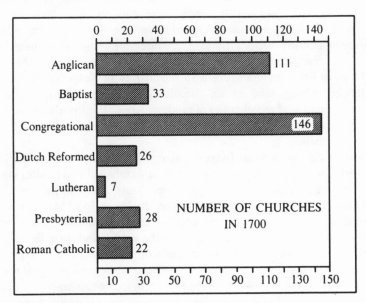

Number of Churches, 1700

extend their empire. This rise to economic prominence of the Netherlands logically meant that profit was to be the major impetus to colonization efforts. Indeed, the Dutch West India Company, which oversaw the initial developments in New Netherland, was organized strictly as a trading and commercial endeavor. The situation was helped as well by Spain's grudging recognition that attempts to regain control over the Netherlands were futile. Energy that might have had to be given to fending off Spanish moves to resubjugate the Netherlands could be channeled into economic and colonial expansion.

Hence, within four years of Hudson's 1609 voyage, a handful of trading centers had been erected on the island of Manhattan, though the first permanent settlers were not to arrive until 1623. Growth, however, was slow. The relative prosperity of the mother country provided little impetus to seek fortune in the New World. As well, the near-despotic power of the early colonial governors and the restrictions placed on the fur trade, the major commercial enterprise, hardly induced even adventurers to come to New Netherland. Religious motives for colonization were almost entirely lacking. The toleration that had made the Netherlands a virtual haven for those enduring religious persecution elsewhere, including for a time the Separatists who eventually came to Plymouth, meant that people were unlikely to be drawn to New Netherland for religious reasons. In addition, the opening decades of the seventeenth century were a time of considerable religious ferment in the Netherlands, capped by the convening of the Synod of Dort in 1618. That synod was to be a landmark event in the history of Reformed (Calvinistic) Christianity, setting standards for orthodox Calvinist belief, especially in its strident affirmation of the doctrine of predestination. In turn, the synod for the moment gave a vitality to Dutch religious life and to Reformed Christianity in Europe in general.

Although the Dutch West India Company did legally establish the Dutch Reformed Church, its colonial governors were hardly inclined to offer vigorous support to its development. In 1626, three years after the first permanent settlers began to build New Amsterdam on the lower tip of Manhattan and a few other scattered communities, two lay religious professionals, *Kranken-besoeckers* (comforters of the sick) came to the colony and were for two years the only ones offering any religious leadership. Consequently, when Jonas Michaelius, the first ordained clergyman or *dominie*, began a five-year ministry in New Amsterdam in 1628, he found the religious situation pretty much in disarray. His successors frequently found themselves devoting as much time to conflicts with the colonial governors over lack of support for the church as to nurturing the souls of the faithful. The patroon system, which in actuality perpetuated a near-feudal structure in the colony and exacerbated class division, also worked against building new congregations and developing a vital Reformed presence in New Netherland.

The situation was complicated as well by the presence of others who gave a degree of religious pluralism to the colony. There were, for example, Puritan settlements on Long Island whose ties were with New England, despite Dutch claims to the area. Dutch Lutherans organized a congregation in 1649, though when a pastor arrived to serve the struggling Lutheran community in 1657, Governor Peter Stuyvesant had him arrested and deported. As well, a handful of French Reformed and some Dissenters from both England and New England (Anne Hutchinson, for example) regarded the Dutch territory as home. The Dutch Reformed Church might have legal establishment, but it did not have strength. Ironically, a stronger Dutch Reformed presence would before the end of the seventeenth century develop not in what once was New Netherland but in West Jersey.

On balance, though, a major reason for the weakness of the Dutch Reformed Church was the lackluster support of the Dutch West India Company in providing for clergy to come to New Netherland. Between the arrival of Michaelius in 1628 and English conquest in 1664, the Dutch West India Company sent only fifteen clergy to the colony. While they had managed to establish about a dozen congregations, there were but six actively ministering when control passed to the English and just three serving in 1673, when the Dutch briefly regained power in the colony. But the transfer of political oversight to the English did not immediately bring any significant change to the dismal religious situation. By then the practical necessity of minimal religious toleration in a colonial endeavor had been generally accepted by the English; that would assume a different dimension in New York when James, duke of York, converted to Roman Catholicism in 1672 and sought to assure toleration for his fellow Catholics.

But what really impeded Christianity's having a vibrant presence in New York was the maintenance under the English of the near-feudal economic and political structure set up by the Dutch. Indeed, the "Duke's Laws" of 1665 that were to provide the first frame of government under English control strongly endorsed the status quo. Over the next two decades, popular resistance to the exclusion of the bulk of the population from the political process, as well as the psychological resistance of the Dutch to accepting English rule, was ultimately to issue in Leisler's Rebellion on the eve of the Glorious Revolution in England that was itself to have profound consequences for the religious life of all British colonies. There was, however, much talk in royal circles of increasing support for churches and clergy and sporadic discussion about the need to replace the established Dutch Reformed Church with the Church of England—discussion that always provoked an outcry among Dutch colonists. But the talk was not followed by action.

British control did mean, however, that there would be some provision for Church of England worship. But for nearly three decades, that would be limited to services conducted by the governor's Anglican chaplain. Not until the era of colonial rechartering that followed the Glorious Revolution would more formal moves be made to strengthen the Church of England in New York. Even then, the result would be disappointing. In 1692, Governor Benjamin

Fletcher began to press the Assembly for a new act of establishment. In September of the following year, the Assembly responded with legislation that later historians have almost uniformly called ambiguous, for it called only for six "good sufficient Protestant Minister[s]" in just four of New York's ten counties.[1] It did not specify that they be priests of the Church of England, and the first congregation to be chartered under the act's provisions, which obtained royal endorsement in 1696, was actually a Dutch Reformed church in Manhattan. But, thanks to the Society for the Propagation of the Gospel, there were some attempts to set up Church of England parishes. The most notable was Trinity parish in Manhattan, which held services as early as 1693 although it was not chartered until 1697. When the colonial governor granted the "king's farm" in Manhattan to Trinity parish, he unwittingly gave it a financial base that would in time make Trinity the wealthiest parish in the United States. Outside Manhattan, a few Anglican parishes were founded, but generally, pluralism and outright religious indifference prevailed until well into the eighteenth century.

## THE LUTHERANS OF NEW SWEDEN

Like other European monarchs of the age, Sweden's Gustavus Adolphus entertained visions of a colonial empire. Swedish attempts to establish a presence on the North American mainland began in 1638 with the founding of Fort Christina on the Delaware River. But during the seventeenth century, probably fewer than a thousand Swedes and Finns came to the area initially called New Sweden. While these immigrants did plant Swedish Lutheranism in the New World, Swedish control of the area (now part of the state of Delaware) was short-lived. The Dutch in New Netherland regarded the region as part of their colony, and in 1655 the Dutch governor Peter Stuyvesant dispatched soldiers who readily brought New Sweden under Dutch authority. After the English seized control of New Netherland in 1664, New Sweden became part of the British domain and was included in the grant given to William Penn in 1681. For two decades after that, the former New Sweden was part of Pennsylvania, finally becoming the colony of Delaware in 1701.

The Swedes were at first more conscientious than either the Dutch or the English in seeking to provide professional clergy to minister to the religious needs of the Lutherans in the area. The need for trained clergy stemmed from two features of Swedish Lutheranism. First, doctrinal instruction, based on Luther's catechism, was central to proper religious training; providing such instruction was a significant part of a minister's duties. Second, the liturgical worship integral to Swedish Lutheranism, focused on the high mass, required a celebrant who was ordained. At least a few of these ministers also took seriously what was in theory part of the rationale for every colonial venture, the conversion of the Indians. For example, John Companius, generally recognized as the most outstanding of the early Swedish Lutheran ministers to serve in America, actually translated Luther's catechism into the language of the Delaware Indians in order to provide them with proper instruction in the faith.

But with the shift of political control first to the Dutch and then to the English, there came a decline in Swedish support for the few hundred Lutherans then comprising the population. By 1690, reports indicate that there were no Lutheran pastors ministering in the area. This situation spurred Swedes at home again to provide clergy and other support for their coreligionists in the New World. If the area was not actually Swedish territory, at least Swedish culture and custom could be maintained through the church. Accordingly, three ministers arrived from Sweden in 1697. One assumed pastoral responsibilities in Wilmington; another undertook ministry to the Swedish colonists who were living in Philadelphia.

The impact of this early Swedish Lutheran presence, however, was to be felt more fully in the eighteenth century. When German Lutherans began migrating to the New World, for example, it was largely through Swedish support that they were initially able to transplant their own Lutheran heritage to a new environment. Because German immigration brought considerably more colonists to America than did Swedish, early American Lutheranism was ultimately to assume more of a German than a Swedish character. But much later, when immigration patterns saw more Swedish Lutherans coming to America, other roots planted in New Sweden were to blossom.

## THE RELIGIOUS COMPLEXION OF THE JERSEYS

While separate proprietary grants in 1648 were designed to create near-feudal colonies in East Jersey and West Jersey, the time was not propitious for their development. No doubt the proximity of New Netherland and New Sweden created psychological barriers to immediate settlement, since both looked to the area as a place for future expansion. A few Dutch efforts to colonize the region just west of the Hudson came to naught for a variety of reasons. Thus in 1664 the Jerseys, along with New Netherland, came under the control of the duke of York, who in turn granted what was then called Nova Caesaria to Sir George Carteret and Lord John Berkeley. While their plans for the Jerseys were not as detailed as those, for example, of Lord Baltimore for Maryland, they did draft a document, *Concessions and Agreements*, that provided both for a framework of government and religious toleration for virtually all Protestant Christians. Enduring settlement in the region, though haphazard, really dates from their assumption of proprietary control. Through a series of complex moves, proprietary control of both East and West Jersey was to change hands yet again, and both were to become royal colonies before the close of the seventeenth century, but by the time those shifts occurred, the religious patterns that were to dominate the area had already been fixed.

The founding of New Ark (now Newark) in 1666 by settlers with strong ties to the New Haven colony paved the way for East Jersey to become a Puritan enclave. Several forces spurred Puritan migration here. Many came from New England both because the prospects of new land offered the hope of greater economic security and the opportunity to establish new settlements held out the possibility of planting afresh the Puritan vision of a covenanted commonwealth that already seemed to be eroding in New England. Others of a Puritan stripe came from England, for in the years immediately following the Restoration in 1660, the time of the so-called great persecution, many most committed to a rigorous Puritanism found themselves subject to harassment and imprisonment at home. East Jersey seemed a haven where the way of purity could be preserved. The same threat of persecution and the promise of religious toleration also drew Quakers and Baptists to East Jersey. Friends, for example, organized a meeting in Shrewsbury in 1670.

Hence the pattern of settlement in East Jersey bore marked resemblance to that designed for New England, with a meeting house at the center of the village and covenant ideology informing both political and religious affairs. Indeed, East Jersey might well have replaced New England as the locus of the ideal Puritan commonwealth had the appointed governors and ultimately the crown given these Puritans a freer hand. Nonetheless, a Puritan influence permeated the religious life of East Jersey well into the eighteenth century—long after East Jersey had been joined with West Jersey in 1702 to create the colony of New Jersey.

In West Jersey, the dominant religious influence in the seventeenth century was to be Quaker. George Fox, founder of the Society of Friends, had traveled through the Jerseys during his colonial tour in the early 1670s. After his return to England he urged some of his followers to consider creating a refuge in West Jersey for the persecuted Quakers. William Penn was among those who sponsored the first group of Friends to come to the Jerseys in 1675, founding the village of Salem on the east bank of the Delaware River. Within three years, around a thousand Quakers had made West Jersey home, and nearly half again as many were to be found in West Jersey when the settlement of Pennsylvania, the Quaker colony par excellence, got under way in 1681. So vibrant was the Quaker presence in West Jersey that the Yearly Meeting organized in Burlington in 1681 retained its prominence even after Philadelphia emerged as the symbolic center of Quaker Pennsylvania; for three-quarters of a century the Yearly Meeting was to alternate between Burlington and Philadelphia. Even in government, Quakers would achieve prominence. By 1682, the majority of proprietors came from Quaker ranks; they were thus able to have renowned Quaker theologian Robert Barclay designated governor. Though Barclay worked through an appointed deputy, he theoretically remained governor until West Jersey became a royal colony in 1688.

The Quaker style combined with topography to create a culture in West Jersey that differed considerably from that of Puritan East Jersey. The rivers and plains of West Jersey favored the development of large agricultural estates. In essence, many West Jersey Quakers were to become near-aristocratic, wealthy landholders dependent on slave labor; in the eighteenth century Quaker involvement in slavery was to cause considerable controversy among Friends and as early as 1688 prompted Pennsylvania Quakers in Germantown, with the encouragement of local Mennonites, to question whether Friends could remain faithful to their own principles if they owned or otherwise promoted slavery. As well, Quaker adherence to endogamy also in the seventeenth century helped assure that the simplicity and quiet piety characteristic of the Friends had a lasting influence on West Jersey life, though theoretically toleration extended to all Protestant Christians. Marriage within the fold buttressed the family ties that allowed Friends to control the political, social, and economic life of West Jersey.

Before the end of the seventeenth century, that toleration was to open doors for many who did not share Quaker values to come to both East and West Jersey. A strong Reformed presence emerged because of increasing numbers of Dutch immigrants who came to the Jerseys and to New York, though no longer under Dutch control, as the century drew to a close. But the wave of the future rested with those who responded to the preaching of Presbyterian Francis Makemie, who began preaching in the middle colonies in 1681. Aided by a steady rise in the number of Scotch-Irish coming to the New World, New Jersey was to become the base from which colonial Presbyterianism blossomed in the eighteenth century. In the eighteenth century, too, these Presbyterians were to join with the Puritans of East Jersey to resist Quaker dominance of the political life of the united New Jersey colony. Quakers may have overshadowed other Christians in West Jersey, as Puritans did in East Jersey, but the seeds of the pluralism that would distinguish those British North American colonies that became the United States were planted in New Jersey before the end of the seventeenth century.

## THE HOLY EXPERIMENT IN PENNSYLVANIA

When one thinks of the Quaker presence in British colonial America, it is not the early endeavors in Barbados, the persecution in New England, the struggling settlements in the Carolinas, or the enduring influence in West Jersey that usually come to mind. Rather, in the popular mind, the Society of Friends is virtually synonymous with Pennsylvania, intended from the start to be a model for what a society founded on Quaker values should be. Both the character of early colonial Pennsylvania and the practicalities of its settlement are inextricably related to the person of its proprietor, William Penn (1644–1718).

Penn was a religious giant of the age, something of a bridge between the ideals of Puritanism and the ideals of the Enlightenment. The son of Admiral William Penn, who had led the naval victory that routed the Dutch from

Jamaica in 1655, the younger William received a solid education and moved in circles that made him friend to both Charles II and James II. As a young adult, Penn showed little inclination toward things religious, but by 1661 he had become attracted to the simple, pacifist Christianity of the Friends, becoming a zealous convert to the Quaker cause in 1666. As a Quaker, Penn too suffered persecution, but turned even that to the advantage of his co-religionists. After publishing a pamphlet attacking the Church of England from a Quaker perspective, Penn found himself in prison in 1669. But while in prison, he wrote what remains a classic of Quaker devotional literature, *No Cross, No Crown*.

George Fox's visit to the British colonies in America in 1672 fostered Penn's interest in establishing a colony based on Quaker principles. When his backing of the Friends who left England for West Jersey in 1675 proved successful, Penn began to formulate plans for a larger proprietary settlement that would both offer religious freedom not only to Quakers but to others who suffered religious oppression and also provide a regular income for Penn and his heirs. In 1681, Penn convinced his friend Charles II to grant him land in the New World in lieu of a rather large debt the king owed originally to Admiral Penn. By July that year, Penn's deputy governor had already taken control of the territory, and before the end of the following year, Penn himself had arrived, a colonial assembly had met, and Penn's *Frame of Government* had been adopted.

Pennsylvania was a near-instant success as a colony if success is measured by the ability to attract settlers. For several decades Pennsylvania colonists enjoyed greater harmony in their relationship with the Indians in the area, thanks to Penn's insistence that they be treated fairly and equitably. Then, too, the *Frame of Government* was extraordinarily generous in its provisions for religious freedom. The "Holy Experiment," as Penn called it, would be open to all who believed in God, though at first the majority of those who flocked to "Penn's Woods" were devout Quakers. Penn was also a tireless promoter of his experiment, advertising widely on the European mainland for colonists and offering them land at bargain prices. Land and religious toleration were quickly to join to bring many non-Quakers to Pennsylvania. In 1683, for example, the founding of Germantown outside Philadelphia followed Penn's granting some eighteen thousand acres to six German Mennonites (although the first thirteen families actually to settle in Germantown also included some Dutch Quakers). Pluralism and ethnic variety were thus part of Pennsylvania's story from the outset.

But part of the story is also linked to the sectarian mind set of the Friends and the difficulties attendant on adjusting from being an oppressed minority to a controlling majority and then to a controlling minority. George Fox's call for the devout to return to the simple Christianity of the New Testament, to heed the "Light of Christ within,"[2] gained plausibility in part because it stood in stark contrast to the perceived formalism and sterile doctrine of the Church of England. The early Quakers needed the Anglican establishment as a foil to their vision of the plain and sober truth of the New Testament. The persecution Fox, Penn, and countless other Quakers endured also served as a powerful cohesive force among the faithful. As long as the Church of England remained as both a real and symbolic opponent of the Quaker truth, Quakers had a potent means of asserting their self-identity, if only by contrast to those who had destroyed the simple essence of Christianity. In Pennsylvania, where Quakers assumed the position of power, it quickly became difficult to operate as a leaven to effect change in the larger social order. Here Quakers were the social order. Even in the eighteenth century, when Quakers became a numerical minority in Pennsylvania, they still confronted the anomaly of being the dominant force in all dimensions of colonial life. This difficulty became magnified when commitment to Quaker principles conflicted with the exigencies of governing as, for example, when the perceived need for defense conflicted with Quaker pacifism. Another aspect of the same general problem emerged in the process of socializing those born in a Quaker culture to the belief and practice of the Friends. One level of commitment was required when identifying oneself as a Quaker meant a having a distinct experience of the light within, abandoning virtual automatic membership in an established church, and accepting the real possibility that persecution would follow. But what of the commitment when all one knew was the plain truth of the Quaker way and when identification with the Friends did not involve a public break with an established church and there was no threat of persecution?

These concerns are evidenced in several trends and movements under way in the last years of the seventeenth century that were to have more serious ramifications in the eighteenth century. One is the result of Penn's policy of opening the colony to all who believed in God. The influx of Germans that began with the grant to the Mennonites who formed Germantown was to bring an ever-increasing number of non-Quakers to Pennsylvania. When the War of the League of Augsburg (with its American phase known popularly in the British colonies as King William's War) erupted in Europe in 1688, many Germans—sectarian and Reformed alike—sought relief from the ravages of war by becoming part of the "Holy Experiment." Before the end of the seventeenth century Germans were joined by what was to be a steady immigration of Scotch-Irish to both Pennsylvania and New Jersey. Indeed, when the incorrigible Francis Makemie organized the first colonial presbytery early in the eighteenth century, Philadelphia became its headquarters. A growing number of colonists were also Baptist, and in 1707, Philadelphia would also become the locus for the first Baptist association organized in North America. As well, in 1694, plans were laid to hold Anglican services according to the *Book of Common Prayer* in Philadelphia, leading to the building of Christ Church the following year and the arrival of Thomas Clayton as the first permanent rector in 1697. So quickly did Anglicanism gain a foothold in the heart of Quaker Philadelphia that Clayton was able to write in 1700 that "in less than four years' space from a very small number her [the Church of England's] community consists of more than five hundred sober and devout souls."[3]

A major controversy within the Quaker fold undoubtedly helped spur Anglican growth even as it pointed out many of the tensions inherent in Quakerism's
struggle to make the shift from a sectarian minority to the controlling force in
Pennsylvania life. That controversy centered around George Keith (1639–
1716), a Scots Presbyterian who had become a zealous convert to the Friends'
cause. In 1691, the year George Fox died, Keith launched a sustained attack on
the Pennsylvania Quaker establishment in which he accused the Friends of
abandoning the rigorous discipline that Fox had encouraged and compromising
Quaker belief. In other words, Keith thought the Quakers had fallen into the
trap of cultural accommodation that often accompanies the transition of a
sectarian movement as second and third generations assume positions of
influence.

Keith's manner of attack, however, was likewise not in keeping with the
Quaker heritage; the truth contained in his criticism was obscured by his
abrasive style and the conviction of some that Keith was merely trying to
assume Fox's role as the recognized leader of the Friends. But clearly there had
been compromise. Governing had raised questions about the practicality of
rigid insistence on the pacifism fundamental to the Quaker way. Germans in
the frontier regions of Pennsylvania, for example, were concerned about protection and defense when the War of the League of Augsburg spilled over to the
American colonies and brought pressure on their settlements from the French
and their Indian allies to the west. Even in Philadelphia, Quaker magistrates
were increasingly resorting to force to maintain social order. Keith also identified shifts occurring within the Quaker meeting itself. While Fox had promoted
study of Scripture and emphasized the role of Christ as redeemer of humanity, Keith and his associates rightly discerned that Quakers in Pennsylvania
had put so much stress on immediate revelation—the light within—that scriptural authority had weakened and doctrinal unity was giving way to a crass
individualism.

The controversy over Keith's criticisms was also symptomatic of other internal problems that were to become more serious in the eighteenth century. The
disciplined life associated with the Quakers had brought considerable commercial success to many Pennsylvania Friends, as it had to New England Puritans.
The same predicament was thus confronting the Quakers as it did the Puritans:
How could material success and an ethic of world-denial be joined together?
More and more it seemed that economic prosperity rather than the spiritual life
consumed the energy of Friends. Historian Frederick B. Tolles aptly captured
the shift in his classic description of the transition as being one from "meeting
house to counting house." At the same time, there appeared to be an erosion of
commitment among the younger generations; gone was the enthusiasm of the
first generation as those who received spiritual nurture in Quaker families came
to regard membership in the Society of friends more as a birthright than a
costly commitment.

But if Keith's assault on Pennsylvania Quakerdom had highlighted serious dilemmas, his offensive style provoked an equally sharp reaction more than it did collective self-scrutiny. In 1692, the Yearly Meeting disowned Keith because of the divisions his attack had brought. When the London Yearly Meeting, to which Keith had carried his cause, likewise disowned him, schism followed, and Keithians formed a new religious body that called itself "Christian Quakers and Friends." The controversy had other political and religious ramifications. For example, Penn lost proprietary control of the colony from 1691 to 1694, perhaps because of the turmoil surrounding Keith, though Keith's supporters were to remain a vocal dissenting minority in Pennsylvania politics long after Penn had regained power. Within a few years, many of Keith's followers had abandoned his sect to identify themselves with the fledgling Baptists, and the movement itself disintegrated as a distinct religious entity even more when in 1700 Keith himself converted to the Church of England and then became the first itinerant missionary employed by the Society for the Propagation of the Gospel to work in North America after his ordination to the Anglican priesthood. Ironically, in time William Penn's sons were also to return to the Church of England.

In the eighteenth century, German and Scotch-Irish immigration would witness so many non-Quakers making Pennsylvania their home that the Friends would become a minority, albeit a culturally, economically, and politically dominant one, in their own "Holy Experiment." The difficulties attendant on using Quaker principles to inform public policy would also bring fresh challenges, and the problem of cultural accommodation would become more acute.

## THE MIDDLE COLONIES AS PARADIGM

Although religious pluralism had gradually (and reluctantly) become the order of the day in late seventeenth-century New England and even in the Southern colonies, where the Church of England enjoyed legal establishment, William Penn's vision of his colony as a haven for the religiously oppressed and a home for any who believed in God was intentionally fostering such pluralism from the start. So, too, the presence of Dutch Reformed in New Netherland and an enclave of Scandinavian Lutherans in what had been New Sweden made pluralism a fact of life in the middle colonies even after Great Britain had added these areas to its own colonial empire.

In the seventeenth century, few recognized that this pluralism would in retrospect make the middle colonies a paradigm for the shape of the religious life of those British North American colonies that would become the United States. But the simple fact is that Reformed Christians, Friends, Lutherans, Puritans, Anglicans, Baptists, German sectarians, Presbyterians, a small number of Roman Catholics, and a smattering of folk of other religious persuasions were able to exist side by side in relative harmony and without serious disruption of the social order. In demonstrating that religious pluralism did not undermine political control or the common good, the middle colonies destroyed the popular conviction dating back to the days of the Protestant Reformation that religious uniformity was necessary for social order. That principle, with its logical concomitant—broadly based religious toleration—would receive greater recognition in the eighteenth century. But the seeds had been planted and strong roots established in the seventeenth-century patterns of the middle colonies.

# 19

## AWAKENING AND REVOLUTION
## IN NEW ENGLAND

The years of the eighteenth century leading to the move toward independence for those British North American colonies that became the United States were tumultuous ones in New England. Many of the seeds planted in the seventeenth century began to blossom, but often in ways unintended or unimagined by those who cultivated them. Pluralism, always a problem to the covenant ideology of the Puritans, more and more became the order of the day, further undermining the vision of a holy commonwealth united in a commitment to religious purity and public order. Fresh challenges to Puritan religious thought came as Enlightenment currents associated with the Age of Reason began to penetrate the intellectual life of the colonies and its clergy. Many continued to see signs of decline in commitment to the Puritan Way.

But in the second quarter of the eighteenth century, a religious revolution swept across not only New England but through virtually all British colonies in the New World. A revival of religion so pervasive in its impact that it became known as the Great Awakening, this religious revolution also had ties to evangelical currents in Britain, for it transpired as revivals came to Calvinist Scotland and as John and Charles Wesley were spearheading the Methodist revivals in the industrial regions of England. Yet not all welcomed the Great Awakening as a rebirth of commitment to the Puritan vision; some saw the religious enthusiasm it unleashed as a threat to religious and public order. In time the revivals were to divide New England Puritans as much as they sparked fresh interest in things divine.

All these forces were part of a larger tapestry into which political and imperial forces were woven. More and more the colonies were drawn into the competition of Britain with its rivals in colonial expansion. For New England, the hostility between the British and French, who controlled neighboring Canada, loomed the largest. As colonies became pawns in the game of empire, questions began to emerge about the nature of colonial relationships with the mother country. Most centered around the issue of determining precisely what control a distant king and parliament ought to have and what independent authority colonies should possess. Given the near-tribal character envisioned for the New England Puritan colonies, issues that seemed political and economic were bound to have religious ramifications, and religious leaders (especially the clergy) were drawn into political affairs as they sought to discern the implications of Puritan belief for public policy. When the colonial militia and British regulars engaged in combat at Lexington and Concord, Massachusetts, in April 1775, a struggle began that was to dismantle much of Britain's North American colonial empire, lead to the creation of a new nation, and cause considerable rethinking and restructuring of Christianity in the Northern Hemisphere of the New World.

## THE EIGHTEENTH CENTURY DAWNS

Perceptions of decline in colonial religious life, particularly concerns that the symbolic center of the Puritan colonies—Massachusetts Bay—had come too much under the sway of mercantile interests and nonorthodox religion, came to the fore in Connecticut in 1701. On the surface, the issue that brought these perceptions into focus was the conviction that Harvard College, the only school for training Puritan clergy in New England, had forsaken Puritan orthodoxy. Hence in October 1701, the General Court of Connecticut acted favorably on a petition drafted by three concerned clergy and granted a charter to a collegiate institution that developed into Yale University once it established a permanent home in New Haven. If Harvard had gone astray, Yale at least could be a bastion of orthodoxy. With the support of a sympathetic, elected (not appointed) colonial governor and the absence of a dominant mercantile class, Yale supporters quickly moved to shore up orthodoxy in the areas under Connecticut influence. One sign of that attempt was a synod of clergy and laity that gathered at Saybrook, Connecticut, in the autumn of 1708. When the General Court enacted into law the resolutions adopted by the synod, known as the Saybrook Platform, Connecticut and Yale became the functional and symbolic centers of Puritan orthodoxy and would remain such until after an independent United States came into being. But the Saybrook Platform itself contained some departures from the ways of seventeenth-century New England Puritanism. Although doctrinally the platform grounded Connecticut Christianity in the Calvinist tradition of the Westminster Assembly of the previous century, it authorized an organizational structure for the churches that was more presbyterian than congregational in form. That in time would draw Connecticut Christians even further away from their fellow New England Puritans and closer to the Presbyterians who were gaining strength in the middle colonies.

No doubt part of the reason why Connecticut Puritans felt that Massachusetts Bay had abandoned commitment to the ways of the founding generation came from the inroads being made at Harvard by Enlightenment thought, a dreaded rationalism to orthodox Puritan minds, and the gradual but steady growth in Boston of both Anglicanism and the more liberal Puritanism associated with the Brattle Street Church. In 1702, SPG missionaries John Talbot and George Keith, the former Quaker, traveled through Britain's North American continental colonies, bolstering the Anglican presence in New England. Although most of the congregations they and their successors started were small and relied heavily on SPG financial support, in Boston (where Talbot and Keith began their journey) a thriving King's Chapel already signaled the growth of Anglicanism in the heart of the old Puritan commonwealth. By 1735, Boston boasted three Anglican churches, all of them attracting some of the city's most influential residents as parishioners; all would continue to flourish until war disrupted colonial religious life in the 1770s.

Thanks to Yale and a standing order reinforced by the Saybrook Platform, the Church of England made little headway in Connecticut. But in Connecticut an incident occurred that dramatically signaled the rising respectability of Anglicanism in areas dominated by Puritans. In 1722, following a period of several years of probing works of Anglican theology, Yale rector Timothy Cutler and a handful of other Connecticut Puritan clergy announced their conversion to the Church of England. That the head of the institution founded to buttress Puritan orthodoxy could come to doubt the validity of the New England theology, renounce his ordination (since it did not come at the hands of bishops), and seek reordination as a priest in the Church of England suggested how pervasive pluralism was actually becoming in the haven of Puritanism. Cutler, for example, was to return to New England in 1723 to begin a stunning forty-two-year ministry as rector of the Anglican North Church (Christ Church) in Boston, while some of his fellow converts returned to help the expansion of the Church of England in both New York and Connecticut.

In neighboring Rhode Island, Anglicanism was also establishing a presence. Under the aegis of the SPG, worship according to the *Book of Common Prayer* became available to a small congregation in Newport as early as 1698. In about two decades' time, three other Church of England congregations had been organized in the colony. While significant Anglican growth in Rhode Island came later, these four churches received considerable moral support and encouragement when George Berkeley arrived in the Newport area in 1729 for what became a two-year stay. Later a renowned philosopher identified with idealism and a bishop of the Church of England, Berkeley intended his visit to be much shorter, more of a stopover as he awaited SPG funding to start a missionary school for the indigenous peoples of Bermuda. When that support was not forthcoming, he returned to England. Nevertheless, his stay granted this fledgling Anglican presence much prestige.

In the early eighteenth century, too, ways of thinking associated with the

Enlightenment were beginning to gain ground in New England. The Enlightenment's emphasis on reason, natural law, and common sense was destined to undermine much of the foundation of Puritan covenant ideology. But the process was a gradual one. Works by Enlightenment thinkers were readily available to Harvard students in the opening decades of the eighteenth century and found their way into the collection of presumably more orthodox Yale. Over the years, sermons by ministers trained at both schools contain increasing numbers of references to Enlightenment philosophers, slowly imbedding in the consciousness of people in the pews the basic tenets of rationalism. Simply put, many ministers were convinced that part of their task was to demonstrate what John Locke (1632–1704) titled his influential work: *The Reasonableness of Christianity* (1695). Indeed, Locke was the single most important Enlightenment figure in terms of impact on American thought. For example, Jonathan Edwards, who was to be the premier colonial Christian theologian and philosopher, built much of his thinking on principles derived from Locke. The full force of Enlightenment thought did not become apparent until later in the century, when political thinkers in those colonies that declared their independence from Britain in 1776 began to seek intellectual justification for their actions and articulate a theory behind a new form of government. At the time, what appeared to have far greater repercussions was the revitalization of religion that came with the Great Awakening.

## RELIGIOUS AWAKENING COMES TO NEW ENGLAND

Occasional revivals of interest in religion were far from unknown in Puritan circles. In 1721, for example, revivals came to several Puritan congregations in Connecticut. In Massachusetts, in the inland Connecticut River valley where the population was growing rather rapidly, Solomon Stoddard witnessed five "harvests" during his sixty-year pastorate in Northampton. But the revivals that came in the 1730s and 1740s were different in that they spread not only throughout New England but ultimately affected religious life in all the colonies in Britain's North American empire. At the same time, they were part of a broader movement, for this "great and general awakening" occurred as the evangelical revival that gave birth to Methodism was sweeping through the industrializing areas of England and religious renewal was bringing fresh life to the churches in Scotland. The consequences of the Great Awakening also distinguish it from earlier, more localized revivals, for the effects of the Awakening were ultimately felt in the political sector, in the ways colonists understood their corporate identity, in education, in the distribution of both economic and political power, and in virtually every aspect of social organization in British North America.

Historians have long debated what prompted the Great Awakening. Because in New England (and in Virginia) the force of the Awakening was felt first in the more inland areas, some have seen the revival as a response to the social dislocation that came with carving out new lands for settlement and the need to provide for an expanding colonial population. Others have stressed the growing political and economic tension between the coastal regions and the back country for dominance in colonial affairs as a prime factor in prompting revitalization of religion. Some have seen the Awakening as a response to the religious pluralism that had reluctantly become a matter of course after minimal toleration became required in the new colonial charters implemented after the Glorious Revolution; religious revival became a last-ditch effort to restore the now-idealized religious ways of the past. Yet others have seen in the Awakening a reaction of the people to a clergy perceived as more concerned with their status as a professional elite than with the nurture of individual souls; the emotions released in the revivals were a powerful antidote to the arid intellectualism of later Puritan preaching. Those whose religious life gained new direction in the revivals and those whose preaching prompted dramatic conversions, of course, saw the Awakening as the work of the Holy Spirit convicting folk of sin and nudging them to salvation. In this instance, undoubtedly all these factors worked together to generate a renewed interest in things religious.

In New England, stirrings of the Awakening came in 1734 when popular interest in religion accelerated while Jonathan Edwards (1703–1758), who had succeeded his grandfather Solomon Stoddard as pastor in Northampton, was preaching a series of sermons on the doctrine of justification by faith. Before long, this "surprising work of God," as Edwards called it,[1] had spread to neighboring Massachusetts towns along the Connecticut River valley as far as New Haven. When after about three years this revival began to wane, hopes remained high that a fresh visitation of the Spirit would quickly follow as news came to New England of similar revivals in other colonies as well as in England and Scotland.

What transformed these hopes into reality was the preaching tour of George Whitefield (1714–1770), who arrived in Georgia in 1739 on his second visit to British North America. The "Grand Itinerant," Whitefield was an associate of John and Charles Wesley in the Methodist revivals in England when he came to Georgia on his first visit in 1738, ostensibly to raise funds for an orphanage in Savannah. But this second visit would see him travel throughout those colonies that became the United States, presumably on behalf of the orphanage, but everywhere holding crowds spellbound by his powerful oratory. Sailing from Charleston, South Carolina, in September 1740, Whitefield came first to Newport before heading on to Boston, where the crowds who flocked to hear him numbered in the thousands. Reported the *Boston Weekly News-Letter* in its 25 September 1740 issue:

> Last Thursday Evening the Rev'd Mr. Whitefield arrived from Rhode-Island, being met on the Road and conducted to Town by several Gentlemen. The next Day in the Forenoon he attended

Prayers in the King's Chappel, and in the Afternoon he preach'd to a vast Congregation in the Rev'd Dr. Colman's Meeting-House. The next Day he preach'd in the Forenoon at the South Church to a Crowded Audience, and in the Afternoon to about 5000 People on the Common: and Lord's Day in the afternoon having preach'd to a great Number of People at the Old Brick Church, the House not being large enough to hold those that crowded to hear him, when the Exercise was over, He went and preached in the field to at least 8000 Persons.

At every stop, Whitefield provoked a sensational response; even the normally staid Jonathan Edwards was reported to have wept profusely as Whitefield preached in his Northampton church. Everywhere, folk eagerly examined the state of their souls, with hundreds upon hundreds feeling in their hearts what hitherto had been apprehended in their heads—the marvelous grace of God electing them to salvation.

Other itinerants followed Whitefield to New England, hoping to stoke the fires he had rekindled. Most notable were the Presbyterian Gilbert Tennant, who was also part of the Awakening movement in the middle colonies, and the more notorious James Davenport. Both, but especially Davenport, aroused greater hostility than had Whitefield, though both drew crowds and secured many converts to the faith. Especially disturbing was the stinging criticism Tennant and Davenport leveled at the settled pastors, for both claimed that the sorry state of religious affairs in New England stemmed from many of the clergy themselves being "unconverted" and therefore hardly able to foster authentic religious sensibilities among their parishioners. So fanatical and arrogant were Davenport's attacks that both Massachusetts and Connecticut authorities finally ordered him to leave.

While many pastors rejoiced in the dramatic intensity with which their flocks now devoted themselves to matters of the soul, some harbored serious doubts about the benefits of the revival. Some concern no doubt stemmed from the attacks of Tennant and Davenport on the spiritual state of the clergy. But other concerns ran more deeply. One was the practice of itineracy itself. The New England Way had long been predicated on having a settled clergy who labored for a lifetime among people joined together by the church covenant. The whirlwinds stirred by itinerants who came and went, leaving behind many who were in an emotional frenzy about their own spiritual condition, seemed to undermine that structure. Then, too, questions arose regarding the authenticity of religious experience that was so emotionally charged. Were not conversions merely a response to the drama of the moment? Was it not dangerous to coerce those who had long numbered themselves among the elect to doubt the authenticity of their own less emotional religious experience? At the center of criticism of the Awakening stood Charles Chauncy (1705–1787), pastor of Boston's First (Old Brick) Church since 1727. To Chauncy, the Awakening was little more than a sham, a "spirit of error" designed to destroy the orderly work of God in slowly moving those who were among the elect to a saving knowledge of divine grace. Nonetheless, later historians have estimated that clergy who supported the revivals outnumbered their opponents by a margin of three to one, with the venerable Jonathan Edwards at the helm.

The Awakening left many enduring marks on New England Christianity. Most obvious was an increase in church membership. For generations, many pious men and women had delayed owning the church covenant because they lacked absolute certainty that they were indeed among the elect. Their religious sensibilities heightened and their souls assured of God's work, an estimated twenty to fifty thousand now joined the ranks of the regenerate. More subtle was the way in which both proponents and opponents of the revivals actually undercut the doctrine of election itself. The classical Puritan conviction that humans could do nothing to effect their own salvation began to erode as revivalists urged their listeners to respond to God's work and acknowledge God's saving grace. Did that not mean that there was a human dimension to salvation in the act of acknowledging the work of grace? For antirevivalists like Jonathan Mayhew (1720–1766), "the right of private judgment" in matters of religion that was promoted as an antidote to the presumed emotional excesses of the revivals in its own way also undermined the Calvinist notion of election. This approach, strongly influenced by Enlightenment currents, also granted to the individual a primary role in religious matters because it made individual rational acceptance of religious truth the starting point of the spiritual life.

In turn, elevating the role of the individual in the process of salvation was destined to challenge the notion that a single covenanted church should serve a single community. Did not those who felt their faith faltering under the ministrations of "unconverted" clergy have a right to form a voluntary association and call their own pastor? Was not the true church just such a voluntary association of believers rather than an agency supported by law that had authority over all citizens of a community? This spirit of separatism and concern for a pure church comprised only of true believers was to have several consequences. In several cases, it led to schism as those converted in the revivals separated from established congregations in order to have a pure church. It also prompted many congregations to abandon the Half-Way Covenant and restore more stringent requirements for church membership. But it also gave a boost to the small number of Baptist congregations that had long argued that the true church was one made up of believers who banded together on a voluntary basis.

The techniques of evangelism used by Awakening itinerants also caused many Christians in New England as elsewhere to seek new fields for spreading the Gospel. In this case, the prime missionary field was the native Indians for whose conversion Puritans had long felt responsible in theory, but whose presence as potential enemies of the European invaders had provoked ambivalence if not neglect in fact. For example, Eleazar Wheelock (1711–1779), an ardent supporter of the Awakening in Connecticut, undertook missionary work among Indians in what became New Hampshire that led to the establishment in 1754 of an Indian school that developed into Dartmouth College.

But the Awakening also had much broader ramifications. The revivals symbolized by George Whitefield's preaching tour mark the first large-scale intercolonial event. Itinerants carried news of this surprising work of God from community to community and in some cases from colony to colony. The net result was the development of a communications network that would prove exceedingly useful a few decades later when the colonies that became the United States declared their independence. At the same time, clergy communicated across the Atlantic. Jonathan Edwards, for example, corresponded with counterparts in Scotland who were struck by the renewed interest in religion there that paralleled events in Massachusetts. Whitefield returned to England to continue his career as an evangelist, though he soon parted company with Methodists John and Charles Wesley who, in Whitefield's mind, were too willing to abandon the Calvinist understanding of election for a doctrine of free will.

As colonists began to communicate with one another to a greater degree than before, they also began the process of rethinking their identity as a people and posing some of the same questions in the political sector that had arisen in the realm of religion. It was an easy step to transfer the challenges to the authority of a settled clergy believed "unconverted" to the authority of political leaders, particularly those in distant England who seemed to put self-interest ahead of the welfare of the colonists themselves. While one cannot accurately measure the degree to which the Awakening thus influenced the uneasiness that would soon mark the North American colonies' relations with crown and parliament, analysts of colonial life generally concur that the Awakening was a catalyst in giving birth to a colonial identity that increasingly defined itself as distinct from Britain and its empire.

But the Awakening in New England also brought to the fore America's premier religious thinker of the eighteenth century: Jonathan Edwards, who remains in the minds of many the most significant theologian-philosopher native to the North American continent.

## THE THOUGHT OF JONATHAN EDWARDS

The thinker who is the Jonathan Edwards known to the late twentieth century may well be a different thinker from the one known to clergy, ministerial students, and ideological disciples in the eighteenth century. Several factors account for this seemingly odd state of affairs. First, many of Edwards's writings—even some that originated as collections of sermons preached to the Northampton congregation—were not published until after his death. Nor were some of Edwards's more personal writings, his extensive notebooks that he began to keep as an adolescent and his fragmentary thoughts on a wide range of topics that were scratched on scraps of paper, accessible to those who called themselves Edwardseans. Hence it is only in retrospect that the contours of his thought have become apparent. Then, too, because some of Edwards's work originated during the Awakening, antirevivalists were quick (probably too quick) to dismiss it and to ignore his more sustained treatises. Others saw primarily the Jonathan Edwards who sought in some works to offer a logical defense of doctrines basic to Calvinism and too readily classified him as merely a defender of the rigid orthodoxy with which Calvinism was becoming identified even in the eighteenth century. Some later commentators, struck by the way in which Edwards's writings reveal a thorough familiarity with the thought of John Locke and of the Cambridge Platonists, have attempted to divorce Edwards from his Reformed heritage. None of these views alone captures the theological genius who was Jonathan Edwards, though there is an element of truth in them all. Even together, they are only suggestive of a thinker who remains elusive and complex.

Two posthumously published works offer a convenient lens through which to examine Edwards's thinking: the *Dissertation Concerning the End for which God Created the World*, which appeared in 1765, and the *History of the Work of Redemption*, based on a series of sermons preached in 1739 and first published in 1774. Both works place at their center the glory of a providential God; indeed, revealing the glory of God is God's aim in creation as well as the culmination of God's work in history. All revolves around God's glory, and all ultimately redounds to God's glory. The drama of salvation is part of this larger revelation of divine glory, since for Edwards salvation was both an inner sense (his phrase was "sense of the heart") or apprehension of this glory as well as an active participation in the unfolding revelation of God's glory in redeeming humanity.

During the years of the Awakening, Edwards sought to explicate the nature of authentic religious experience, especially in the wake of criticism of the revivals as crass emotionalism run amok. In *The Distinguishing Marks of a Work of the Spirit of God* (1741) and *Some Thoughts Concerning the Present Revival of Religion in New-England* (1743), he vigorously defended the genuineness of the type of conversion experience associated with the Awakening, arguing that God may work in extraordinary ways as well as in the more mundane, less emotion-charged fashion that antirevivalists saw as fundamental. Edwards conceded that emotion could be misleading and was not itself an accurate indicator of the vitality of religious experience. One must continually look inward or examine the heart to discern whether the Spirit is stimulating the sense of God's providential glory. If one is not dependent solely on God's grace, then the experience—however powerful—may be a sham. Such was really the theme of Edwards's most famous revival sermon, "Sinners in the Hands of an Angry God" (1741), though subsequent generations often misinterpreted it as a precursor of the "hellfire and brimstone" harangues of a later age.

As the Awakening ebbed, Edwards in 1746 published his most sustained analysis of authentic religious experience, his *Treatise Concerning Religious Affections*. Still a classic treatment of the nature of religious experience, this work forcefully claims that the locus of genuine piety is indeed the heart, but also provides several tests or "signs" that facilitate distinguishing between mere emotion and religious affections. The most important was the twelfth and final sign Edwards delineated. That sign directed attention to Christian practice: "Gracious and holy affections have their exercise and fruit in Christian practice."[2] If the heart did not prompt some transformation of behavior that led to consistent, observable conduct reflective of Christian virtue (itself the subject of another work published posthumously), then true conversion had not occurred. After all, visible conduct was the only aspect of another's life that one could actually see. But there is, of course, a danger in staking the authenticity of religious experience on outside observation: Is not the determination of what actions reveal genuine faith arbitrary? Edwards's insistence on the necessary connection between piety and practice logically led him to abandon the Half-Way Covenant so strongly endorsed by his grandfather and predecessor Solomon Stoddard, and objection to his expectations finally resulted in his dismissal from his Northampton pastorate in 1750. But what Edwards sought was to avoid both the antinomianism that revival critics regarded as the natural consequence of emotional excess and also a rigid legalism that replaced a genuine sense of the heart with strict rules for proper conduct.

In two major theological works, Edwards tied his understanding of the religious affections and their connection to practice to doctrines central to the Calvinistic base of Puritanism. *A Careful and Strict Enquiry into . . . Freedom of the Will* (1754) relentlessly demolished the Arminian notion that the will was free to choose between good and evil actions. Volition, according to Edwards, was itself determined by something prior—motivation, or the sense of the heart. In *The Great Christian Doctrine of Original Sin Defended* (1758), Edwards argued that because of the fall of Adam, the sense of the heart among all humanity is misdirected. It is bound to self-love and the perception that humans are not totally dependent on divine grace. Both are hallmarks of depravity. Left to its own devices, then, the will is not free to choose the good or to relish divine glory. Nor will the affections consent to Being as intended at creation. All therefore depends on God's redirecting the affections, on a "divine and supernatural light" enabling humans to see God's glory, on God's transforming the heart through the operation of irresistible grace.[3] That transformation is precisely the work of redemption that has been under way since the fall and, in Edwards's mind, the Awakening was a powerful manifestation of God's glory in effecting such redemption.

Edwards put the finishing touches on these two works after leaving Northampton and undertaking missionary work among the Indians at Stockbridge. The years at Stockbridge proved the most intellectually creative for Edwards. In 1757, he was called to succeed his son-in-law, Aaron Burr, Sr., as president of the College of New Jersey (later renamed Princeton). Burr had died in a smallpox epidemic, and eager to demonstrate his conviction that scientific advance was also a sign of God's glory (contrary to much popular conviction that disease was a sign of God's judgment), Edwards was inoculated for smallpox. The inoculation, however, was unsuccessful, and Edwards contracted the disease and died on 22 March 1758, shortly after his inauguration as president of the college.

## LIBERALIZING CURRENTS IN NEW ENGLAND

If Jonathan Edwards sought to give fresh life to the vital piety and doctrine essential to the Puritan pursuit of purity in his support of the Great Awakening and in his writing, others drew on different intellectual currents in their own attempts to make the Puritan Way plausible for a new age. Edwards was not the only heir of Puritanism to absorb the philosophy of John Locke; nor was Locke the only thinker associated with the Age of Reason whose writings found their way into New England college libraries or the collections of the clergy. But the impact made by those who imbibed Enlightenment ideas, those who espoused what the age called a "catholick Christianity," came into sharper focus during the Awakening and after when many of the most outspoken critics of the evangelical thrust freely drew on Enlightenment constructs in their attacks on the revivals and went on to apply those constructs to a reshaping of Puritan ideology. In the religious sector, two key figures were Charles Chauncy (1705–1787) and Jonathan Mayhew (1720–1766).

Chauncy, settled at Boston's prestigious First Church since 1727, was the most vocal of the opponents of the Awakening. His *Seasonable Thoughts on the State of Religion in New-England* (1743) stands as a direct rebuttal of Edwards's *Some Thoughts on the State of Religion in New-England*. For Chauncy, the emphasis revivalists placed on the immediate work of the Spirit in providing assurance of one's salvation opened the door for both the dreaded Arminianism and antinomianism. As well, looking to itinerant preachers to stir souls undermined the regular ministry of the settled clergy and thereby shattered the patient reliance on God's orderly work through the traditional means of grace as the most viable approach to salvation. The way the fiery oratory of preachers like George Whitefield caused even those who had owned the church covenant to doubt their election to salvation brought unnecessary and unwarranted emotional turmoil to many. Clearly, the Awakening was part of the "spirit of error" of the times.

But Chauncy's position itself was destined to help demolish the Puritan foundations of New England Christianity he thought he was defending. At its base, Chauncy's argument also espoused individualism, but of a different sort than that promoted by evangelicals who stressed the individual conversion experience. In Chauncy's view, God endowed individuals with the ability to understand the truth of Christianity and therefore to accept it as the path to salvation. Through rational persuasion and reliance on the traditional means of grace, individuals would recognize the work of God in electing them to salvation. Yet the long-range consequences of Chauncy's position was not that different from the effect of the individualism promoted by revivalists, for it too led to a questioning of seemingly arbitrary authority in all areas of life. In its original context, the authority Chauncy and his compatriots challenged was that of the itinerant evangelist who saw only one style of religious experience as authentic, but in time the challenge would take on political ramifications and help fuel that discontent with British colonial policy that finally led to calls for American independence. Hence when war with Britain did erupt, Chauncy became a staunch advocate of the colonial cause.

The Awakening also drove Chauncy to think through other theological implications of his position. In the 1750s, after the Awakening had ebbed, Chauncy drafted several manuscripts in which he moved in the direction of universalism. That is, he argued that God's design in history was finally the salvation of all people, not just a handful who were numbered among the elect. While this view seems an obvious contradiction of basic Calvinist doctrine, it really is the logical concomitant of the individualism that lay behind Chauncy's critique of the revivals. After all, if God worked with individuals in a manner that was appropriate to their personalities and life experiences, did it not stand to reason that God worked this way with all people and therefore desired to bring all to salvation? Chauncy understood the radical nature of his thinking and refrained from publishing the manuscripts in which he developed this notion of universal salvation until the 1780s, when the intellectual climate was more in flux. But his universalism reveals precisely how much diversity marked eighteenth-century Puritanism; it also helped pave the way for the emergence of Unitarianism in the opening decades of the nineteenth century.

Jonathan Mayhew's rationalism was more blatant. In 1749 he published an anthology, simply titled *Seven Sermons*. In one sermon, "The Right and Duty of Private Judgment," he proclaimed that because in creation humans had been given the power to reason, each person had the responsibility to measure religious truth claims and accept only those for which there was adequate rational evidence. Attempts to secure uniformity of belief were therefore destined to fail as people exercised their natural right to private (individual) judgment. Mayhew readily saw where his position was leading and in a sermon preached in 1754 claimed that Massachusetts laws that attempted to squelch religious dissent were themselves contrary to reason. Private judgment meant that pluralism must prevail.

Mayhew also saw the implications of his notion of individual religious freedom for the political realm. His well-known *Discourse Concerning Unlimited Submission and Non-Resistance to the Higher Powers*, preached in 1750 on the anniversary of the execution of Britain's King Charles I, insisted that citizens had a duty to resist political authority that was destructive of human liberty. When a ruler "turns tyrant," he wrote, "and makes his subjects a prey to devour and destroy instead of his charge to defend and cherish, we are bound to throw off our allegiance to him and resist"—just as Mayhew's Puritan forebears had resisted the presumed tyranny of Charles I.[4] Then, in the furor that surrounded passage of the Stamp Act in 1765, Mayhew preached another incendiary sermon on the right and duty to secure liberty in the wake of tyranny until what he called the "snare" of despotism was "broken."[5] New England Puritans would recall the ramifications of Mayhew's emphasis on political liberty more than they would his call for private judgment in matters of belief as tensions between colonies and mother country mounted.

## ISAAC BACKUS AND THE BAPTISTS

The pluralism unwittingly nurtured by the Great Awakening had yet another manifestation in the growth of Baptist churches, not only in New England but throughout the North American colonies that became the United States. Central to that story in New England is Isaac Backus (1724–1806). Scion of a prosperous Connecticut farm family and nephew (by marriage) of Jonathan Edwards's sister, Backus had a relatively quiet conversion experience in 1741 during the height of the Awakening. Dissatisfied with the religious style of the Congregational church in Norwich, Connecticut, Backus began traveling in the southern part of New England seeking opportunities to preach in churches sympathetic to the revivals. In 1748 he accepted a call to what would be a pastorate lasting more than half a century at the Separate Congregational Church in Middleborough, Massachusetts. Within a few years, Backus decided that the Baptist insistence on believers' baptism by immersion was the only understanding faithful to Scripture. Accordingly, he and a handful of other congregants were immersed in 1751. In but five years, the Separate Congregational Church provided the core for the Middleborough Baptist Church.

What drew Backus into public view was his dissatisfaction with the legal arrangements that supported Congregational clergy through tax monies. On the one hand, it was difficult, though not impossible, for one's religious taxes to be channeled to another specific congregation. The procedures placed Baptist churches and other independent congregations at a disadvantage. On the other hand, Backus and his fellow Baptists recoiled in principle at the very prospect of supporting clergy through taxes. Their Baptist perspective decreed that local churches were voluntary associations, with clergy to be supported by voluntary contributions. Relying on the power of the government to tax was nothing other than coercion, a denial of rights of conscience, and an assault on the freedom to believe as one chose. Simply put, it imposed one understanding of the church on all and forced citizens into acceptance. When a cluster of Baptist churches organized the Warren Association to coordinate their resistance to this form of oppression, Backus became the Association's leading spokesman. As such, he penned numerous tracts and treatises promoting full liberty of conscience and traveled widely throughout New England and elsewhere attempting to persuade governmental bodies to cease using their coercive power to support any organized religion. Backus even carried his case to the first Continental Congress in 1774. In retrospect, historians have tagged the untiring efforts of Isaac Backus to secure full religious liberty for Baptists among the most important in cementing what we now call the "separation of church and state" as a basic principle in the nation that became the United States.

Backus's ministry also spurred the formation of other Baptist congregations. In 1740, there were only twenty-five churches of Baptist persuasion in New England. By the time the struggle for American independence erupted, that number had more than tripled. As well, from New England the Baptist gospel began to spread elsewhere. Brothers-in-law Daniel Marshall (1706–1784) and Shubal Stearns (1706–1771), both converted during George Whitefield's second New England preaching tour in 1745, quickly gravitated toward Baptist sentiments and undertook to carry the Separate Baptist message South. Marshall first undertook missionary work in Virginia (in an area now part of West Virginia), but in 1755 he went with Stearns to the Piedmont region of North Carolina where their itineracy resulted in the formation of nearly fifty Separate Baptist congregations by the dawn of the American Revolution.

George Whitefield, Jonathan Edwards, and the other evangelists who stirred the Awakening may have believed they were calling people back to the Reformed teachings of Calvin that undergirded the Puritan passion for holiness. But with rationalist critics arguing for the right of private judgment and paving the way for Unitarianism and Baptists promoting both their understanding of the gospel and the principle of religious liberty, the result of the revivalist preaching was to assure that religious pluralism would carry the day and endure as a lasting characteristic of American Christianity.

## OF EMPIRE AND EPISCOPACY

What brought the Awakening to a close in New England and elsewhere was not so much the fragmentation that came as Charles Chauncy mused about his unpublished universalist treatises and Isaac Backus continued to call for freedom of conscience. Rather, by the mid-1740s, events that at first glance appear to have little connection with Christianity began to displace religious passion as a primary concern among the people in British North America. Many of those events revolve around the ongoing struggle for dominance in North America between the French and the English; others reflect a growing uneasiness with British colonial policy once the French had been defeated and Britain extended her empire to take in what we know as Canada.

France and Britain had long been rivals in their respective efforts to control areas of the North American continent that were not part of the Spanish empire. The rivalry was exacerbated by the English Protestant hostility to the Catholicism that commanded the allegiance of the bulk of the French population. Always there was the suspicion that the French, usually in consort with the Spanish, were plotting revolt in England that would topple a monarchy required to be Protestant since the Glorious Revolution. While there had been sporadic confrontations prior to the 1750s, most of the actual fighting occurred in Europe or in the Caribbean rather than on the North American continent. By and large, however, colonists in British areas proclaimed their patriotic loyalty to the mother country when conflict arose. Nevertheless always there lurked the fear that the French and their native allies would attack settlements in British areas, especially on the frontier.

When military confrontation between the British and the French again erupted in 1755, the North American mainland saw some of the primary action in what became known as the French and Indian War. New England militia fought alongside British regulars, though they were regarded as inferior to the professional British army; clergy preached sermons designed to promote patriotism as troops left for combat. When the struggle ended in 1763, the British had virtually expelled the French from North America and the Caribbean. But now crown and parliament faced the dilemma of paying the cost of the war and of maintaining and controlling a considerably larger empire. The most viable solution seemed to be an increase in taxes and the introduction of new taxes. Colonists in New England began boycotts of British merchandise and organized protests, especially of the dreaded stamp tax in 1765—all with considerable support from clergy and churches. Many thought the new colonial policy spelled the total destruction of the New England economy, though these claims are no doubt exaggerated. Sermons preached when the Stamp Act was repealed suggest the depth of colonial fears. Jonathan Mayhew, for example, saw the tax as a noose that would have strangled not only the economy but all colonial liberty. The pastor at Pepperell, Massachusetts, Joseph Emerson, called repeal a deliverance from slavery. Yet there was a hope that calm would prevail.

These hopes were shattered when rumors circulated that Parliament planned to settle a Church of England bishop in New England. Some believed the move likely as a consequence of French Canada's having become a British possession in 1763. In keeping with prevailing colonial policy, the Church of England received legal establishment in Canada, and colonial administrators were drawn only from the ranks of Church of England members. But the Protestant population in Canada was minuscule in comparison with the French Catholic population and would remain a decided minority for years, despite some increase from among Anglicans and Tory sympathizers who fled to Canada from those colonies that became the United States during the era of the American War for Independence. The rumors of a possible episcopal appointment stirred New Englanders' memories of persecution of their Puritan forebears at the hands of Archbishop Laud in the seventeenth century and quickened fears that an Anglican bishop in the New World would exercise the same combination of spiritual and civil authority that bishops enjoyed in Britain. Little matter that colonial Anglicans, except perhaps in the South, were eager for such an appointment in order to provide more viable leadership and to facilitate such matters as confirmation and ordination that required the ministrations of a bishop. In New England, Puritan clergy took to their pulpits and the press, attacking the proposal as an assault on religious liberty. Perhaps the most vocal was Charles Chauncy, who published several works defending the New England Way and condemning episcopacy.

For a variety of reasons, the proposal came to naught. Most likely it was simply forgotten as British authorities felt greater pressure to increase revenues to finance the government of a growing empire. But fears of religious oppression mounted again in 1774 with the passage of the Quebec Act. From the British point of view, the Quebec Act was an exercise in pragmatism. Much of the population of what had been French Canada was Roman Catholic. Even though Protestant sentiments prevailed among members of Parliament, there was much risk in alienating the former French colonists now that Britain was in control. Hence the new law guaranteed "the free exercise of the religion of the Church of Rome" in Quebec and provided for tax support for the Catholic churches there.[6] New Englanders had long regarded Roman Catholicism and particularly the pope as representing even greater tyranny and oppression than the Church of England and its bishops. What would be the next step? Legally establishing the Church of England in other colonies? The widespread conviction that a tyrannical Parliament had embarked on a course that would snuff out what Puritan Christians of every stripe saw as their religious liberty merged with the growing discontent with British political rule. Hence when cries for independence echoed through New England, most Congregationalists, Presbyterians, and Baptists gave their support to revolution.

## NEW ENGLAND IN 1776

As the colonial period in British North America drew to a close, Christianity in New England was caught in a maze of tensions. Many were distressed at the pluralism that clearly prevailed, for the presence of Baptists, Quakers, Anglicans, and even Jews meant that the notion of a holy commonwealth united in the pursuit of purity had crumbled. Yet some recognized that liberty to pursue the Puritan path of holiness meant granting that same liberty to others who had different notions of how one embarked on the journey to salvation. Even within the circle of those who still gave lip service to the Reformed tradition grounded in Calvinism tension prevailed. Among evangelicals and so-called liberals alike, the doctrine of election was disappearing as both parties espoused different brands of individualism—one the immediate work of the Spirit in the heart of the individuals to bring about redemption, the other the right of private judgment in matters of belief.

The presence of non-Puritans in New England also generated tensions. The Baptists, following the lead of Isaac Backus, were adamant in their insistence that the Puritan establishment, however fragmented, was just as tyrannical in its attitudes toward dissenters as Congregationalist and Presbyterian descendants of Puritans saw the Church of England and Rome. They may well have been accurate in their criticism. A smaller minority saw the tensions between all Christian affirmation and the way colonists regarded the native Indians and the Africans forced to immigrate as slaves. In New England, the most prominent person giving voice particularly to concerns about slavery was Samuel Hopkins (1721–1803) of Newport, Rhode Island. In 1776, Hopkins addressed his *Dialogue Concerning the Slavery of the Africans* to the same Continental Congress that issued the Declaration of Independence, noting that slavery was "very inconsistent" with Christian affirmation.

But in 1776, concerns in the political sector muffled the tensions within Christianity. Once the move to independence was under way, nearly all in New England, except for some of the adherents of the Church of England, set aside their differences to unite behind the American cause. Yet the fact of pluralism, the theological distinctions that were developing, the concerns over the proper relationship of church and state, questions about slavery and treatment of Native Americans, would all again come to the fore in the new United States.

# 20

## SOUTHERN AND CARIBBEAN CHRISTIANITY IN THE EIGHTEENTH CENTURY

As in New England, the eighteenth century brought considerable transformation to British colonies in the Caribbean and the Southern area of the North American mainland. Here, in theory at least, the Church of England generally enjoyed legal establishment, though as the century began, its strength did not equal its status. Such establishment was also to mark the foundation of the last of the British colonies organized on the North American mainland, Georgia. But in the eighteenth century, Anglicanism received a boost from the efforts of clergy and missionaries who operated under the aegis of the Society for the Propagation of the Gospel. Yet the Church of England in the colonies still differed from the establishment at home, and the century was to accent some of those differences, especially with regard to the power exercised by lay vestries and the absence of a bishop to oversee the work of the churches.

In the South, much more than in the Caribbean, the Great Awakening that brought such monumental upheaval to Christianity in New England was also to have an enduring impact, helping graft an evangelical dimension onto Southern religious life. The evangelical presence in Southern Christianity resulted as well from new patterns of migration, particularly the coming of Separate Baptists and Presbyterians along the eastern slopes of the Appalachian mountain chain. As in New England, the Awakening and the evangelical impulse would have ramifications for the political and economic life of the Southern colonies.

As well, the coming of other Christian groups helped make pluralism a fact of religious life in the area. Among the most significant groups, in terms of long-range impact, whose presence grew considerably in the eighteenth century were the Moravians. Thanks to the Moravians and others, Christians in the

334

South and Caribbean were nudged into re-examining their commitment to Christianizing both African slaves and Indians. In the process, difficult questions emerged here as elsewhere about the contradictions inherent in Christian affirmation and the maintenance of a slave-labor system.

Enlightenment influences also crept into Southern religious life, but in a manner quite different from their impact in New England. For Jonathan Edwards and other New England divines who were even more captivated by some Enlightenment ideas, the influence was more that of offering a fresh philosophical basis for supporting or refashioning traditional Christian doctrine. In the South, the Age of Reason was to have a more radical result as many Southern thinkers, especially those who were to be prominent in political life during the era of American independence, quietly abandoned traditional Christian thought for strains of Deism. Enlightenment and Awakening impulses were to work together, however, in cementing acceptance of the religious pluralism that already dominated Southern religious life.

When tensions between North American colonies and mother country grew in the 1760s and early 1770s, Christianity was to be part of the revolutionary cultural complex in the Southern colonies, but again in a different fashion than in New England. The association of the Anglican communion with England (the very fact that it was formally the Church of England) meant that the Southern religious establishments would be inextricably linked to the very forces of oppression identified with crown and parliament, and the majority of Anglican clergy in the South were disinclined to support independence. Hence the political tensions of the age, instead of imposing an artificial unity on the various Christian groups as in New England, were to highlight differences between them and issue in disarray for the Church of England. This disarray in turn accelerated the rise in prominence of more evangelical groups with roots in the Awakening and in the internal migration that brought Separate Baptists and others to the upcountry areas.

## ANGLICANISM AND THE WORK OF THE SOCIETY FOR THE PROPAGATION OF THE GOSPEL

What growth and stability came to Anglicanism in the Southern colonies in the first three-quarters of the eighteenth century resulted largely from the labors of commissary James Blair and missionaries sponsored by the Society for the Propagation of the Gospel (SPG). In Virginia, for example, Blair and the SPG worked together to provide ordained clergy for numerous Anglican parishes. When Blair died in 1743, all but two Anglican parishes in Virginia had a professional ministry, a situation radically different from that which prevailed at the opening of the century, when approximately half the parishes were without clergy. The established church in Virginia did reap some benefits from its support by the House of Burgesses. In the opening years of the eighteenth century, laws designed to ensure conformity served to make dissenters feel unwelcome, though many simply moved farther South to the Carolinas. Nevertheless, at least until the age of the Great Awakening, most of the leading families of the colony were nominally identified with the Church of England; the names of many who served in the House of Burgesses are also found on vestry rosters of colonial parishes. Indeed, the lay vestry became a key ingredient in Virginia Anglicanism, and the prerogatives of the vestry were zealously guarded. Since vestries frequently determined monetary settlements for rectors, they had ample means to control the clergy and were thus able in most cases to assure that the professional ministry reflected the interests of the parish constituency. As a result, few rectors, for example, were willing to raise troublesome questions about the incompatibility of Christian affirmation and the maintenance of a slave-labor system, and the feeble efforts of SPG missionaries and parish clergy to evangelize the African peoples were thus frequently thwarted. In the 1760s, when proposals to designate an Anglican bishop to serve the colonies resurfaced, members of the Church of England in the South were lukewarm if not outright hostile to the idea, largely because it represented a potential threat to the power lay vestries exercised.

In the Carolinas, the SPG faced a greater task in securing an Anglican presence, for the Church of England there began the century in an even weaker position. In 1701, the year the North Carolina assembly finally granted legal establishment to the Church of England, the SPG dispatched John Blair from England to visit the colony. Blair helped set up vestries, appoint lay readers in churches where there were no vestries, and exercised such priestly functions as baptizing children before returning to England. Here, however, political vicissitudes impeded passage and implementation of complementary legislation recognizing the vestries until 1741. Consequently, even though legal establishment prevailed, it did not become as deeply entrenched as in Virginia.

The Church of England made stronger gains in South Carolina, though not without controversy. There the assembly in 1704 enacted legislation that required complete conformity to the Church of England and also created a legal establishment. The latter act was what generated controversy since it not only dealt with the practical matters of outlining parish boundaries, organizing vestries, and providing tax support for the church but also created a commission of laity to oversee the clergy. Naturally, the clergy resisted the latter move. Samuel Thomas, who had come to South Carolina in 1702 as the first SPG-sponsored missionary, insisted after he returned to England in 1705 that the SPG refuse to send missionaries to the colony until the lay commission was abolished. The assembly repealed the law the following year, yielding to pressure from crown and parliament. Thereafter the SPG resumed its ministry, often attracting very well-qualified missionaries; in 1707, the bishop of London appointed the first commissary to serve in the colony. Within twenty years, thirteen parishes had been organized, though those in more rural areas lacked the prosperity and stability that came to parishes in the coastal region (especially Charleston).

Despite the impressive work by the SPG and the benefit of legal establishment, Anglicanism in the Carolinas did not become a vital force in the religious life of the region. Even before the beginning of the eighteenth century, dissenters of various stripes had begun to migrate to the Carolinas from Virginia because of the stricter laws against nonconformity that prevailed there. Indeed in some areas—perhaps in South Carolina as a whole—dissenters actually constituted a majority. Quakers, Baptists, and Presbyterians all made their way to North Carolina, with Quakers for a time early in the eighteenth century exerting considerable influence in the colonial assembly. By 1700 a Baptist congregation was flourishing in Charleston, the area where South Carolina Anglicanism was the most secure. Just before the close of the seventeenth century, the immigration of French Huguenots who were fleeing their homeland in the wake of the repeal of the Edict of Nantes brought another dissenting presence to South Carolina, though in time many of the Huguenots and their descendants would be absorbed into the Anglican communion. In part, the endurance of the Church of England in the Carolinas stemmed from its legal establishment and the dominance of Anglicans in political and economic affairs. There is precious little evidence indicating that Anglicanism offered a dynamic faith for most of those who were prominent in the public arena. Rather, affiliation with the Church of England became more and more a nominal allegiance seen as a routine concomitant to social standing.

The founding of Georgia, the last of the British colonies to be established on the North American mainland, provided challenges of a different sort for the SPG and the Church of England generally, both because of the circumstances of the colony's founding and the ambivalent support offered to SPG missionaries by local authorities. Although SPG founder Thomas Bray remained active with the society for only a few years after its founding, he retained an interest in several philanthropic and evangelizing activities. Two particular concerns were the inhuman conditions those trapped by poverty confronted when consigned to debtors' prisons and the lackluster efforts of Anglicans to bring the Christian gospel to African slaves in North America and the Caribbean. Those interests led to his becoming acquainted with General James Oglethorpe, who would ultimately lead the initial settlement of Georgia in 1733, and a group of associates Bray organized to advance those interests continued to work with others after Bray's death to secure governmental support for founding a colony between South Carolina and Florida.

But ensuring the viability of Georgia was not an easy proposition. In its first twenty years, the population grew to only three thousand, of whom about a thousand were slaves (though slavery was illegal prior to 1749), and growth would remain small throughout the colonial period. Then, too, the first decades of Georgia history were marked by frequent skirmishes with the Spanish settlements to the south that complicated attempts by an incompetent colonial administration to bring stability to the area. Nor was the colony readily able to establish a sound economic base. In view of all this, it is remarkable that there was any organized religious life at all.

The colony's trustees did provide for a chaplain under the auspices of the SPG, but the SPG's second appointee served only briefly because of lack of support from the colonial administration. Ironically, though, SPG missionaries gave Georgia its niche in colonial religious history, for in 1736 Charles and John Wesley began their ministries in Frederica and Savannah, respectively. Soon to be renowned for their leadership in the Methodist revivals in England, neither brother had a successful ministry in Georgia, largely because at this time both identified with a legalistic high-church Anglicanism that was ill suited for colonial life. Charles went back to England after only four months; John struggled for almost two years before admitting failure. But John Wesley did come into contact with adherents of two pietistic groups during his sojourn in Georgia, the Moravians and the Salzburgers (Lutherans who founded one of the few economically prosperous settlements in colonial Georgia, at Ebenezer). These associations would directly influence Wesley's own religious awakening after his return to England and help give birth to the Methodist movement.

Nonetheless, the SPG continued to send missionaries to Georgia. But even the transfer of colonial administration in 1752 from the proprietors to the crown and the legal establishment of the Church of England in 1758 did not bring much advance. A major problem was recruitment of well-qualified clergy, for few were willing to leave England to serve in a colony noted as a haven for paupers and European dissidents. While criticism of Anglican colonial clergy was widespread everywhere in the South during the colonial period, only in Georgia was that criticism generally on target. Those who did come, however, tended to be so fanatically devoted to things English that during the era of independence, the Church of England was very nearly destroyed by the exodus of Loyalist clergy from Georgia. The same was true for North Carolina.

In the Caribbean, the story of the Church of England in the eighteenth century is primarily one of maintaining a relatively weak status quo. Here too, nominal allegiance rather than vital faith was the order of the day among white colonists, whose primary interests were in expanding the sugar economy and securing larger numbers of African slaves to work the plantations. Had it not been for the legal establishment of the Church of England in the British Caribbean, Anglicanism most likely would have experienced considerable erosion. But here too the stimulus to religious renewal resulted from pluralism, for in the eighteenth century Moravians, Baptists, and then Methodists came to the Caribbean, bringing a more vigorous, evangelical understanding of Christianity with them and also directing considerable energy to work among the African population.

## THE MORAVIAN PRESENCE

One of the ostensible aims of the SPG was to evangelize among the native Indians as well as the African slaves. But the acute need to provide clergy for parishes (and frequently to assist in their financial support) dominated the work of the SPG in the colonial period. The first sustained effort to bring Christianity to the Indians was undertaken by Moravian immigrants from Germany, whose presence highlights the importance of ethnicity in understanding the contours of Christianity in British North America.

Moravian roots lie in the Hussite movement of the fifteenth century. Although Roman Catholic authorities during the Catholic Reformation or Counter-Reformation had attempted to rout out this evangelical, pietistic group, the *Unitas Fratrum* or Renewed Church of the United Brethren (more formal names for the Moravians) existed as an underground movement until they took refuge early in the eighteenth century in Saxony on lands owned by Count Nicholaus Ludwig Zinzendorf (1700–1760). Under Zinzendorf's influence, the Moravians blended features of Lutheran pietism with their own intense passion for evangelization. Indeed, this commitment to spreading the Christian gospel spurred the Moravians to regard Georgia and other areas of British North America as mission fields ripe for the harvest. In the 1730s, Moravian efforts got under way in Georgia, Pennsylvania, and South Carolina; two decades later, Moravians were to commence what became an enduring presence in North Carolina as well. In Georgia the initial work, guided by Augustus Gottlieb Spangenberg (1704–1792), focused on the Creeks and Cherokees, though the major Moravian efforts would finally center on the Six Nations of the Iroquois in Pennsylvania (after Bethlehem and Nazareth became the focal points of Moravian settlement).

Moravian success among the Indians brought opposition, however. In some areas, critics were suspicious of Moravians because of their non-English background and accused them of being agents of the papacy or of rival France. The Moravian refusal on religious grounds to swear oaths of allegiance also made them politically suspect. Then, too, merchants eager to reap profits from trade with the Indians, especially in providing the Native Americans with liquor, bemoaned a decline in business among those drawn to Moravian missions. The most difficult time for Moravian work came during the French and Indian Wars when British colonial authorities suspected the Moravians of collusion with the enemy even as Indian allies of the French launched attacks on Moravian mission settlements.

Early in the 1730s, Moravians also began to direct missionary efforts among the African slaves in the West Indies, first in colonies under Dutch dominion. The initial labors began in 1732 on St. Thomas, and by 1735 Moravians were seeking converts among the Arawak Indians and Africans in the Dutch-controlled areas along the northern coast of South America. By 1754, Moravians had extended their evangelizing enterprise to British Jamaica, where work among the slaves achieved only modest success despite initial support from some of the planters. At first, work on Antigua, begun in 1756, was likewise hardly prosperous, but the ministry of Peter Braun, who came to Antigua in 1789, ultimately made this mission one of the Moravians' most fruitful. Prior to 1776, Moravians also initiated work on Barbados; as in the Jamaica mission, success was limited. After 1760, Methodist missionaries also came to the British West Indies and in time gained considerably more converts to Christianity than did the Moravians.

But the Moravians did bring into focus the failure of Anglo-Christianity to carry out its presumed mandate to evangelize among the native American Indians and the Africans forced into slavery. On the mainland of British North America, what finally spurred greater interest, especially in bringing the Christian message to slaves, was the Great Awakening.

## THE GREAT AWAKENING IN THE SOUTHERN COLONIES

Georgia, of course, was the site of Awakening evangelist George Whitefield's initial work in North America, and it was in Savannah in January 1740 that he began his tour that would bring religious revitalization to most of British North America. Whitefield first came to Georgia in 1738, ostensibly to help establish an orphanage at Bethesda. He returned to Georgia the following year and laid plans for his ambitious itinerary through the colonies to raise funds for the orphanage. His tour, which caused such an uproar in New England and the middle colonies, included several stops in the Southern colonies, but without the same degree of enthusiasm or excitement among his audiences as evidenced elsewhere. In some cases, Whitefield faced outright opposition. Anglicans in Charleston, for example, effectively blocked Whitefield from receiving invitations to speak at churches in the area, and Whitefield himself was to note that in the South there was "no stirring among the dry bones" of nominal Christians.[1]

But Awakening did come to the South, albeit in a different form and with somewhat different consequences than elsewhere. Much of the difference relates to new patterns of settlement that were to lead to what historian Rhys Isaac called the "transformation of Virginia," a designation appropriate as well for the effects of new movement into the Piedmont regions of North and South Carolina.[2] European invaders in the seventeenth century had concentrated their settlements along the coast and along rivers east of the fall line marking the limits of their navigability. In the opening decades of the eighteenth century, only a few—mostly small landowners—had come into the fertile valley between the Alleghenies and the Blue Ridge. But after 1730 there was to be a significant migration into that area comprised mostly of Scotch-Irish and Germans coming south from Pennsylvania. Their presence was ultimately to lead to much political tension, as the newcomers sought an appropriate voice in colonial governance and met resistance from those in whose hands power had been concentrated for generations. Their presence was also to imprint an evangelical style on Southern Christianity that has endured to the twentieth century. The story of the Great Awakening in the Southern colonies belongs more to these settlers, especially to Separate Baptists and Presbyterians, than to itinerants like Whitefield and is thus less a tale of revival than, in Sydney Ahlstrom's words, "an immense missionary enterprise."[3]

Early signs of evangelical stirrings along the Blue Ridge of Virginia came in the work of William Robinson, commissioned by the New Brunswick (New Jersey) presbytery—itself aligned with the revival cause—as a missionary to western Virginia and the Carolinas. While there were already a few Presbyterian clergy in the area, they were decidedly of an "Old Side" nonrevivalistic bent. Robinson's itineracy in 1742–1743 garnered a significant positive response, leading other "New Side" Presbyterians such as Gilbert Tennent to make preaching tours in the area. But greater expansion of a revivalistic Presbyterianism was to come farther east, in Virginia's Hanover County. There Samuel Morris, a deeply committed layman, had for several years led a small revival endeavor that was to move into the Presbyterian orbit when the dynamic Presbyterian preacher Samuel Davies (1723–1761) came to Hanover County late in the 1740s. For more than a decade Davies was to evangelize tirelessly, not only among the white population of Hanover County but also among Africans and Indians. When Davies left Virginia to assume the presidency of the College of New Jersey (Princeton) after the death of Jonathan Edwards, this revival movement quickly faded, and in time many of those who identified with Davies's evangelical Presbyterianism would be absorbed into the growing Baptist movement.

For many years, historians of the Awakening looked primarily at the ministry of Samuel Davies as the focal point of the Great Awakening in the South. More recently, however, greater attention has been given to revivalism associated with the Separate Baptists who drew even larger numbers of those settling the Southern frontier than did the Presbyterians. Baptists had come into the back country of Virginia shortly after 1700, and there are records of organized Baptist congregations in both Virginia and North Carolina before 1730. These early Baptists trace their religious lineage to the English General Baptists, folk who rejected much Calvinist doctrine and espoused the more Arminian notion of the involvement of the human will in salvation. While the later organization of the Baptist movement in the South was to revolve primarily among these General Baptists (later called Regular Baptists), the burst of evangelical Baptist growth came from the Separate Baptists.

The key individuals whose missionary work boosted the Baptist cause, Shubal Stearns and his brother-in-law Daniel Marshall, had religious roots in the Great Awakening in New England. Stearns, for example, traced his conversion experience to George Whitefield's second tour of New England in 1745 and journeyed south to the area around what is now Winchester, West Virginia, in 1754. Marshall, after laboring briefly as a missionary among the Mohawk

Indians, joined Stearns later that year. At first, their evangelizing efforts reaped only modest success, but in 1755 they made their way to the North Carolina Piedmont. Within five years, these indefatigable itinerants had organized at least ten congregations. Stearns and Marshall by no means restricted their work to North Carolina. They were instrumental in promoting the Baptist gospel in both the Virginia back country and South Carolina, and in 1771, the year Stearns died, Marshall moved on to Georgia, where he organized the first Baptist congregation in that colony.

While Baptist expansion was impressive, it did not occur without opposition that was as enmeshed in political difficulties as in religious hostility from the established Church of England. Simply put, population growth on the frontier greatly exceeded that of the more longstanding settlements along the coast. But political power, particularly representation in the colonial assemblies, had not shifted to reflect the new demographics. Of course, those who long wielded the reins of political power were generally at least nominally affiliated with the established church. Hence those on the frontier were perceived as both a political and a religious threat to the status quo. While moves to quash the Baptist movement often formally revolved around laws prohibiting dissent, they were equally efforts to contain demands for equal representation in the colonial assemblies. In Virginia, attempts to crush the Baptists got under way in 1768, but with little success. By 1776, Baptist congregations could be found in approximately half the counties in Virginia. In North Carolina, repression was temporarily more successful as military force was used in 1771 to put down the rebellious Regulators, frontiersmen agitating for their presumed political rights.

The Baptist victory on the southern frontier had numerous long-term consequences, the most important of which was stamping an evangelical cast on Protestant Christianity in the South. Revival techniques became a matter of course, as did reliance on a ministry that depended more on individuals who could testify to a profound personal religious experience than on those who received education for professional ministry. A continuing suspicion of formal creeds permitted Baptists to fuse apparently contradictory theological positions; on a popular level, many espoused both the Arminian notion of freedom of the human will in the matter of salvation and the Calvinist idea of predestination. Renowned Baptist leader John Leland, who came to Virginia in 1776 and labored there for fifteen years, captured that doctrinal fusion when he wrote: "I conclude that the *eternal purposes* of God, and the *freedom of the human will*, are both eternal truths; and it is a matter of fact, that the preaching that has been most blessed of God, and most profitable to men, is *the doctrine of sovereign grace in the salvation of souls, mixed with a little of what is called Arminianism*."[4] By the late 1760s, the older General Baptists and the Separate Baptists had begun to work together, though the upheavals that came with the American Revolution delayed formal merger until, in the aftermath of the independence movement, Baptist unity seemed essential in the struggle to dismantle the Anglican establishment and assure religious liberty.

As vital as was the Baptist presence in nurturing Southern evangelical Christianity, other religious impulses in time furthered the cause. In 1763, for example, Anglican Devereux Jarratt (1733–1801) began an evangelical ministry within the established Church of England following his ordination in London. Brought to a vital faith by Presbyterian friends, Jarratt believed that the evangelical style was compatible with Anglican belief and practice and soon found himself at the center of an Anglican revival movement in Dinwiddie County. Within a few years, Methodist itinerants had come into the area and launched their own revival efforts. Since the fledgling American Methodist movement saw itself as an extension of Anglicanism (Methodist founder John Wesley himself never left the Church of England), Jarratt and the Methodists often worked together, and a combined revival in 1776, the year American independence was declared, marked the high point of evangelical Anglicanism in the colonial period. Indeed, in 1776 nearly 80 percent of colonial Methodists in North America were to be found in the South.

In New England, the Great Awakening had prompted some rethinking of ministry to the native American Indians; in the South, the evangelical awakening stimulated similar concerns. But here the more significant impact was in the evangelizing of Africans caught in the system of chattel slavery that provided the base for much of the region's agricultural economy.

## SLAVE CHRISTIANITY IN THE COLONIAL PERIOD

From its inception in 1701, the SPG had as one of its aims carrying the Christian gospel to African slaves, but in reality SPG missionaries found their time and energy consumed in ministry to the white Anglican population and consequently did little more than urge owners to be mindful of their duty to seek the conversion of their slaves. But that the slaveholders were reluctant to do, for they feared that conversion and subsequent baptism would bring a de facto equality and thereby shatter the master–slave relationship. At the same time, the slave system was designed to undermine the indigenous religions Africans brought with them to the New World, for separating Africans who shared a common tribal religious and kinship heritage became a powerful mechanism to break the humanity of Africans and mold them into subservient slaves. That process, however, was never as successful as slaveowners believed, for in the slave quarters remnants of tribal rituals endured and in time fused with the evangelical Christianity of the Awakening era to give a distinctive cast to black Christianity in British North America. In some areas where there was a heavy concentration of slaves, such as the sea islands off the coast of Georgia and South Carolina, more of the West African religious patterns endured.

Work among the Southern slave population was another way the evangelical Awakening of the eighteenth century gradually undermined the established order. Many who preached to the slaves began to recognize the horrors of chattel slavery, though few called for abolition—at least in the eighteenth century—since they recognized that to do so would arouse the opposition of the slaveholders and likely bring an immediate end to their work. But in evangelizing among the Africans, these preachers helped plant the religious roots of the abolitionist movement that would blossom in the nineteenth century and instilled in their slave converts abiding notions of liberty and freedom. Among those associated with Awakening currents, Presbyterian Samuel Davies, for example, welcomed slaves in his revivals and churches, and the records suggest that several hundred responded to his ministry in Virginia in the 1750s. Baptists also eagerly sought to take the message of Christian salvation to African slaves, as did Methodist itinerants once they moved into the South. Methodist work among slaves was also prominent in the British West Indies after 1760 when white lawyer-planter Nathaniel Gilbert, from Antigua, and two of his slaves returned there after having heard John Wesley's preaching while visiting in England. In Antigua, Methodists and Moravians worked together among the slaves, with the result that the island became a center of Protestant Christianity with the majority of its adherents drawn from the ranks of African slaves.

In many ways, the evangelical style of the Awakening was more suited for ministry among slaves than the formalism associated with the Church of England. The emphasis on feeling, on intense personal religious experience, evoked a more powerful response than decorous worship according to the *Book of Common Prayer.* Evangelicals preached a simple gospel of the heart that resonated with the experience of those denied access to education, and the acceptance of emotional expression in evangelical circles to some extent drew on the rich tradition of African ritual patterns. No doubt, too, the promise of heavenly reward for those who accepted the message of salvation went a long way to assuage the oppression encountered under slavery. In time, slaveholders would twist the Christian emphasis on obedience to the ways of God into a message of compliance with the orders and whims of human masters and attempt to use Christianity as a means to keep slaves in bondage.

African converts in turn helped shape what has been called the "invisible institution," that singular expression of Christianity molded by the experience of slavery. Since evangelicals regarded that any Christian called to preach was qualified to do so, African Christians began to proclaim the gospel to one another as they labored in the fields and gathered together in their quarters at the close of the day. While this "invisible institution" would become a more vital dimension of black Christianity in the nineteenth century, after the Great Revival of the opening years of that century gave fresh impetus to the evangelical cause, it began among those who responded to the Baptist and Methodist preachers in the age of the Awakening.

The evangelical movement among blacks and whites alike indirectly benefited from the lack of religious vitality within much of Southern Anglicanism. With allegiance to the Church of England more nominal than a symbol of deep religious commitment and the established church itself more and more identified with the colonial "aristocracy," Anglicanism was hardly poised to minister to the spiritual needs of those on the periphery of the social order, whether Africans or white migrants moving into the upcountry. Evangelicalism filled the void left by the religious establishment. But even among those affiliated with the Church of England, the intellectual currents of the Age of Reason were challenging traditional notions of what it meant to be religious in very different ways than the evangelical movement challenged the prevailing order of both church and society.

## ENLIGHTENMENT RELIGION

Many of the individuals of the mythic "founding generation" of the United States drank deeply from the wells of the Enlightenment, including George Washington and especially Thomas Jefferson. Of course, others known more for their contributions to politics than to religion from other regions of British North America were equally as influenced. One thinks immediately of New England's John Adams, whose concerns for political philosophy bore a distinct Enlightenment cast, and of Pennsylvania's Benjamin Franklin, whose years of living in Europe as a representative of the colonies brought firsthand acquaintance with many who sought to unravel the implications of the Age of Reason. Thomas Jefferson (1743–1826), however, left behind the most extensive written records that treat religion, that reveal his understanding of a Christianity transformed by the Enlightenment.

For all of them, the primary aim of Christianity was not so much the salvation of souls as the inculcation of moral virtues that would create a responsible citizenry. This rationalist approach readily cast aside the dogma of Calvinism, particularly the notion of predestination, and exalted in its place a human being free to follow reason wherever it led in the pursuit of truth. Whatever smacked of superstition, whether Scripture or sacraments, was quietly left behind. Hence Jefferson felt free to edit portions of the Christian Scriptures, excising all that reeked of the irrational and retaining only that which promoted a reasonable public morality.

One sees Enlightenment influence even in the way Jefferson, Washington, and others spoke of God. Their language derived more from the sense of order that Enlightenment folk thought prevailed in nature than from sacred writ. God was Providence and Supreme Ruler who oversaw the grand events of time and place, not the personal lord of patriarchs and prophets who protested injustice and rewarded the righteous while punishing the wicked. Hence it is not inaccurate to label Jefferson, Washington, and their ideological compatriots Deists who affirmed the existence of a divine architect of the universe because such was useful in advancing public morality. Christ was respected rather than revered, the exemplar of the morality that could be intuited by all rational human beings more than the divine Son of God whose crucifixion paved the way for human salvation. This moral philosophy accordingly downplayed doctrinal and denominational differences; such obscured the elements common to all forms of Christianity—indeed to all religions—that focus on moral behavior.

In retrospect, what was critical about this Enlightenment religion was the way it dovetailed with the emphasis on individual responsibility and freedom of choice directly or indirectly advocated by the evangelicals rooted in the Awakening who would have rejected totally its ideological underpinnings. It was the individual who in freedom chose to follow reason; it was the individual in freedom who chose to accept or reject the offer of Christian salvation. Thus for the enlightened as well as the evangelical, particulars of belief became a matter of the private sphere. Virtue and morality in the public sphere could flow as easily from one as from the other. Hence the public philosophy of a Jefferson could be endorsed by virtually all and set the stage for those British North American colonies on the brink of revolution to become, in Sidney Mead's rephrasing of Gilbert Chesterton, a "nation with the soul of a church."[5] Reason and faith alike demanded freedom, whether it be freedom from a tyrannical religious establishment and its bishops or freedom from a tyrannical king and parliament who no longer promoted the common welfare of all. Few, of course, admitted that chattel slavery was incompatible with the life of reason, just as few more orthodox Christians recognized the incongruity between faith and slavery. But when revolution came, Enlightenment and evangelicalism set aside any such concerns and joined hands in the cause of American independence.

## THE SOUTHERN COLONIES IN 1776

Christianity in the South in 1776 was rather different than it had been in the opening years of the eighteenth century, when the Society for the Propagation of the Gospel laid plans to boost the cause of the established Church of England and extend its ministry to Indians and slaves. But the transformation that occurred frequently drew on trends and patterns rooted in the first century of colonial conquest. Despite legal establishment, Anglicans could never eliminate the presence of religious dissent, and by 1776, pluralism in the sense that multiple Christian bodies would exist side by side had become as firmly entrenched in the South as it had in New England. Pluralism resulted in part from the migration of groups with an ethnic-religious base such as the Moravians. In part it came with the rapid rise of the Baptists, the presence of more and more Presbyterians, and then the arrival of Methodist itinerants who would imprint an evangelical style on Christianity in the South. The evangelicalism of the Awakening endowed Southern Christianity with an abiding appreciation of the place of feeling and emotion in religion. It made the revival an enduring feature of the Southern religious landscape and the conversion experience the basic starting point of the religious life. Ironically, in time evangelicalism would itself become something of a de facto religious establishment in much of the South and in the twentieth century encounter many of the same problems confronted by the Church of England in the eighteenth.

Connections between Anglicanism and the mother country meant that independence would not only lead to the loss of establishment privileges but would also leave the Church of England in the United States in disarray as many clergy—and not a few of the laity for whom Anglican affiliation was more than a nominal matter—identified with the Loyalist cause and sought refuge elsewhere. When the age of revolution closed, the Church of England confronted a more severe shortage of clergy than had ever prevailed in the colonial period. But the reliance on lay vestries and the reluctance to grant seemingly limitless power to priests and bishops that had kept the Church of England relatively weak would become important components in rebuilding what became the Protestant Episcopal Church in the United States.

The religious freedom from religious establishment sought by Baptists and the intellectual freedom favored by Enlightenment rationalists would come together to bring an end to any legal establishment of a single religious denomination in the South once new structures of government were in place. That same freedom would provide greater impetus in the nineteenth century for evangelicals, especially Baptists and Methodists, to step up their labors among the African slaves. In turn, the "invisible institution" that was born in the slave experience would likewise continue to meet the religious needs of those yet denied freedom in the new nation and become a vital ingredient in the mounting movement toward abolition of chattel slavery.

Next to the evangelical style, what most endured from Christianity in the South in the eighteenth century was the Enlightenment morality fostered by the likes of Jefferson and Washington. The emphasis on morality and public virtue reflected not only the major thrust of "rational Christianity," but also the basis on which the new nation began to build a common identity distinct from that which had prevailed when this region had been part of the far-flung British colonial empire. Indeed, Enlightenment morality became a public religion. This civil religion was never to displace Christianity but would exist alongside the churches almost in a symbiotic relationship with them in the Republic that would make its motto "In God We Trust."

# 21

## THE MAKING OF REFORMED AMERICA: CHRISTIANITY IN THE MIDDLE COLONIES IN THE EIGHTEENTH CENTURY

Forces that shaped Christianity in New England, the Southern colonies, and the Caribbean in the eighteenth century also had a lasting impact on Christianity in the middle colonies in British North America. But there additional factors were to add to the diversity of Christian expression in a region where pluralism had already made deep inroads in the seventeenth century. A steady influx of immigrants from Germany brought ever greater ethnic richness to Quaker Pennsylvania and adjacent areas. Some, such as the Dunkers and Mennonites, hoped to find in the British North American empire simply the space to live out their beliefs without undue influence from others. Others, such as the German Reformed and Lutherans, infused religious life in the middle colonies with the pietism that had enlivened Christianity at home. Meanwhile, the Quakers themselves saw their political influence (but not their economic influence) wane as mounting concern over relations with the French and their Indian allies and then the surge for American independence challenged the Quaker commitment to pacifism and nonviolence. Then too there came increasing numbers of Scotch-Irish immigrants (the most numerous group after 1700), who brought with them an abiding commitment to Calvinist doctrine tempered by the philosophy of Common Sense Realism that would soon dominate American philosophy.

The Church of England, enjoying the privileges of establishment in New York, made significant gains there, especially in areas on Long Island and in Westchester County, as well as in New Jersey and Pennsylvania. Anglican growth in the middle colonies was to spur interest in securing appointment of a

Church of England bishop to oversee the spiritual welfare of communicants and spark a controversy that would be felt throughout the British colonies that became the United States. Roman Catholicism was also to make fresh inroads in the middle colonies in the eighteenth century, confronting considerable hostility in New York but reaping the benefits of the broad toleration characteristic of William Penn's "holy experiment" in Pennsylvania.

The revivals of the Great Awakening that transformed New England religious life in the 1740s and nurtured the evangelical presence in the Southern colonies a decade later likewise swept through much of the middle colony region. Among those of Presbyterian persuasion, the revivals were to have especially profound repercussions. On the one hand, the stimulus they gave to religious activity and commitment would join with the effect of increasing immigration of persons in the Reformed heritage to make the middle colonies the center of Reformed Protestantism in British North America, creating what Fred Hood has called "Reformed America."[1] On the other hand, the call for conversion characteristic of revival preaching would also prompt controversy and division as the more doctrinaire recognized the threat to the notion of predestination implicit in the evangelical message.

By the time American independence was declared, the middle colonies had become a virtual paradigm of the religious complexion of the new nation. While the same forces were at work throughout the nation, nowhere was pluralism more firmly entrenched than in the middle colonies; nowhere was the emphasis on personal religious experience—whether the quiet awareness of the Quaker light within, the pietistic inner assurance of divine forgiveness, or the intensity of evangelical conversion—more taken for granted as the focus of the religious life.

## THE MANY FACES OF CHRISTIANITY IN PENNSYLVANIA

Much of the transformation that marks the Quaker story in Pennsylvania and nearby New Jersey in the eighteenth century has roots in both the presence of ever-larger numbers of non-Quakers and the character of the Quaker testimony itself. In its origins, Quakerism exemplified many of the qualities generations of sociologists have assigned to the "religious sect." That is, Quakers viewed themselves as a minority called out from among a corrupt church and society to act as a leaven, an example of what the Christian life was all about. Quaker pacifism and nonviolence, while central to Quaker self-understanding in the early generations, represented as much a challenge to the accepted modus operandi of societies and nations as it did a positive doctrine in its own right. Consequently, the very nature of the Quaker experience left believers ill equipped to be an unofficial religious and political establishment in Penn's colony. When the population was small and space for expansion seemingly limitless, this sectarian perspective was better able to translate its spiritual

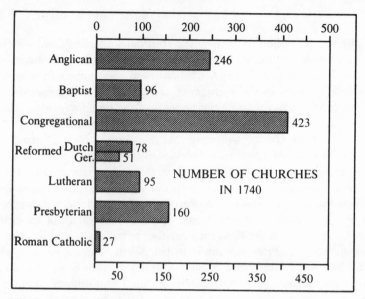

Number of Churches, 1740

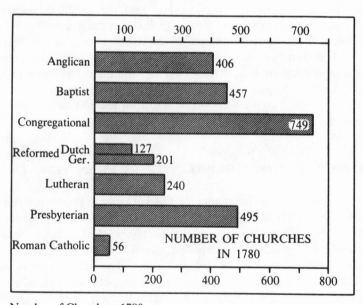

Number of Churches, 1780

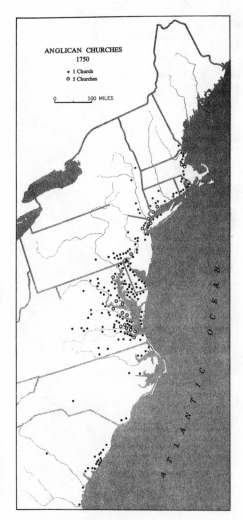

Anglican Churches, 1750                    Baptist Churches, 1750

ideals into public policy, especially in welcoming other persecuted minorities
within its borders where they could live in relative isolation from others.

But the growth of the colony could not but raise nettlesome issues. Settlers
who lived on the fringes of colonial settlement, while often sharing the sectarian mind set of the Quaker colonial leadership, felt very different threats
from the Indian groups being gradually displaced and the slow movement of
the French southward from Canada than did Quaker merchant families ensconced in comfortable Philadelphia homes. Would Quaker legislators not
provide for their defense? Was not security part of the invitation to join the

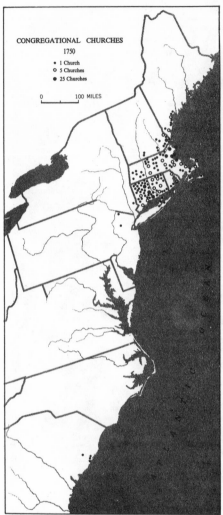

Congregational Churches, 1750

Lutheran Churches, 1750 (One Church also on St. Simon's Island, Georgia)

"holy experiment"? Then, too, as crown and parliament called for taxes and militia to support the imperial struggle with the French and their Indian allies three times prior to midcentury, the tension inherent in espousing the "peace testimony" while leading a colonial government troubled many Friends. By midcentury, even though Quakers still dominated the colonial assembly, they were clearly a minority of the population; pressures from the majority combined with those from crown and parliament to force a decision. When the final colonial confrontation between Britain and France erupted in 1756, Quakers reluctantly gave up the reins of government in an attempt to remain faithful to

Presbyterian Churches, 1750

Reformed Churches, 1750

their belief. But they did not retreat from dominance in the economic life of the colony. The shift was one, in Frederick B. Tolles's classic phrase, from meeting house to counting house, for Quaker merchants continued to control much of the colonial economy. But that shift was in time to raise other internal questions, since to some it appeared that economic success had replaced the simple life of following the inner light and that accommodation to the ways of the world had occurred despite retreat from the political sector. It was perhaps easier to maintain the Quaker sectarian critique of society as part of a persecuted minority than as part of an economic elite.

Roman Catholic Churches, 1750

At the same time, some Friends were intent on exposing the manifold ways in which nominal Christians failed to put into action the implications of their faith. In the eighteenth century, none was more committed to forcing Quakers and others to see their shortcomings in this arena than John Woolman (1720–1772). Clerk of the Friends' Quarterly Meeting in Burlington County, New Jersey, for nearly forty years, Woolman in 1746 began travels that would continue for the rest of his life to urge not only Quaker communities but also those living in New England, Virginia, and the Carolinas to recognize the evils of slavery. Indeed, Woolman was the most outspoken colonial critic of slavery, and his *Considerations on the Keeping of Negroes*, written in two parts in 1754 and 1762, remains the foremost eighteenth-century American statement on the inhumanity of slavery and the slave trade. Woolman also argued that the French and Indian war represented a divine judgment against a people more committed to greed and riches, epitomized by the presence of slavery, than to the simple truth of Christianity, and his *Plea for the Poor* eloquently argued for the wealthy to use their resources for the benefit of those in need. While Woolman's labors led many Rhode Island Quaker shipowners to cease using their ships for the transport of slaves, his major achievement lay in convincing the Philadelphia Yearly Meeting of Friends to adopt measures that prohibited members from owning slaves.

John Woolman was a signal voice within the Quaker fold whose condemnation of Quaker acquiescence to the ways of the world revealed the difficulty of retaining a sectarian criticism of culture when the sect itself dominated the political and economic sectors. External forces, especially the growth of ethnic German sects in Pennsylvania, raised similar issues from another perspective. While many of these groups were sympathetic to the Quaker peace testimony (indeed, many shared the Quaker aversion to war and things military), their growth was one factor that propelled concerns for the security of colonial frontier settlements.

Quakers and Mennonites had worked together to make Germantown, then a village outside Philadelphia, a thriving settlement even before the close of the seventeenth century and had in 1686 built a common meetinghouse where joint services were held until 1690. But the growth of both groups had led to the construction of separate facilities, with the Quaker meetinghouse opening in 1705 and the Mennonite counterpart in 1708. The Mennonites took an active interest in political matters only briefly, and as Mennonite immigration (particularly from Switzerland) increased in the early decades of the eighteenth century, they gradually withdrew from public life. They also began to withdraw geographically, so that by 1760, when Mennonite immigration to the New World dropped to a trickle, the rural frontier area of Lancaster County had become the locus of the Mennonite presence in Pennsylvania. To the same area came spiritual cousins of the Mennonites, the more conservative followers of Jacob Amman known as the Amish, beginning in 1727. Both shared the Quaker aversion to war, and both remained opposed to the use of military power in any form. But their presence on the frontier, where the French and Indian threat was more pronounced, provided ample fuel for critics of Quaker politicians accused of failing to provide adequately for the defense of the people. Thus unwittingly these historic "peace churches" helped bring the demise of the "holy experiment" in a governmental sense when Quakers left the colonial assembly during the Seven Years' War.

By then numerous other clusters of German immigrants, most of a pietistic strain, had also found a home in Pennsylvania, adding to the pluralism characteristic of the colony. Among the earliest to arrive were those popularly known as the Dunkers, more formally called the Church of the Brethren. Founded by Alexander Mack (1679–1735), the Dunkers owed their designation to the practice of baptism (or rebaptism) by triple immersion in flowing water, but they also revived several other early Christian practices such as foot-washing. In 1719, the first Dunkers migrated to Germantown under the leadership of Peter Becker, though they did not organize as a community until 1722. By the end of the decade, virtually all the Brethren had made the transatlantic journey to North America, forming communities not only in Pennsylvania but also in neighboring Maryland and New Jersey. To the Dunkers belongs the distinction of publishing in 1743 the first Western-language Bible printed in North America. From the Dunker fold also emerged what became a vibrant German cultural communitarian endeavor, the Ephrata Community, led by Dunker convert Conrad Beissel (1691–1768). A model for later communitarian endeavors, the Ephrata Community insisted on separation of the sexes, attempted to develop a self-sufficient community economy, and distinguished itself by celebrating a literal Sabbath on Saturday. Largely because of the charismatic personality of Beissel, Ephrata for a time appeared well on its way to dominating the German Christian presence in Pennsylvania. But its reliance on Beissel's leadership was also its downfall, for the community began to disintegrate after his death and completely dissolved within thirty years.

The influence of the Moravians has been more enduring. Although these German pietists originally intended to settle in Georgia, several of the initial group of Moravian migrants that arrived in 1735 made their way to Philadelphia and from there ultimately made their spiritual center in Bethlehem, so named by Moravian founder Count Nicholaus Ludwig Zinzendorf in 1741. Zinzendorf had a broad ecumenical vision, hoping that the simple devotional and communal life of the Moravians (known in Europe as the Unitas Fratrum) would transcend the divisions in doctrine and practice that defined European Protestant Christianity, but those divisions were so deeply imbedded in colonial life that the Moravians for a time became more a communitarian endeavor withdrawn from the larger society. The Moravians, however, did mount an impressive ministry among the Indians throughout much of British North America until the French and Indian Wars, then frontier skirmishes as European conquest moved ever westward, and finally in the nineteenth century the United States policy of Indian removal made such work virtually impossible. Close ties with fellow believers in Europe also hampered Moravian growth in North America since the American communities for decades helped support the work of the Unitas Fratrum across the Atlantic. But the devotional life of the Moravians, especially as expressed in hymnody, has had a continuing influence on both American and European Christianity.

For a time, another German pietistic sect, the Schwenckfelders, benefited from the commitment of Zinzendorf to a path of simple spirituality. Named after Kaspar Schwenckfeld von Ossig (1489–1561), a Christian mystic of the age of the Reformation, the Schwenckfelders represented a small, scattered movement existing under threat of persecution in Catholic areas of Germany when they sought refuge on Zinzendorf's estate in the mid-1720s. Although the Schwenckfelders received a land grant in Georgia in 1734, at Zinzendorf's urging they began to migrate to Pennsylvania instead. But unlike the Moravians or the Dunkers, the Schwenckfelders did not busy themselves with organizing churches or establishing communitarian settlements. Rather, their emphasis on inner spirituality worked against any form of institutionalization, with the result that the Schwenckfelders did not even erect any buildings for worship until the time of the American War for Independence, and the ongoing emphasis on individual cultivation of the religious life has kept both numbers and influence small.

Not all German immigrants to Pennsylvania in the eighteenth century came from the pietist ranks. While a handful of German Lutherans had come to Pennsylvania in the early days of colonial settlement there, the major Lutheran migration came after the mid-1730s when Lutheran leaders in Halle (Germany) laid plans to send a missionary to the colonies. While Lutherans in Pennsylvania had long been asking for assistance, what probably prompted action was the arrival of the Moravian Count Zinzendorf in Pennsylvania, since Zinzendorf himself claimed to be a Lutheran pastor. The individual dispatched to oversee Lutheran work in the colonies was Henry Melchior Muhlenberg (1711–1787), who arrived in Charleston, South Carolina, in September 1742. After visiting the Salzburger Lutheran community in Georgia, Muhlenberg headed to Philadelphia, where he began a ministry among Lutherans that would continue until his death. Adopting the technique later associated with the Methodist circuit riders on the frontier, Muhlenberg launched an aggressive agenda of regularly traveling among the enclaves of Lutherans in eastern Pennsylvania and Maryland, teaching, preaching, counseling with other pastors of Lutheran persuasion, and supervising the construction of churches. In 1748, Swedish and German Lutheran pastors and lay delegates who accepted Muhlenberg's invitation to come to Philadelphia for the consecration of St. Michael's Church formed the Pennsylvania Ministerium. This event, which marks the beginnings of the formal organization of American Lutheranism, came at a propitious time, for records indicate that the following year alone, more than ten thousand German immigrants entered the colonies through the port of Philadelphia. Although the early work of the ministerium was somewhat irregular, the association of Muhlenberg and the German Lutheran community with the Swedish Lutherans of New York (led by Karl Magnus von Wragel from 1759 to 1768) brought considerable stability to the American churches and left them well prepared for expansion southward into Virginia and North Carolina in the 1770s.

## ANGLICANS AND CATHOLICS IN THE MIDDLE COLONIES

New York was not only the organizational center for the Swedish churches, it was also the symbolic heart of the Anglican presence in the middle colonies since there it enjoyed the privileges of legal establishment. As elsewhere in the British North American colonies that became the United States, the Church of England in the middle colonies in the eighteenth century owed much of its vibrancy to the labors of those who served under the Society for the Propagation of the Gospel. In the decades prior to the American Revolution, for example, more than fifty SPG missionaries promoted the Anglican cause in New York alone. Their efforts were largely responsible for laying a solid foundation for the Church of England on Long Island and in Westchester County, just north of the city of New York. In New York, too, the SPG also began ministry among the Native Americans—Indian missions had been one of the original aims of the society. But these efforts were generally unsuccessful prior to the close of the French and Indian Wars since the colonial government frowned on them, believing most Indians were allied with the French enemy.

In Pennsylvania, for the first two decades of the eighteenth century much of the Anglican work revolved around the ministry of Evan Evans, a Welsh priest sent to Philadelphia by the bishop of London. As rector of Christ Church in Philadelphia from 1700 to 1718, Evans was able to draw some Welsh immigrants into the Anglican communion and to bring many of the disgruntled Quaker followers of George Keith into the church as well as to help organize Anglican churches in outlying areas in both Pennsylvania and Delaware. After Evans retired from Christ Church in 1718, SPG missionaries carried on Anglican work in the area until the American Revolution, though only a handful of parishes outside Philadelphia itself functioned on a regular basis.

Perhaps the most significant strengthening of Anglicanism in the middle colonies in the eighteenth century came in New Jersey. In 1702, the year West Jersey and East Jersey were united into one crown colony, former Quaker George Keith and John Talbot arrived as the first SPG missionaries. Talbot's ministry began with the founding of an Anglican parish in Burlington, but it took him throughout New Jersey in an effort to organize Anglican churches. His strident royalism and his commitment to a high church perspective frequently embroiled Talbot in controversy, but he early on recognized that if Anglican work were ever to flourish in Britain's North American colonies, it was essential that there be a resident bishop to administer the work and provide communicants with the full range of liturgical offices integral to the Anglican understanding of the church. That vision was to bring another Anglican into public view, for Thomas Bradbury Chandler, rector of St. John's Church in Elizabethtown, New Jersey, who was to become an ardent Loyalist during the Revolution and later the first Anglican bishop of Nova Scotia, became an outspoken advocate of the need for a bishop. What first brought Chandler into the fray was the colonial response to a sermon preached by the bishop of Landaff at the anniversary meeting of the SPG in England. The sermon renewed the call for establishing an American episcopate and quickly brought printed attacks in the colonies, the most strident of which came from liberal Boston Congregationalist pastor Charles Chauncy. In the late 1760s and early 1770s, Chandler wrote three treatises in which he tried both to build the case for the necessity of an American Anglican episcopate and to disarm critics by assuring them that a colonial bishop would have only ecclesiastical duties and none of the civil responsibilities exercised by bishops in England that many New England colonists associated with repression of their forebears. But support for a colonial bishop was basically limited to Anglicans in the middle colonies; even Southern Anglicans were wary of having a bishop in residence since they recognized that the ecclesiastical authority of a bishop would weaken the control of lay vestries in Southern parishes. The controversy ended, however, without the appointment of a colonial bishop once the American Revolution made political rather than religious matters the priority.

Without a bishop, of course, candidates for the priesthood in the Church of England had to travel across the Atlantic for ordination. Indeed, until well into the eighteenth century, the College of William and Mary in Virginia remained the only academic institution in the colonies sponsored by Anglicans and hence the only school where prospective Anglican clergy might receive appropriate preliminary training for the priesthood. Anglicans and others with an interest in education in the middle colonies sought to rectify that situation. In 1740, largely at the behest of Benjamin Franklin, a charter was obtained for the Philadelphia College and Academy, although little came of the school for more than a decade. It was not until 1754, when Anglican priest William White became provost and spearheaded efforts the following year to secure a new charter, that what became the University of Pennsylvania became a viable educational institution. Also in 1754, a royal charter was granted to King's College (now Columbia University) in New York. Support from Anglicans was vital to the establishment of both schools, and both in varying degrees reflected the educational theories of Bishop George Berkeley, who had resided in Rhode Island from 1729 to 1731. But neither institution was characterized by the same intensity of religious orientation that had marked the early years of other colonial colleges, yet both became important conduits for training many who would help shape American Anglicanism in the late eighteenth and early nineteenth centuries.

The middle colonies as well provided the base for what expansion occurred in the eighteenth century among Roman Catholics in that part of British North America that became the United States. While Catholic roots in Maryland remained important, in the eighteenth century Pennsylvania became more significant as a center of colonial Catholicism, and New York became the primary locus of unsuccessful efforts to stamp out popery in the colonies. The continuation of a small but vital Catholic presence in Maryland resulted largely from the work of the Jesuits and a handful of Franciscans. Using slave labor, the Jesuits were able to cultivate a large estate close to the Pennsylvania border, where they built not only a small church and rectory but also a secondary school. Even after Pope Clement XIV abolished the Society of Jesus in 1773, Maryland Jesuits made plans to secure their land holdings, and several remained in Maryland as secular priests. Nonetheless, Roman Catholics remained a small minority in the colony that had been founded to provide them a place where they could practice their religion freely.

William Penn's policy of broad religious toleration in his "holy experiment" made his proprietary colony a more congenial home for Catholic immigrants, though pressure from the crown forced Pennsylvania to adhere to laws prohibiting Catholics from voting or holding public office from 1705 until after the Revolution. But it was in Philadelphia in 1733 that the first regular Roman Catholic parish church, St. Joseph's, was built; a second parish church would open in Philadelphia in 1763. Both buildings are still standing. German Jesuits who arrived in 1741 opened a small school outside Philadelphia and expanded pastoral work as far west as Lancaster. Throughout the colonial period, German immigrants would provide the core of Pennsylvania's Catholic constituency, though the total number of Catholics in Pennsylvania at the time of American independence was probably no more than a few thousand.

The story is rather different in New York, where Catholicism was forced underground by repressive colonial policies. In the later seventeenth century, two Catholic governors served New York after it became a British colony under the authority of the duke of York, who encouraged religious toleration. Catholic Thomas Dongan, governor from 1683 to 1685, welcomed English Jesuits to the colony, initially to combat the ministry of French Jesuits among the native American Indians in the colony. But the upheaval in New York during the age of the Glorious Revolution and Leisler's Rebellion led to New York's becoming a crown colony and the subsequent introduction of policies oppressive to Catholics. Legislation in 1701, like that which followed in Pennsylvania four years later, prohibited Catholic colonists from voting or holding public office, and shortly thereafter colonial policy forbade Jesuits and Catholic priests from entering the colony. The 1740s witnessed such popular anti-Catholic activity in New York that until after the Revolution there were no attempts to have public Catholic worship in the colony, though there is evidence that occasionally Mass would be celebrated in secret in private homes. But neither repressive policy nor hostile public opinion succeeded in eradicating the Catholic presence in New York, and the small Catholic community that surreptitiously survived provided a solid base for the considerable expansion of New York Catholicism in the nineteenth century, when the number of Catholic immigrants coming into the area mushroomed.

## AWAKENING CURRENTS IN REFORMED AMERICA

While most historians look to George Whitefield's tours of the British North American colonies in 1739–1740 as the pivotal event in the religious revival of the Great Awakening, many would see its roots in the middle colonies as early as the 1720s among a group of Dutch Reformed churches. Theodore Jacob Frelinghuysen (1691–1748) arrived in New Jersey's Raritan River valley in 1720 as pastor to Dutch colonists in the region. Soon his calls for conversion sparked a revival among the handful of Dutch Reformed churches there, and a pietistic strain took hold among those whose theological base was firmly Calvinistic. Frelinghuysen's concerns for conversion and for the negative effects of formalism in religion had a deep influence on Gilbert Tennent (1703–1764), who became pastor of the Presbyterian church in New Brunswick in 1726, and through Tennent on Tennent's father and two brothers, all of whom became prominent evangelists. Because there was a shortage of Presbyterian clergy in the colonies to serve the growing number of Scotch-Irish immigrants, Gilbert Tennent quickly became something of an itinerant, ministering to congregations from New Brunswick to Staten Island. By the 1730s pietistic stirrings were sweeping through them all.

Gilbert's father, William Tennent, Sr. (1673–1746) was especially taken with the need to provide training for Presbyterian preachers who would continue to nurture the seeds of vital faith planted by Gilbert and his other sons and started a modest seminary at Neshaminy in 1726. Ridiculed as a "log college" by its detractors, in time this educational endeavor would provide the impetus for founding the College of New Jersey. In its beginnings, the revival party supporting the "log college" found an ally in Jonathan Dickinson (1698–1747) and his followers, whose ties were with New England Puritans.

But some of the same criticisms levied against Awakening revivals in New England soon were heaped on the Tennents and their associates by those suspicious of the evangelical surge, sometimes known in Presbyterian circles as "subscriptionists." There was the usual condemnation of presumed emotional excess in the revivals, but some believed the evangelicals were guilty of egregious doctrinal error. Simply put, the evangelical call for conversion seemed to acknowledge a human role in the process of salvation and therefore was thought to undermine the Reformed Calvinist insistence that salvation was the work of God alone, who predetermined who would be among the elect. Then too came concerns that the itinerant revivalists undercut the work of parish clergy in ministering to the spiritual needs of their flocks, a concern that would come to the fore early in the 1740s. Among the Reformed churches there had long been an emphasis on proper education for clergy; antirevivalists in the middle colonies in 1738 sought to require clergy candidates who were not university graduates to be examined by a special committee of the synod. This move was widely viewed as an attempt to discredit the work of the "log college," where more than a dozen men of evangelical persuasion had received their training. But despite criticism, the revival impulse continued and moved in a crescendo when George Whitefield came to Philadelphia in 1739 on his second tour of the colonies.

The skeptical Benjamin Franklin testified to the dynamism and charisma of Whitefield and his message when he recounted in his *Autobiography* his impression of Whitefield:

> He had a loud and clear voice, and articulated his words and sentences so perfectly that he might be heard and understood at a great distance, especially as his auditories, however numerous, observed the most exact silence. He preached one evening from the courthouse steps, which are in the middle of market Street and on the west side of Second Street, which crosses it at right angles. Both streets were filled with his hearers to a considerable distance. . . . I computed that he might well be heard by more than thirty thousand. This reconciled me to the newspaper accounts of his having preached to twenty-five thousand people in the fields, and to the ancient histories of generals haranguing whole armies, of which I had sometimes doubted.
>
> By hearing him often I came to distinguish easily between sermons newly composed and those which he had often preached in the course of his travels. His delivery of the latter was so improved by frequent repetition that every accent, every emphasis, every modulation of voice was so perfectly well turned and well placed that, without being interested in the subject, one could not help being pleased with the discourse, a pleasure of much the same kind with that received from an excellent piece of music.

Whitefield's visits to Philadelphia helped cement the ties between those of New England heritage associated with Jonathan Dickinson and the Presbyterians, thereby giving the revival party a sense of solidarity. But Whitefield and the revivalists garnered considerable lay support in 1739–1740, and many willingly identified themselves with the pietistic surge building within the Reformed churches. By 1741, however, crisis loomed in Presbyterian circles. The particular episode that brought matters to a head was Gilbert Tennent's preaching of his inflammatory sermon "The Danger of an Unconverted Ministry" in Nottingham, Pennsylvania, a town in another presbytery. While the surface issue may have been the challenge to Presbyterian church order in Tennent's engaging in evangelical work outside the presbytery in which he held membership, no doubt all the criticisms of the revivals—coupled with Tennent's challenge regarding the religious state of the clergy—lurked in the background. The notoriety Tennent gained from this sermon would go with him when he ventured to itinerate in New England, where the issue of the religious character of clergy was even more provocative.

In May 1741 the meeting of the Synod of Philadelphia revealed the depth of divisions among Presbyterians, and the proceedings themselves reveal an uncharacteristic lack of order among those attending. The upshot was that antirevivalists (the "Old Side," as they were popularly dubbed) were in the majority and declared themselves the legitimate synod. The "log college" revivalists, many of them "New Side," thus believing themselves expelled, regrouped and formed their own presbytery, while others affiliated with the New York Presbytery. But the future was to rest with the New Side, which was soon sponsoring ministers to serve Presbyterians in western Pennsylvania and to the south in Virginia. Never the zealots that the Old Side claimed, New Side ministers also moved quickly to provide the proper education for potential clergy. In 1746, largely thanks to Jonathan Dickinson, a charter for a college was obtained, and classes were begun the following year at Dickinson's parsonage in Elizabethtown. The fledgling institution appeared on shaky grounds for nearly two decades, mostly because a series of presidents (including New England's Jonathan Edwards and Virginia's Samuel Davies) died. But by 1768, when the Scots divine John Witherspoon (1723–1794) agreed to take the reins of leadership, the future Princeton University had become a vital center of learning and a symbol of the dominance of the New Side in Presbyterian life. In time, Witherspoon would be the only clergyman to sign the American Declaration of Independence.

A decade before Witherspoon arrived in Philadelphia in August 1768, the schism between the Old Side and New Side had been amicably healed, perhaps because the Old Side had become stagnant and the New Side had experienced rapid growth. In 1758, a reunited Presbyterian synod convened in Philadelphia with Gilbert Tennent himself as moderator. Not all the Old Side were willing to accept what seemed capitulation to the evangelical party; some left the Presbyterians and joined the Anglican communion. But with a reunited structure and a college to educate its clergy, the Presbyterians in the middle colonies were poised to meet the religious needs of the thousands of Scotch-Irish immigrants who poured into the colonies in the eighteenth century. So rapid was the growth of the Scotch-Irish that on the brink of the Revolution Benjamin Franklin estimated they comprised roughly a third of the population of Pennsylvania alone. While some Presbyterian immigrants preferred to maintain the traditions of the Church of Scotland or of some of its dissident groups when they came to the colonies, most found their way into churches that blended the Reformed theological heritage with the distinctively American emphasis on religious experience and conversion. Together the Awakening and immigration made the middle colonies and adjacent areas the heart of a "Reformed America."

In time another Christian body would benefit from the evangelical style New

Side Presbyterians imprinted on the religious life of the middle colonies. In 1766, the first Methodist society was organized in New York City. Five years later, the renowned Francis Asbury began a ministry in North America that would pave the way for Methodism's rapid growth in the century following the Revolution. But when hostilities erupted between colonies and mother country, Methodists in all British North America numbered barely more than three thousand. Yet the ethos encouraged by Presbyterian evangelicalism provided a fertile environment for the Methodist brand of Christianity that stressed heart over mind, inner experience over intricate theologizing.

## THE MIDDLE COLONIES IN 1776

Perhaps nowhere in those British colonies that became the United States was religious pluralism more evident at the time of independence than in the middle colonies. Largely because of the example of William Penn and the broad toleration Penn encouraged in his "holy experiment" in Pennsylvania, thousands of German and then Scotch-Irish immigrants had come to Pennsylvania. While Lutherans made their way to Pennsylvania and nearby New Jersey, many of those from Germany sought to transplant in the New World the more pietistic and sometimes communitarian religious life that had left them on the religious and social periphery in their homeland. Their presence meant that ethnicity would be a vital component of the religious life of the new independent nation. It also meant that the once-dominant Quakers would gradually retreat from public affairs, while retaining economic prominence in Pennsylvania, and begin a gradual process of inner transformation to adjust to changing circumstances.

As the population of the middle colonies grew, many began to migrate south into Virginia and then into the Carolinas, bringing religious diversity and ultimately an evangelical dominance to the one area of British North America where a nominal Anglicanism enjoyed the strongest religious establishment. In the middle colonies, evangelicalism also became the order of the day, thanks to charismatic figures such as Gilbert Tennent, who readily adapted the Calvinist theology of the Reformed tradition to meet the religious needs of those yearning for a certain experience of the work of God in their lives. While the evangelical approach brought temporary schism among colonial Presbyterians, it was ultimately to dominate Reformed America, albeit in a more moderate form that sought to draw together the strengths that came from the Reformed emphasis on an educated clergy with the vital faith born of personal religious experience.

As the independence movement gained popular support among some religious and many political leaders in the middle colonies, Anglicanism suffered much the same fate it did in the neighboring colonies to the south. Identified with the crown, the Church of England became a suspect institution. Many of its most outspoken proponents, such as Thomas Bradbury Chandler (who had so vociferously stated the case for appointing a colonial bishop), aligned themselves with the Loyalist cause and were forced to flee to Canada, England, or other British territories. Catholics, still a minority in their original colonial haven in Maryland, found Pennsylvania a more congenial site for developing their own religious institutions even as they were excluded from full participation in public life and forced underground by oppressive policies in New York. Yet the Catholics of the middle colonies would become the nucleus for a strand of Christianity that would witness extraordinary growth in the first half of the nineteenth century.

In retrospect, the middle colonies seem a paradigm for the religious complexion of the new American nation. While pluralism prevailed everywhere, it flourished most vitally in the middle colonies and finally demonstrated that the long-held fear that religious diversity precluded political stability was unfounded. In the middle colonies, too, the social conscience that would characterize much of American religious history was nurtured not only in the pacifist convictions of Quakers and German pietists, but in the critique of slavery that was gaining ground especially in Quaker circles thanks to the labors of John Woolman. As well, from the quiet pietism of the Amish to the more aggressive evangelicalism associated with the New Side Presbyterians, the Christianity prevalent in the middle colonies cultivated the emphasis on personal religious experience that remains a hallmark of American religious life. Reformed America was America in miniature.

# NOTES

CHAPTER 2

1. Luis Weckman, *La herencia medieval de México*, 2 vols. (Mexico: 1983), 1:36, note 3.
2. James Muldoon, "Papal Responsibility for the Infidel: Another Look at Alexander VI's *Inter Caetera*," *Catholic Historical Review*, 64, n. 2 (April 1978):183.
3. Quoted in León Lopetegui and Félix Zubillaga, *Historia de la Iglesia en la América Española* (Madrid: 1965), 270.
4. *Hernan Cortes: Letters from Mexico*. Translated and edited by Anthony Pagden, with an introduction by J. H. Elliott (New Haven: 1986), 333.
5. Robert Ricard, *The Spiritual Conquest of Mexico*. Translated by Lesley Byrd Simpson (Berkeley: 1966).
6. Quoting Ramírez Cabañas, *Spiritual Conquest*, 307.
7. Robert Padden, "The *Ordenanza del Patronazgo*: An Interpretive Essay," *The Americas* 12 (April 1956):340–341.
8. Louise Burkhart, *The Slippery Earth: Nahua–Christian Moral Dialogue in Sixteenth-Century Mexico* (Tucson: 1989), 15.
9. See the examination of origins of this legend in Lesley Byrd Simpson, *Many Mexicos* (Berkeley: 1966), 43–44.
10. Michael C. Meyer and William L. Sherman, *The Course of Mexican History*, 2nd ed. (New York: 1983), 56.


CHAPTER 5

1. This chapter is based in large part on my lecture " 'Are They Not Men?': Las Casas and the Pro-Indian Movement in the Sixteenth Century," *Archbishop Gerety Lectures 1986–1987* (South Orange, N.J.: 1987).
2. Bartolomé de las Casas, *Historia de las Indias*, book 3, chapter 4, quoted in Marcel Bataillon and André Saint-Lu, *El Padre Las Casas y la defensa de los Indios* (Barcelona: 1981), 81. Translation by the author.
3. Lewis Hanke, *The Spanish Struggle for Justice in the Conquest of America* (Boston: 1966).
4. Las Casas, *Historia*, book 3, chapter 84, in Bataillon and Saint-Lu, *El Padre Las Casas*, 114–115.
5. Gonzalo Fernández de Oviedo y Valdés, *Historia general y natural de las Indias*, 8:131–132, in Benjamin Keen (ed.), *Readings in Latin-American Civilization: 1492 to the Present* (New York: 1967), 88–89. Translation by Professor Keen.
6. Quoted in Hanke, *The Spanish Struggle for Justice*, 92.
7. Ibid.

8. Quoted in Bataillon and Saint-Lu, *El Padre Las Casas*, 300. Translation by author.

CHAPTER 6

1. Willis Knapp Jones (ed.), *Spanish American Literature in Translation: A Selection of Prose, Poetry, and Drama Before 1888* (New York: 1966), 208–209.
2. C. R. Boxer, "A Great Luso-Brazilian Figure," in Lewis Hanke (ed.), *History of Latin American Civilization: Sources and Interpretations*, vol. 1: *The Colonial Experience* (Boston: 1967), 247. My treatment of Vieira is based almost entirely on Boxer's excellent work.

CHAPTER 8

1. Gibson, *The Aztecs under Spanish Rule*, 118.
2. Meyer and Sherman, *The Course of Mexican History*, 460–461.

CHAPTER 9

1. Cited in Jean Delumeau, *Le péché et la peur. La culpabilisation en Occident (xiiie–xviiie siècles)* (Paris: 1983), 334.

CHAPTER 10

1. John Webster Grant, *Moon of Wintertime* (Toronto: 1984), 245.
2. Quoted in ibid., iii.
3. Francis Parkman, *The Jesuits in North America in the Seventeenth Century* (Toronto: 1900), 131.

CHAPTER 11

1. Cited in Jean Delanglez, *Frontenac and the Jesuits* (Chicago: 1939), 46.
2. "Native American Religions," in Charles H. Lippy and Peter W. Williams (eds.), *Encyclopedia of the American Religious Experience* (New York: Scribner, 1988), I, 149.

CHAPTER 12

1. Camille de Rochemonteix, *Les Jésuites et la Nouvelle-France au xviie siècle* (Paris: 1896), tome 2, 325.
2. Peter Kalm, *Travels into North America* (Barre, Mass.: 1972), 380.
3. Ibid., 397.
4. Ibid., 426–428.
5. Ibid., 430.

CHAPTER 13

1. Quoted in John S. Moir, *Church and State in Canada 1627–1867* (Toronto: 1967), 33.

2. Adam Shortt and Arthur G. Doughty (eds.), *Documents Relating to the Constitutional History of Canada, 1759–1791* (Ottawa: 1918), 168–169.

3. Ibid., 191–192.

CHAPTER 15

1. Quoted in Mark A. Noll, "The European Roots of American Christianity," in *Eerdmans' Handbook to Christianity in America*, edited by Mark A. Noll, Nathan O. Hatch, George M. Marsden, David F. Wells, and John D. Woodbridge (Grand Rapids, Mich.: William B. Eerdmans, 1983), 21.

2. A. G. Dickens, *Reformation and Society in Sixteenth-Century Europe* (New York: Harcourt, Brace & World, 1966), 174.

3. Sydney E. Ahlstrom, *A Religious History of the American People* (New Haven: Yale University Press, 1972), 176.

CHAPTER 16

1. Sydney E. Ahlstrom, *A Religious History of the American People* (New Haven: Yale University Press, 1972), 184.

2. William Stith, *An Appendix to the First Part of the History of Virginia* (Williamsburg, Va.: W. Parks, 1747), 2.

3. Quoted in Perry Miller, *Orthodoxy in Massachusetts* (Gloucester, Mass.: Peter Smith, 1965), 139.

4. John Winthrop, "A Model of Christian Charity," in *The American Puritans*, ed. Perry Miller (New York: Columbia University Press, 1962), 83–84.

5. Mark A. Noll, "Puritans and Historians," in *Eerdmans' Handbook to Christianity in America*, edited by Mark A. Noll, Nathan O. Hatch, George M. Marsden, David F. Wells, and John D. Woodbridge (Grand Rapids, Mich.: William B. Eerdmans, 1983), 31.

6. Nathaniel Ward, "The Simple Cobbler of Aggawam," *American Puritans*, 96–97.

7. Quoted in Mark A. Noll, "Varieties of American Christianity Before the Great Awakening," *Eerdmans' Handbook*, 34.

8. Edward Johnson, "Wonder-Working Providence of Sion's Saviour," *American Puritans*, 28–36.

9. Mark A. Noll, "The Practice of Religion in Colonial America," *Eerdmans' Handbook*, 65.

10. Rhode Island Historical Society, *Collections*, 4 (Providence: Rhode Island Historical Society, 1838), 228–230.

11. Edwin S. Gaustad, "Anne Hutchinson," *Eerdmans' Handbook*, 46.

12. Quoted in Rufus M. Jones, *The Quakers in the American Colonies* (New York: Russell and Russell, 1962), 111.

13. Quoted in Ahlstrom, 161.

14. Noll, "Varieties," 43.

CHAPTER 17

1. Quoted in Sydney E. Ahlstrom, *A Religious History of the American People* (New Haven: Yale University Press, 1972), 192.

2. Quoted in Carl and Roberta Bridenbaugh, *No Peace Beyond the Line: The English in the Caribbean, 1624–1690* (New York: Oxford University Press, 1972), 148.
3. Ibid., 378.
4. Ibid., 386.
5. In John Tracy Ellis, ed., *Documents of American Catholic History* (Milwaukee: Bruce Publishing Co., 1956), 100–101.
6. Maryland Archives, *Proceedings and Acts of the General Assembly*, 1 (Baltimore: Maryland Historical Society, 1883), 244–47.
7. Ahlstrom, 191.
8. Quoted in ibid., 191.

CHAPTER 18

1. Quoted in Sydney E. Ahlstrom, *A Religious History of the American People* (New Haven: Yale University Press, 1972), 216.
2. William Penn, "Primitive Christianity Revived, in the Faith and Practice of the People Called Quakers," in *The Select Works of William Penn*, 3 (New York: Kraus Reprint Co., 1971), 474.
3. Quoted in Ahlstrom, 216.

CHAPTER 19

1. Jonathan Edwards, "A Faithful Narrative of the Surprising Work of God," in *The Great Awakening*, edited by C. C. Goen, *Works of Jonathan Edwards*, 4 (New Haven: Yale University Press, 1972).
2. Jonathan Edwards, *A Treatise Concerning Religious Affections*, edited by John E. Smith, *Works of Jonathan Edwards*, 2 (New Haven: Yale University Press, 1959), 383.
3. Jonathan Edwards, "A Divine and Supernatural Light," in *Works of President Edwards*, 8 (New York: Burt Franklin, 1968), 3–20.
4. Jonathan Mayhew, *A Discourse Concerning Unlimited Submission and Non-Resistance to the Higher Powers* (Boston: D. Fowle and D. Gookin, 1750).
5. Jonathan Mayhew, *The Snare Broken* (Boston: Edes and Gill, 1766).
6. Quoted in Mark A. Noll, "Christians and the Birth of the Republic," in *Eerdmans' Handbook to Christianity in America*, edited by Mark A. Noll, Nathan O. Hatch, George M. Marsden, David F. Wells, and John D. Woodbridge (Grand Rapids, Mich.: William B. Eerdmans, 1983), 133.

CHAPTER 20

1. Quoted in Sydney E. Ahlstrom, *A Religious History of the American People* (New Haven: Yale University Press, 1972), 315.
2. Rhys M. Isaac, *The Transformation of Virginia, 1740–1790* (Chapel Hill, N.C.: University of North Carolina Press, 1982).
3. Ahlstrom, 315.
4. John Leland, "A Letter of Valediction on Leaving Virginia, 1791," in *The Writings of the Late Elder John Leland*, edited by Louise F. Green (New York: G. W. Wood, 1845), 172.

5. Sidney E. Mead, *The Nation with the Soul of a Church* (Macon, Ga.: Mercer University Press, 1985).

CHAPTER 21

1. Fred Hood, *Reformed America: The Middle and Southern States, 1783–1837* (University, Ala.: University of Alabama Press, 1980).

# BIBLIOGRAPHY

## IBERIAN CATHOLICISM COMES TO THE AMERICAS

Alden, Dauril. *Royal Government in Colonial Brazil*. Berkeley: University of California Press, 1968.

Bannon, John Francis. *The Spanish Borderlands Frontier, 1513–1821*. New York: Holt, Rinehart and Winston, 1970.

*Bartolomé de las Casas in History. Toward an Understanding of the Man and His Work*. Ed. Juan Friede and Benjamin Keen. DeKalb: Northern Illinois University Press, 1971.

Bolton, Herbert Eugene. *Rim of Christendom: A Biography of Eusebio Francisco Kino, Pacific Coast Pioneer*. New York: Macmillan, 1936.

Boxer, Charles R. *The Dutch in Brazil*. Oxford: Oxford University Press, 1957.

Burkhart, Louise. *The Slippery Earth: Nahua-Christian Moral Dialogue in Sixteenth-Century Mexico*. Tucson: University of Arizona Press, 1989.

*The Church and Society in Latin America*. Ed. Jeffrey A. Cole. Center for Latin American Studies, Tulane University, 1984.

Cook, Sherburne F. *The Conflict between the California Indian and White Civilization*. Berkeley: University of California Press, 1976.

Gannon, Michael V. *The Cross in the Sand: The Early Catholic Church in Florida, 1513–1870*. Gainesville: University of Florida Press, 1965.

Gibson, Charles. *The Aztecs under Spanish Rule: A History of the Indians of the Valley of Mexico, 1519–1810*. Stanford, Calif.: Stanford University Press, 1964.

Greenleaf, Richard E. *Zumárraga and the Mexican Inquisition: 1536–1543*. Washington, D.C.: Academy of American Franciscan History, 1961.

————. *The Mexican Inquisition of the Sixteenth Century*. Albuquerque: University of New Mexico Press, 1969.

Guest, Francis F., O.F.M. "An Examination of the Thesis of S. F. Cook on the Forced Conversion of Indians in the California Missions." Reprint from *Southern California Quarterly*, Spring 1979, 61, No. 1.

————. *Fermín Francisco de Lasuén 1736–1803: A Biography*. Washington, D.C., 1973.

Hanke, Lewis. *The Spanish Struggle for Justice in the Conquest of America*. Boston, Toronto: Little, Brown, 1965.

Haring, Clarence. *The Spanish Empire in America*. New York: Oxford University Press, 1947.

Lafaye, Jacques. *Quetzalcoatl and Guadalupe: The Formation of National Consciousness in Mexico, 1531–1813*. Trans. Benjamin Keen. Chicago: University of Chicago Press, 1976.

*Latin American Women: Historical Perspectives*, Ed. Asunción Lavrin. Westport, Ct.: Greenwood Press, 1978.

Lavrin, Asunción. "The Role of the Nunneries in the Economy of New Spain in the Eighteenth Century," *Hispanic American Historical Review* 46, n. 4 (November 1966):371–393.

_____. "Values and Meaning of Monastic Life for Nuns in Colonial Mexico." *Catholic Historical Review* 58, n. 3 (October 1972):367–387.

Lea, Henry Charles. *The Inquisition in the Spanish Dependencies*. New York: Macmillan, 1908.

Lockhart, James. *Spanish Peru, 1532–1560: A Colonial Society*. Madison: University of Wisconsin Press, 1968.

Lockhart, James, and Stuart Schwarz. *Early Latin America: A History of Colonial Spanish America and Brazil*. New York: Cambridge University Press, 1983.

Maccormack, Sabine. "The Heart Has Its Reasons: Predicaments of Missionary Christianity in Early Colonial Peru," *Hispanic American Historical Review* 65, n. 3 (1985):443–466.

Martin, Luis. *The Kingdom of the Sun: A Short History of Peru*. New York: Scribner, 1974.

_____. *Daughters of the Conquistadores: Women in the Viceroyalty of Peru*. Albuquerque: University of New Mexico Press, 1983.

Mecham, J. Lloyd. *Church and State in Latin America*. Chapel Hill: University of North Carolina Press, 1966.

Meyer, Michael C., and William L. Sherman. *The Course of Mexican History*, 2nd ed. New York: Oxford University Press, 1983.

Miller, Robert Ryal. *Mexico: A History*. Norman: University of Oklahoma Press, 1985.

Mörner, Magnus. *The Expulsion of the Jesuits from Latin America*. New York: Knopf, 1965.

Muldoon, James. "Papal Responsibility for the Infidel: Another Look at Alexander VI's *Inter Caetera*," *Catholic Historical Review* 64, n. 2 (April 1978):183.

Phelan, John Leddy. *The Kingdom of Quito in the Seventeenth Century: Bureaucratic Politics in the Spanish Empire*. Madison: University of Wisconsin Press, 1967.

_____. *The Millenial Kingdom of the Franciscans in the New World: A Study of the Writings of Gerónimo de Mendieta, 1525–1604*, University of California Publications in History, No. 52. Berkeley: University of California Press, 1956.

Poole, Stafford. "War by Fire and Blood—The Church and the Chichimecas in 1585," *The Americas* 22 (October 1965).

_____. "The Church and the Repartimientos in the Light of the Third Mexican Council, 1585, *The Americas* 20 (July 1963).

_____. *Pedro Moya de Contreras: Catholic Reform and Royal Power in New Spain, 1571–1591*. Berkeley: University of California Press, 1986.

Ricard, Robert. *The Spiritual Conquest of Mexico*. Trans. Lesley Byrd Simpson. Berkeley: University of California Press, 1966.

*Sexuality and Marriage in Colonial Latin America*. Ed. Asunción Lavrin. Lincoln: University of Nebraska Press, 1989.

Simmons, Charles P. "Palafox and His Critics: Reappraising a Controversy," *Hispanic-American Historical Review* 46, No. 4 (November 1966):394–408.

*Sixteenth Century Mexico: The Work of Sahagún*. Ed. Munro S. Edmonson. Albuquerque: University of New Mexico Press, 1974.

Soeiro, Susan A. "The Social and Economic Role of the Convent: Women and Nuns in

Colonial Bahia, 1677–1800, *Hispanic American Historical Review* 54, n. 2 (May 1974):209–232.

Sweeney, Ernest S., S.J., "The Nature and Power of Religion in Latin America: Some Aspects of Popular Beliefs and Practices," *Thought* 59, n. 233 (June 1984):149–163.

Taylor, William B. "The Virgin of Guadalupe: An Inquiry into the Social History of Marian Devotion," *American Ethnologist* (1986):9–33.

Tibesar, Antonine, O.F.M. "The Alternativa: A Study of Spanish-Creole Relations in Seventeenth Century Peru," *The Americas* 11 (January 1955):229–282.

_____. *Franciscan Beginnings in Colonial Peru*. Washington, D.C. Academy of American Franciscan History, 1953.

Wagner, Henry Raup, with the collaboration of Helen Rand Parish. *The Life and Writings of Bartolomé de las Casas*. Albuquerque: University of New Mexico Press, 1967.

Warren, Fintan B. *Vasco de Quiroga and His Pueblo-Hospitals of Santa Fe*. Washington, D.C.: Academy of American Franciscan History, 1963.

# FRENCH CATHOLICISM COMES TO THE AMERICAS

Alexander, Hartley Burr. *The World's Rim: Great Mysteries of the North American Indians*. Lincoln: University of Nebraska Press, 1953.

Arsenault, Bona. *Histoire des Acadiens*. Québec: Le Conseil de la vie française en Amérique, 1966.

Audet, Louis-Philippe. "La paroisse et l'éducation élémentaire 1608–1867," *Rapport de la Société canadienne d'Histoire de l'Eglise catholique* (1947–1948):101–124.

Axtell, James. *After Columbus: Essays in the Ethnohistory of Colonial North America*. New York: Oxford University Press, 1988.

_____. *The Invasion Within: The Contest of Cultures in Colonial North America*. New York: Oxford University Press, 1985.

Bailey, Alfred G. *The Conflict of European and Eastern Algonkian Cultures, 1504–1700*, 2nd ed. Toronto: University of Toronto Press, 1969.

Baillargeon, Noël. *Le Séminaire de Québec de 1685 à 1760*. Québec: Les Presses de l'Université Laval, 1977.

_____. *Le Séminaire de Québec sous l'épiscopat de Mgr de Laval*. Québec: Les Presses de l'Université Laval, 1972.

Bernard, Antoine. *Histoire de la Louisiane*. Québec: Université Laval, 1953.

Blain, Jean. "La moralité en Nouvelle-France . . . ," *Revue d'Histoire de l'Amérique française* 27:3 (1973):408–416.

Bosher, J. F. *The Canada Merchants 1713–1763*. Oxford: Clarendon Press, 1987.

Brown, George, David Hayne, Francess Halpenny, et al. (eds.). *The Dictionary of Canadian Biography*, 12 vols. Toronto: University of Toronto Press, 1966–1990.

Brunet, Michel. *Les Canadiens après la conquête, 1759–1775*, Montreal: Fides, 1969.

Burt, A. L. *The Old Province of Quebec*. New York: Russell and Russell, 1933, 1970.

Campeau, Lucien. *Etablissement à Québec (1616–1634)*, vol. II in *Monumenta Novae Franciae*. Quebec: Les Presses de l'Université Laval, 1979.

_____. *Fondation de la mission huronne (1635–1637)*, vol. III in *Monumenta Novae Franciae*. Quebec: Les Presses de l'Université Laval, 1987.

_____. *La première mission d'Acadie (1602–1616)*, vol. I in *Monumenta Novae Franciae*. Quebec: Les Presses de l'Université Laval, 1967.

_____. *La mission des jésuites chez les Hurons 1634–1650*. Montréal: Les Editions Bellarmin, 1987.

_____. *Les Grandes Epreuves, 1638–1640*, vol. IV in *Monumenta Novae Franciae*. Montreal: Les Editions Bellarmin, 1989.

_____. "Mgr de Laval et le Conseil souverain 1659–1684," in *Revue d'histoire de l'Amérique française* 27:3 (1973):323–359.

Casgrain, H.-R. *Sulpiciens et prêtres des Missions étrangères en Acadie, 1676–1762*. Quebec: Bruneau et Kirouac, 1897.

Catta, Etienne/ *Le Révérend Père Camille Lefebvre (1831–1895) et la renaissance acadienne*, 3 vols. Moncton: La Province acadienne des Péres de Sainte-Croix, 1983.

Champlain, Samuel. *Oeuvres de Champlain*, Quebec: Editions du Jour, 1973.

Charlevoix, F.-X. de. *Histoire et description générale de la Nouvelle-France*. . . . Paris: Nyon Fils, 1744; Montreal: Edition Elysée, 1976.

Chinard, Gilbert. *Les réfugiés Huguenots en Amérique*. Paris: Société d'édition "Les Belles Lettres", 1925.

Choquette, J. E. Robert. "French Catholicism in the New World," in Charles H. Lippy and Peter W. Williams (eds.), *Encyclopedia of the American Religious Experience* (New York: Scribner, 1988), I, pp. 223–238.

Conrad, Glen R. (ed). *The Cajuns: Essays on Their History and Culture*. Lafayette, La.: Center for Louisiana Studies, University of St. Louis, 1978.

Daigle, Jean. "L'Acadie, 1604–1763," in Jean Daigle, *Les Acadiens des Maritimes: études thématiques*. Moncton: Centre d'études acadiennes, 1980.

Delacroix, S., et al. *Histoire universelle des missions catholiques*, 4 vols. Paris: Librairie Grund, 1957.

Delanglez, Jean. *Frontenac and the Jesuits*. Chicago: Institute of Jesuit History, 1939.

_____. *The French Jesuits in Lower Louisiana (1700–1763)*. Washington, D.C.: Catholic University of America, 1935.

Delumeau, Jean. *Le péché et la peur. La culpabilisation en Occident (xiiie–xviiie siècles)*. Paris: Fayard, 1983.

_____. *La Peur en Occident (xive–xviiie siècles)*. Paris: Fayard, 1978.

Desjardins, Paul. "Le projet de mission du Père Aulneau chez les Mandanes," *Rapport de la Société canadienne d'Histoire de l'Eglise catholique* (1948–1949):55–69.

Devèze, M. *Antilles, Guyanes, la mer des Caraïbes de 1492 à 1789*. Paris: S.E.D.S., 1977.

Dickason, Olive. *The Myth of the Savage and the Beginnings of French Colonialism in the Americas*. Ottawa: O. P. Dickason, 1984.

Dollier de Casson. *A History of Montreal, 1640–1672*. Translated and edited by Ralph Flenley. New York: E. P. Dutton and Co., 1928.

Donnelly, Joseph P. *Jean de Brébeuf 1593–1649*. Chicago: Loyola University Press, 1975.

Du Creux, François. *The History of Canada or New France*. 2 vols. Toronto: The Champlain Society, 1951.

Eccles, W. J. *Canada under Louis XIV 1663–1701*. Toronto: McClelland and Stewart, 1964.

_____. *Frontenac the Courtier Governor*. Toronto: McClelland and Stewart, 1959.

_____. "The Role of the Church in New France," in W. J. Eccles, *Essays on New France*. Toronto: Oxford University Press, 1987.

Ellis, John Tracy. *Catholics in Colonial America*. Baltimore: Helicon, 1965.

Fortier, Alcée. *A History of Louisiana*, 4 vols. New York: Manzi, Joyant and Co., 1904.

Francis, R. Douglas, Richard Jones, and Donald B. Smith. *Origins: Canadian History to Confederation*. Toronto: Holt, Rinehart and Winston, 1988.

Frégault, Guy, *Le xviiie siècle canadien*. Montreal: HMH, 1968.

————. *La guerre de la conguête*. Montreal: Fides, 1955.

Gill, Sam D. "Native American Religions," in Charles H. Lippy and Peter W. Williams (eds.), *Encyclopedia of the American Religious Experience* (New York: Scribner, 1988), I, pp. 137–152.

Gosselin, Auguste. *L'Eglise du Canada depuis Monseigneur de Laval jusqu' à la conguête*, 2 vols. Quebec: Laflamme-Proulx, 1911.

————. *L'Eglise du Canada après la conguête*, 2 vols. Quebec: Laflamme, 1916–1917.

————. *Vie de Mgr de Laval*, 2 vols. Quebec: L.-J. Demers et frères, 1890.

————. *La Mission du Canada avant Mgr de Laval (1615–1659)*. Evreux: Imprimerie de l'Eure, 1909.

Grant, John Webster. *Moon of Wintertime: Missionaries and the Indians of Canada in Encounter since 1534*. Toronto: University of Toronto Press, 1984.

Griffiths, Naomi. *The Acadians: Creation of a people*. Toronto: McGraw-Hill Ryerson Limited, 1973.

Harris, R. Cole (ed). *Atlas historique du Canada*, I, *Des origines à 1800*. Montreal: Les Presses de l'Université de Montréal, 1987.

Jaenen, Cornelius. "Amerindian Views of French Culture in the Seventeenth Century," *Canadian Historical Review* 55, n. 3 (September 1974): 261–291. Reprinted in Robin Fisher and Kenneth Coates (eds.), *Out of the Background: Readings on Canadian Native History*. Toronto: Copp Clark Pitman Ltd., 1988.

————. *The Role of the Church in New France*. Toronto: McGraw-Hill Ryerson Ltd., 1976.

————. *Friend and Foe. Aspects of French-Amerindian Cultural Contact in the Sixteenth and Seventeenth Centuries*. Toronto: McClelland and Stewart, 1976.

Jenness, Diamond. *The Indians of Canada*. 5th ed. Ottawa: Queen's Printer, 1960.

Kalm, Peter. *Travels into North America*. Barre, Mass.: The Imprint Society, 1972.

Lanctôt, Gustave. *Montréal sous Maisonneuve 1642–1665*. Montreal: Librairie Beauchemin Limitée, 1966.

Latreille, André, et al. *Histoire du catholicisme en France*, 2 vols. Paris: Spes, 1957.

Le Clercq, Chrestien. *First Establishment of the Faith in New France*. Trans. John Gilmary Shea. New York: John G. Shea, 1881.

Lauvrière, Emile. *Tragédie d'un peuple*. Paris: Librairie Henry Goulet, 1924.

Lescarbot, Marc. *Histoire de la Nouvelle-France*, 3 vols., Paris: Edition Tross, 1866.

Marie de l'Incarnation. *Ecrits spirituels et historiques*, edited by Dom Albert Jamet, 4 vols. Quebec: 1929–1939.

————. *Correspondance*, Ed. by Dom Guy Oury. Solesmes: Abbaye Saint-Pierre, 1971.

Mealing, S. R. (ed.). *The Jesuit Relations and Allied Documents: A Selection*. Toronto: McLelland and Stewart, 1963.

Moir, John S. *Church and State in Canada 1627–1867*. Toronto: McLelland and Stewart, 1967.

Neatby, Hilda. *Quebec: The Revolutionary Age 1760–1791*. Toronto: McClelland and Stewart, 1966.

Nish, Cameron (ed.). *Histoire du Canada documentaire*, vol. 1, *Le Régime Français 1534–1760*. Scarborough: Prentice-Hall, 1966.

O'Neill, Ch.-E. *Church and State in French Colonial Louisiana: Policy and politics to 1732*. New Haven: Yale University Press, 1966.

Parkman, Francis. *The Old Regime in Canada*. Toronto: George N. Morang and Company, 1901.

————. *The Jesuits in North America in the Seventeenth Century*. Toronto: George N. Morang and Company, 1900.

Plante, Hermann. *L'Eglise catholique au Canada*. Trois-Rivières: Editions du Bien Public, 1970.

Rennard, J. *L'histoire religieuse des Antilles françaises, des origines à 1914*. Paris: Société de l'histoire des colonies françaises, 1954.

Rochemonteix, Camille de. *Les Jésuites et al Nouvelle-France au xviie siècle*, 2 vols. Paris: Letouzey et Ané, 1895–1896.

————. *Les Jésuites et la Nouvelle-France au xviiie siècle*. Paris: Alphonse Picard, 1906.

Sagard, Gabriel. *Le grand voyage au pays des Hurons*, 2 vols. Paris: Tross, 1865.

————. *Histoire du Canada*, 4 vols. Paris: Tross, 1866.

Saint-Vallier, J.-B. *Catéchisme du diocèse de Québec*. Paris, 1702.

————. *Rituel du diocèse de Québec*, 2 vols. Paris, 1703.

————. *Estat présent de l'Eglise et de la colonie française dans la Nouvelle-France*. Paris, 1688.

Schlarman, Joseph Henry. *From Quebec to New Orleans: The Story of the French in America*. Belleville, Ill.: Buechler Publishing Company, 1930.

Shortt, Adam and Arthur G. Doughty. *Documents relating to the Constitutional History of Canada, 1759–1791*. Ottawa: The Historical Documents Publication Board, 1918.

Taveneaux, René. *Le catholicisme dans la France classique 1610–1715*, 2 vols. Paris: Société d'édition d'enseignement supérieur, 1980.

Thwaites, Reuben Gold. *The Jesuit Relations and Allied Documents: Travels and Explorations of the Jesuit Missionaries in New France, 1610–1791*, 73 vols. Cleveland: Burrows Brothers Company, 1896–1901.

Trigger, Bruce. *Natives and Newcomers: Canada's "Heroic Age" Reconsidered*. Kingston and Montreal: McGill–Queen's University Press, 1985.

————. *The Children of Aataentsic: A History of the Huron People to 1650*. Kingston and Montreal: McGill–Queen's University Press, 1976.

————. "The Historians' Indian: Native Americans in Canadian Historical Writing from Charlevoix to the Present," *Canadian Historical Review* 67, n. 3 (September 1986): 315–42. Reprinted in Robin Fisher and Kenneth Coates (eds.), *Out of the Background: Readings on Canadian Native History*. Toronto: Copp Clark Pitman Ltd., 1988.

————. *Histoire de la Nouvelle-France*, I, *Les vaines tentatives 1524–1603*. Montreal: Fides, 1963. II, *Le comptoir 1604–1627*. Montreal: Fides, 1966. III, *La seigneurie des Cent-Associés 1627–1663*. Montreal: Fides, 1980.

————. *L'esclavage au Canada Français*. Québec: Les Presses universitaires Laval, 1960.

————. *The Beginnings of New France 1524–1663*. Toronto: McLelland and Stewart, 1973.

————. *L'Eglise canadienne sous le Régime militaire 1759–1764*, 2 vols. Montreal: Les études de l'Institut d'histoire de l'Amérique Française, 1956.

————. "Les communautés de femmes sous le régime militaire (1759–1764)," *Rapport de la Société canadienne d'Histoire de l'Eglise catholique* (1955–1956):33–52.

————. "La servitude de l'Eglise catholique du Canada français sous le régime anglais," *Rapport de la Société canadienne d'Histoire de l'Eglise catholique* (1963):11–33.

## CHRISTIANITY COMES TO BRITISH AMERICA

Adams, Doug. *Meeting House to Camp Meeting: Toward a History of American Free Church Worship from 1620 to 1835*. Austin, Tex.: Sharing, 1981.

Anderson, J. M. S. *The History of the Church of England in the Colonies and Foreign Dependencies of the British Empire*, 3 vols. London: F. and J. Rivington, 1845–1856.

Balmer, Randall. *A Perfect Babel of Confusion: Dutch Religion and English Culture in the Middle Colonies*. New York: Oxford University Press, 1989.

Baltzell, E. Digby. *Puritan Boston and Quaker Philadelphia*. New York: Free Press, 1979.

Battis, Emery. *Saints and Sectaries: Anne Hutchinson and the Antinomian Controversy in the Massachusetts Bay Colony*. Chapel Hill: University of North Carolina Press, 1962.

Benes, Peter (ed.). *New England Meeting House and Church*. Boston: Boston University Press for the Dublin Seminar for New England Folklife, 1979.

Bercovitch, Sacvan. *The Puritan Origins of the American Self*. New Haven: Yale University Press, 1975.

Bossy, John. *The English Catholic Community, 1570–1850*. New York: Oxford University Press, 1976.

Bowden, Henry W. *American Indians and Christian Missions: Studies in Cultural Conflict*. Chicago: University of Chicago Press, 1981.

————. "North American Indian Missions," in *Encyclopedia of the American Religious Experience*, edited by Charles H. Lippy and Peter W. Williams. New York: Scribner, 1988. 3:1671–1682.

Brown, Willard D. *A History of the Reformed Church in America*. New York: Board of Publication and Bible School Work, 1928.

Bushman, Richard L. *From Puritan to Yankee: Character and the Social Order in Connecticut, 1690–1765*. Cambridge: Harvard University Press, 1980; first pub., 1967.

Butler, Jon. *Awash in a Sea of Faith: Christianizing the American People*. Cambridge: Harvard University Press, 1990.

————. "Enthusiasm Described and Decried: The Great Awakening as Interpretive Fiction," *Journal of American History* 69 (1982):305–325.

Carthy, Mary Peter. *English Influences on Early American Catholicism*. Washington, D.C.: Catholic University of America Press, 1959.

Cayton, Mary K. "Social Reform from the Colonial Period through the Civil War," in *Encyclopedia of the American Religious Experience*, edited by Charles H. Lippy and Peter W. Williams. New York: Scribner, 1988. 3:1429–1440.

Cherry, C. Conrad. *The Theology of Jonathan Edwards: A Reappraisal*. Bloomington: Indiana University Press, 1990; first pub., 1966.

Coalter, Milton J., Jr., and John M. Mulder. "Dutch and German Reformed Churches," in *Encyclopedia of the American Religious Experience*, edited by Charles H. Lippy and Peter W. Williams. New York: Scribner, 1988. 1:511–523.

Commager, Henry Steele. *The Empire of Reason*. New York: Oxford University Press, 1982; first pub., 1977.

Corrigan, John. "The Enlightenment," in *Encyclopedia of the American Religious Experience*, edited by Charles H. Lippy and Peter W. Williams. New York: Scribner, 1988. 2:1089–1102.

DeJong, Gerald F. *The Dutch Reformed Church in the American Colonies*. Grand Rapids, Mich.: Eerdmans, 1978.

Dickens, A. G. *The English Reformation*. New York: Schocken, 1987; first pub., 1964.

Dillenberger, Jane, and Joshua Taylor (eds.). *The Hand and the Spirit: Religious Art in America, 1700–1900*. Berkeley: University Art Museum, 1972.

Dillenberger, John. *The Visual Arts and Christianity in America: The Colonial Period Through the Nineteenth Century*. New York: Crossroad, 1984.

Donnelly, Marian Card. *The New England Meeting Houses of the Seventeenth Century*. Middletown, Ct.: Wesleyan University Press, 1968.

Dorsey, Stephen P. *Early English Churches in America, 1607–1807*. New York: Oxford University Press, 1952.

Ebeling, Gerhard. *Luther: An Introduction to His Thought*. Trans. R. A. Wilson. Philadelphia: Fortress Press, 1970.

Ellinwood, Leonard. *The History of American Church Music*. New York: Morehouse-Gorham, 1953.

Ellis, John Tracy. *Catholics in Colonial America*. Baltimore: Helicon, 1965.

Endy, Melvin B., Jr. *William Penn and Early Quakerism*. Princeton, N.J.: Princeton University Press, 1973.

Ferguson, Charles W. *Methodists and the Making of America*. Austin, Tex.: Eakin Press, 1983; first pub., 1971.

Gaustad, Edwin S. *The Great Awakening in New England*. New York: Harper, 1957.

George, Carol V. R. *Segregated Sabbaths: Richard Allen and the Rise of Independent Black Churches, 1760–1840*. New York: Oxford University Press, 1973.

Gewehr, Wesley M. *The Great Awakening in Virginia, 1740–1790*. Durham, N.C.: Duke University Press, 1930.

Glatfelter, Charles H. *Pastors and People: German Lutheran and Reformed Churches in the Pennsylvania Field, 1717–1793*, 2 vols. New Oxford, Pa.: Pennsylvania German Society, 1979–1981.

Good, James I. *History of the German Reformed Church in the United States, 1725–1792*. Reading, Pa.: D. Miller, 1899.

Hall, David D. *Worlds of Wonder, Days of Judgment: Popular Religious Belief in Early New England*. Cambridge, Mass.: Harvard University Press, 1989.

Hambrick-Stowe, Charles. *The Practice of Piety: Puritan Devotional Disciplines in Seventeenth-Century New England*. Chapel Hill: University of North Carolina Press, 1986; first pub., 1982.

Hatch, Nathan O. *The Sacred Cause of Liberty: Republican Thought and the Millennium in Revolutionary New England*. New Haven: Yale University Press, 1977.

Heimert, Alan. *Religion and the American Mind: From the Great Awakening to the Revolution*. Cambridge, Mass.: Harvard University Press, 1966.

Hennesey, James. *American Catholics: A History of the Roman Catholic Community in the United States*. New York: Oxford University Press, 1981.

————. "Catholicism in the English Colonies," in *Encyclopedia of the American Religious Experience*, edited by Charles H. Lippy and Peter W. Williams. New York: Scribner, 1988. 1:345–355.

Henry, Stuart C. *George Whitefield: Wayfaring Witness*. New York: Abingdon, 1957.

Hofstadter, Richard. *America at 1750: A Social Portrait.* New York: Random House, 1973.

Holland, DeWitte T. *Sermons in American History: Selected Issues in the American Pulpit, 1630–1967.* Nashville, Tenn.: Abingdon, 1971.

Holmes, David L. "The Anglican Tradition and the Episcopal Church," in *Encyclopedia of the American Religious Experience*, edited by Charles H. Lippy and Peter W. Williams. New York: Scribner, 1988. 1:391–418.

Howe, Daniel Walker. "The Impact of Puritanism on American Culture," in *Encyclopedia of the American Religious Experience*, edited by Charles H. Lippy and Peter W. Williams. New York: Scribner, 1988. 2:1057–1074.

Hughes, Thomas A. *The History of the Society of Jesus in North America: Colonial and Federal*, 3 vols. in 4. New York: Longman Green, 1907–1917.

Isaac, Rhys M. *The Transformation of Virginia, 1740–1790.* Chapel Hill: University of North Carolina Press, 1982.

Jones, Rufus M., et al. *The Quakers in the American Colonies.* New York: Russell and Russell, 1962; first pub., 1911.

Kendall, R. T. *Calvin and English Calvinism to 1649.* New York: Oxford University Press, 1979.

Koch, G. Adolf. *Republican Religion: The American Revolution and the Cult of Reason.* New York: Henry Holt, 1933.

Lingle, Walter, and John Kuykendall. *Presbyterians: Their History and Beliefs.* Atlanta: John Knox Press, 1978.

McLoughlin, William G. *New England Dissent*, 2 vols. Cambridge, Mass.: Harvard University Press, 1971.

McNeill, John T. *The History and Character of Calvinism.* New York: Oxford University Press, 1954.

Marietta, Jack D. *The Reformation of American Quakerism, 1748–1783.* Philadelphia: University of Pennsylvania Press, 1984.

Marini, Stephen A. "The Great Awakening," in *Encyclopedia of the American Religious Experience*, edited by Charles H. Lippy and Peter W. Williams. New York: Scribner, 1988. 2:775–798.

Marty, Martin E. *Religion, Awakening and Revolution.* Wilmington, N.C.: Consortium, 1977.

Maxson, Charles H. *The Great Awakening in the Middle Colonies.* Gloucester, Mass.: Peter Smith, 1958; first pub., 1920.

May, Henry F. *The Enlightenment in America.* New York: Oxford University Press, 1976.
————. *Religion and the Enlightenment in America.* New York: Oxford University Press, 1991.

Miller, Perry. *Nature's Nation.* Cambridge: Harvard University Press, 1967.
————. *The New England Mind*, 2 vols. Cambridge, Mass.: Harvard University Press, 1983; first pub., 1939, 1953.

Morgan, Edmund S. *Visible Saints: The History of a Puritan Idea.* Ithaca, N.Y.: Cornell University Press, 1965.

Nelson, Clifford. *The Lutherans in North America*, rev. ed. Philadelphia: Fortress Press, 1980.

Noll, Mark A. "The Bible in American Culture," in *Encyclopedia of the American Religious Experience*, edited by Charles H. Lippy and Peter W. Williams. New York: Scribner, 1988. 2:1075–1087.

Norwood, Frederick A. *The Story of American Methodism: A History of the United Methodists and Their Relations*. Nashville: Abingdon Press, 1974.

Nuesse, Celestine Joseph. *The Social Thought of American Catholics, 1634–1829*. Washington, D.C.: Catholic University of America Press, 1945.

Ozment, Steven E. *The Age of Reform, 1250–1550: An Intellectual and Religious History of Late Medieval and Reformation Europe*. New Haven: Yale University Press, 1980.

Pelikan, Jaroslav. "Lutheran Heritage," in *Encyclopedia of the American Religious Experience*, edited by Charles H. Lippy and Peter W. Williams. New York: Scribner, 1988. 1:419–430.

Perry, William S. *The History of the American Episcopal Church, 1587–1883*, 2 vols. Boston: J. R. Osgood and Co., 1885.

Raboteau, Albert J. "Black Christianity in America," in *Encyclopedia of the American Religious Experience*, edited by Charles H. Lippy and Peter W. Williams. New York: Scribner, 1988. 1:635–648.

————. *Slave Religion: The "Invisible Institution" in the Antebellum South*. New York: Oxford University Press, 1978.

Rose, Harold W. *The Colonial Houses of Worship in America, Built in the English Colonies before the Republic, 1607–1789, and Still Standing*. New York: Hastings House, 1964.

Sachse, Julius F. *The German Sectarians of Pennsylvania, 1708–1800*, 2 vols. Philadelphia: Printed for the Author, 1899–1900.

Salisbury, Neal. *Manitou and Providence: Indians, Europeans, and the Making of New England, 1500–1643*. New York: Oxford University Press, 1982.

Schmucker, Samuel Simon. *The American Lutheran Church*. Philadelphia: E. W. Miller, 1851.

Shea, John Gilmary. *The History of the Catholic Church in the United States*, vol. 1. New York: J. G. Shea, 1886.

Simpson, Alan. *Puritanism in Old and New England*. Chicago: University of Chicago Press, 1961.

Stoeffler, F. Ernest. *Continental Pietism and Early American Christianity*. Grand Rapids, Mich.: Eerdmans, 1976.

Stoever, William K. B. "The Calvinist Theological Tradition," in *Encyclopedia of the American Religious Experience*, edited by Charles H. Lippy and Peter W. Williams. New York: Scribner, 1988. 2:1039–1056.

————. *"A Faire and Easie Way to Heaven": Covenant Theology and Antinomianism in Early Massachusetts*. Middletown, Ct.: Wesleyan University Press, 1978.

Stout, Harry S. *The New England Soul: Preaching and Religious Culture in Colonial New England*. New York: Oxford University Press, 1986.

Sweet, William Warren. *Religion in Colonial America*. New York: Scribner, 1942.

Thompson, Ernest T. *Presbyterians in the South*, 3 vols. Richmond, Va.: John Knox Press, 1963–1973.

Tipson, Baird. "Calvinist Heritage," in *Encyclopedia of the American Religious Experience*, edited by Charles H. Lippy and Peter W. Williams. New York: Scribner, 1988. 1: 451–466.

————. "New England Puritanism," in *Encyclopedia of the American Religious Experience*, edited by Charles H. Lippy and Peter W. Williams. New York: Scribner, 1988. 1:467–480.

Tolles, Frederick B. *Meeting House and Counting House: The Quaker Merchants of Colonial Pennsylvania*. Chapel Hill: University of North Carolina Press, 1948.

Trinterud, Leonard J. *The Forming of an American Tradition: A Re-Examination of Colonial Presbyterianism*. Freeport, N.Y.: Books for Libraries Press, 1970; first pub., 1949.

Tuveson, Ernest Lee. *Redeemer Nation: The Idea of America's Millennial Role*. Chicago: University of Chicago Press, 1968.

Vaughan, Alden T. *New England Frontiers: Puritans and Indians, 1620–1675*. Boston: Little, Brown, 1965.

Walzer, Michael. *The Revolution of the Saints: A Study in the Origins of Radical Politics*. Cambridge, Mass.: Harvard University Press, 1965.

Weeks, Louis. "Presbyterianism," in *Encyclopedia of the American Religious Experience*, edited by Charles H. Lippy and Peter W. Williams. New York: Scribner, 1988. 1: 499–510.

White, James F. *Protestant Worship and Church Architecture: Theological and Historical Considerations*. New York: Oxford University Press, 1964.

Williams, Peter W. "Religious Architecture and Landscape," in *Encyclopedia of the American Religious Experience*, edited by Charles H. Lippy and Peter W. Williams. New York: Scribner, 1988. 3:1325–1339.

Woolverton, John F. *Colonial Anglicanism in North America, 1607–1776*. Detroit: Wayne State University Press, 1984.

Worrall, Arthur J. *Quakers in the Colonial Northeast*. Hanover, N.H.: University Press of New England, 1980.

Yoder, Don. "Sects and Religious Movements of German Origin," in *Encyclopedia of the American Religious Experience*, edited by Charles H. Lippy and Peter W. Williams. New York: Scribner, 1988. 1:615–634.

Yrigoyen, Charles I., Jr. "United Methodism," in *Encyclopedia of the American Religious Experience*, edited by Charles H. Lippy and Peter W. Williams. New York: Scribner, 1988. 1:539–553.

Ziff, Larzer. *Puritanism in America: New Culture in a New World*. New York: Viking, 1973.

# INDEX

## G

Gallican movement, 140
Gálvez, Jose de, 112
Gama, Vasco da, 15
Gante, Pedro de, 32, 42
Garcés, Julian, 33
Garnier, Charles, 165
Gaulin, Antoine, 224
Gausted, Edwin S., 278
General Court of Connecticut, 318
*General History of the Things of New Spain*
(Sahagún), 33
Genocide, in New World, 125
Gentlemen of Saint-Sulpice, 139, 173–
175. *See also* Sulpicians
Georgia, 25, 300, 337
Geraldini, Allesandro, 19
Germain, Charles, 227
German Reformed (church), 348
Germans, in Nueva Granada, 63
Germantown (PA), 312, 313, 335
Gerson, Jean, 140
Gibraltar, awarded to Britain, 110
Gibson, Charles, 123
Gilbert, Nathaniel, 344
Gill, Sam D., 188–189
Gitchi Manitou, 180
Glorious Revolution, 259, 283, 294,
360
Góngora, Carlos de Sigüenza y, profile
of, 92–94
Gonsalves, Antônio, 15
*Good News from Virginia* (Whitaker), 290
Good, Sarah, 284
Goupil, René, 165
Granada, Luis de, 14
Gravier, Jacques, 208
Great Awakening, 317; causes of, 320–
321; in New England, 320–332; as
political catalyst, 324; in Southern
colonies, 334, 340–343
*Great Christian Doctrine of Original Sin
Defended, The* (Edwards), 326

Great Lakes, missionary activity on,
205–207, *206*
Guale Indians, 25, 92
Guarani Indians, 17, 65, 114
Guenet, Marie, 168
Gustavus Adolphus, King (Swe.), 308
Gustavus Vasa, King (Swe.), 251
Guyart, Marie, 148, 167–168
Guzmán, Domingo de, 7
Guzmán, Nuño de, 31

## H

Habsburgs, 5, 95, 109
Habsburg-Valois wars, 5
Half-Way Covenant, 282, 323, 326
Hanke, Lewis, 80, 87
Harvard College, 279, 318
"Hat and Cloak" riots, 114–115
Hasinai Indians, 116
Hein, Piet, 101
Hennepin, Louis, 210
Henrietta Maria of France, 266
Henry IV, King (Fr.), 136, 138, 143
Henry VII, King (Eng.), 141
Henry VIII, King (Eng.), 135, 253–254
Henry the Navigator, Prince, 14–15
Hidalgo, Francisco, 116, 119
Hieronymites, 8, 83
*Historia Eclesiástica* (Mendieta),
*Historia natural y moral de las Indias*
(Acosta), 60
*History of the Indies* (Las Casas), 83
*History of the Work of Redemption*
(Edwards), 325
Holden, Achilles, 21
Holy Roman Empire, 134
Hood, Fred, 349
Hooker, Thomas, 276, 278
Hopi Indians, 78
Hopkins, Samuel, 333
Hordes, Stanley, 78
Hospitalers of St. Joseph, 173